JOURNAL OF
RUDOLPH FRIEDERICH KURZ

JOURNAL OF
RUDOLPH FRIEDERICH KURZ

An Account of His Experiences Among Fur Traders
and American Indians on the Mississippi and
the Upper Missouri Rivers During
the Years 1846 to 1852

Translated by
MYRTIS JARRELL

Edited by
J. N. B. HEWITT

UNIVERSITY OF NEBRASKA PRESS · LINCOLN

International Standard Book Number 0–8032–5713–9
Library of Congress Catalog Card Number 70–100814

First Bison Book printing: October 1970

Bison Book edition reproduced from Bureau of American
Ethnology Bulletin 115, Smithsonian Institution, United
States Government Printing Office, Washington, D.C., 1937.

Manufactured in the United States of America

CONTENTS

Picture section follows page 366

FOREWORD

The accompanying narrative Journal of the noted Swiss artist, Rudolph Friederich Kurz, of Bern, Switzerland, was recorded in the German language during the years from 1846 to 1852, which the author spent at the western trading posts of the great fur companies on the Mississippi and the upper Missouri Rivers, from New Orleans to St. Louis and Fort Union.

Through the interest of Mr. David I. Bushnell, Jr., a typed copy of the Journal in the German language, and a script and a typed translation of it into English by Myrtis Jarrell,[1] are now in the archives of the Bureau of American Ethnology, Smithsonian Institution, Washington, D. C.

The typed German text consists of 455 pages (inclusive of three supplements), large legal cap in size; the English translation of 780 pages of ordinary typewriter size (including the appendices).

The original German manuscript of this interesting Journal is now in the Historical Museum in Bern, Switzerland.

Rudolph Friederich Kurz was born in Bern, Switzerland, about January 8, 1818, and he died there in 1871. From his Journal it is learned that he had two brothers, Louis and Gustav.

Through the courtesy of the staff of the Legation of Switzerland in Washington, D. C., the following biographical note concerning Mr. Kurz has become available for use here—namely, from

"Dictionnaire historique et biographique de la Suisse", to wit:

"Kurz, Rudolph Friederich, 1818–1871, peintre anamalier et paysagiste, vécut quatre ans chez les Indiens du Miscissippi supérieur; maitre de dessin à l'école cantonale de Berne 1855–1871; membre fondateur et premier directeur de l'école d'art.

Références:

Sammlung bernischer Biographien, volume I;

Dictionnaire des artistes suisses;

E. Kurz: Aus den Tagebucheren des Malers F. Kurz;

Volumes d'esquisses au Musée historique de Berne."

---

[1] TRANSLATOR'S NOTE.—Owing, no doubt, to omissions in the copy of the Kurz manuscript, references in the manuscript proper to certain additions in the supplements have no corresponding references on the pages of the latter, so I was unable, in every instance, to verify the references in the manuscript.

From evidence which the Journal itself supplies it appears that at least portions of it were recast and rewritten as late as the year 1856, so that his comments on events and persons of the period covered by the manuscript express his own matured opinions and observations.

Mr. Kurz witnessed a number of historically important events in the valley of the Mississippi River. While in this great western region he learned much of the final westward migration of the Mormon people resulting from the bitter hostility of the white people with whom the Mormons came in contact.

He likewise witnessed the great rush westward of the money-mad to California after the reported discovery of gold there. His comments on these events are sometimes rather caustic, but they appear to be based on his own observations. Mr. Kurz is especially critical in his remarks on the causes and the conduct of the Mexican War, which had broken out just before he reached this country.

Mr. Kurz lived at several of the great trading posts of the fur companies on the Missouri River, being occupied at times as a clerk, especially at Forts Berthold and Union, and so came into direct contact with the daily lives of the Indians, of the carefree traders, and of the officers of these trading posts.

It was this intimacy with the private lives of these several classes of people which supplied him with the data he so interestingly incorporated in his narrative, since he witnessed conditions which have long ago passed into oblivion along with the buffalo.

At all times he evinced a deep sympathy for the Indians in their struggle against the destructive encroachments of the white man, and so he willingly excused the Indians for their foibles.

Mr. Kurz indulged in severe criticism of Mr. George Catlin, the artist, even charging that Catlin did not hesitate to victimize "Uncle Sam" in the sale of his paintings.

Mr. Kurz, in explaining his presence in America, writes in his Journal: "From my earliest youth primeval forest and Indians had an indescribable charm for me." He continues: "Man's habitations spread over the whole earth; there are churches and schoolhouses without number; yet where are men found dwelling together in unity? Where does sober living prevail, or contentment? I longed for unknown lands, where no demands of citizenship would involve me in the vortex of political agitations." Continuing, he remarks: "Twelve long years I spent in preparation for my professional tour."

Such considerations, among others, moved Rudolph Friederich Kurz to leave his homeland to seek in an unknown country for the attainment of his ideals.

So, Mr. Kurz sailed from Havre on the *Tallahassee*, commanded by Captain Hoddard. His objective was Mexico, although he knew that war had broken out between that country and the United States. Notwithstanding this information, he kept on to New Orleans, under the impression that Mexico would submit as soon as General Taylor crossed the disputed boundary, the Rio Grande.

But upon his arrival in New Orleans on December 24, 1846, he learned that, according to the plans of President Polk, the war was to continue. This knowledge caused Mr. Kurz to change the field of his proposed operations. So, on January 1, 1847, he embarked from the city of New Orleans on board the steamer *Amaranth* for St. Louis, which place he reached January 17.

The editor has not felt it incumbent upon him to make any material change in the text of the Journal, except to make the spellings of tribal names in it conform to the standard of orthography adopted in the Handbook of American Indians, Bulletin 30 of the Bureau of American Ethnology. He has, however, in one or two places expunged passages reporting mere hearsay which might be held to be obnoxious to certain bodies of people. In all other respects the Journal has been left in the language of the translator, Myrtis Jarrell.

J. N. B. HEWITT.

JOURNAL OF RUDOLPH FRIEDERICH KURZ

AN ACCOUNT OF HIS EXPERIENCES AMONG FUR TRADERS AND
AMERICAN INDIANS ON THE MISSISSIPPI AND THE UPPER
MISSOURI RIVERS, DURING THE YEARS 1846 TO 1852

TRANSLATED BY MYRTIS JARRELL

EDITED BY J. N. B. HEWITT

I remained an entire week in New Orleans to recover from seasickness, to make drawings of scenes in the native forests nearby, and,
in the meantime, to determine upon definite future plans.

On Christmas day I set foot for the first time in the American
forest primeval. As it was winter, I could not expect luxuriant
vegetation such as one finds in the warm seasons, but, I must say,
the extensive cypress swamps and brakes behind the city toward Lake
Pontchartrain were totally different from anything I had ever seen
before. As that region is marsh, cypress and water oak are found
there almost exclusively, and denuded of foliage at that season, their
only adornment was festoons of Spanish moss. The climber I saw
most frequently was the blackberry. On the ground I found odd
outgrowths from the cypress roots concerning the origin of which,
according to what I read afterwards in William Bartram's "Journey
Through Louisiana", I had a mistaken idea. Botanists there call
those formations cypress knees. To me they seemed to be cypress
stems broken off and worn away by rain or by the action of water
during the frequent floods.

From my earliest youth primeval forest and Indians had an indescribable charm for me. In spare hours I read only those books
that included descriptions and adventures of the new world; even
my own beautiful homeland pleased me best in its records of primitive times, when sturdy shepherds and huntsmen, with their noble
forms unconcealed—like the "woodmen" in heraldry or the Germans
of Tacitus—roamed freely in the virgin woods where dwelt the
aurochs and the stag, the bison and the gazelle, the wild boar and the
unicorn, the chamois and, what is more, the dragon. Now primeval
forests exist only in inaccessible mountain fastnesses; cultivation ex-

1

tends even to the snow-capped peaks. Man's habitations spread over the whole earth; there are churches and schoolhouses without number; yet where are men found dwelling together in unity? Where does sober living prevail? Or contentment? I longed for unknown lands, where no demands of citizenship would involve me in the vortex of political agitations. I longed for the quietude of immemorial woods where no paupers mar one's delight in beauty, where neither climate, false modesty, nor fashion compels concealment of the noblest form in God's creation; where there is neither overlordship of the bourgeois nor the selfishness of the rich who treasure their wealth in splendid idleness, while the fine arts languish.

When I was allowed to devote myself to painting, those longings became all the more intense for the reason that, from the moment I determined to become an artist, my life purpose was fixed: I would devote my talents to the portrayal of the aboriginal forests, the wild animals that inhabited them, and to the Indians. From that moment I had an ideal—a definite purpose in life to the attainment of which I might dedicate all my powers. To depict with my brush the romantic life of the American Indian seemed to me a subject worthy of the manifold studies I was to undertake. In fact, the comprehensiveness of the plan proved my greatest difficulty, because, in the study of art, landscape and animals require each a special training that is only little less important than that demanded for the representation of human beings. Many years would be required of me, if I was to attain to mastery in a single one of these subjects. Nevertheless, my enthusiasm for art, my perseverance and untiring patience—self-will, as this trait is often named—gave me fair hopes of realizing my aims.

I spent 12 years in preparation for my professional tour. During that time I had wavered between this country and that in trying to make up my mind which would be the best field for my work. It was not merely a question as to which zone afforded the most luxuriant landscape and the greatest variety of wild animals, but, above all else, which country afforded, also, the most perfect type of primitive man; for, as my studies progressed, my ideals became more exacting, my aims more lofty: I aspired to attain to the excellence of antique art—yes, still more, to equal Raphael's master works. Accordingly, it was no longer my purpose to portray the Indian as an end in itself but to employ that type as a living model in the portrayal of the antique. Baron Alexander von Humboldt, whom I had the honor to meet in Paris in 1839, recommended Mexico as the country above all others that would serve my purpose best. The lofty cordilleras, the luxuriant vegetation of the tropics, the Comanche Indians, the buffalo, etc., were all there together—un-

surpassed in any other geographical zone. In Brazil and in Suri-
nam, it is true, vegetation was much more abundant, but, on the
other hand, the wild animals were less varied in kind and the Indians not so finely formed. Furthermore, the North American Indian, inasmuch as he has to exert himself to a greater degree for his
livelihood, has far more intelligence and energy than his southern
brother.

In 1839 I decided in favor of Mexico and, so eager was my desire
for travel, I would have set out thither at once had not my friend
Karl Bodmer restrained me with his good advice. He wisely urged
me not to be in too great haste, but first to become so practiced in
the drawing of natural objects and in the true representation of
animals and of mankind that the matter of technique would no
longer offer the least difficulty. Then I should be able to discern
quickly the natural characteristics peculiar to the region in question
and to portray the forms with facility and ease. It is an undoubted
fact that, when one has to labor painfully with drawing, perspective,
and the combining of colors while sketching or painting an object or
scene, life and action suffer thereby. One must have a practiced
hand and an experienced eye to be able to indicate with a few swift
strokes the preeminent characteristics of an object, which he can
keep in mind upon painting the same or else recover always with
ease. The ability merely to make sketches would not avail me. I
must devote myself to prolonged study in art.

Now, with regard to the contents of my journal: No scientific descriptions of natural life, as studies of mine, will be found therein.
That work has been admirably done by recognized scientists such as
Audubon, Prince Neu Wied, and others. My pictorial representations
are more complete, more accurate in so far as the animals are portrayed together with the terrain that offers the best setting for them,
and the Indians are represented not only in their ceremonial garb
but also in the dress of everyday life. An artist depicts but one
moment of an action, though there may be many more ideas as well
as descriptions of habits and customs that, while not suitable to his
purpose, are interesting and justify an account of the whole action.
On the other hand, the pictorial delineation is supposed to be a
clearer, more complete picture than the most perfect description in
words.

My chief task in this work was to give from my own observation
a sincere portrayal of the American Indian in his romantic mode of
life, a true representation of the larger fur-bearing animals and of
the native forests and prairies. The pictures are intended to be true
to nature but chosen from the standpoint of the picturesque and depicted in an aesthetic manner. They are intended to satisfy natural-

ists as well as artists, to broaden the knowledge of the layman and serve at the same time to cultivate his taste.

1846

In the autumn of 1846 I believed myself sufficiently prepared to attain success in my life work; longer delay seemed unnecessary. Because of the political unrest at that time, I left Bern without regret. I went direct to Havre—Paris I knew already from a 3 years' stay there some time earlier—and engaged passage on the *Tallahassee*, of which boat Captain Hoddard was in charge. The voyage was, on the whole, favorable. I suffered the entire time from seasickness, but for that I was prepared. What I found most unpleasant was the motley crowd of emigrants I was obliged to mingle with for such a long time. The revolting scenes I, among others, was forced to look upon turns my stomach even now. In spite of the fact that war had just been declared between the United States and Mexico, I pressed on to New Orleans with the expectation that Mexico would surrender as soon as General Taylor had taken possession of the boundary in dispute, i. e., the Rio Grande. Upon my arrival in New Orleans on December 24, however, it was perfectly manifest that, according to Polk's plans, the war would continue. In the meantime there was no prospect whatsoever of comfortably sketching scenes in the war zone. I should have been obliged to enlist with the forces of one country or the other; either enter the ranks or take the risk of being treated as a spy by both of them. My sympathies were not sufficiently enlisted either for Mexico or Uncle Sam to jeopardize my life, when my purpose in going to Mexico could be only halfway accomplished.

I was much inclined to go to Texas and remain there until the war was over. I was strongly advised against that plan, however, by my friend, L. V., on account of the great number of lawless ne'er-do-wells who made that part of the country unsafe. Moreover, Texas was within the theater of war. Though the country surrounding New Orleans interested me with its cypress woodlands, Spanish moss, and low fan palms, the sudden and extreme variations in temperature were, I thought, not at all conducive to health. That which displeased me, however, was the public sale of slaves. These transactions made the city so distasteful that I would not even consider spending the winter there in the interest of my art. I was urged on to other scenes; first, to St. Louis; from there, the way lay open before me along the Santa Fé trail across the prairies to Mexico, by way of Fort Laramie to California, or up the Missouri to the Sioux, Crows, etc., or, last of all, up the Mississippi River to the Chippewa or the Winnebago.

1847

So, on New Year's Day, 1847, I left the city of New Orleans on board the *Amaranth* for a voyage up the Mississippi to St. Louis. I found many German immigrants below and, among them, several of my earlier fellow-passengers. One of them tarried too long making purchases in Memphis and his family was compelled to leave for St. Louis without him. The consternation of the latter can be imagined; the man had all the money with him. Did they ever find one another again, I wonder? From day to day the weather grew colder and the landscape more wintry. Cypresses, orange trees, and Spanish moss became more and more rare. The muddy stream below Cairo, at the mouth of the Ohio, is so wide and the banks, for the most part, so flat, that I could see from the boat little that was picturesque. The days were short. On deck the sharp wind was so cold that one felt quite content to sit, with an interesting book, beside the iron stove in the cabin. A. Murray's Prairie Bird afforded me some very pleasant hours. There were not many passengers; that time of year was the least favorable for travel. Above Cairo we found a snow-covered landscape and the river partly frozen. The only navigable water was in midstream—in a channel, as it were, that became continually more difficult on account of the drifting ice that kept up a constant din, rubbing against the sides of the keel, plunging defiantly among the paddle wheels, then reappearing, bobbing and bouncing out of the eddies.

On January 12, a night of Egyptian darkness, we lay to at Devil's Hole to get some firewood. Next morning drifting ice was so thick about the boat that we found it impossible to work our way out. We were frozen in. All our efforts to break the ice with hand-spikes and turn the boat were equally as futile as our attempt to agitate the water by ceaseless working of the rudder. Fine prospect! Nothing but the swelling of the waters or a thaw could help us out of the dilemma. The captain took advantage of the circumstances to "rope us in." He gave us only two scant meals a day for which he charged us a dollar extra. It was no fault of his, he said, that we were fast bound in ice; superior force was denied him.[1] The only dwelling in our neighborhood was on the farm of a woodcutter whose supplies, for a number of people icebound for an indefinite time, were reckoned to be as meager as those of the ship's company; consequently, we had to submit. This was all the more severe on us because of the time of year: in winter one has a keener appetite; furthermore, several meals a day make the time seem less long and

---

[1] Travel by steamboat in America is usually very reasonable, comfortable, and satisfactory. The fare is, on an average, one dollar per 100 miles with bed, 3 good meals a day, and, as a rule, luggage free.

wearisome. As for me, I was bent on adventure of any kind whatsoever, so I attempted to beguile the time by taking a turn in the
forest, knee deep in snow. But I was annoyed by the extra expense:
my purse could not hold out as long as my courage and endurance.
Depletions of the purse are not to be disregarded; hence, I found
that outing a most vexatious adventure.

To make matters worse, the river fell, and in consequence we
were, for the first few days, aground. No exertion on the part of
the crew could avail anything. Meanwhile, I made my first acquaintance with the American log cabin and the backwoodsman. The
fellow chewed tobacco incessantly, spitting his brown juice right and
left. The mother smoked a pipe as she swayed back and forth in
a rocking chair, a piece of furniture as indispensable, it seems, as a
bed. The log house is built usually with only one room; the huge
fireplace serves for kitchen. The entire family and their guests
sleep in that room; its only vestige of ornamentation was found in
pieced-together bed coverings called quilts. There is no trace of
running water, vegetable gardens, flower gardens, or orchards, and,
as compared with ours, the same might be said of their stables and
granaries. The people themselves were most friendly and seemed
to be contented with their lot, because they were easily satisfied.
As to their appearance, they did not look healthy. Even the native-
born Americans are not exempt from fever. The freshly broken
forest land is by no means salutary for any one. The backwoodsman, therefore, is wont to be a tall, gaunt man with hollow chest
and pale, almost ashen, complexion.

The food of these people consists, three times a day, of black
coffee with a bit of brown sugar, fried ham and hominy (boiled
maize), corn bread, and molasses. The children are very fond of
crumbling their corn bread in warm ham gravy. Although they
possessed cows and chickens, milk and eggs were a rarity in winter.
The backwoodsman seemed not to have the least idea of stall feeding; it was far too much trouble for him to arrange, particularly
in the depths of the forest. Furthermore, he cared too little about
cattle to put himself to the inconvenience of giving them the necessary attention; consequently, the poor beasts presented, in winter,
a sorry sight, shocking to a native of Switzerland. At a zigzag
fence that enclosed the house lot the cows had to stand exposed to
the wind, snow, and rain. With shoulders and hoofs thrust forward
and their gaunt backs covered with a crust of snow, half-starved,
benumbed with cold, their only possible comfort the smell of corn
nearby, they seemed to me the embodiment of misery. The horses
were protected during severe weather for the reason that the backwoodsman's wife was especially fond of horseback riding. "Visiting"—that is, riding around to visit the neighbors—is for the

farmer's wife what "shopping" is for the city woman. As excuse for this negligence toward his poor cattle the farmer declared that the beasts were better adapted to the out-of-doors than to stall feeding and, accordingly, Nature had provided especially for them; there was forage enough under the snow. With regard to wild cattle that is, in a way, true, but not when it is a question of domestic animals.

Every beast loses in instinct in proportion to what it gains by training. The farmer gave a peck of corn more to a cow with a young calf (also, to a sow with a litter of pigs), so that the animals would not stray too far. He accustomed the cow to stay near the house, where she longingly and with bovine patience looked forward to having the corn, that she constantly smelled in the nearby corncrib, at last between her teeth. If she preferred to be independent and wander around for food, not appearing again in the evening, then the farmer went after her and brought her back with a whip and many a "hulloa" and "damn." If this treatment of cattle were confined to the backwoodsman only, it might be explained, for he cannot grow hay in the forest and has to feed his cattle on corn. But the same thing is true in the West: one rarely sees even a well-to-do farmer there who cuts winter forage, and not even then unless he lives near cities or towns, where he can sell the hay at a good price.

After 6 long days and what seemed still longer winter nights, the river rose and burst the ice layer. We were delighted to hear the sounds of its cracking and splitting. But, after all, it was only in midstream that the ice had broken up. In order to open a way for us into that channel, the captain had two sailors put his small boat on the ice crust at right angles to the bow, then had four other sailors (hands) cut an opening for the boat with axes and pull it lengthwise, back and forth, against the ice in an effort to break through. He had the same experiment tried at the keel. Soon we had the satisfaction of seeing the thick crust of ice cut away and an opening made for us into the navigable water. Still the bow of the *Amaranth* had to be raised and the steamer had to be turned around. Even the passengers joyfully lent a hand to turn the capstan and to shove the boat forward. Floating ice greatly hindered our sailing and also damaged the boat by its constant bobbing and bouncing against the keel and beating against the paddle wheels. We were often obliged to stop altogether for fear that the largest of the ice blocks might shatter the blades. That continual friction of the ice against the boat caused an incessant noise like the beating of grain on a threshing floor.

What interested me particularly was the sailing trim of American steamers. For inland voyages they are exceedingly well arranged both for comfort and for practical use. In contrast with ocean steamers, they are built very broad and flat beneath the keel, in order that they may be heavily loaded with all sorts of goods and commodities without sinking the vessel too deeply into the water. The entire space in the hold between the capstan and the boilers is constructed to accommodate an inconceivable cargo of different sorts of wares that, oftentimes, overflows to the lower and to the upper (hurricane) decks, both of which are reserved for such uses. The intervening or saloon deck is given up wholly to passengers: about three-fourths of its length in the forepart of the boat is called the gentlemen's cabin, but serves also for the dining saloon; in the rear—farthest removed from the boilers, and regarded, therefore, as the safest quarters—is the ladies' cabin. The latter is usually fitted up more luxuriously than the men's cabin, from which it is shut off by glass doors. Only those gentlemen who are acquaintances or friends of the ladies on board have entree to their cabin.

This custom of separating the two sexes in that way impresses a foreigner unpleasantly and also exerts an influence upon men's manners that is distinctly disadvantageous. Not allowed to shorten the long hours of a voyage in agreeable intercourse with ladies, to be enlivened by their charming company and refining influence, the men, restricted to their own devices for amusement, spend the time playing cards, drinking, chewing tobacco, smoking, talking politics, or they resort to the idle employment of whittling. Whether this custom has been established by Americans precisely for the purpose of being able to follow undisturbed those passions and practices I have mentioned or whether the highly cultivated American ladies feel that they can not run the risk of attempting to elevate the stronger but less refined sex without suffering some harm to themselves, I cannot decide.

As a drawing of one of these steamboats will be given later, I omit any detailed description. The jovial Negroes on the plantations afforded us much amusement. New Year's week the Negroes spend as a holiday, and such a round they have of visiting, exchange of gifts, drinking, fiddling, and dancing! It is a pleasure to observe them. When I witnessed their merriment and drollery in servitude, I could not help thinking them a fortunate people.

On the morning of January 17 we could see through the clear cold atmosphere the tower and courthouse in St. Louis. How different the feeling with which a traveler approaches an unknown city where he has but a passing interest, from that emotion which one experiences when setting out to seek one's fortune.

St. Louis appealed to me. I found the city much larger than I had expected. I made a number of pleasant acquaintances among people from my own country. As artist, I had no chance at all there: daguerreotypists completely crowded out portrait painters; lithographers needed only printers—no draughtsmen; to get a position as instructor in a girl's school I had to be a married man; to be employed in a boy's school I had to be a Romanist. On the other hand, as house painter I might have met with success. But I grew dizzy at the thought of hanging high up on houses and steamboats, either bronzed by the sun or rocked by the wind. If I had been willing to settle down in St. Louis I might have been able to make a good income as decorator. But Indians—I had already seen several—appealed to me much more than business affairs. I found out soon enough that I was far too visionary, too unpractical to succeed in that new land as a businessman, however well equipped I might otherwise be in the knowledge of languages as well as in other acquirements.

I was lacking, moreover, in those qualities that fit a man for the sedentary life. My desire was now to travel and to contemplate the deep woods, to study the buffalo and the red man. Two opportunities were offered me: a campaign in Mexico; a position with a firm of furriers. On the one hand, the attraction of the cordilleras was very great, but I could not make up my mind to fight the Mexicans who had done me no injury or to defend a country that was waging the war without just cause—plainly for conquest only.[2] Besides, I could have accomplished, under those circumstances, only a few sketches. I could not have done my work thoroughly or completely. My other chance was to go as clerk with a fur trader, some time during the summer after the melting of the snow had opened the upper Mississippi to navigation. Meanwhile, the forests on the Cahokia, opposite St. Louis, began to burgeon. I forgot everything else in my wonder at the loveliness of that display. During the following summer my resolution to devote myself exclusively to the study of the native forests was unalterably fixed.

---

[2] At that time there were 10 regiments of volunteers in the United States. Any man who aspired to be an officer put up a notice at his recruiting office, where men could be enrolled for his company. When he got together a dozen volunteers, he had them march daily through the streets, making great noise with fife and drum to arouse enthusiasm and beat up recruits. If this future captain (who, by the way, had hardly held a gun in his hand so far as military training was concerned) could bring together from 70 to 80 men, he reported them with his muster roll to the Secretary of War in Washington. He had no fear of being refused his brevet as captain, for, whether the would-be officer were or were not qualified for the command, he had the number of men required for his company. As these aspirants for commissions were compelled to have funds for recruiting purposes, acquaintances usually stood together, advanced the sum necessary, and distributed the commissions among themselves. For the higher commissions one was obliged to have "protection." In this country that means no more than being a political demagogue. As a matter of course, only Democrats received the higher commands. It is a question whether such lawyers, newspaper men, and counting-house clerks would become good soldiers at once; for instance, one of the generals ordered an earthwork thrown up in front of a trench! While it is perfectly true that American volunteers make up for lack of training in their dash and bravery, one wondered what sort of Mexican army was going to be defeated by such soldiers.

On February 15 I had a chance to see a parade (a turn-out show) in St. Louis to celebrate the eighty-third anniversary of the founding of the city. Government officials, the oldest inhabitants, Free Masons, Odd Fellows, school children, firemen with their brilliant fire engines, hunters in the dress of mountaineers, and militia—all marching in procession with different bands of musicians. Another thing I must not neglect to mention was a model of the first steam-boat that appeared at St. Louis (*General Pike*, 1817) which was carried on the shoulders of sailors. In the evening there were bon-fires in the streets, "transparents", sky rockets, enthusiastic speeches, much eating and drinking.

On March 24 Mr. Alfred Michel invited me to go with him on a business trip to Nauvoo. Upon mentioning his highly respected name I cannot do otherwise than express my gratitude, also, for his many kindnesses to me. We went up the Mississippi on the "crack" boat *Tempest* to Keokuk, a small town near the lower rapids, and made a detour by land to Montrose, where we found picturesque groups of native settlers encamped at Des Moines. A skiff took us across to Nauvoo. The temple there could be seen at a considerable distance. Nauvoo is well known as the scene of the struggle between the Mormons and the Suckers (inhabitants of the State of Illinois), when each contestant, in gallant self-defense, was forced to give up houses, improved lands, and, so far as the former is concerned, even the State itself. They went from there to the upper Missouri in the State of Iowa, where they founded the flourishing city of Kanesville. That place is now their rallying point before they wander on to Salt Lake in what has since become the State of Utah.

Much has been written already concerning the cause of the con-flict but the accounts are, as a rule, partisan. The Mormons were first driven out of Jackson County in Missouri because they, as Democrats and aliens, were set upon by the Whigs and natives and maligned with all the rancor of political ill will.

Nowhere in the world are such attacks the practice in politics as in North America; in no other country is a political opponent ex-posed to such venom, to such base methods as in the United States. The Whigs had, at first, the upper hand in Jackson County but they were put in the minority by the Mormons. Any one who is ac-quainted with the violent political practices of Americans knows that in no election—that of President no more than that of a dis-trict official—are personalities respected or lies or absurdities dis-regarded. Knowing this, he can fully understand how little basis of truth there was for the Whigs' accusations. And to what means the people in Missouri resorted in order to expel the Mormons!

The militia marched upon them; the general, to avoid a clash, assured the Mormon leaders upon his word of honor that, if they would surrender arms until they had crossed the border, they would be allowed to withdraw in peace. They accepted General Greene's terms honorably, and never saw their weapons again.

Whether Joe Smith, the first Mormon prophet, actually found the Golden Tablets containing the history of the lost tribes of Israel or whether, as is said, he indulges in spiritual hallucinations is, in the abstract, of no significance; for the Book of Mormon contains only an account of the sufferings, endless wanderings, and battles of the lost tribes somewhat in the style of the Book of Kings and the Book of Judges in the Old Testament. It includes no articles of belief. The book may be regarded as harmless in itself; it merely proves, so it is said, that the North American Indians are descended from the Jews.

Neither the teaching nor the practices of the Mormons that are held to be, for the most part, obnoxious, were cited in the objections raised against the sect until their adherents increased to such degree that the "Elders" assumed too much importance. The leaders in the church, by an improper use of appearances, bring their followers into discredit. The laity also have several wives, though they do not often happen to mention the fact. This abomination they attempt to justify by reference to the Scriptural teaching: God gave Hagar to Abraham because Sarah was barren. Interpretations of Holy Writ so absurd as that bring Christianity to scorn. That the Omniscient One should bestow Hagar upon Abraham, in order to preserve his race, when He knew that, later on, a child would be born to Sarah in her eightieth year! Besides, the Bible denies to no man the right to possess more than one wife; and, moreover, polygamy is said to be customary among the North American Indians.

There is still another reproach brought against the elders, namely, they are said to defraud well-to-do members of their wealth by exacting loans and tithes under all sorts of pretenses for the good of the church. This may be true in certain instances but I met so many Mormons in good circumstances that I did not believe the elders guilty, in this respect, of abusing their power. I was even less inclined to believe that report for the reason that in making proselytes material prosperity is regarded as the principal appeal rather than different opinions in matters of faith.

Generally speaking, the Mormons are honest and industrious. Of this, their enterprises in Nauvoo, their rapid progress in the wilderness, are striking examples. Their temple at Nauvoo (since destroyed by fire) is the only building in the United States showing originality in design and construction. All others are either imitations of the Gothic and rococo styles or, oftentimes, an extraordinary combination of both. This Mormon temple proves what an industrious people can accomplish in a short time by uniting their forces. It was a structure in quadrangular form built of solid limestone. At the western end the entrance admitted to a lofty vestibule over which rose a small tower. There was very little ornamentation; only a sort of decoration, about 6 feet from the floor and extending all the way round, that reminded me of runic inscriptions. Unfortunately, I have lost my sketch of that building.

On the ground floor there was a large stone basin drawn by 12 life-size oxen carved in stone. In that basin repentant sinners, male and female, bathed naked in the presence of the prophet and thereby washed away their sins.

I was not an eyewitness. Those tales were told by people who had lived as good neighbors to the Mormons in Nauvoo. It seemed to me, however, that women and girls who would permit improper advances in the church could not prevent the same sort of liberties outside the church; consequently, they would be branded by public opinion as dissolute. Such is not the case. The only reproach that can be brought against them is that they seemed overfond of dress, in the selection of which they did not always show good taste. In Savannah, later on, I often listened to one of the Mormon preachers by whom I was really edified. I enjoyed, especially, too, the singing of the choir. When they met together for choir practice one evening in every week, I found real pleasure in hearing them sing. What made this particularly enjoyable was the fact that in the western part of the United States choir music was so seldom heard. Whatever singing one hears in the West is usually among the negroes. The American, who is not of a musical temperament as are the French and Germans, rarely devotes his vocal powers to anything more than psalms, unless he should indulge in light or ribald songs.

In Savannah there lived also a Mormon named Rains, who was a farmer. He had two wives, each living in her own house but both on the same farm. He was twice summoned before the court at Savannah on a charge of bigamy. As his wives did not appear against him, however, and as no one else could prove that he had the second woman for wife, therefore could not testify to the fact on oath, he had to be released both times, notwithstanding that everybody was convinced of his guilt. Under such circumstances one is led to doubt the honesty of the jury. In the first place, when Rains was accused of bigamy but was not committed, the jury dared not pronounce him guilty, even though he could have been committed, at least, on the charge of adultery. He might have been brought before the court a second time for his immorality but no one would trust himself to do that, because the wording of the charge was not "adultery" but "bigamy." Furthermore, according to American law, the offence must be affirmed on the oath of an eyewitness. Now, there were people who had sufficient evidence against Rains but would not make use of what they knew, for the reason that, on farms, such loose living was allowed and known as "bundling." [3] A similar case came up later in St. Louis in the summer of 1852. I was present in the courthouse at that most remarkable trial. A certain man named Johnson was accused of incest.

The witnesses were able to testify on oath to all possible proof but, since they were not eyewitnesses to his acts, he was acquitted. Americans can't do such a thing—Oh, no!

Another important undertaking on the part of the Mormons, which was interrupted by their exodus, was the projected 6 miles of railway from Nauvoo to Warsaw to avoid the rapids. Through the Mississippi River there extends a ledge, all the way from Keokuk to Warsaw, that leaves only from 3 to 4 feet of navigable water; at low water navigation is impossible. Even small steamers with a draft of more than 3 feet are forced, therefore, to make use of so-called "lighters", i. e., they unload their commodities in barks which they tow up to Montrose and then, having passed the rapids, load their boats again at Keokuk. This condition of things is a great hindrance to navigation; consequently, for the sake of improving facilities for transportation and at the same time of having the work done to their own advantage, i. e., on their side of the river (the eastern or left side), the Mormons decided to construct a short railway line from Warsaw to Nauvoo. The present plan for a canal would cost more but would, at least, dispense with the trouble of unloading the boats.

The Suckers acted in a manner equally dishonorable toward Joe Smith as did the militia general in Missouri.

The Mormons in Nauvoo were accused of violating the law; for example, they were charged with certain practices concerning marriage, civil rights, etc., that were not in accord with the laws of the State of Illinois. Joe Smith offered to appear before the court and defend both this teaching and his practices. Though the governor sent him a company of rangers for bodyguard, the prophet was nevertheless set upon by the mob and murdered in his bed.

We journeyed back to St. Louis on the *Laclede*. That steamer and the *Tempest* were at that time the fastest and best-equipped boats on the Upper Mississippi. Service, meals, rate of speed, left nothing

---

[3] Not an unusual custom of the times in Pennsylvania and elsewhere.

to be desired. To travel on such steamers is a real delight: One has all the comforts of good food and lodging, swift motion, tranquillity, conversation, and scenery for a reasonable price (on an average of $2 per 100 miles).

April: By this time the trees were in full burgeon everywhere but not yet in their perfection. So far I had had to satisfy myself with studying the bark and trunk of the different varieties of trees and the stems of vines and parasitic plants. The result was that the latter proved so interesting that they put the trees out of my mind almost altogether. That forest in Illinois, opposite St. Louis, surpassed in luxuriant vegetation, diversity in plant groups, and in its great variety of trees all other woodlands I have ever seen.

Along the banks of the quiet little Cahokia River, every step of the way, I found a constant variation of picturesque woodland scenes: Oaks, elms, poplars, willows, nut trees, locusts, maples, persimmon trees, their boughs laden with parasitic vines, were clustered on the borders of the stream, their loveliness reflected in the clear waters as in a mirror. What distinguishes these native forests from others is the rank growth of creepers and climbing plants and the dead trees. The wanderer, at every step, encounters the striking contrasts of death and abundant life, profusion and decomposition, lavish bestowals and advantage withheld, flaunting pride and payment exacted. He treads a narrow path made by no conveyance of man nor laid out for man's convenience; it marks the track of the deer, whose course no fallen tree nor the thickest copse can hinder.[4]

As soon as the foliage is in full leaf the mighty trunks themselves are hidden from view by rank luxuriance of creepers and twining plants. The latter, strange to say, are distinguished by no choice assortment of blossoms; the whole living force of the vines is expended in foliage. As most of the trees on the Cahokia were known to me already, I devoted my entire attention to the different varieties of creepers and climbers. I was at once struck with the fact that no ivy appeared among them. They were, for the most part, perennial vines. I noted, furthermore, that certain trees, like cottonwood and poplar, support these vines hardly at all, while others, like "sweet locust", are almost smothered by them. This observation led me to suppose that the climbing species or suckers thrive best on trees having thin foliage. Whether the sap of the tree, entering into the vine

---

[4] The Virginia or white-tailed deer, a very graceful animal, is still found in this part of the country; here and there the horns of elks are found but no longer any trace of the buffalo, though a hundred years ago they were numerous. Indian women in Illinois used to weave a fine web out of wool from the buffalo's hump. Of that kind of weaving there is no longer any trace among the tribes of the upper Missouri; their only thread is obtained from the tendon taken from the dorsal muscle of the deer. After this has been dried and beaten they separate the fibers, coarse or fine, according to the purpose for which they are to be used.

through the many suckers that press into the bark, makes any difference in this respect I can not say. My artistic study of trees and plants was confined rather more to outward appearances and, in that regard, I was so enraptured by their indescribable loveliness that I came near forgetting, not only the rest of the world, but even to do my sketching. Interlacing with one another and intertwining about the trees these vines made a sylvan decoration the richest as well as the most graceful that one can imagine. The festoons sway with the gentlest breeze and loosen themselves from the support of twigs. Sometimes, under a gust of wind, garlands as thick as a man's arm are detached and hang suspended from the boughs to the ground like the rope of a sail.

The trees become so impoverished by the dense shade and exhausting effects of this parasitic growth that they not infrequently decay and fall to the ground; whereupon, the parasites, as if the tree existed for support, even take fresh growth in the débris of the wreck. Sometimes old trees, collapsing under the burden of an ever-increasing mass of vines, form regularly shaped mounds that resemble high walls; sometimes, deep declivities of a great green ledge; sometimes, sylvan bowers with vaulted roof—hidden recesses of the serpent kind. In fact, the presence of these decayed or dead trees, which marks the chief distinction between primitive and cultivated forests, serves the purpose of beautifying the former in a most picturesque manner. In the darkness of night, when one cannot at once distinguish objects clearly, one is often startled by the bizarre forms that the suspended vine garlands seem to assume. So strangely intertwined are they that, in the dusk, they look like fallen giants who, though overthrown, still threaten with long uplifted arms.

In this forest wild animals are hardly found at all; turtles, frogs, wild ducks, wild geese, doves, both gray and white, herons, and the white-tail (Virginia) deer are only worthy of mention. As is usual in localities where heat and moisture produce abundant vegetation, the mosquitoes are excessively disagreeable both because of their multitude and their bloodthirstiness. I was forced, frequently, to visit the same spot several times, because they stabbed my face, hands, and body with such fury that, with all my enthusiasm, I could not sustain their attacks long enough to finish my sketch at one sitting.

At the end of May Mr. Michel most kindly invited me the second time to go up the Mississippi with him. On my first voyage the forests were not yet in full leaf; therefore I was unable to prepare sketches, except of some bluffs above Alton. These bluffs begin near Alton with what is called the Pia [5] rock, well known from an Indian tradition and an age-old, half-disintegrating hieroglyphic

---

[5] Piasa : A mythic being, representing the meteor or firedragon.

drawing of a colossal eagle, which is said to have played in early days a role similar to that of our dragon, and is reputed to have had, also, his St. George and his secret nook in a fen.

The bluffs extend along the left bank of the river all the way to Warsaw. They are not lofty but oftentimes original in form and beautiful in color. Between them are wild glens and ravines, where one sees grotesque forms of trees, masses of rock, and bowlders that have fallen from the heights above. The Mississippi is beautifully clear until it mingles with its tributary, the Missouri, which is invariably muddy for the reason that throughout its entire tremendous length it flows through alluvial soil. Therefore only as far as Illinoistown, opposite St. Louis, can one follow the clear stream; after that the waters become turgid and dark.

May 29. This afternoon I had my first experience in one of those accidents that, owing to negligence on the part of engineers, so frequently occur on North American steamers. Our boat, the *Providence*, stopped several hours at Rock Island City in Illinois to unload lumber and other freight. Soon after we left there, as we were striving against gale and current in our course around Rock Island, we were startled by a detonation like the discharge of a twelve-pounder and the bursting forth of steam. The engineer had neglected to supply the boilers with sufficient water and an explosion was the result. I had just sat down on the saloon deck, directly above the boilers, with the intention of sketching that old American fort on Rock Island (Fort Armstrong). Another man was sitting near me. Vapor from the outpouring steam blackened both of us with soot and we were deluged with water.

As all the passengers were rushing back toward the ladies' cabin, thinking that part of the boat to be the safest place, I ran along with them. I did not know whether, at the next moment, we should be hurled to death in mid-air, gulped down by the river, or consumed by fire. My first view of the terrified men and women, hurtling against one another, crying and shrieking, was almost laughable. As far as I was concerned, I felt that, as I could swim, I had nothing to fear, except that I might be blown into the air. Otherwise I was all the more easy in mind because I had no luggage with me. When the explosion occurred several of the ladies, on account of the oppressive heat, were enjoying a siesta in their staterooms; accordingly they rushed out on deck negligée, looking charming in their light garments and with hair unbound.

That impression was immediately dispelled by another so horrible that I hope I may never see the like again; the second cook and a 17-year-old German girl, together with her younger brother, were brought up on deck frightfully burned. They were carried into the cabin, so that their horrible suffering might be alleviated.

Their poor black bodies, burned almost beyond recognition, were rubbed with oil and when that remedy proved ineffectual, with raw potatoes, scraped into a soft mass and applied to soothe the pain. There were others below more or less scalded; a total of 14 people were injured, 4 of whom died that night.

The boilers had too little water and in consequence became overheated; two of them were rent. Boiling water was thrown backward at least 30 feet and struck the people near the cooking stove with full force. A small boy lying directly beneath the boiler was not hurt. In spite of the fact that the engineer, who unfortunately escaped unhurt, might justly have been held responsible, the captain insisted he be given a written acknowledgment to the contrary, in order that he might not lose the insurance on the ship and the ship's cargo. The fact is, the captain was engaged in a card game at the time of the accident and more interested, no doubt, in his cards and stakes than in the proper management of his boat, on the safety of which he most likely relied too much. He is to be held blameworthy, I presume, only in so far as he is responsible for the negligence of the ship's crew. His companions in the card game signed at once the written statement exonerating him.

The *Providence*, being unfit for further travel, had to be taken back to the landing place we had just left. We passengers were obliged to wait for the arrival of another boat before we could proceed farther on our journey. Next morning we were glad to see, in the distance, between the river and the forest, a cloud of smoke slowly but steadily approaching. After some hours a steamboat came into view; the name *Red Wing* I could already decipher with the aid of my telescope. By and by she came alongside, took us on board, and as much of our freight as could be carried besides. It is always lucky, in such instances, if one's passage is not paid in advance. Otherwise, one is likely to lose the entire amount. If one has luggage one need not pay the fare until the day before arriving at one's destination.

The Upper Mississippi far surpasses the Missouri and the Ohio in picturesque scenery—has many more islands abounding in beautiful woodlands, which sometimes take the form of long, narrow strips of forest opening out here and there into pleasing vistas; sometimes they seem nothing more than detached clumps of trees that, presently, widen to such extent that they can hardly be distinguished from the mainland. Not infrequently a beached steamboat proves the most suitable accessory to the landscape. Still farther north the river becomes but a series of small lakes, where picturesque scenes, famous for their beauty, may be enjoyed all the way from the foot of the bluffs to the Falls of St. Anthony.

At the head, or highest point, of Rock Island the upper rapids begin and, just as the lower rapids near Keokuk do, make navigation difficult. Due to the rugged, rocky bed, the waters are always in great agitation. The river was very high as we came on; consequently, though there was really less danger under such circumstances, we went forward very slowly and with much difficulty. When shall I ever forget Rock Island and that group of apparently coldblooded Fox Indians who wrapped themselves so snugly in their blankets and watched us with such curiosity! The Upper Rapids are 30 English miles in length and are formed, just as the Lower Rapids are, by a rocky ledge that extends from one bank of the river to the other.

On June 2 we arrived at Galena (in German, Bleierz) on the Fever River. The city is well known for its lead mines, the profits from which caused the Black Hawk War. Lead is found in a single narrow stratum that extends 8 miles along the right bank, at the foot of a precipitous hill just where this tiny stream flows into the Mississippi. On and near the hill are a great number of dwelling houses that by means of a steep flight of steps are brought into connection with the city below. The Fever River is rightly named: it is a shallow stream with little or no fall; therefore it engenders miasma and mosquitoes by thousands. Farther upstream the river is not navigable for steamboats, and even to this point by only the smaller boats. At the landing place there was a queer sort of ferry: flatboats propelled with the hands, without the aid of rudder, horse, or steam. There is no current, therefore no resistance to overcome. A rope is suspended over the water at about half a man's height. The ferryboat is attached to the rope at both ends by means of sliding rings. The ferryman's method of setting the boat in motion is to take firm hold of the rope and thrust the boat forward or backward with his feet. He begins at the fore end (which is the rear end on his return trip, for the ferryboat is never turned around) and pushes forward until he reaches the stern, then runs back to the fore end and catches hold of the rope again, and proceeds as before.

For two days I rambled about the neighborhood of Galena. The weather was ideal. I made sketches of many interesting places. In the vicinity lies the battlefield, which was pointed out to me, where Capt. Zachary Taylor, afterwards President of the United States, defeated Black Hawk. To this day opinions concerning that war differ much, even among the Americans themselves. Some maintain that Black Hawk was altogether in the wrong, because Keokuk, chief of the Fox Tribe, had concluded a treaty with the United States concerning the cession of lands and Black Hawk should have accepted that agreement. Yes; but in accordance with the laws of which nation? According to Indian decree? In the first place, any one who is acquainted with Indian customs knows that a chief has no authority as regent; may never ordain a thing done, notwithstanding the fact that the members of his tribe, at certain times and under certain circumstances, may confer upon him supreme command, in some instances bow absolutely to his will. In the event that one member, who is quite his equal, does not willingly agree to be subordinated to him, the chief as such has no power over that person. If, in accordance with our ideas, Keokuk had had the authority of regent, then Black Hawk and his followers would have been bound to accede. But the former chief had no such authority; he was empowered to conclude a treaty only for himself and his faction— never at any time for the Fox nation as a whole. So long as Black Hawk and his adherents did not agree to the cession of lands no one had a right to take possession of them until his share had been apportioned. That had not been done.

Furthermore, Keokuk was not even chief by tribal decree. He was installed as such by the United States simply because he was a good friend to the Americans; in consequence of this the Foxes separated into factions, one of which was favorable to Americans, the other to the English. For that reason the treaty accepted by Keokuk was not binding in any sense upon the adverse party.

Thus far Black Hawk was within his right to fight for the graves of his forefathers. He might with justice look upon the Americans as robbers and treat them accordingly. From the moment, how- ever, when Black Hawk was defeated on the field of battle, and made a treaty with General Atkinson, binding himself and his followers to surrender the lands in dispute, he was put in restraint. Never again would he be allowed to contest that transaction in arms against the Americans. One can only say, what has been said before, that right as established by the strong hand will prevail only so long as the weaker contestant is obliged to yield to superior force without question as to the justice of his claim. The same observation applies also to decisions contested by armed forces in revolution, though according to the generally accepted view in such instances the defeated force is always in the wrong.

In connection with the Black Hawk War one further fact is worthy of mention: according to the stipulations of the treaty with Keokuk, the Fox Indians were granted permission to withdraw at once to their former lands but the white owners of lead mines were unwilling to submit to that provision and shot the Indians down like wild beasts, just as, later on, the gold seekers did in California.

As I had visited lead mines and silver mines before at Huelgoat and Pullonen in Brittany, and furthermore, had little time now

at my disposal, I did not go to the mines at Galena. As soon as
Mr. Michel had accomplished his business undertakings we returned
on the *Wareagle* to St. Louis.

On November 19 in the same year I accompanied Mr. Michel to
New Orleans, where he intended to establish a commission house.
On that visit I saw many Choctaws at the market. The men were
selling wild game (rabbits, turkeys, venison) and the women, seeds,
grain, and healing herbs.

The most important event during my stay in New Orleans, and
that which I most enjoyed, was the public appearance there of the
hero of Buena Vista. I shared the universal jubilation upon his
passing through the streets on his old gray horse. My enthusiasm
was not so much for his unexcelled achievements in war as for the
man who, in spite of Polk's mean treatment of him, proved himself
capable of such glorious examples of military greatness as his vic-
tories at Palo Alto and Resaca de la Palma against General Arista
on the 8th and 9th of May, against Ampudien at Monterey on the
21st of September 1846, and against Santa Anna on February 22,
1847. Notwithstanding that Polk had left him in the lurch, had
transferred his best troops to Gen. Winfield Scott in order that this
man might also win laurels; * * * I was glad that, in spite of
Polk, old Zach [6] had the best prospects of being President of the
United States. I was very glad of this, although I would myself
sooner be a Democrat than a Whig. The throng that filled the streets
was something dreadful and the exultation of the people indescribable. What impressed me particularly was the comparatively small
number of good-looking white women. Among the great numbers
of feminine onlookers at the windows, those of the colored race
seemed, as a rule, the handsomer.

Two weeks later I returned to St. Louis, taking with me several
new studies of forest scenes in Louisiana and Arkansas. This winter
voyage up the Mississippi was even more adventurous than my first
one. Page, the captain and owner of the boat (the *Hannibal*), was
so extraordinarily pious that he thought it a sin to travel on Sunday; therefore he anchored Saturday evening at a safe but very
lonely place and built a fire. There we remained the entire Sabbath
day and until midnight. Any one who cared for extempore sermons had the chance three times during the day to hear them. I was
sorry that it was a season when the forests were not in leaf; I should
have had such excellent opportunity for sketching. As it was, however, the trees with their draperies of Spanish moss presented a
dusky, original appearance that, when seen through the river mists,
was peculiarly effective. Near the close of day crashing peals of
thunder sent me scurrying back to the boat.

---

[6] Gen. Zachary Taylor.

That pious captain played a trick on us at Cairo. Upon hearing the news that the Mississippi north of its junction with the Ohio (at Cairo) was frozen over, Page determined not to risk sailing his precious ship in ice-blocked waters but, notwithstanding his obligation to those on board, to unload passengers and freight and return to New Orleans. He was kind enough, however, to wait one day longer (meanwhile, he unloaded the freight). By that time the *Oswego*, coming up from Louisville, arrived and took us aboard for St. Louis. Oh, you wretched old *Oswego;* never shall I forget you as long as I live!

The Ohio was overflowing its banks—exceedingly high and swift. The swollen waters swept along with them a multitude of fragments from houses demolished by the flood, fences, uprooted trees, and the dead bodies of cattle. In the midst of all that the more daring river craft were scouring the waters to appropriate from the wreckage whatever was of value. The delta was nothing more than a deep morass; there was no place where we could saunter about; so we had to content ourselves, as far as entertainment was concerned, with watching the river pirates from the hurricane deck.

The little *Oswego* did not please me at all; the besmeared appearance of the cabins discouraged any hope of good service; on small, cheap boats there is never congenial company, so there was no other choice for me and my unfortunate fellow passengers but to betake ourselves to the poop with its old stern wheel (instead of two paddle wheels, one on each side, this boat had one at the rear). Yet, when we had to make up our minds whether we would wait at an inn for a more comfortable steamer or continue the journey on the *Oswego*, I decided in favor of the latter.

As I said before, the swollen waters of the Ohio were causing widespread devastation. The current was so swift and strong that it pressed back the waters of the Mississippi and, under the low temperature at the time, that backwater quickly froze. Though the ice crust was quite thin, it retarded considerably the cheaply constructed *Oswego*. In addition to that hindrance, the boat, being heavily loaded, was forced to a strain beyond its worn-out strength and had to stop almost every minute while some damage to the machinery or to the wheel was being repaired. At Chester we stuck fast again; the old machinery could do no more.

Again we were forced to wait for another steamer and pay dearly for our short journey from Cairo to Chester (60 English miles). Fortunately, we were not delayed very long—not an entire day. On first view, I had little hope of finding a place on the *Boreas No. 3* that arrived a few hours later from New Orleans. From a distance the boat seemed to be overcrowded. However, most of those on board were German immigrants, not cabin passengers. Quite a number of them lodged on the floor in front of the main cabin in an open space between the stoves, where they had the comfort of some heat and were protected by a strip of canvas from the wind. They were cold, notwithstanding. The older people and little children remained nearly all the time under the protection of their wraps and blankets, but some of the young girls declared every time in favor of the main cabin where the crowd was. There they allowed themselves to be stared at, in the hope of attracting a beau.

It is extraordinary how universally the opinion is held among immigrant girls (no nation excepted) that there are precious few of their sort in the United States and that nothing is so easily managed as getting married—one need only possess a pretty face. Now, luckily, every one of them believes herself to be in possession of that attraction; therefore, not one of them considers the possibility of failure. Whether she understands that most necessary qualification of all, i. e., the English speech, is immaterial. Eyes are eloquent and, where they do not avail, gesticulations assist. Such girls as that were found almost always standing together in the saloon (they have no right to sit down nor were there any seats for them, if they had). They giggled if a man stared, especially in their direction. If he said something to them, the words of which they could not understand, they had not the least doubt in the world as to his meaning, nevertheless. The young man was deliberating upon the possibility of his being accepted whether he had money or not.

It is natural that immigrant girls from Europe should stand on so little ceremony in the matter of accepting husbands on short acquaintance, without courtship. They imagine, more or less justly, that the life of an American woman is one of leisure and comfort. They are therefore quite ready to be married to an American, even though they may not be able to converse with him. Besides, they find extended courtships are by no means the custom in the United States, particularly in the West.

If a young man calls twice on a girl he is expected to declare himself. If he is accepted, he plans to marry at once. If he is not accepted, he is supposed to discontinue his visits, for the reason that he might otherwise prevent others from paying suit to the girl and, it may be, rob her of a love that might lead to marriage later. That is essentially practical. In the first place, it is notoriously true that during courtship both parties reveal their most amiable qualities and only after marriage let their contrary traits be known. That is why, in spite of long courtships, there is so much complaint in Europe. Now, in the United States, a man conducts his love affairs without illusions. He does not indulge in dreams of an angel but assumes, simply, that both parties to the contract have faults that must be borne. Therefore, since he does not surrender himself to passionate overfondness, he is not likely to suffer disappointments so grave. Inasmuch as the simpler mode of life here as well as better means of supporting a family enable a young man to settle early, it usually happens that both men and women marry their first love. If the union should result unhappily, the civil compact can be dissolved with the greatest ease; quite frequently, the ease with which a man vanishes ("vamooses") into a distant State, settles down under an assumed name, and may marry again.

We travelers from the *Oswego* found no vacant cabins and in consequence had to be satisfied at night with mattresses on the floor, an upturned chair for headrest, and a blanket. That we slept in our clothes goes without saying; in the first place, we were cold and, besides, we felt so insecure about everything. There were 80 cabin passengers; two tables had to be served at all meals.

As soon as a meal is ready to be served on American steamers the steward reports this to the captain or his clerk; whereupon one or the other goes to the ladies' saloon and invites them to the table. Then the steward rings a bell. Upon that announcement, the unmarried men may go in and wait, standing, as patient as sheep, until the ladies, or perhaps only one lady, finishes her toilette, sweeps to the table on the arm of her cavalier or her husband, and sits down; then, and not until then, the remainder of the gentlemen take their seats. This American comedy in manners is observed as well at the inns and is meant to show the high respect American gentlemen pay the fair sex, surpassing, in that regard, even the world-famed gallantry of the French and winning for themselves the distinction of being called the most enlightened people. The result is, they encourage American womankind in vanity and laziness. Every woman expects the greatest consideration. She is unwilling to work. The instant a young wife is obliged to set about any task she reproaches her husband: "I am forced to do the work of a negress. You ought to be ashamed!" An American woman is never seen working in the field.

A country girl dresses herself just as girls dress in the city (there is no difference in the style of dress). All she knows about domestic affairs is to cut out and make her clothes, to piece bedquilts, to cook, only in the most rudimentary sense, i. e., to make coffee and boil hominy (soup is unknown in the country), to fry ham and eggs, and bake corn bread. The acme of her ambition in the culinary arts is mince pie.

In connection with my remarks concerning the form so punctiliously observed with regard to the ladies, I must record this: I was present when 40 men were obliged to stand 8 minutes behind their chairs because of one woman's tardy appearance. When the captain entered the saloon to invite her to the table she went at once to the mirror to see whether her hair was in order, then moistened her delicate fingers to give it a better gloss, smoothed out the folds of her skirt, took still another survey with evident pleasure in the tout ensemble, then she sailed in, no doubt with the consciousness that many men (one of whom, at least, was worthy of her) were gazing upon her with admiration. Under the influence of such flattering vanity she gave us a look that plainly said: "As reward for your patience, you stupid men, you may now behold what is truly beautiful. Look at me!"

Many people may regard such observations as of petty significance. So they would be, if American wives would stay in their place and not be perpetually striving, little by little, to supersede the men in everything, even in politics. It has happened often enough in our modern day that women form unions for their emancipation, nay, what is more, convene congresses, where they deal with men as though they were bears and demand nothing less than political equality. What is the cause of this ambition on the part of idle women? Nothing more than the submissiveness of their husbands. They find household matters uncongenial. They think their duties as wives and mothers allow them too little scope. They would rather read newspapers and novels than to do any work. Do young girls desire political privileges? Not at all. A girl's desire, above all else, is to be married, as a matter of course. What a privilege that some one is going to be allowed to work for her! I do not mean to assert that the female sex is not endowed with requisite qualifications for governing but I think women should call themselves happy in that they are not required to employ their abilities in political affairs. They should be satisfied with their sway over the hearts of their husbands. Through that influence they get, also, control in public affairs, at least indirectly. If they insist upon having all the rights that men possess, then they must assume men's duties and obligations.

The many shocking instances of indecent assault, more numerous in this country than in any other, are due in large measure to this division between the sexes and the undue claims of women. To the same cause may be traced those frequent desertions on the part of parents—either a mother or a father leaves children and helpmate in the lurch. Furthermore, the vice of polygamy may be cited as another result.

Before the *Boreas No. 3* reached St. Louis another call was made upon her for help in time of need; the *Atlantic* for two days had been stuck fast in the ice, all the firewood had been consumed, and on account of drifting ice in the river, no more could be procured. After we had given her a "lift" and supplied her with wood she was soon afloat once more. We had no further adventure before landing, but witnessed a comic byplay in the ladies' saloon; one woman accused another of having filched her purse and her breast-pin and of having hidden them under a pillow. There was much gabble and cackle but nothing proved.

On December 24 we were again in St. Louis—14 days on the way.

1848

During the first 3 months of the year 1848 I painted a number of horses from life. I saw them all day long, standing before my window. American horses are bred from no particular stock but are a product of much cross-breeding. They are, on the whole, excellent for riding but not strong enough for draft horses. Indian ponies—dwarfed horses—resemble in many respects the spirited but somewhat delicate Breton trotters. Between whiles I read diligently, in St. Louis newspapers, those highly interesting accounts that were appearing at the time, of the Mexican War; visited the courts of justice, and listened to political speeches in order to become acquainted with American conditions. Further remarks on that subject I postpone until the end, when I leave the United States. By that time, my judgment, matured through a protracted stay and comprehensive observation of things, will be more just.

The winter of 1848 was not very cold—at least, not cold enough to freeze the Mississippi from shore to shore at St. Louis. That occurs only in very severe weather. During these months, while I was waiting for the coming of spring, when the waterways farther north would be open to navigation, I had time to consider plans for the future. As my private affairs are of little interest to the public, I leave out prosaic accounts of my activities in the way of earning a livelihood, with the exception of this observation: in the United States, just now, a painter in the fine arts has no prospects whatsoever. He is looked upon as a "windbag," an intriguer, a "humbug." A house painter, on the contrary, makes a good income. In saying this, I bring no reproach against the Americans; they are republicans—that means, the political life of the nation absorbs, to a great degree, their energy of mind and their interest. Furthermore, the nation is young; the ambition of the people is to become a great country, to get the mastery, so that they can dictate to European powers. And lastly, the inhabitants outside the cities are a farming class, who have no taste for the works of art. They regard such things as extravagance.

As the purpose of my stay in America was to accomplish certain aims in the study of art, all plans for employment in other directions for the sake of earning my bread (my supply of funds was already low) had to be subordinated, necessarily, to that purpose. I found out soon enough that I could never do anything so antagonistic to my true nature as to go into business, even for the length of time required to earn enough money to get forward independently as an artist. That a man cannot serve two masters was never more truly verified than in me. If my penchant for portraying aboriginal nature in art had made me dissatisfied with what my own beautiful country could offer, now that I had actually seen primeval woods and the wild beasts, Nature's true children, that desire of earlier years had become a passion. I was so happy not to have been disappointed in the woodlands and forests: they were, I found, far more rich, included more that was original, and the Indians were of a more noble type than I had ever dreamed.

I had already accomplished something in the pursuit of my aims: primeval woods, prairies, and river I had observed at every season of the year—torpid under the benumbing influence of frost, brimming with life under the influence of warmth. Now I longed to study Indians and wild animals.

The war with Mexico still interfered with my visit to that country. The upper Mississippi, as far north as Galena, afforded much picturesque scenery, to be sure, but few buffaloes or stags; furthermore, the Indians in those far northern districts, owing to the severe climate, were of stunted growth and, for the studies I wished to make, wore too many clothes. The Missouri region, therefore, attracted me especially. That region offered more, in reality, that an artist could turn to account than northern Mexico or the Lake region of North America, but not what I cared for especially. However, in the event that the Indians there did not satisfy my expectations I had still a choice between the Independence trail to Santa Fe and the one leading from St. Joseph to the Rocky Mountains, Oregon, and California.

I decided to go to St. Joseph on the Missouri. There I should certainly find Indians enough: The region in the midst of which the town was situated was open Indian country, belonging to the Kickapoo, and the town itself was a rendezvous for fur traders of Missouri and Nebraska, just as Independence was a center for Santa Fe fur traders and, at an earlier date, St. Louis for the entire fur-trading region of the West.

Before I left St. Louis, perhaps forever, I made sketches of some remains in the city that date from the most remote Indian epoch, and others from the days of Spanish rule. There were two tumuli in the form of huge terraces, both of which, for the reason that dwelling houses had been built upon them, could be recognized as such only from traditional report. The former residence of the Spanish governor, now a German brewery, Washington garden to the south of Third Street, was an unpretentious building of limestone with veranda and high wall. Not far from this house on South Main Street is the oldest chapel or church; it is of wood with stone foundation. The entrance is at the end toward the street and the door is reached by a flight of steps. This elevated entrance was contrived, probably, to avoid entering directly from what was frequently little more than a bog. The chapel has no tower but a cross above the door. The walls are timbered beams joined together as in a blockhouse. On the river shore, north of St. Louis, there is a round Spanish watchtower with stone walls of great thickness—no loopholes.

I left St. Louis April 5 aboard the *Tamerlane*, under command of Captain Miller. The boat was heavily loaded with tradespeople, for the most part, who were going up from St. Louis taking their supplies along on the same boat with themselves. During the entire winter tradesmen in St. Louis can receive no goods from the East and can send away just as little fresh corn, hemp, and tobacco. The opening of the waterways, therefore, is an important event for the cities along the Missouri and will be always, until railway lines have established connections with the East.

The Missouri is invariably muddy. Owing to a lack of mineral matter in the soil, both in the bed of the stream and in the banks, the river tears away the shore on one side and deposits the sediment on the other, according to the direction of the current. That is what gives the Mississippi its "coffee and milk" color below Alton. Strictly speaking, the Missouri deserves to bear its name all the way to the Gulf of Mexico, for it is of greater length, breadth, and depth than its eastern brother. But its immense length was not known at all to the first French travelers, to whom we are indebted for our earliest information concerning this part of the country; they knew the Missouri only at its broad estuary. The muddy condition of the water makes the stream a dangerous route for steamers for the reason that trees are easily uprooted by the current from the loose soil—there is no stony substance in the soil— and they sink into the river bed, where every shoot can ram itself into the soft earth in such a way that it bores through the most solid hull that comes in contact with it. These offshoots from the submerged trees are called "snags." Those that are completely hidden under water cause the greatest peril. Sometimes, in places where a strong current tears away an entire strip of forest, the river is so blocked with those tree trunks that boats can wind their way through the channel only with the most careful steering.

Therefore if the pilot sees a heavy tree trunk floating toward the side of the boat and finds it impossible to avoid, he has an especial warning bell rung, so that the engineer will adjust the wheel in a way that prevents the blades from being shattered by the tree. No damage is feared from a trunk of light weight.

The average speed of a steamboat going upstream is 10 miles an hour; going downstream, from 10 to 20 miles, according to the condition of the river and the power of the engine. For instance, the average boat makes the voyage from New Orleans to St. Louis in 13 days; a "crack" steamer in only 5 or 6. From St. Louis to New Orleans the worst conditioned vessel needs not more than 9 days to make the distance (1,200 miles). From St. Louis to St. Joseph (500 miles) steamers require as much time as from New Orleans to St. Louis, because, owing to "snags" and shifting sandbanks, they do not run at night.

On that account the steering wheel on these river boats is fixed high up, so that the pilot can keep a sharp lookout over a wide expanse of water. To discover these completely submerged obstructions he has to watch closely every variation of the water surface. As may be inferred, the boats do not travel upstream at night unless there is a brilliant moon. Even then only the most experienced pilots who have made constant study of the changes in the river and variations in the current dare attempt to steer them. Our first pilot on the *Tamerlane*, Laberge by name, had been at the wheel on the Mackinaw boats by means of which the fur traders dispatched their hides and pelts to St. Louis long before the upper Missouri was navigated by steamboats. He was, of course, one of the best pilots on the Missouri.

The uprooted trees assume still other, though less dangerous, positions in the Missouri (also in the lower Mississippi), i. e., they do not lie stationary on the bed of the stream but are balanced by the current in a way that gives them a saw-like motion; hence they are called "sawyers." There is also much driftwood which, when it is heavy, does great damage to the paddle wheels.

We progressed slowly but without accident. I was in no haste, and, on the hurricane deck, I enjoyed the beautiful weather exceedingly. The consciousness of being actually on the voyage up the Missouri, drawing nearer and nearer each day to the buffaloes, deer, and bears, was intoxicating.

"Ye, who have yearn'd alone, my grief can measure." [7] My longings were soon to be satisfied. The dreams of my youth were to be realized. My life purpose in art was to be accomplished.

---

[7] "Nur wer die Sehnsucht kennt, weiss was ich leide."—GOETHE.

On April 18 at 11 o'clock at night, while the ship's black crew were singing a jubilee song, we docked at St. Joseph. In my eager gladness I went in search of an inn, although I should have fared just as well if I had spent the rest of the night on board.

St. Joseph, once the trading post of Joseph Robidoux, is situated at the foot of the Black Snake Hills on the left bank of the Missouri. Though the town was founded only six years ago there are evidences already of a rapidly expanding and flourishing city. In spite of the fact that there are many new buildings, both of wood and of brick, houses, either for homes or for business purposes, are hard to get. Upon my arrival the principal streets were much enlivened by fur traders and immigrants on their way to regions, as yet little known, in Oregon and California. The rich gold mines were not then discovered. Only the most daring fur traders had penetrated into that far country and, following in their wake, a rough, lawless set of adventurers, eager for gain and best pleased with what the strong hand won, traveled the same trail in armed bands with pack mules and covered wagons.

A black bear, captured and enchained, gave me the welcome opportunity to study his kind. He was absolutely black; not even a trace of gray or brown, even on his upper lip.

July 12. To-day an Iowa farmer brought into the town a live badger,[8] in a piece of hollow tree, to exhibit him for sale. I bought the animal for $4 and kept him about a month in my bedroom, providing him daily with meat, bread, and fresh fruit. He was quite well-behaved toward me but during the night scratched out great pieces of plastering at the foot of my bedroom walls. Now and then I allowed him to run in the outlying fields to get some exercise and to amuse me with his way of digging in. He could not run any faster than I usually walked. If I went along behind him he moved straight ahead; if I walked beside him then he tried to escape in the opposite direction. In less than 10 minutes he would burrow his whole length into the rich, loose soil and then I had to pull him out by his tail. When he was set upon by dogs it was a matter of no importance to him so long as they made a frontal attack; but as he was not able to turn his head, on account of his stiff, thick neck, the instant he was attacked from the side he was lost. He was skilled in the art of biting; he had a queer sort of bark somewhat like that of a fox. After I made repeated drawings of him I was obliged to have him killed; the damage he did was so far in excess of his good uses. I had his pelt tanned, in order to use it for a hunting bag, but

---

[8] According to Audubon, the American badger differs from the species found in Europe only in its jaw teeth. It appears so to me in the drawing.

it proved to be too greasy to be of service. However, I brought it home with me.

Indians of various tribes—the Potawatomi, the Foxes (Musquakee), Kickapoo, Iowa, and Oto—one sees constantly in this town, particularly at the landing where they take the ferryboat to cross the river. They conduct themselves in a very dignified manner. Now and then, to be sure, when one of them has drunk too much of the forbidden whisky, he is somewhat quarrelsome, but no more so than an intoxicated white man; nor is an Indian under those conditions any more dangerous than a drunken American. The latter is armed, as a rule, with bowie knife or revolver and is quick to use his weapon upon the slightest provocation.

Throughout the entire summer bourgeois or the heads of firms, clerks, and other engagees or employees of the different fur companies crowded the streets and public houses of the town. St. Joseph is for them now what St. Louis was earlier—their rendezvous. Here all staple commodities are supplied from St. Louis, but horses are bought up for the purpose of selling them to the Indians on the upper Missouri and on the Platte or Nebraska. There packs of buffalo hides (as many as 10 packs at a time) are reshipped on the steamers, the empty mackinaw boats sold and their crews discharged. Those people are called Mountaineers,[8a] a name associated with many dangerous adventures, much painful endurance, but also with much romance and pleasure. The Mountaineers like best to dress themselves in clothes made of tanned deerskin, embroidered and fringed. One recognizes them, therefore, at sight; knows who they are and whence they come. They are stared at as though they were bears. Not infrequently they have no other apparel then their leather costume, for after a long stay any other clothing would be entirely worn out.

It seldom happens, however, that these engagees have ever seen the Rocky Mountains, much less braved their dangers. But, on the other hand, they are compelled to work very hard in cold, rain, and storm. The Canadian engagees, guides in the Canadian woods, mangeurs de lard,[8b] are known to have swaggered through the most breakneck dangers in which they were inclined to play an important role. However, they cannot reckon courage as the most striking of their fine qualities. They have far too much regard for their own safety to fight for an employer about whom they constantly complain, because he demands work done in return for his money. Later on, when I reached the upper Missouri, I observed a great many of

---

[8a] See footnote 9 below.

[8b] "Manquiro de lard" appears to be miswritten for "mangeurs de lard." This habit of devouring lard has led to the sobriquet "greaser", applied now broadly in the west. Sylva Clapin, Dictionnaire Canadien Français, says of the phrase "mangeurs de lard," "a surname given by our ancient bush-runners to a new initiate, who, after having endured the first hardships, often misses the bread and the bacon of the paternal table."

these swaggerers. In that distant region, beyond the pale of law, I have often seen them cry out in alarm at the mere sight of a stranger in the distance and take to flight—even throwing aside their weapons or implements as if those instruments of defense did not belong to them. They are, on the other hand, the most good-tempered people and especially good patrons of the innkeepers if they have any part of their wages left when they reach home. Few of them are provident enough to put aside any part of their earnings to buy house and land or to settle down to their earlier employment.

Since gold has been discovered in California and lands have been granted on the part of the United States Government to settlers in Oregon, fur traders are in the background at St. Joseph. Now thousands upon thousands of gold seekers and immigrants en route to Oregon throng the taverns and streets in spring. The coming of the Montagnards [9] is no longer an interesting event.

In the summer of 1848, however, they were still the heroes of the day and took great delight in their triumph. Four of them whom I knew were much superior to the usual engagees in their good manners, their love of truth, and in enterprise. All four were Canadians; their names were Lambert, François Desolles, Michaux, and Wiskom. They were all inspired with the same purpose: to save enough money to become owners of land and of their homes. That common aim united them. For lack of means they could not be independent traders; for lack of training they could not be employed as clerks. At best, they could only serve as interpreters, for which their knowledge of the Sioux tongue qualified them. They were a far better type than the usual engagees, servants, and day laborers. As soon as the winter, or fur season, was over they left the fort, where they had been employed as trappers or traders, came to St. Joseph to spend the summer and, incidentally, to buy a good saddle horse cheap.

In the autumn they packed provisions and some gifts for their Indian wives and rode away to the trading post, where they thought they could get the best prices for their horses. At the time of which I speak they had a profitable business in horse trading, because they bought the animals at such a low price ($20 to $30) in St. Joseph. But when the bands of emigrants to California increased to such numbers they were forced to pay more than twice as much for a horse, which the Indians were no longer in a position to purchase from them for the reason that they could not get together a sufficient number of buffalo hides.

The four engagees having arrived at a trading post are no longer free to trade on their own account but only in the interests of the

---

[9] Montagnards are the discharged engagees or employees of the various fur companies and have formed the crews of the mackinaw boats which have discharged their loads of furs. They were called mountaineers, although very few of them have ever seen the Rocky Mountains.

proprietor or of the company to whom the post belongs. Wherever they find employment for the winter there they remain and sell their horses to the bourgeois or person in charge. They dare not trade horses to the Indians themselves, at least for buffalo hides (under no circumstances in exchange for Indian women), because, in doing that, they would violate the chartered rights of the licensed fur traders. So they sell their beasts to the bourgeois at the current price for horses at the post in exchange on St. Joseph or St. Louis. Then the bourgeois trades the animals for buffalo hides, whereby he never fails to make his profit.

All four engagees are enthusiastic for the Indian life. On the whole, the French more than any other European nation adapt themselves most readily to the Indian customs and mode of life; their easygoing temper, their courage, gallantry, and la gloire are inherent virtues of the Indian. Lambert is also a "bravo"; he has often fought with the Sioux in their battles against enemies and distinguished himself for gallantry in action. Therefore he is entitled to wear the crest in recognition of his heroic deeds: Porter les plumes, parcequ'il compte coup. This word "coup" has been adopted in the English speech. It is used to designate distinguished or heroic action in recognition of which an Indian is entitled to wear an eagle feather in his hair and to have the same emblazoned in Indian fashion on his buffalo robe. So far as Lambert is concerned, however, the winning of such trophies is a mere fancy; his ideal in life is to retire, in the course of time, as a landed proprietor.

My intercourse with these Mountaineers was very pleasant. Those with whom I talked were half-breeds who gave me much information and taught me, besides, the Indian language of signs which, however much their dialects may differ, is the same throughout all tribes on the Missouri. This knowledge of the sign language was of the utmost importance to me, even in St. Joseph, for I came in contact there with Indians from so many different tribes that I was at first hopelessly confused by their various dialects.

One of my hobbies was to collect Indian weapons, decorations, and apparel. Before I had learned the sign for "swap" I rarely succeeded in making a purchase unless I had an interpreter. The reason was, as I found out, that, in my bungling manner, I had made the sign meaning "give." When a man presses the desired object to his breast and gives the Indian a questioning look he is requesting a gift; when he indicates or points out the article he wishes, then strikes his right forefinger twice across his left forefinger, he means barter or trade. I soon became better acquainted with the Indians, when I was able by means of signs to purchase moccasins, bows and arrows, tobacco pipes, embroidered purses, bracelets, and clothing. For a very slight compensation I was enabled thus to proceed with my studies. The Iowa I found especially friendly. The Fox Indians and the Potawatomi were far more reserved. The Iowa have been a well-disposed tribe from the first; there is no record of any hostile act on their part toward the white race. Both of the other two, on the contrary, have waged bloody wars for the retention of their lands, especially the Potawatomi. Whether, as some people assert, those two tribes are to be regarded for that reason as more warlike is a question. The Potawatomi, as a related tribe to the Chippewa, fought during the War of the Revolution with the English against the Colonists.

After the Treaty of Ghent they remained still loyal to the English by whom they were won over with gifts and instigated to uprisings until, upon their last great attempt under Tecumseh, they were left in the lurch by the English under command of General Proctor and were forced to surrender their landed properties and to withdraw. In accordance with the terms of the treaty of 1814, they were allotted lands, known in the State of Missouri as "the Platte Purchase," that extended from the estuary of the Platte toward the northwest, even to the confines of their enemies, the Sioux. But, though they excelled all other tribes in the art of tilling the soil and in the breeding of cattle, they were not yet to settle down in peace. A part of the tribe was removed to lands beyond the Missouri, on the Kansas River. How long they are to have the benefit of that retreat only time will prove. As to the questions whether this continual displacing of tribes from their farms is a benefit or a menace to civilization and whether a benefit or a menace to friendly relations with the Americans, that is easily answered. The Fox Indians have not been inveterate foes of the Americans. That they came in conflict at all was the fault of the English, whose plan was to make the Indians a cat's-paw to pull their own chestnuts out of the fire. That explains the position taken by Black Hawk, who builded his hope on the English, and also why Tecumseh was put in chains.

This strife between the Indians and the Americans caused unrest among the Iowa; they had never existed in great numbers—were never a large tribe. Therefore, when they saw the white men pressing westward even to their own boundaries, they knew the Americans too well to risk a losing fight. Besides, being allied with the French, not the English, they were always friendly in their dealings with the white race. That they were brave warriors the records of their history prove. Less than twelve years ago they fought the Missouri Indians at King's Hill, not far from St. Joseph, and won the battle.

By the treaty of 1814 the Iowa were granted a strip of land south of the Potawatomi. They lived in a village on Black Snake River 3 miles from St. Joseph. Those possessions they were obliged to give up, however, and to withdraw to territory across the Mississippi. They then came into conflict with the wandering tribes of Shawnee and Pawnee. What a fate for the Iowa! No game in their hunting grounds. No courage to break up land and establish themselves in settled habitations; they were continually dispossessed; and now, directly through their territory lay the great trail to California and Oregon. Their fate was easy to foresee. They themselves realized it only too well.

Indians one meets here and in the surrounding country are, to be sure, no longer a true type of the savage. They have acquired much from living neighbors to the white man and, more's the pity, little that is good. How could it be otherwise? Do so-called Christians set them good examples? In the main, however, the Indian retains his traditional usages and customs; consequently, I found quite enough to study and to sketch. The stalwart forms, the race color, their tents of skins, their dances and games, their family life, all conform to our traditional conception of the Indian. The dress of the women, except in the matter of the material of which it is made, is unchanged; the "robe" and the blanket are still in vogue. The horses and saddles, flints, knives, and tomahawks of steel are innovations, and some articles of food as well.

Differences of physiognomy and distinctions in dress that set apart Indians of one tribe from those of another one does not notice at first. Only after rather close observation one learns to distinguish characteristics of one tribe from those of another with the same ease with which one recognizes natives of France, Spain, Germany, England, or the Jewish race, notwithstanding that the distinctive characteristics of each are very difficult to express in words.

The manner of dress among Indians varies quite as much and sets them as distinctly apart from us as their copper-colored skin. As a rule, the men wear only breechcloths, moccasins, and woolen blankets; otherwise, they are nude. Sometimes they wear leggings, i. e., trousers of deerskin, that are cut differently according to the tribe to which the wearer belongs; that denote tribal differences also in the way they are made and ornamented. The Indian women wear, nowadays, a short, bright-colored calico shirt (this garment is worn also now and then by the men) made with collar and with sleeves that are finished with cuff or wristband; they wear, besides, a sort of underskirt of red or blue woolen material that reaches to the calf of the leg and is held in place about the hips by a leather or woven girdle. Sometimes women use the same material for a kind of leggings that extend only to the knee and are fastened with knee bands, the straps and bands being often varicolored and richly ornamented with coral. On their arms they wear any number of bracelets, often as many as twenty, of brass wire that they themselves embellish in a really tasteful manner with files.

The fall of the Indian's blanket is similar to that of the Roman toga, but more graceful, because the drapery of a blanket is not so full—is less baggy in appearance. To put the blanket on, one takes hold of the longer upper edge with both hands, and bending forward, draws it up somewhat above the head, so that its weight is distributed equally on both sides, and therefore it does not drop when the belt (usually a strap of tanned buffalo hide) is worn to confine the folds about the hips. Though Indian women always belt their blankets, men never do except on their wanderings. In the under side of the belt or girdle at the back there is a slit through which a knife, in its sheath, is carried. Beneath the folds of the blanket, above the belt, women carry their children or other belongings. The blanket serves both as covering for the head and, in a way, as veil. When the women are at work it is allowed to fall over the belt in order that they may move their arms freely. As I have said already, men use belts but rarely. In the vicinity of their villages the braves adopt a manner of wearing their blankets that is peculiar to themselves. For instance, in order to have free use of the right hand and to reveal the tattoo marks, usually on the right breast, they take hold of their blanket or robe on the right side, draw it from under the right arm across the body to the left hip; the other half of the robe is brought forward with the left hand which remains covered and holds that part, brought under from the right, in its proper place.

Often these braves carry a fan in the right hand as they strut about the village dressed in this way. That style is followed, however, only in warm weather. As these coverings are ornamented with one or more colored stripes along the border of their narrower sides that fall straight down in front, those stripes always attract one's attention. The buffalo robe is worn in the same way as the blanket, i. e., lengthwise around the body, the head end brought over from the right, the tail end carried forward from the left. But, as buffalo robes are much heavier than blankets, the women use little leather straps that are drawn through the robe and fastened, somewhat like the fastenings on a mantle, at the throat. This helps to place the weight of the robe on the shoulders. Blankets, as well as bison robes, are sometimes painted, but they are not as artistic, because the woolen surface does not admit of detailed drawing. One sees, usually only on the back, red or yellow hands; these denote "coups"; and red or yellow hoofprints, which denote horses stolen. If the hoofprints are blue or black they indicate that the horses were presented as gifts. The blanket is, as a rule, the Indians' only bed covering. Their pouch is made use of as a pillow. Having taken off their moccasins and loosened their girdles or belts, they are ready for bed.

The blankets, however, Indians are beginning to use as material for coats, similar to the blanket coat worn by Americans. They give to these garments the shape of a paletot with hood but without buttons. They are held in place only by means of the belt. The garment is cut in such a way that the colored stripes are used for ornamentation. The straight edge with the stripes forms the lower part of the coat; nay, even the strokes denoting the quality (1, 2, 3, point blanket) are left in view; and stripes outline shoulder seams and extend along the base of the hood. This kind of coat I saw among the Herantsa,[9a] the Crows, Assiniboin, Cree, Sauteurs, both for children and young and old men; women and girls, on the contrary, do not wear them. The hood is pulled up in bad weather and here and there one sees on the peak of one of these a feather for decoration. Indians wear white, red, green, sky blue, and indigo blue blankets. Special sizes are woven for children.

After a more extended acquaintance with the various tribes one becomes observant and notices definite marks of distinction. For instance, the Potawatomi skin is much darker than that of other tribes in this region, their features less noble, their bearing not so stately. They wear their hair loose and unkempt. The men are fully clothed. They wear, usually, a coat and leggings of tanned deerskin, the leggings having a broad, double projecting seam that distinguishes the wearer from members of any other tribe.

Frequently they wind around their heads and loins woolen scarfs or sashes that are embroidered with beads in a design of arrow heads in different colors (called, therefore, ceinture à fleche). The same design, both in drawing and in color, appears also in old Mexican paintings; the colors, in most instances, are white, black, and red.

The Iowa are a more cleanly people than the Potawatomi; they are also of a brighter color, handsomer, and more stately in bearing. The men stiffen their hair with grease or loam and wear it pulled back from the forehead in such a way that the brow, being entirely exposed, appears very high. They do not wear the shirt of deerskin nor do their leggings have the broad projecting seam, but the latter are often trimmed with beads. On the whole, they wear very little clothing; in midsummer, with the exception of the breechcloth and blanket, they wear no clothes at all. So I had at last my long-desired opportunity to study the antique from living models.

Even during the first month of my stay in St. Joseph I had chances every day to study Indians that came in bands from the

---

[9a] They were the Hidatsa ; also called Belantse-etea. These are only dialectic variants of the name Hidatsa.

different neighboring tribes. It was the time when the yearly payments were made for the land extorted from them. As soon as the father received the money for himself and members of his family (the Iowa received $8 a head from the United States Indian Agent) they came to St. Joseph to make their purchases, because they could supply their needs there at more reasonable rates than with the traders. Still many Indians were in debt to the latter and, in that case, the traders had the first claim for payment.

The Indians came in increasing numbers, pitched their tents of skins (or, as often happened, of white cotton cloth) in the depths of the forest on their side of the river and had themselves ferried across to St. Joseph. The first two occasions upon which I crossed to the Indian settlement in that flatboat I came back in a most unexpected way. The first time, a numerous band of Potawatomi was on our bank, waiting to be put across. I had already bartered for several articles and was just in the act of trading with one of those Indians who had bought a rifle and therefore was offering his bow and well-filled quiver for sale. We could not come to an agreement; he entered the flatboat together with many other members of his tribe and all their horses, while I remained on shore watching the animated scene.

As the boat was shoved off, the Potawatomi shouted to me, "Trade." I sprang into the boat among the horses, in order to conclude the bargain on the other side of the Missouri. Then, as the ferryman told me that boats would be on the river until late in the evening, I went, with perfect ease of mind, in the forest to observe the Indian settlement at nearer view. My attention was especially attracted to some young people who were racing American horses they had recently bought. These beautifully formed naked savages riding bareback in a horse race along the sandy river shore I thought as fine a sight as the Grecian horseman at the Parthenon, and much more alive and intelligent. Their settlement I found not less interesting. There were tents just set up in readiness for new arrivals; others unpitched and bound on the horses in readiness for the tribe departing. I remained such a long while in the midst of these sights so welcome to me that it was evening before I returned to the shore. There I found a group of Americans and Indians waiting patiently but in vain for the ferryboat. Such a violent wind was blowing on the river that, let us shout "over" as lustily as we could, the ferryman would not attempt to cross while the waves were so high. At last, after a long delay, the wind fell and we were taken over, or rather we ourselves lent a hand to get the flatboat to the other shore, for the river, even then, was very rough.

I was attracted, the second time, to the Indians' side of the stream by the escapade of a young Fox brave whom I could not see enough of. It happened this way: I had been sitting for a long while on the shore, observing a group of elderly warriors [10] of the Fox Tribe who were partaking freely of the whisky bottle while waiting for another person of importance with whom they would be ferried across. Their women were already asquat in the boat with their goods and chattels. Suddenly a superb young brave, elegantly attired, came galloping down the steep river bank and with a bound landed in the boat with such force that the women started up screaming. As I was drawing near to get a closer view of the splendid horseman and his charger the young warrior dismounted, in order to keep his horse under control during the crossing, but the fiery animal, startled by the Indian's throwing his red blanket over his shoulders, leaped out of the flatboat. I caught him at once by the bridle and quieted him. Neither by entreaties nor blows, however, could his owner get him again on the ferryboat; he shied at the red blanket, and just having been purchased from a farmer, he was not yet acquainted with the sounds of Indian speech.

What picturesque poses these two Fox Indians took! In order to spare the beautiful horse further blows I gave the Indian to understand that I would induce the animal to go aboard the flatboat; for the brave's eyes were blazing, his "blood was up"; he needed but little more annoyance to bring his knife into play. Stroking the stamping, snorting beast and speaking kindly in English, I soon pacified him and led him into the boat, and kept hold of the rein until we arrived on the other side. The handsome brave swung himself at once into the saddle and with a friendly Hou! Hou! he disappeared in the forest.

Forms more beautiful than those I found among the Iowa Indians I can not imagine, though I have been accustomed during my studies from life for many years to all that is finest in the human form. Another advantage was their habit of wandering about in a nude condition, which contributed much toward the proud, easy bearing, as well as to the natural, graceful movements that characterize the Indian. No individuals of the white race can compare with them in that regard. The Iowa arrange their hair in one or two braids on the crown of their head and fasten thereon some eagle feathers or other headgear. The women, on the contrary, part their hair above the brow, draw it backward and bind it at the neck; then they braid with that queue a cloth, either varicolored or else richly embroidered. The younger girls, the elite among them, at least, arrange their hair in two braids, one on each side of the head, that hang sometimes

---

[10] One of these Indians wore a beautiful collar with a bear's claw, for which he asked $12. That seemed to me too dear a price, so I postponed the purchase of such a badge of distinction until a later time.

at the back, sometimes in front, and are also often adorned with bright-colored bands and beads.

Every Indian has straight black hair, dark brown eyes, copper-colored skin, more or less dark, rather prominent cheek bones, and small hands and feet. They rarely allow their beards to grow; in fact, they have hardly any hair at all on their bodies and the little that appears they very carefully pull out. When standing, an Indian's feet point directly in front of him; therefore, the foot-prints of an Indian can be easily distinguished from those of a white man. Any one who has had to walk a great deal through tall grass or along narrow paths that animals use will understand at once the advantage of placing the feet in that way.

Indians, including both sexes, have no tendency to obesity. Their distinctive physical characteristics are, further, a robust, low-arched chest and strong, compact limbs. Their attitudes and movements are never awkward. Their hands, which are perfectly flexible and supple from their constant practice in the sign language, they use in a manner particularly graceful. How often I have wished I was a sculptor that I might memorialize in stone the stately pose of certain figures and the masterful fall of the blanket.

The Oto, in speech as well as in outward characteristics, are a kindred tribe to the Iowa. According to certain American philologists the Iowa belong to the Dakota Tribe.[9b] From what I know of their language that conclusion is incomprehensible to me. That the Iowa in later years lived in the territory of the Dakota, west of the Missouri, proves nothing. They were forced to withdraw to the other side of the river by the combined tribes of Sauk and Fox Indians.

The Sauk and the Fox Indians shave the hair entirely from the crown of their heads and arrange what is left at the back in such a way that it looks like a tuft or brush. Some of them leave the long hair on their crowns for a support on which to fasten their head adornments. The braves have a proud warlike mien. They have this, at least, in common with the Potawatomi: they love the Americans just as little. They have no outlook for the future that inspires hope. Their thoughts dwell more on the past, when they were independent and free. Their daughters are not as beautiful as the maidens among the Iowa; consequently not so much exposed to the temptations of the white man.

In the late autumn of 1848 the Missouri froze over to such a depth that a four-horse team or sleighs laden with wood could cross without the slightest danger. This icebound passageway gave to many Americans easy access to the Indians' forests, where they collected

---

[9b] I. e., the Siouan stock.

enormous amounts of firewood and took it away without compensation to the owners and sold it in the city. Finally the chief of the Kickapoo [11] (the land of the Iowas begins at Wolf River) complained to the United States land agents, who then had a prohibitory order issued. The Americans act as though they think the Indian domain is at their disposal for hunting and fishing as much as they like without being called to account; but if an Indian should be met hunting, on what is really his own ancient native ground that he has recently parted with, a bullet or a beating will certainly fall to his share.

Near the end of the year 1848 about 30 lodges of Iowa Indians camped in the forest across the river from St. Joseph.

They came to get the benefit of the clippings and cuttings of meat and the wastage incident upon the hog-killing season. Since they must live by hunting, the winter is a difficult time for the Indians, and particularly grave in those forests where wild animals are well-nigh exterminated. The buffalo and the elk have retreated long since to regions farther west. Following the chase under such conditions, in the frosts and mists over ground covered with snow and ice, is extremely hard.

The chief of that band or kindred tribe of 30 Iowa families, or lodges, was called Kirutsche. During the summer he had often visited me for several days at a time and taught me the Iowa dialect. So I was already very well acquainted with him. He took much pleasure in my eagerness to learn. Kirutsche was a man of middle age, agreeable in manner, not tall but extremely agile. He had seen a great deal of the world; had been received by Louis Philippe himself in Paris.

As soon as Kirutsche was encamped and the entire settlement in order, he came over immediately to invite me to a dance that was to be given in his honor the next evening by some of his friends. I accepted his invitation with delight.

It was the evening of December 15. As I was crossing the frozen stream an ice-cold wind swept across the river, driving before it a cloud of snowflakes.

In the forest I found many converging paths and did not know which one would lead to Kirutsche's tent. As soon, however, as I was well into the wood, out of the howling wind, I heard the measured beating of a drum. Following in the direction of that sound, I arrived in a short time at the lodge. I had expected to find a tent of skins similar to those I had already passed, but this, I saw, was a hut constructed of withes in elliptical form and overarched with rush mats. At the top there was an opening for light and for the

---

[11] The Kickapoo a hundred years ago were the southeastern neighbors of the Sauk. According to Lieutenant Pike they inhabited the region at the mouth of the Missouri in 1805.

egress of smoke and cut low in one of the long sidewalls was another that served for door. The latter was covered, as by a curtain, with an animal pelt.

While I was standing before the hut, enjoying this interesting picture, in the twilight, of Indians' habitations in the primeval forest, I saw the form of a full-grown Indian come hurtling through the doorway. Naked, as he was, he fell in a snowbank and lay there, affording great amusement to the women and children who had gathered around him. He had drunk too much whisky and was in consequence hurled out of the hut for disturbing the company.

When I wished to go through the narrow door I found a great tall Indian stationed there as guard. He was unwilling to let me in. Kirutsche's squaw, who had already seen me, called to her husband, however, and he came at once to greet me. Kirutsche bade me sit down beside his beautiful 16-year-old daughter Witthae.

Notwithstanding my enthusiasm for the moment, I realized that my highest aims were being fulfilled; that after all my patient endurance, after all reverses, hindrances, and weary persevering years, I was at last in the midst of Indians; that I had found living models for my study of the antique; notwithstanding my heightened feeling under the consciousness of all this, I had to admit that this charming Indian girl made a deep impression on me. We could exchange very few words, to be sure; though she understood English, she was not willing to attempt conversation in that language; I could speak still less "Pachotschie." We had to converse, therefore, by means of signs, and eyes. To express my good will I presented some small gifts that I had taken along with me for that purpose. It was then that I learned what I often put to the test later on: that one becomes acquainted with Indians much more quickly if one does not understand their speech.

My beautiful neighbor did not absorb all of my attention, however, to the exclusion of the dance. Around a large fire that was burning in the center of the lodge sat twenty men and young blades (called "bannerets" by the Canadians and "bucks" by the Americans, because, at that age, their only occupation seems to be strolling about with girls). At the upper end Kirutsche sat on the floor, just as all Indians sit, with his legs crooked under him. Beside him were grouped his special friends and two drummers who to the measured drumbeats sang loud a repetition of "Oh!"

Two young men leaped, one behind the other, around the open space between the fire and the circle of onlookers; each of them holding back the blanket with his left hand, carried in his right a slender whistle made of bone with which, inclining now to the ground, now toward the heavens, then toward the fire, then toward the guests, he blew a succession of harsh tuneless sounds. The entire scene was in the highest degree animated and picturesque. I studied it very carefully in all its details, got the impression complete, so that, immediately afterwards, I was able to make a sketch true to life.

Then, varying the movements, the two performers (they really cannot be called dancers) went slowly round the circle and addressed themselves to each of the older guests or to those who were actually taking part (as distinguished from the mere spectators). With the right hand they indicated the person to whom they would speak, said something flattering, whereupon the latter would reply "Hau" or "Hun" (both words drawled, the last one very nasal and strongly aspirated; they are abbreviations for "yes"). After they had spoken to every one in the circle and had repeated the bounding and whistling act, the two young men and the drummers were relieved from further duty. However, before the new performers came into action whisky was served, in a wooden cup, to inspirit the guests.

To avoid accidents, in case of inebriation, Witthae collected all the knives (no Indian, man or woman, ever fails to carry a knife at the belt) and hid them.

Between whiles, Kirutsche sat down beside me to chat and to make me better acquainted with his daughter. I made him a present of some lead and gunpowder that he greatly needed. Then he said something to Witthae, who immediately took out of her pouch (which served also for pillow) a daguerreotype and showed it to me. Both she and her father were immensely pleased when I recognized at once a likeness of the chief.

"Paris—Louis Philippe—big King—French", said Kirutsche; and made the sign meaning "received as a gift." Witthae pressed the picture into my hand, giving me to understand that she was presenting it to me. Her mother (Wuotschimm) made known to me with nods and winks that I might kiss her daughter, but Witthae, seeing that I was about to put my arm around her, sprang up laughing and slipped out of the tent. Then all had a great laugh at me. But I was only saying to myself: "Just wait a bit!"

In about three hours the whisky flagon was empty, the people were tired, and the guests began to disperse. I was hoping all the while that Witthae would come back, but I hoped in vain. To search for her in other tents I did not like to do. As finale, an old witch of a woman who had become intoxicated gave a solo dance to the universal amusement of the spectators.

With her long hair wildly disheveled, she stood with back bent and elbows akimbo, moving her arms alternately backward and forward, while with feet close together she hopped, now to the right, now to the left, keeping time to the measured drumbeats and her own outcry.

Then I had to search out my way home through the forest. There was sufficient light, I admit, to show huge, dusky objects rising out of the snow but not enough to enable me to find a path. I wrapped my riding cloak close about me and stamped cautiously along in the direction of the river, sometimes climbing over a fallen tree, sometimes wading kneedeep in a snowdrift, but exulting all the way over the thought of having spent an evening in a lodge.

For three months I was a regular visitor at that camp and spent many a day and night in the variously constructed dwellings. The tents were, for the most part, conical in form and made of skins in the usual Indian fashion. There were among them, however, some lodges constructed of osier twigs or withes and covered with rush mats. There were others, besides, constructed with pieces of ·bark with a roof of the same material; i. e., strips of bark laid across the top. The last-named hut could be used only when roof and sides were covered with snow.

In this Indian settlement I observed customs and modes of life. I sketched also as much as was possible during the cold winter season.

In severe weather I remained indoors, made portrait sketches of interesting faces, and tried to learn the language as quickly as possible. My linguistic attempts gave occasion for a great many jokes and much pleasantry. I wrote the words down, always, in order to learn them by rote and the better to impress them. My reading their words off in that way afforded the Iowa much diversion. I was never able to get a copy of the dictionary in "Pachotschie" that their missionary (a Protestant) had compiled for the purpose of teaching the language in the schools. When attempting to write the pronunciation of words correctly I made use of all the languages I knew: For instance, the Iowa dialect has the English th, many nasal sounds from the French, the German u, r, i, but no sound for f or l. On the whole, I found the dialect a soft, melodious language.

1849

On New Year's morning an old squaw came to sell me a quiver of many good arrows; her husband now has a gun. After the sale was effected she took me aside and gave me to understand, partly with words, partly by signs, that she had a young and beautiful girl she wished me to marry. I was to come in the evening and see her. Being fond of these people and having given no occasion for mistrust or quarreling, I did not once consider the danger of rambling about the forest at night among so-called savages.

Curious and on the alert for any adventure, I went at nightfall along the way I now knew well to the tent designated. There I found the old woman with her entire family squatting around the fire. She bade me sit down beside an exceedingly young but attractive girl, and made the sign meaning, "That is your wife!" The girl was yet a child; at least, no more than 13 years old. Anene shrouded herself in her shabby blanket and began to sob from fright. I was much embarrassed. I tried to calm the shy girl and to comfort her with gifts of candy and other trifles. Meanwhile the old squaw sent for a young Indian who had learned very good English in Johnson's school in Kentucky. Now the transaction began: First, the marriage contract, namely, to the mother a pony, and in addition a new woolen blanket; to the bride a complete outfit of new clothes, good food, and no beatings(!); to the remaining relatives a sack (70 pounds) of meal. I was struck dumb with amazement; accordingly the old woman, thinking, from my silence, that I was satisfied with the terms, desired to have mentioned, as an afterthought, some sugar and coffee for herself. Then, quite unexpectedly, came Witthae with her younger sister, Niukigreme, and sat down just behind me. Witthae had heard about the transaction and now came to let me know that she was aware of what was going on. I gave her but one look; she gave me but a glance, yet that revealed what she had been careful, until now, to conceal.

She and her sister ran out again without having spoken a word. Then Anene ran out; for fear, most likely, of having her ears boxed by the jealous Witthae. Nor would she come back again; her mother might send for her as much as she liked, she would not come.

After waiting a long time in vain, I took myself off. In the wood outside I came into a tempest; trees were crashing, snowflakes falling thick and fast, and the night had become so black that darkness seemed almost palpable. Under such circumstances it was impossible to find my way home without a lantern. So I returned to the fire. Kennachuk, Anene's brother (all members of the same band or lodge call one another brother and sister, father and mother, whether that relation really exists or not) prepared a place for me to sleep and gave me a pillow. I wrapped myself in my cloak and lay down, but it was far into the night before I went to sleep. I had too much to think about; though this affair was at an end, I was sure of Witthae instead.

In just such manner as I have described the Indians give girls in marriage—or sell them, if they do not consent of their own free will. One or two horses is the price that makes a binding contract. When horses are not included, the marriage has no binding force either for the wife or her parents.[12]

---

[12] As horses were not originally known to North American savages, the bargain made with commodities must also have been valid. With the coming of the horse an Indian woman advanced in value.

In the event that the daughter runs off, she must take the horses back to the son-in-law; either his own or other horses equally good. For $30 I might have had Anene! Reasonable purchase! That is, if she were worth anything at all.

I was often surprised to hear young Iowa speak such good English. I asked Uotschetsche, one of the young men, whether they were taught so well at the mission. He said not so; but at Johnson's school in Kentucky. That man Johnson appears to be a great friend to the Indians (a rare exception among Americans). Out of his own means he has founded a school for Indian boys, where the youths are taught the English language, reading, writing, arithmetic, some geography and history. Whether they receive also religious training I do not know. I have found not the slightest trace of Christian belief in the schoolboys; still less, of better moral standards.

When the boys at Johnson's school reach a certain age they are required to learn a trade. However well meant that may be, the plan will not prove a success so long as the Indians are not given the same political rights as the white population in America. What is the use of being shoemakers, tailors, etc., when one is discriminated against as an isolated class? In their present state of poverty their old clothes serve them very well: are, really, more suitable to the conditions under which they live.

I would say that such training would not serve its purpose even in the useful trades, such as blacksmiths, armorers, tanners, rope makers and similar occupations, because an Indian skilled in such a trade would never work for an American; the latter would not receive him as a partner; he would never be able to establish himself as his own master for lack of capital; and among his own people he could not find sufficient employment or sufficient pay.

When these Kentucky protégés come back to their tribes they soon learn the truth as to their prospects. They then become the most unhappy, the most indolent, the most disregarded among their people. With their new-fashioned ideas they find no means of support; they are not farmers, huntsmen, or protectors; still less, warriors. In a word, they are ruined as Indian braves.

Judging by the many examples that I have observed, I shoud say that, notwithstanding his good intentions and self-sacrifice, Colonel Johnson has accomplished no good end. Nor will he as long as his fellow-countrymen do not receive the Indians as their social equals. Indian blood would certainly do the Americans no damage; Indian blood is purer than that of thousands of native-born Americans as well as of naturalized immigrants. The Indian, as the real natives of the land, would have a more ardent attachment to the soil, a deeper love for the nation, than, for instance, the Irishman who never surrenders his loyalty to the Emerald Isle.

The American is an aristocrat only skin deep. That sort is more foolish, more absurd in his pretensions and more immoral than an aristocrat by birth. The nobles have rendered excellent service. Real nobility serves as incentive to honor and distinction, but never when good birth is judged only by the difference in color of a man's skin.

At the end of January 1849 the first gold seeker showed himself in St. Joseph. For a long time I, and many other people as well, had regarded this much-discussed discovery of gold as a make-believe on the part of the United States Government to get the newly acquired region of California quickly populated. However, when a certain Widmer arrived here in the autumn, having been sent on by Solothurn von Sutter in California to conduct his wife and daughter over the prairie, no one could longer doubt the truth of the reports. The first arrivals from the East were two rich merchants from New York. They had traveled in a sleigh direct from their home to this place (more than 3,000 miles), in order to be the first to reach California. As they traveled westward the gold fever mounted; they were wealthy speculators—not duffers.

In the main, I think most of the gold seekers of this year had more ample means than those of later years; it was the more necessary also, because nobody hereabouts was prepared for such a large number of emigrants. The prices of provisions, cattle, and goods became exorbitant.

The farmer fixed no price for his products but advanced them higher and higher with each new band of adventurers. A bushel of corn, formerly only 15 cents, advanced to $1; a barrel, containing 5 bushels, was $5. Ham, formerly from 3 to 7 cents a pound, was now 12 cents; butter, from 8 to 25 cents. Oftentimes bread could not be had at all. Half of the farmers were again on their feet financially. Many of them, in spite of their preemption rights, were so poor that they could not pay the State for their land when the payments fell due; therefore a law had to be passed for their relief, whereby they were allowed to make payments in installments. But for that measure, most of the elderly farmers in the upper counties would have been bankrupt and their properties, together with the improvements they had made on them, would have fallen into the hands of speculators.

When the Missouri was open to navigation in the middle of February several thousand of these adventurers, all in a heat from gold fever, streamed into St. Joseph from all parts of the more northerly States, from the south by way of Panama, and many from Europe besides. Here the steamboat stopped and unloaded passengers, mules, horses, cattle, vehicles, and commodities. The landing place was animated to an extraordinary degree.

The city was packed so full of people that tents were pitched about the city and along the opposite bank of the river in such numbers that we seemed to be besieged by an army. Every house lot that was enclosed became a stable and brought in money to the owner. Widmer also came back; as Sutter's family had taken the route through Panama, instead of coming to Highland, he was now conducting a large company of gold seekers.

Because of the advance in prices, many poor emigrants felt compelled to give up their plans, at least for that year. They were obliged to return home or else remain here and seek employment. Many more, because they were unacquainted with this new mode of life and the conditions under which they must travel, wrecked their draft animals and for that reason had to turn back. Most of them made the mistake of loading their wagons too heavily and also of having begun their journey across the prairie too early, before the grass was high enough. These last-mentioned emigrants were forced, at best, to make a detour with their horses, mules, and cattle that greatly overtasked their teams. Instead of beginning with a maximum speed of 14 miles a day they went oftentimes twice that distance—by far too much, when setting out on a long journey. These ill-advised beginnings caused much laughter on the part of observers but were anything but pleasant for the emigrants themselves. Attempts to drive the obstinate wild ass caused, frequently, a great hullabaloo.

Many a time I have seen one single ass turn to scorn a dozen of those inexperienced drivers. They might jerk and pull as much as they pleased, the ass would not budge until they had mastered the art of driving in the right way. With oxen matters were often quite as bad; until their drivers learned how to put on the yoke, could crack the whip and knew which side was meant by "tschi" and which by "ho" the beasts gave occasion for much cursing and swearing.

Not less entertaining was the horror many of these emigrants had of the Indians, and even of the pioneers. They went about the streets heavily armed. They never failed to carry pistols (revolvers) and long knives in their belts. The inhabitants of St. Joseph, on the contrary, had more to fear from these adventurers than they had to fear from us.

And their golden dreams! Not one of them would return with less than $50,000! In California, that El Dorado, gold could be scratched out with the nails, without difficulty, with almost no work at all. There was no need of taking money along, if one but had his outfit; Indians one paid with the whip. After the fare was paid for being ferried across the Missouri, there was no further need of money, they

said. Under illusions, created by gold fever, they did not consider
that on the way out they might be forced by accidents to trade or to
barter; that they would not be given their food and clothing in
California; that they, even in the gold region, might suffer for lack
of money. In their delirium brought on by gold fever they did not
consider these matters at all.

Play and drink was the order of their day. In proportion to the
promiscuous throng, however, there was not much quarreling, horse
stealing, or swindling. "Oh, Californy, you are the land for me",
was their song, their rallying cry, their constant thought. It happened, however, that a conductor who had been engaged by several
bands of emigrants gambled away their combined funds instead of
providing the necessary outfit.

That was a jolly, stirring time. They tarried in St. Joseph until
June. Our tradesmen did a splendid business. About the same time
the Mormons assembled near Kanesville, 8 miles from Council Bluffs,
in readiness to wander on to Salt Lake and found their new Zion.
The quiet that followed this hubbub was almost unbearable. To
make the contrast all the more noticeable, most of the tradespeople
were off on new speculations and the farmers were busy on their
lands making preparation for the next migration to the west.

These travelers brought cholera with them from St. Louis; in
consequence, several of our population lost their lives. Up to this
time I had been perfectly well, even immune from cholera, although
my young partner who slept in the same bed with me had such a
severe attack that his convulsions awoke me. He died; I remained
in good health still.

On June 4, about 10 o'clock at night, a frightful storm broke over
the city and caused great destruction. Such a flood of rain streamed
down the street in front of the house where I lived that the swift
current made it dangerous for any one to stand there. Black Snake
River demolished dikes, bridges, and houses; my dwelling was surrounded by water that found no outlet. During the whole night I
was forced to work strenuously to keep the tide from rising further.
Next morning I was wretchedly cold in spite of the summer heat;
even at midday I was freezing cold. My illness became more grave.
I had an attack of bilious fever and spent several dreadful nights
entirely alone, without assistance. In my delirium I fancied the
house was falling in, that the bed was sinking under me. When I
became once more rational, I found that I had fallen out of bed and
was clinging convulsively to the fireplace.

But ill weeds grow apace. In a few weeks the doctor had allayed
the fever. As an after effect, my feet were so terribly swollen
that they felt like lead; standing or walking was painful. The
thought of having to submit to slow death from dropsy was ex-

cruciating to me. So near the fulfillment of my aims and not to be able to accomplish them! I would rather shoot myself than to watch the steady swelling of my legs. But the water did not rise further; after three long months I was again restored to health.

When I was strong enough once more to crawl up Black Snake Hill and stand beside the grave of little La Fleur I looked out over the widespreading view of that Indian domain—the forest with which I associated such a throng of memories—and felt my heart quicken again with purpose; I took courage anew. "Poland is not yet lost", I said to myself. "Never despair!"

Indians who came to see me in the autumn served as models for sketches and portraits. First came six of the most notable Fox Indians with their interpreter, asking that I put down in writing for them a message to the squire in this place through whose assistance they might get some horses that had strayed. As I wrote their signatures, each in his turn touched my quill pen as a sign that he consented to or authorized what was written. I took the greatest pleasure in those grandees; they bore themselves with a dignity so natural, so distinguished, that I was filled with admiration. With all sorts of pretexts I tried to detain them; I found in them delicate tact in manners, nobility of feature, and dignity in bearing. Unfortunately I did not take down their names. It occurred to me afterwards how frequently I forgot names, my memory having been too much overtaxed with the multitude of new matters.

From a trader I bought a painted buffalo robe. I had one already in my possession that was adorned with a sun, but the figures in the other were still more interesting.

The so-called "Indian summer" was wonderful that autumn; cold weather began late. It was the 22d of December before the Iowa came and spread their tents. The river was not yet frozen over and the poor Indians did not have enough money to pay the ferryman. They waited the livelong day, gazing with longing at the city across the stream. I was waiting most impatiently the hour of their arrival. Several whom I knew shouted across to me, "Istamantugra wagyachere." I sprang into a skiff and was rowed across. Then all begged to be taken back with me. First of all, I inquired for Kirutsche. He was not there. Then I went into all the tents to see whether other intimate acquaintances of mine had come. I selected the handsomest for models, so that I might go on with my studies. Until the river froze, I was obliged to be ferried across each time when I wished to paint a portrait of any one, and also to pay the person's fare back.

One evening, when the wilderness was irresistibly beautiful, I wandered in the forest, paid some visits, listened to the enamored lads as they made love to the girls with their flutes or made signals by blowing through their clenched fists. I, too, had a trysting place with the dainty little Niukogra near a hollow tree on the bank of the Missouri, whose waters refreshed this entire region. Several small herds of the most noble wild animals came there to graze, happily unconscious of their woeful fate.

The moon never shone so brilliantly, the trees never seemed so huge, nor life so romantic as at that spot. I sat there for a long time with the dear little wanton on the trunk of a fallen tree, under the spell of the moon, mirrored in the stream before us, and of her languishing eyes. I asked many questions but wrote nothing down. We sat there until late into the night, then went into the tent, wrapped ourselves in a cloak or blanket, and those who could fell asleep.

1850

On January 1 I began the New Year well by remaining in camp the livelong day and sketching both the exterior and interior of tents. At last, January 9, Kirutsche came, but at first he was alone. He made a proposal to me: if I would marry his daughter, Witthae, and establish myself in their domain, I should receive from his tribe more than 2,000 acres of land, secured to me by authority of the chiefs and the United States land agent. Kirutsche had spoken to me about this before. He wished to work; standing with folded arms was of no use. Neither did working by himself advance him at all; he had, then, to support all his relatives. He could not possess anything for himself alone, nor could he save anything, while the others were hungry. In order that he might derive some benefit from his labors, he wished me to form a partnership with him in the purchase of a stone-cutter's business that we knew of and work it ourselves.

On making the proposal he said emphatically that I was never to begin giving any of our possessions to the others, because they would then constantly beg without doing anything for us in return. The Iowa, he said, were not yet accustomed to agricultural labor. Their landed property, moreover, was not secured to them as mine would be, if the title was signed by the United States land agent; land so secured the Iowa could no longer offer to the United States for sale. I must admit that the plan rather appealed to me; to Witthae still more. I knew that what he told me about the land was true (improvements are included in the terms only that the land may not be obtained by speculators and thieves for their own advantage, but by settlers). The greatest difficulty was how to rid ourselves of the hungry Indians. Well, we would plant no corn. They could not take the stone from us. Besides, the stone-cutter's place was on the Missouri, a long distance from their village. He who ventures nothing, gains nothing, I thought; in all matters, there is much to be said on both sides. Furthermore, my parents-in-law pleased me quite well; they were industrious, good-tempered, and honest.

So, when Witthae came with her mother on January 10, I received her as my wife. Her mother served hot coffee, fried meat, and bread.[13] White Cloud, chief of the Iowa, came as guest to witness our union. Next day I purchased her outfit that she might clothe herself in new garments throughout. I bought the usual short shirt or blouse of red calico, a woolen underskirt and pantalettes, a red blanket, a choice of large pearl beads for necklaces, and many colored bands for her hair and for her costume. Later I bought wool for knitting and smaller beads for girdle and garters.[14] Though Witthae herself would rather have adopted the European mode, I preferred that she dress as an Indian girl. I liked the Indian style of dress both for its charm and its utility.

Everything went well until the mild winter weather made further slaughtering of hogs inadvisable; then, since the Iowa could no longer profit by the bits of meat trimmed from the slaughtered swine, one family after another went away—Kirutsche and Wuotschime among them. Floating ice made their passage across the river very dangerous. Soon Witthae began to feel like a captive bird. She had no one but me to entertain her. All my efforts to cheer her up proved unavailing. She became melancholy, obviously homesick. She gazed continually with tear-dimmed eyes into the distance beyond the river. Wrapped in her blanket she sat, dreaming of her earlier freedom; paying no attention to my assurances that I would take her over to her people as soon as the weather permitted.

Luckily, her mother's sister came one evening, bringing her daughters with her. Witthae was once more cheerful. In the hope of relieving my wife from further attacks of homesickness I invited her aunt to remain with us a while and help us to spend the time until we should settle down in a place nearer Witthae's people. It was arranged, moreover, that Kirutsche was to come to us upon his return from a visit to some friends in the Fox Indian tribe and assist us, when we transferred our residence to the land promised.

Then, imagine my astonishment, some mornings later, when I found that my bird had flown. Witthae had gone, taking her relatives and her belongings with her. I was in the front room shaving, when, all at once, it occurred to me that there was an unwonted stillness in our living room. After I had finished I went in there. I

---

[13] The women are especially fond of coffee drinking. They think it conserves their strength.

[14] She had, most likely, the same costume, originally of soft deer skin.

could hardly believe my eyes, in spite of undoubted proof to the contrary. There was no possibility of doubt: their goods and chattels had been taken along with them. I pondered: should I hasten after her, stop her, plead with her to be gracious and come back to me? Never! I loved her; I had taken her in sincerity with good intention; I had treated her well; I hoped, therefore, that she would come back. But at evening she had not returned. I thought it beneath my dignity to go after her.

Two weeks later my mother-in-law came, but did not bring her daughter. She said Kirutsche would bring her back.

"If she does not wish to come of her own accord, she may remain at home," I told her mother. Wuotschime was very much grieved. I held to my resolve. That was the end of my romantic dream of love and marriage with an Indian. Brief joy!

Now, all at once, St. Joseph was spoiled for me. I went 14 miles farther north to the town of Savannah. If the emigrants to California had appealed to me more I should have supplied myself with funds to go out with them, try my fortune in El Dorado, and then, with additional wealth, be all the more able to complete my work in art. But the gold seekers appealed to me even less this year than last. The route along which they traveled west was now known, as well as the expense of the necessary outfit and the best means of getting forward rapidly. The multitudes on the way to California, therefore, were poorer men, on the whole, and much more avaricious than the first adventurers. "Gold or death; gold, by all means", was their war cry. The farmers withheld their forage crops, for they knew that most of the gold seekers, in their fevered haste, would come on too early and be obliged to tarry a while in St. Joseph until the prairie grass was sufficient for their draft animals.

The emigrants were in great distress: The grass simply would not grow; the weather was unfavorable. As waiting in the city cost so much, they dispersed themselves on the farms, where, though they found food just as dear in price, they did not have to pay for the ground on which to pitch their tents. Many farmers, for the sake of exorbitant profits, sold so much of their produce that they themselves had nothing left and, oftentimes, had to wait until the next harvest. Swine were so rare and so dear that there were no pork houses the next winter; all hog meat had to be ordered from St. Louis, sometimes from Cincinnati.

As I have said, if the emigrants this year had pleased me better, I should have gone with them, for the possession of gold would have been a great assistance in the accomplishment of my purpose. Furthermore, I might have gone from California to Mexico and have been able to follow my original plan to study the Comanche.

But, in the first place, what assurance had I that I should accomplish this three months' journey in safety or that I should be successful in California, either in trade or in delving for gold? One had only to be acquainted with the majority of these wanderers and realize their passion for gold to form a very good idea as to one's chance. If a man were lucky enough to stuff his pockets with gold dust was he certain of keeping any of it? When people undertake a journey of 3,000 miles on foot with a wheelbarrow what avaricious greed must urge them on! Of what doubtful undertakings are such men not capable!

Almost every newspaper brought accounts of murders in the "diggings." My principal reason for not going, however, was my knowledge of conditions in Missouri: I knew that I could continue my studies among Indians and the wild animals in native forests nearer at hand. I did not need to wander so far west. If I had gone to California I should have profited, even at best, only by the opportunity to travel; I should not have been able to finish my studies. Often one does not value what one sees every day and, precisely for that reason, one goes forth to seek at a distance what can be had near at hand.

April. Savannah, although founded 8 years earlier than St. Joseph, is, on account of the latter's advantageous situation on the river, not nearly so large or important. In this land, the size of cities, not favorably situated either on a railway or navigable stream, is determined by the business enterprise of the region round about them. The fruits of the field are profitable or not, according to the transportation cost to a better market. Many farmers, too far removed from markets, do not harvest their crops except to feed and clothe themselves and their families; therefore they are unable ever to better their condition.

The rapid growth of St. Joseph has caused the abandonment of Jamestown (Jeintown), a former settlement on an eminence halfway between St. Joseph and Savannah. Competition was too great.

The empty tavern and some heaps of rubbish are still there as testimony to the town's early downfall.

St. Joseph was founded just eight years ago (laid out in 1842) but already takes precedence over all neighboring towns, even Weston. St. Joseph's favorable situation on the Missouri makes it a rendezvous for Mountaineers as well as the rallying point for emigrants to Oregon and California. When direct connection with the Mississippi is established by the projected railway to Palmyra the town will have every prospect for a bright future, unless the great continental from New York to San Francisco takes a route that leaves St. Joseph aside. In that event the growth of the town will be brought to a standstill; its very existence may be endangered. St.

Louis' early bright prospects are becoming daily more clouded. Trade with the North is now diverted almost entirely to Chicago. If, in spite of all efforts and sacrifices on the part of her citizens, St. Louis should not be made a principal station on the great continental railway, this emporium of the West, the future seat of the United States Government, would pass as a tale that is told.[15]

St. Joseph, as well as St. Louis, is indebted to the fur traders for its beginning. In 1834 Joseph Robidoux, as I have mentioned already, bought this trading post from the American Fur Co. and from this point carried on an exchange trade with the neighboring Indian tribes. His first house stood at the end of a ridge near the mouth of the Black Snake, as the stream is called from its tortuous course through the black shadows of the woodland. Canadians called the place at an earlier time, Le Post du Serpent Noir. Robidoux's old storehouse is still standing; it looks like a stall. In fact, the place is now used for that purpose. His dwelling house was on the other side of town. On its site now stands a tavern that was built by County Clerk Fowler.

As soon as the increasing number of country towns and farms began to close in upon Joe Robidoux and to create competition in the fur trade he decided to buy 160 acres to which he held preemption rights and to sell the land for city property. At first he sold lot for lot at very reasonable prices, in order to induce people to buy them; for instance, he would sell a lot for $10 or for a yoke of oxen. Then, according to the convenient location of the plots in question, he steadily advanced the prices. He is now an immensely wealthy property holder, but his 60 papooses, his seven white children, and several brothers in rags and tatters continually consume his substance. Two years ago the city lots had advanced threefold in value.

Now a building lot with 40 feet front and a depth of 140 feet, abutting in the rear on an alley, is worth from $300 to $600.

In Savannah I had an especially good opportunity to observe some of the religious carryings-on: camp meetings, baptism by "sprinkling" or "ducking in mud holes" was the order of the day. It was certainly a sight that reflects little credit on these so-called Christians. This religious mischief is sometimes carried to such extremes that an impressionable woman with a delicate nervous organism is driven out of her mind by the frantic rage of the preacher! Each claims to be right; each threatens with hell and

---

[15] St. Louis' prospects have been much improved by the railway line from Cincinnati; at the time I wrote the above, Illinois, out of jealousy, refused to grant the railway company right of way. But universal condemnation of that course brought the Suckers to a better mind.

damnation. This sort of thing influences many of their adherents to seek other churches.

On August 7 I bought a dainty black mare with white feet— all four white. She is a genuine mustang. What a joy to wander about the forest, where Fashion carries me to distances I could not otherwise accomplish and so widens the sphere of my observations. With Fashion's aid I have been able to visit often the Hundred-and-Two River (so named because it is said to be 102 miles long), to bathe in its clear waters, to sketch groups of trees on its shores that are hardly surpassed by those on the Cahokia.

Potawatomi from Kansas and those on the land known as the "Platte Purchase" visited one another frequently. I made sketches of some of them and, in exchange, furnished the young fellows with 10-cent pieces of rods out of which they make arrows for the hunting season.

At 20 feet they hit small objects with great accuracy; at a greater distance the least movement of the air may exert an adverse effect. At 100 feet they fly the arrows with great skill but can not be sure of piercing the heart of the animal.

In the autumn newspapers began to publish articles about a plan that was being considered by the United States Government, in connection with the highway to California and Oregon, to enter into negotiations with the Indian tribes concerned and for that purpose to invite the most notable men among them to a conference next summer at Fort Laramie. At once it occurred to me that I might enjoy an agreeable adventure and at the same time make it profitable if I would occasionally buy good horses, ride about the country on horseback, sell the animals at a profit next spring at Salt Lake, then, on my return, attend, if possible, that most interesting assembly at Fort Laramie and witness the signing of the treaty.

1851

The speculation in horses did not succeed particularly well. Farmers held back their corn and hay for the expected emigrants; the maintenance of my five pads came too high. Finally, because of bad news from California, not nearly so many adventurers came in the spring, but many more Oregon farmers who brought their cattle and provisions with them.

Then, of course, horses declined in value. I lost a great deal of money. The cost of feeding the animals was out of proportion to the amount their work brought me. I was too fond of them and spent too much taking care of them.

One misfortune after another induced me to sell the horses and give up the idea of going to Salt Lake. First, I suffered the loss of an excellent mare that I lent to an acquaintance who wished to attend a Christmas ball at Rochester. After he had run a race on a bet, after the manner of Americans, and over a rough, frozen road, he left my fine animal standing in front of a public house all in a sweat and without the protection of a blanket. In spite of all efforts to save her, the mare died from pneumonia. I suffered another mishap in a pasture where I allowed my four horses to exercise on a beautiful March day. A boy took great delight in playing tricks on the spirited animals and, to give himself further amusement, set a dog on them just to see them run an extended course. Having become once frightened, they did not stop running for several miles, until they were far into the forest. After a long search I came up with them at last but, as I drew nearer, calling gently to them, and was sure of getting hold of at least one of them, whinnying, they turned abruptly about, extended their legs, shook their manes and, in a trice, had disappeared from view.

For the reason that Lily, one of my mares, appeared to be going in the direction of the place where she had been bred, I thought I should find all of them next morning at her old home. So early in the day I hired a horse and rode over there, through a region that was unfamiliar to me. My road, a most romantic one, led through a magnificent forest, over two beautiful streams, and across a waste. Not a trace of my horses anywhere! Then I remained at home two days, hoping that my runaways might be induced by hunger to return or else that some news might come to me concerning their whereabouts. But they did not return. No news came. On the fifth day after their flight I hired another horse and rode to the place where two other mares of mine had been bred, i. e., to the "Round Prairie" on the high road to Fort Kearney near Newark. There, fully 9 miles from the city, I heard specifically that they had been seen. Fortunately, they had kept together and were so wild and spirited that no one could catch them; otherwise I should certainly have lost one or the other. A young farmer who had seen the two colts and knew the range of their earlier pasture mounted his horse and helped me trace them. For several hours we followed them from one farm to another. It was perfectly evident that they wanted to play with their former companions and were searching for them, and as the brutes went visiting around in their old neighborhood and tarried here and there with their former playmates we drew constantly nearer.

Still following the trace we came, late in the evening, into the highroad again, where dust made it impossible any longer to distinguish their tracks.

Well, I spent the night in Newark. Next morning, the sixth day of their "spree," I was up with the sun to follow any trace I might find on the highway. Over a wide stretch I searched but could find neither on the right nor on the left any tracks made by sixteen feet. I did find a place beside the road where they had lain down together, but on what night? That was a puzzle too difficult for my wits to solve. My only possible clue was fresh dung. After breakfast I mounted my hired pad with the intention of going home, hoping that my straying animals would instinctively return, finally, to the place where they had received good nurture and rich forage. Upon my inquiry at a farm on the highway I was told that toward sunset the previous evening four horses—according to the description, they must be mine—were seen prancing along the way in the direction of Savannah.

A little farther on, where the road from Marysville branches off from the highroad to Fort Kearney, I heard from a countryman living there that during the night four horses wanted to rest on the straw lying in front of his fence, that the roan mare (my Bet) had already lain down but, for fear that their presence might tempt his own beasts to break out, he had driven them away. Which way they went he did not know.

"Home, of course, to their own comfortable stalls," I said to myself.

I rode rapidly back to Savannah in happy expectation. There I found no trace of my runaways' return. So, after I had eaten, I had to mount a fresh horse and renew the search. Following my latest clue, I rode until the evening in all directions, through forest and over plain, without result. Vexed and tired, I returned to the Savannah road. Suddenly I was aroused from my ill-humored reverie by hearing some one call out as I was passing a farm, "Hulloa, Dutchman!" Turning my head, I saw a man sitting on his fence. He called out again, "Look here! Are them your horses?" Sure enough, there they were, evidently half-starved. There was no grass. At best, they could only have fed on tender buds just appearing on the shrubs. Besides, they had been racing about the country without rest.

Several hours earlier, the man said, those hungry horses had stopped at his fence, cast longing looks toward his stacks of corn, and then made known their desires by an eager neighing. He took them in, because he had heard that I was searching for them. The birds were caught, to be sure, but I had trouble still to get them in hand. So wildly they ran about, so persistently parried our efforts on every hand, that I thought they must be possessed with the devil.

Finally we got them in a corner and held them in fear by cracking a whip until I had bridled them. I saddled the filly, because she remained uncontrollable longer than the others. Then I paid the man for his assistance and set out home on a gallop. Never in my life have I ridden as fast; the horses seemed really running a race with one another to see which could reach home first. I thought I should be jerked off the saddle.

I had hardly got my team of four in good condition again when they ran away with me and plunged with the vehicle down a hill. To practice driving a four-in-hand and to accustom the horses to that mode of traveling I took drives every day in the vicinity. I got excellent practice on the usual American roads, for they abounded in stumps, steep slopes, and many running streams, but to learn how to manage with sloughs, ditches, narrow passes, curves, and the turning of corners I chose the forest road to Nodaway Island, to the Hundred-and-Two, and along the Little Platte River, all the way out to the parade ground. The horses pulled so well together, traveled with such uniform gait, were so instantly responsive to the rein, always stood so quietly when halted, backed without plunging, trotted so well without need of the whip, and the roan mare proved such an excellent lead horse, I was planning with much pleasure to take a journey with them to Deseret.

In April I drove alone to St. Joseph to talk over plans for the journey with my future traveling companion. On my return, about 3 miles from Savannah, the offside horse cast a shoe on her left rear foot. I stopped immediately, for she seemed to be limping. Since no one was there to take the reins, I threw them lightly on the seat cushion and went to examine the hoof. In spite of the care I took, stroking her soothingly and speaking gently, the instant I attempted to raise her foot she gave a leap and off and away all of them went over stock and stone, up hill and down dale, as if in a mad pursuit. I tried at once to seize the bridle rein of the lead horse but, in running, I stumbled over a stump and fell. When I got up I saw the vehicle plunging on—here a cushion hurled away, there my cloak. "Adieu, je t'ai vu!" I thought. "Confound it all!"

I ran after them, of course, as fast as I could. I had an idea that they were stuck fast in the forest. Sure enough, below the first hill, I found Bet wallowing in the dust, trying to get free from the harness and the long lines that were wound about her. Having set her free, I ordered her to get up. She could hardly stand! She was trembling in every limb and spread her feet wide apart for fear of falling. She had lost her head entirely. I led her away from the road and tied her tight and fast at a spot where there was grass; then I went in search of the others. About a hundred feet farther on I found Lily, Bet's companion, standing, bewildered, in the road.

Aside from a wound in her left rear shank, inflicted, most likely, by the pole, she had suffered no injury. I swung myself lightly upon her back and went on after the two shaft horses and the hack.

I found them at the top of the last steep hill as one approaches Savannah. Fortunately they could go no farther; they had hardly come out alive from the creek below. The two horses were caught in some bushes and the vehicle was jammed against a tree. The horse on the right had thrown her hind leg over the pole and was evidently forced to stop. The vehicle had most probably been carried on until it was held fast by striking the tree trunk.

I disentangled the beasts from their harness to see what damage had been done. Lily had suffered no injury—was only lamed. The hack could stand on its wheels, to be sure, but many screws were gone. I went back to bring Bet, the cushion, and my cloak. Then, having harnessed Lily and the colt together, I led them slowly home. The horses had to be cared for and doctored; the vehicle and harness had to be mended.

Finally, at the end of April I was ready for my journey; my wagon was provided with a canvas top and provisioned with zwieback, smoked meat, butter, eggs, sugar, tea, cooking and drinking utensils, oats and corn meal for the horses, a saddle, a double-barreled shotgun, a hunting knife, and four 30-foot cords with iron pins. The last-named were to be used for tying the horses.

My intended companion on the journey, a young American, was to wait in St. Joseph and be ready to set out with me on the first of May. Notwithstanding that he had detained me with his promises to go, Steiner refused, when I arrived in St. Joseph, to consider taking the trip. He had not the means, he said, to provide his own personal outfit. Now, I had asked nothing more of him than that he bring his own provisions, and, in return for his seat in my wagon, that he look after the vehicle on the journey, while I took care of the horses.

A fine predicament! To travel with four horses and a wagon alone was not to be considered, for both team and vehicle would have to be constantly guarded. To find another trustworthy person to go with me could not be done at once. Therefore, my grand display with four-in-hand came to a sudden end. I determined to sell both wagon and team. But now, when I wanted a purchaser, nobody would buy. Earlier, when I did not wish to part with my horses, I had many advantageous offers.

May 9. Lily and the colt sold in Weston. Bet placed on a farm so that she may grow strong again. Such a fine mare one is justified in giving the best attention; she will certainly bring $60 more. The wagon and harness as well as the large mare, Landy, left behind to be sold, so that on my return I shall have some funds. Trip to Salt Lake and Fort Laramie given up; I should have found no wild animals on the jaunt anyway.

So, I am going up the Missouri, a stream that has already been turned to good account, but not exhaustively. But both Indians and wild animals have been treated rather more from the viewpoint of natural history than from that of their picturesque life; my chief purpose, after all, is the study of primitive conditions. Art galleries and paintings are for me secondary considerations: they will interest me only when my preparatory work shall have been thoroughly accomplished and are to be the means, when I bring out my master works, whereby I prove myself a great artist.

May 11. Left St. Joseph on board the *Sacramento* for Council Bluffs, where I shall wait for one of the two boats that make annual trips to the Yellowstone in the interest of the two fur companies and bring back the commodities that supply their traffic.

May 12. This afternoon we passed a community of Oto and various settlements of half-breeds. One of our deck hands, spying some Indian women in bathing, amused himself by throwing out to them a bottle of whisky with the hope of enticing them out of hiding. His ruse succeeded; they were not willing to let the valuable gift sink to the bottom.

May 13. Arrived this evening about 6 o'clock at Iowa Point near the Bluffs. A forlorn place. None of the houses are built near the river, because the inhabitants so much dread losing their lives by the constant floods.

As a result the town is already a mile from its original site; on the opposite side much of the land is under water. My bed is made on a trestle over which a buffalo robe is stretched. Another buffalo robe serves for coverlet. Hardly a dozen houses are inhabited here; the people are, for the most part, Mormons.

May 14. Crossed over to Belle Vue, Mr. Peter A. Sarpy's trading house for the Omaha. There are still many emigrants in this part of the country. The cattle are driven across the river at this point, an undertaking that gives rise to much drollery. Many of the cows swim back again to find their calves that were thought too young for the journey and had to be sold. The teams are taken across in flatboats with the wagons.

In Belle Vue besides Sarpy's house there was the place where the United States land agent lived (Barrow by name. On account of unauthorized transactions with the Indians, he was removed at that time), the school for Pawnee children (Ellet was the teacher's name), six log houses with adjoining plantations, where half-breeds lived, and the remains (ruin it cannot be called) of Fontanelle's earlier trading post, a picture of which one may see in Neu Wied's Atlas. Farther below a Protestant mission, and beyond MacKinney, a trading place for the Oto and Omaha, a beautiful, far-reaching view over the estuary of the Big Platte or Nebraska.

May 16. In Belle Vue I saw the first Indian huts of clay. I made a sketch of a Pawnee girl beside one of them. Her attire was distinctive for simplicity; a shirt or chemise that came up under the arms and was held there by two straps over the shoulders—et voi la tout! I should have done better to stay in Belle Vue than here in Council Bluffs, but there is no tavern over there; besides, I know no one at all in that place.

May 17. A Mormon girl showed me a man's coat and trousers made of white leather and richly embroidered with silk in Indian fashion. She thought I would allow myself to be influenced to order a similar suit made. That one was ordered especially for a fop here, and is said to have cost as much as $500. I have had frequent opportunities, both here and across the river, to make portraits of Omaha. Each portrait costs me 50 cents.

May 20. Crossed again to Belle Vue for the purpose of visiting a village of the Omaha 6 miles distant. The nearest way is a road running sheer over the bluff by the ruins of Fontanelle. From that height one enjoys a picturesque, far-reaching view up the river toward Kanesville, where it winds through the forest below and far on to the estuary of the Platte, then through a wooded plain toward Papillon Brook that encircles, in part, the height on which the Omaha village is situated. How I was to get across that muddy stream was a puzzle. No sign of a bridge anywhere, only a number of fords where horses had to wade in dark, turbid water up to their paunches, and for that matter, men and women had to cross in the same manner.

I was on foot; furthermore, not exactly inclined to intrust myself to that mudhole and then appear in such a soiled condition in the village. I was going along downstream, hoping to find a fallen tree that would serve me for footlog, when I saw on the opposite side a mother and two boys getting ready to swim. The latter swam immediately over, but the woman wrapped herself again in her blanket, and remained on the bank. She spread on the water a skin or bag the edges of which turned upward, giving it the appearance of a miniature flatboat. The boys gave signs that I was to put my sketchbook and my clothes in that novel contrivance and then swim across. I took off my clothes, except my trousers, and let my belongings be towed as directed; then in I went with a splash and, with a few strokes, was on the other side. I gave the lads a tip, and explained that in a little while I should be there again and might need them. But my knowledge of the Iowa dialect did not avail me; the Omaha have a different dialect. With signs, however, I got on well.

The instant my back was turned—splash—the mother swam to the opposite shore, but not after our manner of swimming, with both hands at once, forward stroke, curving inward to the side. She pulled a stroke with one arm at a time, alternately, in the Indian way. Negroes swim with the same stroke.

When I had put on my clothes again I climbed the hill to the Omaha settlement. Their dwellings consisted both of skin tents (tipis) and clay huts, in the midst of which were scaffolds used for the curing of meat and high enclosures in which they confined their horses for safety. On the side from which I entered the village there was a narrow ditch or trench, whether constructed for defense (a shelter behind which they fired on their enemies) I do not know. At that time it was serving as depository for their "commodities." They mounted the meat scaffold by means of the simplest sort of improvised ladder, i. e., the trunk of a tree about 6 inches in diameter in which steps were cut. A young Indian woman invited me in good English to come into her tent and dry my trousers before the fire. Her name was Betsy. She spoke English quite well; also French and both the Iowa and Omaha dialects. She was what the Americans call "a character" (one of those genial originals).[16] I had news of Witthae, who is married to an Oto and lives in the neighborhood. I took a walk about the village. For a long while I watched the sport of young boys as they practiced hurling the spear with great velocity through a revolving brass ring—lordly figures, notable postures, fine expressions of animation and eagerness.

Before a clay hut sat the personages of the village as spectators and judges, some of them distinguished for their trappings of state, for their inherent dignity. * * * I sketched several portraits. Betsy expressed a desire to accompany me to Belle Vue to buy some bread. We swam together across the Papillon, after she had pushed me into the water, because, with unpardonable curiosity, I looked around to get a glimpse of her in her bathing suit. We then took our way across the plain. From the top of a hill we saw, a long way off, smoke rising from a steamboat coming up the Missouri. I was waiting with much impatience for the boat that was to take me back to Council Bluffs. I had fumed in vain until I was in quite a heat, was "boiling over." Still no emigrants were there; no ferryman appeared. After waiting for two hours my patience was wellnigh exhausted: In the first place I was hungry; in the second place I was plagued with the thought of my possible plight, if this approaching steamer should prove to be the company's boat that I so restlessly awaited and could not take, because I did not have my

---

[16] Decatur told me later about Betsy. Once when there was a famine she had, by her own efforts alone, constructed with some pieces of timber a sort of raft on which she crossed the river, killed a cow with her rifle, cut the animal to pieces, put the meat on her float, and with her stolen booty steered her way back to her people.

luggage with me. Would the captain allow me to go aboard here and then, for my sake, make another stop at Council Bluffs? If I lost this chance what was I to do? Meanwhile the steamboat drew nearer and nearer. Both upper and lower decks were black with human figures. Those people are engagees, I said to myself. Finally, as the vessel came round a curve, I could read with my telescope the name *Statesman.*

As far as I knew, that was not one of the St. Louis line of steamers. On the hurricane deck I could see wagon bodies painted blue and red wheels piled upon them—a sort of vehicle I had identified with Pittsburgh. That must be an Ohio boat, I concluded, bringing emigrants from the East.

In due time it came alongside. The passengers and I peered at each other. Are they emigrants? I asked myself. Mormons? Exactly. Far from halting at the Bluffs, they were going on 30 miles farther up the river to Kanesville or Mormon Landing. At last the agony of suspense was over!

May 25. Was sauntering along the sands near the ferry in the afternoon to make studies of some trees when a flotilla of Mackinaw boats arrived. Charles Martin was at the wheel. While they were waiting here in hope that a steamer would relieve him from further steering I made Martin's acquaintance. I sketched his half-breed sons for his wife—also, for myself. The people with him dressed as half-breeds and wore their hair long.

May 26. Today a horse thief was arrested by the ferryman. The latter had just ferried the man and his stolen horse across, when several emigrants, covered with mud and oozing perspiration, came galloping up to catch the rogue. The ferryman at once mounted a fresh horse and followed the trace of the fugitive, whose horse was already tired out.

To allay suspicion he rode quietly beside the man, took hold of the stolen horse's bridle, and ordered that the animal be given up. The thief grabbed for his pistol but our man discharged his own weapon through the former's coat pocket and wounded him in the hip; whereupon he was obliged to surrender the horse.

June 1. A very ordinary crowd here. President Monroe's verdict only too well confirmed:

"The worst Indians I have seen in my travels are the white people that live on the borders."

*　　　*　　　*　　　*　　　*　　　*　　　*

We had an example, a short time ago, of the manner in which Judge Lynch administers justice. A number of counterfeiters and gamblers (professional card players, oftentimes tricksters and murderers) fled from the States to this place and thought they could here carry on their questionable practices in perfect safety. The farmers in this vicinity were of one mind with regard to them: after having destroyed their molds and their presses they whipped the evildoers in a frightful manner.

Peter A. Sarpy has been here. He proposed that I wait as his guest in Belle Vue until the great company's boat arrives. His brother is a member of the company. He promised to give me introductions. I accepted with gratitude.

June 3. The entire plain is flooded from continual rain. Not an inch of dry ground; therefore this lair also is under water. For three weeks I have waited here. This evening I shall go to Belle Vue.

June 4. Belle Vue. The ends I have in view come nearer their fulfillment. I am living at present in a trading house; I sleep on a buffalo robe; I am again in the midst of Indians who are continually trading with Mr. Sarpy. He lets them have gunpowder, lead, and tobacco on credit that they may be prepared for hunting during the summer. Buffaloes range about 80 miles from this village. In this vicinity the Virginia (white-tailed) deer is still frequently found. Stephen Decatur, a nephew of the celebrated commodore, is employed here now as clerk. He is most courteous and obliging. Two months ago he served as sailor on a ship because, owing to the illness of his comrades on their way to California, he got stuck fast in this region. He was earlier a teacher in the East. There are three other employees: Joseph La Fleche, Sagan Fontanelle, and Peter, an interpreter for the Omaha and Oto. All three are half-breeds.

The Omaha wear moccasins made of elk skin blackened with smoke and usually with an ornamental seam across the back of the foot. The flaps turn outward. Shoes that the Pima wear are somewhat different from these of the Iowa; for instance, they have no flaps around the ankles. The decoration also is of another sort but difficult to describe.

June 8. Six braves from the Omaha tribe came today to let me sketch their portraits in return for a gift. After I had made drawings of Tehnegech and Techidingue in the position they themselves preferred, i. e., sitting on their heels with their faces full front, I told Wäkusche, a very handsome old man of noble bearing, to sit in my armchair, showing him that I wished his head turned somewhat to the side, because in that way his features would be seen to better advantage. He wished, however, to be represented just as others, fullface. Nevertheless I would not consent to that. Whereupon he went outside to take counsel with his comrades as to whether he might allow his portrait made with profile view without prejudice to his honor. Whether the much desired playing cards or his friends' arguments had most weight in overruling his scruples, I do not know. Enough! He came back and sat as I desired.

June 9. Tecumseh Fontanelle was careless with his gun and shot his left arm to pieces. This misfortune caused great wailing among his female relations. He was carried to his mother in the village, so that his friends might suck impure blood from the wound. Mr. Sarpy owns a splendid stallion, white with reddish brown spots. I made a portrait sketch of Waaschamani, a very old former chief of the Omaha. He showed me several testimonials from United States agents, in order that I might know he was a good friend to the white man. I sketched also Aschäwagi (Spotted Horse), a Pawnee chief who is on a visit here for the purpose of exchange and barter. Whenever he brings his wares he puts them in Mr. Sarpy's storehouse and stays with him until his business transactions are accomplished.

June 10. This morning, just as I was beginning a portrait of an Omaha youth, three gentlemen came in, two of whom, W. Picotte and A. Culbertson, I knew already. They are agents in the upper Missouri region for the great fur-trading company. The third gentleman was chief pilot of the Mackinaw boats and also a trader. I talked with Mr. Picotte about my plan to take advantage of their steamboat, if possible, to study Indians and wild animals in the regions of the upper Missouri. He said I should be able to see little or nothing from the boat, for the reason that, owing to the noise a steamer makes, animals were very shy about coming near the shore.

I should see little more than a few gaping Indians; nothing of their woodland exploits, their dancing, or anything of their sports. To see what was really of interest concerning the Indians, he said, I should have to spend two or three years at a fort. That I knew beforehand; however, I had not the means to take up quarters in a fort at my own expense as did Comte d'Otrente, the Irish Palesieux, Prince von Neu Wied, Baron von Barneburg, Audubon, and others. I asked him whether it were possible to get a position as clerk.

"I will see," he said. "In any case, come on board. If you find that you can see as much as you desire, voyaging up the river, then you can return on the boat."

Mr. Culbertson will take me as far at least as Fort Benton, where the Blackfeet live.

June 11. The two agents went downstream in their boats, met the company's steamer and accompanied it up the river. Heretofore the firm (Chouteau, Jr., & Co.) operated their own boat, the *Assiniboin*, and, after that was destroyed by fire, the *Yellowstone*. Since the latter was wrecked, however, they have their goods transported on boats owned by other people. So far all has gone well! I made a portrait of Tamegache, son of the well-known Waschinga. He became lame and surrendered his claims as chief in favor of the young

"Elk." I made a sketch, also, of Tanini, a most beautiful 14-year-old girl. She began to cry from fear (of some charm of witchcraft?). Only the promise of a calico dress could induce her to dry her tears.

June 12. I rode with Joseph La Fleche to the Omaha village and witnessed a buffalo dance [17] around the wounded Tecumseh Fontanelle. We had a hazardous journey, fording the Papillon and clambering up precipitous slopes. The dance of the buffalo troop was held in a large, roomy clay hut. Ten dancers arranged in pairs imitated, in the most natural manner, the way that buffaloes drink, the way they wallow, how they jostle and horn one another, how they bellow— and all the while the performers sprinkle the wounded man with water. All the dancers wore decorated buffalo masks and buffalo tails fastened to their belts in the back. With the exception of the never-failing breechcloth they were nude. A throng of people looked on. Only the "jongleur" or Indian doctor danced alone, and without mask and tail. We went home over the prairie at a gallop. A sharp wind drove the raindrops against our faces and presently a terrible storm broke with crashes of thunder—neither so loud nor so continuous, however, as we are accustomed to hear in our Swiss mountains. The Omaha have suffered so dreadfully from attacks of illness, and from the Sioux, that they could enlist hardly 80 warriors. At present they are exiles from their own territory and live on land belonging to the Oto.

To provide me with a position as clerk, in the event that the captain on the company's boat that we are expecting cannot take me with him, Decatur made me an offer at their trading post, with the Pima, on the Fauquicourt. Sarpy's trader, Descoteaux, is there. The fact that he is a man of bad reputation makes the offer unattractive to me.

June 13. Bought all sorts of materials that I can barter on the boat for Indian relics and add to my collection. Money would be of little use in such trading, because the Indians themselves have no idea of values and all commodities at the forts farther on are very much more expensive.

June 14. Decatur told me a good joke that old Robidoux played, many years ago, on a competitor of his in these parts named Manuel Lisa. Both were traders with the Pawnee. Each of them tried to acquire by trade as many pelts as possible for himself without being at all squeamish as to the means he employed, and, for that reason, they often quarreled. In order to prevent such wrangles and under the conviction that neither had the power to ruin the other, they pledged reciprocally to be "loyal", i. e., if a band of Indians arrived at their trading posts for the purpose of exchange and barter, neither

---

[17] A "medicine" dance to cure him. The buffalo is imitated.

would attempt to take advantage of the other. Manuel Lisa, however, had no intention of trading on honorable terms for any length of time; accordingly, upon an occasion when both of them expected a band of Pawnee he tried to circumvent Robidoux. While he ordered his post supplied in secret with commodities to barter to the Pawnee, he went over to see Robidoux by way of putting him off his guard, by his own presence there to hinder preparations, and to see what was really going on in the other storehouse. Robidoux played the part of unsuspecting host just as well as his opponent played his role; acted just as though he had allowed himself to be really duped. He invited Lisa to drink a glass of champagne to the success of prospective trade; but regretted that on account of his gout he was not able to stoop down, and therefore would have to ask Lisa to fetch the flask from the cellar himself. The latter obligingly raised the trapdoor in the room and went down the steps. Joe let fall the door, rolled a cask upon it, and with mocking words left his opponent imprisoned, in order that he might trade alone with the Pawnee.

On this same occasion I related to Decatur another story I had often heard in St. Joseph about old Robidoux. By his first marriage he had a son, Joe, who inherited from his deceased mother so many building lots in St. Louis that, according to current prices of city property, he was worth about $90,000. Now, Joe, Jr., was a confirmed drunkard and, on account of his bibulous habits, gave his father a great deal of trouble. Some years ago he went into the Catholic church dressed like an Indian, i. e., practically naked, to the amazement of the assembled worshippers. The old man, being in rather poor circumstances financially on account of his great number of children and his unfortunate addiction to cards, took advantage of this opportunity to confine his drunken son, as a punishment, for several weeks in his cellar and refused to release him until Joe, Jr., put in a favorable mood by receiving a glass of whisky after a long fast, signed a deed, already prepared, transferring the property to his father.

Another trick played by old Robidoux. As I have said already, he had a passion for card playing. As he went every spring to St. Louis, and, indeed to New York, for the purpose of selling furs and also of bringing back a new stock of Indian goods he had, on the steamers, plenty of opportunities for gambling. The game usually played is one in which that player wins who risks the highest stake; whether he actually holds the highest cards in his hand is immaterial. The game is called poker. On one of the old man's trips up the Missouri he met with an experienced partner; they were strangers to each other. Robidoux, rather poorly dressed as was his habit, did not impress his opponent in the game as one to be feared, so, after they had been playing for quite a while, the latter, with the intention of springing a surprise, put up a considerable sum. Old Robidoux, however, instead of showing concern, called to the waiter: "Bring that old trunk of mine here! Here are one thousand dollars in cash; I bet 'em all!"

The stranger could not increase the amount; consequently, notwithstanding the fact that he held the better cards, he lost the game and was obliged to give up his high stake of 700 or 800 dollars.

In the summer of 1848 the youngest son of old Robidoux met his death in a tragic manner. When he had finished his course at a college in St. Louis he came direct to St. Joseph. As too frequently happens, his entrance into the world of affairs was a protracted "spree." In his father's town he thought he might give himself up to the convivial life without restraint. Now it happened that just at this time the citizens of St. Joseph were in a state of great excitement over hooded bands of thieves that took away their horses and cattle. A number were caught and, to avoid legal procedure, the inhabitants let them be lynched. In consequence of these occurrences, any one who gave rise to the slightest suspicion after dark had to be prepared for any fate. One night young Robidoux, in exuberant spirits, heightened still more by many a "pop", was leaving the grocery in the dark, at midnight, to go home, when he conceived the desire to play a poor joke on a counting-house clerk, left in charge of the store, by frightening him up with noise. MacD., having no idea who was beating on the storehouse door so late, and having only thieves in mind, opened the window and called, again and again, "Who's there?" Young Robidoux, instead of answering him, pressed close against the lintel to avoid being seen, for neither was MacD. his friend nor Mac's employer one of his father's; both of them were competitors of old Robidoux in trade with the Indians. Recognizing neither the young gentleman nor his companion, in the darkness, but regarding their movements as questionable, he shot young Robidoux from above, directly in the head, and killed him as dead as a rat. Then Robidoux's comrade cried out who they were, but it was too late. I remember perfectly well the scene that followed. Notwithstanding the late hour, everybody on Main Street was waked up; a crowd gathered about the dead body. Old Robidoux was furious. He declared the murder of his son to be the base act of his competitor in trade and wished to lynch MacD.—in fact he himself brought a rope for the purpose. With much difficulty he and his adherents were restrained from committing that deed of violence. MacD., protected by his own friends, gave himself up to the constable. The fellow who was with the unfortunate young Robidoux at the time of his death was required to tell the facts and his statement prevented further bloodshed. MacD.'s employer stood bail for him, so that during the legal proceedings he need not remain in St. Joseph. As was just, he was later acquitted, and then he returned to the town.

New Year's Day, 1851, I spent among friends in St. Joseph. When, on the following day, I went to the house I had occupied during my former residence there (a small log house consisting of one room with a fireplace) I found that my supply of wood was almost entirely consumed. On New Year's eve in the preceding year I gave permission to some negroes, after they had got the consent of local magistrates, to dance in my room. I did this because nobody else would allow them to use premises for that purpose. My permission was limited to that one evening only, and did not include the use of my firewood. My house was not locked, however, and those colored people made merry there on New Year's Day and burned nearly all of it. On my bed I found a small chest, on which, after they had covered it with sand, a pair of negroes had indulged in a very lively dance. As they did not reimburse me for my wood, I took the chest in payment but was obliged to hide it in the fireplace. The master of the negro who owned the chest wrote me a letter in which he threatened to report me for carrying on illegal transactions with negroes. That caused me no anxiety, however. Soon after I had another unpleasant experience with a crowd of boys who, at their mothers' bidding, when some Iowa Indians visited me, threw stones both into my stable and my room. I paid them back with several lashings with my whip.

June 16. Monday. Early this morning Decatur waked La Boue and me with the shout, "The company's boat!" From the steps of the "pickets" I read with my telescope the name *St. Ange.* Notwithstanding, there were our two gentlemen, P. and C.[18] The vessel came to land. A young steer was slaughtered at once to provide meat for the boat's crew; the doves and cats that were to be taken to the ports were caught and put in their cages; some freight was unloaded; and I was granted my request to take advantage of the boat trip up the Missouri. The steamer is really a hospital for victims of cholera—the sick and the dying! My cabin is filled with the effects of people who have died. My box now serves a sick person for pillow. Shall I take this risk? But the boat is already under way, in midstream. "Good-bye, Decatur!" Two engagees took advantage of the boat's stop at Council Bluffs to abscond, after they had already drawn their wages in advance.

June 17. No doctor on board; two more deaths since yesterday! Evans, a professor in geology, prepared the remedy (meal mixed with whisky) that I administer. Father Van Hocken bestows

---

[18] Picotte and Culbertson.

spiritual consolation. Father De Smet is also not well, but he is not suffering from cholera. The engagees drink too much whisky. The deck hands or sailors remain sober; therefore they are in good health.

June 19. In the evening we were forced by a violent tempest to lay to near Black Bird's grave. Such raging wind! Such a flood of rain! Such vivid lightning! The cages containing the doves and the cats were blown into the river.

June 20. Anchored the entire day on the right-hand shore, in order to renovate the boat, to air clothes in the sunshine, to take better care of the sick, and to bury the dead.

June 21. Father Van Hocken dead. He died as a Christian. Had been sick only two hours. It was about 4 o'clock in the morning when I was awakened by his calling me. I found him, half-dressed, on his bed in violent convulsions. I called Father De Smet. We anchored in the evening and buried him by torchlight. Father Van Hocken was to have gone as missionary to the Nez Percés. And I had not sketched his portrait for Father De Smet.

June 22. Stopped a moment at Sergeant's Bluff (Floyd's grave) to greet "La Charité" and "La Verité." This is Iowa territory. They say a city is to be founded here later on.

June 23. Passed Bruyère. We travel slowly; there is no need of haste. As Louis has died, I am now installed as Mr. Picotte's clerk. I am obliged, therefore, to be up early in the morning and wake the engagees, see to the wood cutting, weigh out rations to the cooks—coffee, sugar, crackers, bacon, etc., for each day's "mess": that is my prospects for a good position. At least I get my traveling expenses free of charge.

June 25. Fort Vermilion is abandoned. Schlegel, the bourgeois, came with bag and baggage on board our steamer, to proceed 60 miles farther up the river and establish a new post. His company is forbidden to sell whisky and could not, therefore, compete with trade in the nearby Iowa territory, where whisky can be had. An instance of the effect of civilization upon the fur trade. Civilization under the advance of the whisky flask!

June 26. The Prussian Schlegel drank all my French brandy on the sly, as preventive for cholera. He became intoxicated; as a consequence, Mr. Picotte called me to account. Schlegel and his native mistress were put ashore with all their goods and chattels at the Isle de Bonhomme, where he intends to establish a new trading post in the land of the Sioux. Toward sunset we passed the estuary of the Rivière á Basil; strikingly picturesque scenes.

There are a great many fallen trunks from which firewood can be cut. That night we stopped not far from L'Eau qui Court to have wood cut and also to put off an engagee with Mr. Sarpy's cargo. We had an unexpected visit: a troop of Ponca warriors who, in the deep shadows of the primeval woods, gave us a most welcome concert of their war songs. Then they came on board and, after an exchange of harangues, coffee was served.

July 4. While we were at an extra lunch in honor of the Fourth we came in sight of Fort Pierre. Finally, after our midday meal was over, we reached the fort, W. Picotte's chief trading post for the Teton Sioux. A dozen braves, painted and decorated, guarded the wares that were unloaded from the ship. Most Sioux women still wear their traditional waistcloth. I sketched the fort and the settlement from the deck of the *St. Ange*. Many people and a large part of the ship's cargo were left here. A splendid bull of Devonshire breed is kept at this place for breeding purposes. He is said to have overthrown buffalo bulls more than once.

July 5. At 10 o'clock we left Fort Pierre; the Teton warriors gave us a parting salute. Winter huts in several abandoned Indian villages demolished, for the purpose of using poles and beams for firewood. Since we no longer meet farmers along the river, we have to cut firewood ourselves and carry it aboard. "Au bois! Au bois!" [18a] shouts H. P.

June 27. Cedar Island.

June 28. We met a flotilla of laden Mackinaw boats belonging to our company. We dropped anchor. Fred La Boue assumed chief command at the wheel; he directs the course of the first boat. All of the others must follow in his wake. I saw several Indian women with their children near the helm. Their husbands are coming back again in the autumn on horseback. Most of the others remain in the States and are replaced by our engagees, on the *St. Ange*.

June 29. As we were nearing Fort Lookout this morning Campbell (together with Schlegel, who had come aboard) wished to take the shortest route thither on his favorite horse; for he is a trader there. Owing to the elasticity of the long planks, however, the beautiful bay, in attempting to go ashore, fell into the water. Instead of swimming toward the land, he turned his course midstream in an effort to cross to a pasture he knew. They had to go out in a rowboat to catch him and keep fast hold until we could take him aboard the steamboat, which, on that account, we were forced to land on the other side of the river.

July 2. While we were voyaging along the right bank this afternoon I noticed on shore the walls of a fortification. I thought at once I had found some remains of ancient Indian origin and hastened to Mr. Picotte to question him concerning this remarkable discovery.

[18a] "To the forest, to the forest."

The earthwork dates back to earlier traders from whom the big company purchased it.

When wood was to be cut those places in the forest were chosen principally where leafless cottonwood trees were found in great numbers. At that time I took for granted that those bare tree trunks were denuded of bark and foliage through decay due to age. Audubon and Bachmann, on the other hand, attributed that condition to another cause: one of Audubon's companions discovered that the porcupine is the evildoer. Such a condition had never been observed before, even by such an experienced traveler as Audubon.

July 7. Today for the first time I saw buffaloes. One hundred and eighty years ago they were still to be found in the State of Ohio! Good-by buffaloes, Indians, and fur companies. We came upon several buffalo bulls standing on a sand bank. Owing to the direction of the wind, they did not get our scent; so we approached them so close that we were actually startled and gazed with eyes and mouth agape. One was killed; he ran quite a distance, however, before he fell dead. By means of a long rope he was pulled on to the deck by the engagees with loud hurrah and immediately quartered. Then I had my first buffalo steak.

July 8. Reached Fort Clarke, the Arikara (Riks) village. As Mr. Picotte expected the grandees of this settlement and wished to serve them sweetened coffee and crackers when he presented gifts, I had to remain on board to issue orders, etc. In the village Mr. P. and company were invited to partake of roasted dog as a choice dish. (I should not have exchanged courtesies.) From my station behind Père de Smet's wagon I watched what was going on there as well as at the fort and observed the people with the aid of my telescope. Had an interesting view of about 50 girls and women bathing. As they thought themselves well concealed they were sportive and animated in a natural way. There were several dainty figures among them—so slender yet round, so supple yet firm. How they splashed and romped behind the partly submerged tree that they thought screened them from observation.

Others dreamily dried themselves in the sun in postures and movements so natural and unrestrained, and yet such grace! If only that dog feast had continued until night I should not have been sorry. Mr. P. was escorted back on a pony that had been presented to him. I was obliged to go down to the office and see that the Indians were properly cared for in the main cabin.

Several Mandan accompanied us to their nearby settlement. Fourteen huts, most of them empty; poor remnant of a tribe. A windstorm drove us so violently shoreward that we were compelled to halt near those huts. The boat was actually driven to

the river bank. Several Mandan and Minnetaree (Hidatsa) remained on board and journeyed with us to Fort Berthold, which
they regarded as a great favor. The village now inhabited by the
Arikara belonged formerly to the Mandan. Prince Neu Wied
spent a winter there and Bodmer has a good drawing of it.

July 9. Early this morning Mr. P. told me I was to be prepared
to remain at Fort Berthold. He had just heard that Mr. Kipp, the
bourgeois there, wished to spend the autumn in Canada, and therefore a clerk must be left in charge. However, if Pierre Gareau,
the half-breed interpreter, should care to take charge of the fort
himself I might go on to Fort Union. At midday we saw from
afar the white palisades of an Indian village gleaming in the sunshine. We enjoyed a joke with our redskins on board.

From the deck they could discern in the distance several members
of their race whom they declared at once belonged to a hostile tribe;
they began their war songs, loaded their muskets, and fired at the
foe. We were rounding a neck of land or "bend", as "the lurking
enemy" came bounding into view. We found them to be friends.

Commodities consigned to this post were already disembarked
when I received the message to take my luggage and go ashore.
The steamer departed. I remained on guard near the wares until
they were taken in a two-wheeled cart to the fort. At a little distance off, shy children peered curiously from behind piles of merchandise and made comments on the strangers. In the course of
time I went myself to the fort and met my new bourgeois or chief.
I had seen Mr. Kipp before, in St. Joseph, where he was trading
horses. I observed him, especially, as he was leaving there for
Savannah in a two-wheeled vehicle drawn by two beautiful animals.
After supper with Alexis I took possession of my new quarters. A
dark room, lighted only by a tiny window, the panes of which seem
never to have been washed. A large fireplace and two wooden bed-
steads, which I found upon closer inspection to be inhabited by bed-
bugs. I was induced immediately, therefore, to spread my buffalo
robe on the floor and sleep there.

July 10. What I saw and heard today offers me a rich harvest of
sketches. In the neighborhood in which I now spend my days is an
Indian village of 80 clay huts surrounded by palisades and frequented by billiard players, idle lookers-on, horse traders, and Indian
women engaged in daily tasks.

There are also throngs of troublesome mosquitoes; only by smoking
them with "sweet sage" (Artemisia) can one think of getting any
sleep in the house. This fort, they say, is always alive with Indians,
except in winter, when they hunt the buffalo in surrounding regions.
That is another sight that I shall enjoy.

There is little traveling to and from this post. The Minnetaree or Gros Ventres, as they are called, never go far from their stockades for fear of the Sioux. They are too few to have the protection of different bands of their own tribe. The Indian women here plant fields of Indian corn (maize) and after the harvest, Crow Indians, a related tribe, come to the village. Now that a treaty of peace is concluded, Assiniboin come also to barter for corn—or rather, to beg. The Minnetaree are so reduced by wars and pestilence that Mr. Kipp, in return for 100 buffalo hides, enclosed their habitations with pali sades, so that they might be secure at least against surprise attacks and consequent extermination. Now no huts are visible until one has passed through the entrance to their barricade. Bellangé holds out to me the prospect of witnessing a combat, notwithstanding. For the Sioux, he says, renew their attacks every year.

July 11. I made a trade with Bellangé for two Indian pipe bowls, seven pairs of moccasins, and other things.

July 12. After breakfast the river shore was all astir. Hunters and horses were ferried across by Indian women in flatboats made of raw buffalo hides.

One could see in the distance a shifting dark spot on the plain—it was buffaloes. The assembled hunters had to surround them on horseback and procure fresh meat enough to last for a time. While a few of the animals might escape this danger, they would fall into the hands of the lurking Sioux. Mr. Kipp had provided his runners with excellent marksmen, who undertook the hunt for him in return for a share of the game. They came back soon, their horses laden with fresh meat. They had come upon five buffaloes apart from the herd that the huntsmen intended to surround and they selected the youngest and fattest, overcame him at once, and brought back the meat that we were so much in need of. For 2 days we had had none at all; furthermore, only two meals a day—at 6 o'clock in the morning and 4 in the afternoon. An order of things that brings on the discomfort of an empty stomach. In exchange for a blue blanket and a knife I got from a Mandan a buffalo robe elaborately trimmed with vertical stripes of porcupine quills.

July 13. Sunday. In the afternoon, while I was industriously sketching, a Mandan came hurriedly into my room and begged for my double-barreled shotgun, because one of his comrades had been shot by an enemy. As, in event of an attack, I might need the weapon myself, I refused to let him have it.

I went out immediately to the village to find out what was going on and found the place like a swarming beehive. Warriors and young men in arms were hurrying across the plain, others were mounting their horses, a crowd of women were returning in haste from the fields where they had been grubbing turnips, other women were going out, curious onlookers were standing in groups, eagerly gesticulating, anxiously chattering. An Indian, called Le Boeuf Court Queue, had been shot, they said, by one of the Sioux. He had been at the fort about breakfast time. I wished to trade with him for an old-style tomahawk (an elliptic stone attached to a very tough dried tail of the buffalo bull). I sat on the roof of our house and scanned the village and plain with my telescope. Though it was a gable roof, it was covered with earth instead of shingles; so I could easily walk around up there. The scene before me was most interesting: an increasing number of women and children were returning across the plain; some on horseback, others on foot; some with their sumpter-beasts,[19] others driving loaded "travois" drawn by dogs. Finally, toward sunset, I saw approaching the escort with the dead. Nearer and nearer they came across the plain in the golden shimmering light that soon deepened to violet, then to gray, throwing the dark forms into relief; the nearer they came, the more dull and dead appeared the heavens, until, in the dusk of the twilight, they arrived at the village.

First came the mourning widow, leading the horse across whose back lay her dead husband wrapped in his blanket. Mourning relatives followed, encircled by restive braves whose blood was hot. Now we got some information concerning the "coup."[19a] Le Boeuf Court Queue had gone with his family out on the prairie 3 miles north of the village and had lain down on the ground beside his grazing horse, while his wife and child were grubbing turnips. Suddenly the wife was aware of something moving in the tall grass in front of her and, knowing that they were on the extreme boundary of their fields, where danger might be lurking, she called her husband's attention to it. The Mandan swung himself at once upon his horse, bow and arrow in hand, to investigate the suspicious movement of some low bushes, but hardly was he in range of the enemy's arrow when he dropped dead from his steed. The woman screamed for help. The enemy fled without the scalp—in fact, without having touched the Mandan. The deed, therefore, is not counted a "coup." To shoot a person from a distance and kill him is not regarded among Indians as an heroic act. One must scalp the person attacked. One of the five men who admit having witnessed the deed reports that the enemy took away the Mandan's swift-footed horse.

Having arrived at the burial ground, the dead warrior was taken from his horse and laid on his blanket, his head and chest raised. Relatives sat around him wailing and howling, jerking out their hair, pounding their heads with their fists, tearing their flesh with knife and arrow points until their blood flowed as sacrifice.

---

[19] I. e., burden-bearing beasts.   [19a] See below.

Friends brought blankets, garments, bright colors as funeral offerings. Meanwhile a scaffold was constructed of four stakes held together with crossbeams. Upon this structure the fallen Mandan, attired after the manner of Indian warriors and wrapped in his robe, was laid beneath the covering of a new red blanket. His medicine pouch was fastened to one of the posts. The crowd dispersed— only his widow and his mother remained to wail.

Indians on the prairie do not put their dead under ground; in the first place they have no implements suitable for digging graves and, second, the bodies would have to be buried very deep to be secure from wolves. The sight of those scaffolds erected for the dead is often horrible, even loathsome, when after a time, the wind having loosened the wrappings, crows and ravens continually ravage the body. Bits of putrefied flesh fall below. In the end the posts themselves give way and the remains of the dead, once so respected, so much beloved, so deplored, lie scattered on the ground, the prey of magpies and mice.

July 15. Whenever I might be sketching in my room the Mandan are always in the way; they are never weary of smoking with their friend, Alexis. The latter is here for the purpose of demanding back his horses that the Minnetaree stole, because they thought them property of the Sioux. The fact is, Alexis lives in the domain of the Sioux (Yankton) at Fort Medicine.

On that account and for the further reason that he is, through his marriage with a woman of that tribe, allied with those enemies of the Minnetaree, he will find it a difficult matter, though he has identified his stolen horses, to get them back.

Now that I see so much that is picturesque, so many striking groups that follow one another in quick succession and that I wish to record in sketches while the impression is fresh in my mind, I can not endure being so much disturbed and inconvenienced. To make matters worse, the Mandan and Minnetaree as well are extremely superstitious and they look with dread upon an artist as the forerunner of pestilence and death. They regard drawing and painting as "bad medicine." This is not to be wondered at when one considers the singular coincidences that have confirmed them in that belief. For instance, it was the misfortune of these tribes to suffer their first epidemic of smallpox 20 years ago, when Catlin made his journey to this region; they suffered an affliction equally disastrous from cholera immediately after Bodmer's visit here with the Prince Von Neu Wied; again, fifteen people were carried off by cholera on our boat this year and, though in recent years no devastating pestilence prevailed, coincident with my arrival that dreadful disease made its appearance among the Indians in the regions south of us. I was warned by Mr. P. even while in Belle Vue and forbidden to paint any portraits in their territory, for the reason that I should be held to account, he said, for the least misfortune.

It might be that I should have to atone for any untoward occurrence with my life and might bring upon the company, as my protectors, complications equally disagreeable.

Accordingly, I had been on my guard. I had not asked any Indian to sit for his portrait but had studied them covertly and made only sketches. Notwithstanding their mistrust, however, they were so impelled by curiosity that they would stand in wonder before the drawings and took great pleasure in looking at them and in recognizing Père De Smet, Picotte, and Captain Laberge from some rough sketches I had made of those gentlemen without sittings.

Mr. Kipp installed me today as clerk. I was charged with the task of compiling, according to his pronunciation, a dictionary of the Mandan dialect for Colonel Mitchell. I kept the rough draft for myself and gave him a copy.

After supper—I cannot say just what time it was—I was in my room waiting, when I heard shots and outcries in the village. A woman, who peered through the small window and saw me there, made the sign for throat cutting, across the river. The enemy upon us again already, I thought. A moment later I was on my way to the steep river bank. A crowd was assembled on the landing below to see two skinboats come to land. Two young braves were returning with their first scalps! What exultation among the spectators! Every one was eager to extend the first welcome. The warriors came ashore. Their faces were painted black with the exception of the tips of their noses (sign of their having performed a "coup").

They presented their weapons, immediately upon landing, to those standing nearest them on shore (in token of the first congratulations). One of the bystanders so honored fastened the two scalps (there was no skin attached) to a long pole and strode into line just behind the victorious braves, singing their song of triumph. Proudly they moved forward, betraying no sign of emotion, totally unresponsive to the embraces of their people.

Before I slept I found out all particulars about that heroic exploit. The two young Indians were 19 days on the warpath. They went as far as Fort Lookout, ostensibly on an expedition for scalps, in reality to steal horses. They had already seized four horses when they saw two well-clothed Indian women bending over their work in a cornfield. They rode swiftly by, flying an arrow at the women, and in an instant the deed was done. The older woman attempted to draw a pistol from her belt but did not succeed, because her blanket came in the way and in her too great haste she could not extricate the weapon (rash resort to a pistol has long been a matter of scorn among our Indians). As the attack was made in sight of the wigwams the two heroes satisfied their greed for glory by scalping the unfortunate, shrieking women, and fled to their horses. They were hotly pursued and finally were obliged to abandon their stolen booty, because the horses were too much exhausted to swim across the river. The two scalps were placed beside the dead Le Boeuf Court Queue as an expiatory offering.

As a goodly number of half-breeds live in the vicinity of Fort Lookout it is possible that the two luckless women were of that caste. Judging by the good clothes and the fact that Zephir's wife is the only woman having a pistol in her possession, one may very well suppose, as Alexis himself said, that the women must have been Zephir's wife and daughter. Zephir is now enjoying a pleasure trip on the *St. Ange* in recognition of his long service as interpreter for the company. I am well acquainted with both mother and daughter. In my position here as clerk I have had to measure out to them a great deal of coffee, sugar, etc. Quite recently the daughter bartered her white shawl for 20 pounds of New Orleans sugar. How delighted she seemed that day when she caught sight of the high-priced luxury!

July 16. The Mandan dictionary is finished—600 words. I bought from Mr. Kipp some rare antiquities: A bear's claw, a chaplet, and a crossbow made of elk horn. I paid $5 each. Mr. Kipp is getting ready for a journey to Liberty on a visit to his white wife and children, a trip about which he has for quite a while been undecided. In the meantime his Mandan wife and papooses will stay with her parents in the Mandan village. He did not like my bringing a large trunk filled with wares for the barter trade, because he prefers to have the advantage of all profits made in that way; but when he saw that I had only ornaments, weapons, and clothing, the sort of articles his company does not carry, he said no more. In fact the two gold pieces he received from me today put him in a good humor.

Heretofore he has always been brusque with me. Regarded me, it seemed, as the fifth wheel of a wagon. Assigned me no work to do. Not once has he verified the receipts for goods brought on; was constantly complaining about having so little to do; was sure he should die of ennui without some employment. He acted in a way I thought queer. Finally he said plainly that I would serve my purposes better at another fort. He was talking in that vein when I applied to him for work. I felt uncomfortable to see myself regarded as superfluous when I knew perfectly well how the time could be profitably spent.

Now he has decided to go. He will stay at least three months and return about the time of the first snowfall. Meanwhile Pierre Gareau will have charge of the post. That man can neither read nor write. Neither does he know how to enter on the books sales to the Indians and to the employees, nor to credit the amounts that are received. In fact he does not know how to reckon. At noon, just as we were going to watch the war dance around the two scalps in the village, we discerned on the horizon, beyond the distant forest, ascending clouds of smoke from the steamer *St. Ange*. The boat from Fort Union was arriving. Indian women who are engaged to carry packs of 10 buffalo robes were summoned from the dance, painted and bedecked as they were. The dance itself was interrupted.[20]

Mr. Kipp came in utmost haste and gave over keys and books to me, with no special directions. He put on his hat and coat. The boat was already at the landing. Mr. Picotte came hurrying up to us without coat and hat and bade us bestir ourselves. He was much vexed because nothing was in readiness. The bill of lading should have been at hand when the boat landed. Without the shipping bill, either for the boat's clerk or for himself, how could he tell how accounts stood at the post? He bade me give presents to this and that Indian and charge to his account. I did not know where they were to be found.

"What have you been doing all this time?"

"Mr. Kipp would not assign me any duties."

"And yet he will go away. Has he those bills of lading himself? Then, where can they be?"

At that moment Pierre Gareau and his two wives came upon the scene, prepared also to go aboard the *St. Ange*. "Where in heaven's name are they setting off for?" I asked myself. Pierre informed me in passing that, if Mr. Kipp should have to stay, he was going on a visit to his kinsfolk in the Arikara village. He also gave over his keys to me. Out of the house came Mr. P. without having found the bourgeois. The fact is, the latter's yearning for an inspiring drop or two had attracted him to the boat.

"You have a fine state of things here."

I would have liked to creep away somewhere and hide, for he was certainly right. Nothing was in order, so far, at least, as business affairs were concerned. There I stood alone, in a state of absolute unpreparedness, with all the keys in my possession. Every one else was busy either with the ship's lading or on the boat. Alexis came

---

[20] Indian women in this region carry bundles on their backs by means of broad leather bands that cross upon the breast. Iowa women carry their packs by means of bands across the brow. The difference may be due, however, to the greater weight of the burden here; 10 robes weigh at least 100 pounds.

and told me that Buonaparte would give him back his horses. He
went away. Mr. Kipp was not going aboard but Pierre Gareau.
So—still more. * * * The boat has gone. And I am here for at
least a year. The bourgeois says cholera in the States south of us
hindered his departure. He must look after the Indians who are
suffering from influenza, he says, else they might become wild. If
he went to the States he might die himself. The true reason for his
remaining here, however, is Mr. Picotte's dissatisfaction. He is now
unpacking; comes immediately upon valuable articles, such as castoreum, which he had forgotten to dispose of. That makes him
peevish.

July 18. To the accompaniment of a tambourine, played by an
old man, young Indian women and girls gave a dance in full dress
in our courtyard. They formed an ellipse, facing one another, and
with feet close together they skipped forward and back to the
rhythmic call of "eh, eh." Their cheeks were painted red. A few
wore feathers in their hair. One carried a cavalryman's sabre in
her right hand. The dress of Herantsa [20a] women consists of their
traditional shirt of deerskin or of blue and white striped ticking or
some other cloth made according to their ancient style.

The Crows follow the same mode. Their house dresses are usually
very greasy and dirty. Their full dress shirts or smocks are trimmed
with rows of elk's teeth. A hundred teeth cost as much as a good
horse. This high valuation is due to their being so rare: the elk,
as is well known, has only six incisors in the lower jaw. For the
pleasure of witnessing the dance I am indebted to old Totano.

July 19. P. Gareau is back from Fort Clarke. He declares that
the Mandan have cholera and attribute their misfortune to Pale
Face who so frequently brings them ravaging diseases. "The whites
must have buffalo robes, but Indians can get along perfectly well
without the whites." Mr. P. has bestowed bounties to appease them.
P. G. has fever now. On his return journey he ran down and killed
a bison, and, while overheated, drank a great deal of impure water.
* * * An Indian offered me five robes for my telescope—a good
price, but I cannot spare my glass: it does me invaluable service by
enabling me to enjoy scenes at a distance that I could not get a view
of close at hand. Besides, being so nearsighted, I could not go out
on the prairie without it, in this land where I never know what I
may come upon. Furthermore, my telescope was the last gift I
received from my brothers, Louis and Gustav.

The 67 Assiniboin warriors who were put across the river on
Thursday, the 17th, have marched home on account of bad weather
and want of shoes—most probably! They took the field against the
Arikara but have come back empty handed. Went to walk on the

[20a] Herantsa = Hidatsa; i. e., r = d, a dialectic change.

prairie in hope of finding a certain beautiful person. There were too many people about in the neighborhood taking care of horses. Scalps in plenty at the place of sacrifice. The Herantsa, as the Gros Ventres call themselves (that name is foolish; they have not large paunches), are mistrustful of my sketching; they say it brings the pestilence. What would they think if they should see the scalp of one of their relatives in my possession? I should have to declare it was taken from an enemy; then they would be eager for it themselves.

Many Indians are sick—afflicted with dry cough and pains in the head. Mr. Kipp and family, P. Gareau, and others are also very ill at the fort. Only I, the evil genius ("bad medicine"), am well. For those deaths on the steamer my art is to blame. In reality the dry cold wind that has been blowing continually for 14 days causes this epidemic of colds. Since I came I have enjoyed only 2 warm days. Wind south, southeast, cool and brisk. Chatted for a long while with Bellangé. He has been here many years—knows everything. He is smith, wheelwright, farmer, trapper, interpreter, and trader. He would like to take the position now held by Pierre Gareau, whom he cannot endure. If he could read and write he would be ambitious to supersede me also.

July 20. While I was making a study in my room of a droll shabby dog Le Nain came in and gave me instruction in the Herantsa dialect. I wrote down the words—sharp pronunciation even for a Dutchman. Half of our Indian huntsmen rowed across the river to get fresh meat. For several days now we have had only dried meat. Not many from the village are on the hunt; most of the people there are suffering from cold in the chest and from headache (influenza). Bellangé related many of his adventures. His desire is to distinguish himself especially as beaver trapper. The fellow claims to do too much; I don't believe half he tells me. This year beaver pelts will not bring, he says, $6 a pound—are not sought What a power fashion exerts, even in the most distant, out-of-the-way land! Now that beaver hats are no longer in vogue, the price of beaver pelts has considerably declined. The low value placed on their skins is to the advantage of the beavers. There are said to be a great many of them not far from here but trapping them is too dangerous for Indians. Besides, as the prairie so frequently swarms with warlike bands of Arikara, Crows, Cree, Cheyenne, Sioux, Assiniboin, and even with members of the Blackfeet Tribe, the Herantsa [Hidatsa] dare venture out only in large numbers.

July 21. As there were few Indians about I made sketches of their dogs, of which there is an endless number here. Most of them look like wolves.

Moreover, they do not bark but howl most dolefully. If one dog begins a chorus 100 strong immediately joins him. Continuous cold rains. Our huntsmen rowed across the river. I have worse prospects than heretofore for work in the storehouse. But I will at least show good will. Bellangé gave me further instruction in the Indian language of signs.

July 22. The epidemic grows constantly worse. Hardly an Indian seen outside their village. Fever patients now and then jump into the river in spite of their coughing and sweats. Kipp and Gareau complain constantly of headache, aching bones, and twitching muscles. Kipp held out no hope of my remaining immune from the disease now so prevalent. He repeated this so often that I began to believe he wished me to have influenza. It would relieve his mind to know that meals need not be cooked for me alone; for if I were ill, I should have no appetite. Again made studies of dogs. I realize more and more what an advantage it is to be so well prepared in art that I can readily grasp characteristic feature of the landscape, of animals, and of the human figure. This gives me a mastery I could not possibly attain by studying out with painstaking labor the relations of things. If one knows the genius, one sees one's way, readily, with the individual. Mosquitoes unendurable. Excessive heat, then tempest.

July 23. How fortunately I am placed! What favorable opportunities for studying the Indians!

What I have observed—the hunt, the wild beasts—then I shall have completed my purpose here. That will come in time. Patience overcomes all obstacles. Meanwhile I am quite contented to have found such excellent models among the Indians. The Herantsa Wirussu are a magnificent people—the women possess little beauty of face but are splendidly formed. These Indians have a noble mien that is classic—all about me are living models of the antique. Draped with their blankets, they offer the best of subjects for the chisel. I often wish that I was a master sculptor; but then I should have to forego the pleasure of depicting grandeur in landscape; terrific hailstorms, in the midst of which these red children eagerly rush out and gather the hailstones, as many as possible, in order that they may have clear, cool water to drink. That is a luxury here, where one is dependent upon muddy lukewarm water from the Missouri.

July 26. The 2 days just passed were of absorbing interest. A dozen metisse de la Rivière Rouge (half-breeds from Red River) arrived with a Catholic missionary. They wanted horses, either in exchange or by purchase. They had come from their large settlement, a day's journey from here. All were dressed in bright colors, semi-European, semi-Indian in style—tobacco pouches, girdles, knife cases, saddles, shoes, and whips were elaborately decorated with glass beads, porcupine quills, feather quills, etc., in an artistic work done by their wives and sweethearts, but their clothes were of European rather than western cut.

The young priest, Father Charles Lacombe, began to preach. He found at once much with which to reproach us. Mr. Kipp, living here with squaw and children, had a white family in the States. His half-breed son was not baptized. P. Gareau, living here with two squaws, was sire of several children equally unregenerate. Bellangé has a troop of half-breed offspring not yet baptized. As for me, I was not a Catholic. Things were in a sad state. Every one of the children must be christened forthwith. * * * And that was the utmost that he accomplished. Conditions under which a man had to live in this region, he was told, were not his concern; white women would not live here. * * * As the black-robed priest was quartered in my room I did not escape a lecture. I cut him short, however, with the remark that there was too wide a divergence of opinion concerning such matters and too great a difference in age and experience between him and me to justify his calling me to account. When he found out that I was not a Romanist he refused to sleep in the same room with me. Went to his flock encamped outside.

With Catholic priests I am particularly unfortunate. In St. Joseph I had a misadventure with Scandling, the priest officiating there. Before the assembled congregation, on October 29, 1848, he wished to reject me as sponsor at a christening. I was to be god-father for the son of a Frenchman who was a friend of mine. As I was not a Romanist I called the father's attention to their religious observances and made the condition that he talk the matter over first with his priest in order to avoid any untoward occurrence. I was already at loggerheads with Scandling; in a wine trade he apos-tatized me as a Jew, whereupon I refused to let him have the wine for communion. The day arrived for the christening and I went with the boy's mother and a young man—the other godfather—to the church. I wondered why the father did not appear. When our turn came the priest stepped up in front of me and put several ques-tions in Latin that I was required to answer. As a matter of course I "melted like butter in the sun." I was obliged to say that I was not of his faith. He then objected to my assuming the responsibility of standing sponsor for a Catholic child. I could not blame him for that. I was not a little annoyed, however, that the boy's father had not forewarned the priest. The mother now intervened—made ex-cuses for her husband—and I gave my word never to alienate the child from the faith that has the sole disposal of the means of grace. When the young godfather made a better showing in his examination than I, the clergyman was mollified and the awkwardness of my position much relieved. After the baptism we had to go into an adjoining room to inscribe our names and to give the priest a small fee. My goldpiece I wrapped in paper and laid it beside the church register, thinking in that way to spare the sensibilities of the ecclesiastic. However, when I turned to go away I was stopped by the worthy priest, who remarked that it was customary among his parishioners to leave a slight token of regard for him. I directed his attention to the paper beside the book, whereupon, with much bowing and scraping, he dismissed me with his blessing. By that time I was really too much out of humor to make myself agreeable to fair Theresa—and both of us had looked forward with such pleasure to this meeting.

Among those half-breeds I found a smith who had whisky in his possession. P. Gareau drank until he was intoxicated, then began insulting and fighting everybody who refused to drink with him.

He attacked Indians as well as others, pulled off his shirt, and was of a mind to go into the village and challenge his enemies (members of the opposition) to combat. He was stopped by the soldiers (highly respected braves entrusted with the duty of keeping order in the village or settlement) and brought back. Then I shut the gate.

The priest was sent here by the Bishop of Chicago for the purpose of founding a mission. He wishes to begin that work, but if he desires success he must not set out by antagonizing respectable people whose support at this place he must necessarily depend upon. This is Catholic territory under the jurisdiction of the Bishop of Chicago. Neither Jesuits nor Protestants are allowed to found missions in any part of this region east and north of the Missouri. * * * Now, these Metisse are half Chippewa and half Canadian, Scotch—even Swiss (from an earlier colony of Lord Selkirk's). Early this morning we received news that a band of Sauteurs (Ojibwa, Chippewa)[21] would come from their settlement and make us a visit. Finally, after all members of the group had their festive array in order—according to Indian custom that is of the highest importance—they emerged from a grove of trees and marched forward toward us. There were perhaps a hundred of them, some in trappings of war, some on foot, while others, on horseback, flanked the column.

Five chiefs, carrying ornamental peace pipes or calumets and displaying prominently their trophies in recognition of "coups", formed the vanguard. Behind them marched the soldiers in platoon formation, singing martial airs, beating the drum, and firing their guns.[22] Then came three women dressed in one of their several costumes worn

---

[21] The Ojibwa who used to live in the region of Sault Ste. Marie were called Sauteurs.
[22] Upon occasions of visits on the part of Indians the firing of a volley from their muskets to announce their arrival betokens that they come on a mission of peace.

by Indians in this region.[23]   Last in the procession came a chorus of young men who had not yet won distinction for themselves.   Behind the fort, Quatre Ours, the Herantsa chief, and La Longue Chevelure, the celebrated speaker, awaited their coming.[24]   When they came up the Sauteurs paused long enough to hear their speaker's address of welcome, then singing together they withdrew with swift, proud step to the village and sat down in an open place on a narrow strip of dry ground that bordered what at that time was nothing more than a large ill-smelling pool of slime inhabited by thousands of frogs.

The five chiefs laid their pipes on the ground in front of them in such a way that the pipe bowl pointed to the hut occupied by Quatre Ours and the stem to a wooden fork stuck upright in the earth nearby The pipes were not lighted.   Now, articles of clothing,[25] magnificently ornamented, were brought to the chiefs and laid on the ground in front of their pipe bowls.   There were no presentation speeches but much dignity of port.   During this performance there was continual singing.   I had more than enough of it.   As I wished to make purchases from those half-breeds I betook myself to my room, where I bartered for some beautiful work at a reasonable price, according to what the same articles would bring today.   * * *   The Sauteurs overtook that Sioux who shot Le Boeuf Court Queue and killed the man and his wife.   The woman was so tired she could go no farther, the man remained with her, while the other three took to flight, riding the horse in turn.   * * *   This evening the Sauteurs are off to pitch their camp farther on and hunt buffaloes—courir la vache, as the Canadians say.   One of the Metisse brought a white buffalo robe to sell and received two good racehorses in exchange.   Such a skin is very valuable, for white or dappled buffaloes are very rare.   There are sometimes crossbreeds that are said to be very large, splendid animals.

July 27.   The Metisse have also taken their departure.   Our Indians are over the river again to ensnare buffaloes.   As soon as they catch sight of the animals in the distance the "soldiers" assemble in their hut (socalled assembly lodge) to consider whether they will go on the hunt.   Their decision is reported from the "lodge" by a crier.   Nobody is allowed to take his own course contrary to the decision of the "soldiers" on the buffalo hunt, because, according to the rules of the

---

[23] A skirt of blue cloth that extends to the shoulder and is held in place by 2 broad bands or supporters over the shoulders and a girdle about the hips, both girdle and bands elaborately decorated.

[24] Both chiefs looked particularly self-satisfied in their black dress coats; they wore black suits, European in style, without the traditional shirt or smock, but with breech-cloth; they wore long hair, no gloves, and they carried fans made of eagle feathers.

[25] The garments were for the most part so-called habits de Cheffre, i. e., a sort of gay-colored military coats of red, blue, or green cloth and shirts of soft white deerskin, either laced or richly embroidered with colors.

sport, everyone is to enjoy equal opportunities. I bartered a plug of tobacco to the Metisse for a beautiful bridle; a plug of tobacco and a pound of candy "kisses" for a knife of odd design with broad, tapering blade, together with its embroidered sheath; a red coverlet for a most beautifully ornamented pouch and whip; a pound of coffee and a pound of candy "kisses" to the Sauteurs for a feather ornament; a knife for a boy's tomahawk; and from Bellangé I got six pairs of children's shoes, three pairs of larger moccasins, one pair of gloves for winter lined with beaver, and two ceintures.

July 28. All the talk of this day is about the disappearance of the young and beautiful wife of Nez d'Ours, one of our "soldiers", i. e., one of the braves who are entrusted especially with the protection of the fort and never allow any transactions with the opposition.

While he was bartering with the Metisse during their stay here for the white buffalo robe, a young Mandan buck took advantage of the opportunity to escape with this young woman in a buffalo boat to the Mandan, who live near the Arikara village. The girl is hardly 15 years of age, rather small, to be sure, but beautiful, graceful, and to all appearances modest and unassuming in manner. The elopement of a wife with her lover is a dangerous venture, but nevertheless frequently occurs. However much he may care, Nez d'Ours must treat the matter lightly, else he will be scorned by his comrades as an unworthy brave. At the same time he has the right to demand the return of all gifts and horses that he had bestowed for his unfaithful wife, as well as all that the young Mandan possesses, if he has anything at all, and to give the latter a sound flogging whenever opportunity is offered. In the presence of several Herantsa I killed a young chicken snake [26] that had the evident intention of crawling about the floor under my bed. Hardly had I struck the reptile when one of the Indians fell into my arms and indicated to me that it was for his medicine (talisman). Then he slowly picked it up with two sticks and carried it solemnly to the door. Had the Indian brought the snake into the room? Be that as it may, his superstitious belief had received a rude shock.

July 29. This evening the steamer *Robert Campbell* arrived, bringing commodities for the opposition's company (Primeau, Harney, and Joe Picotte). Their fort is situated on the other (eastern) side of the village. The boat has gone farther up the river again. It left St. Louis on the 2d of July and had met the *St. Ange* on the way at Fort Pierre. Last year the *St. Ange* made the voyage from St. Louis to Fort Union and back in 32 days. This year 2 months were

[26] Chicken snakes are not venomous, neither very often seen. In St. Joseph I saw an unusually large one, 6 feet long, with a body 2½ inches in diameter. Once one of the Iowa came to me wearing wound around his neck the dried skin of a snake of this sort, the head and tail of which were decorated. I purchased it just as a curiosity.

necessary. Why? Because $100 a day is charged instead of a fixed sum for the entire trip. Mr. Kipp is talking again of his desire to travel on the *Robert Campbell* to St. Louis. The old man does not know what he wants to do. It occurs to him at last to unpack his goods and examine them. Summer is not the season for trade in furs. Animals shed their hair or fur at that time; their coats are thick and beautiful only in winter. If I am to remain here, I shall have a great deal of free time for my studies. The bourgeois says he must go to Canada and attend to some pressing business with his two sisters. That arrangement would require my remaining here a year at least. In the meantime I should learn the Herantsa dialect and become acquainted with the people and the business. I might perhaps remain here altogether or at another trading post

I should have to order my effects that I left behind in St. Joseph sent on to me; otherwise I should lose them. I am not conscious of the least yearning for so-called cultured societies, for I am not urged on to this work by ambition to contemplate the most beautiful objects and reproduce them on canvas but I am inspired by my ideal— my adoration of beauty. Here one lives much more at ease, is more free than in the civilized States; the so-called savage is not always disputing about the teachings of religion, about political matters the rights of man, etc., principles concerning which men should have reached some uniform understanding long ago. With the savage, the sound sense with which Nature endowed him has settled all such matters. Cursing, quarreling, such as one hears constantly among us, is never heard among the Indians. Let one but look on when they are playing billiards; the strokes are so nearly equal, the game so close, that the players themselves cannot easily decide which one wins (and they always play for a stake, oftentimes quite high). They then appeal at once to the bystanders as arbiters. There is no swearing, no contention—they lack even expressions for such. Furthermore, insult would inevitably bring definite results; deadly revenge from the person insulted, involving even bloodshed and death. With us affairs of honor are either passed over without punishment or satisfaction is demanded at great cost; the duel is forbidden.

An affront to one's honor stings to the quick—is a much more grave offense than horse stealing—yet what means has one to parry the insult or to get satisfaction? The law. But lawsuits are very expensive, and because so many people are unable to bear the necessary expense involved in punishing an offender by legal action they put up with offenses that would otherwise have deadly results. For that reason I will say nothing in favor of dueling; that is no means of arriving at a just settlement; either the stronger or the more skillful, not the one suffering unjustly, will be the victor. The justice of the court should inflict punishment upon the slanderer at once, without cost, and procure satisfaction for the person maligned if he has been wronged. I exchange two good linen shirts with Pierre Gareau for a most beautiful saddle pad. While I was taking a walk on the prairie today I met a number of interesting children playing in groups near their grazing horses. Several little girls, who had made a shelter from the blazing sun with their blankets, were singing to the rhythm of drumbeats and tambourines. Their song practice soon enticed one of the boys who were also guarding horses, and he taught a little dwarf to dance. I saw small boys quite frequently also at their first shooting practice. With grass stalks for arrows they aimed at the leaping frogs and, when they hit the mark, laughed with delight to see the little white-bellied creatures turn somersaults in their swift movements to escape.

July 30. Mr. Kipp gave me today a packet of newspapers that he had received by boat. The dissension and discord in Europe sicken me. How peaceful is life here!

August 1. The children come frequently to see me, now that they know I gave several of them sugar. My tiny window is often quite filled with cheerful faces that watch me, and entreat for "mantsiqua" (sugar) as I write or sketch. A girl of 14 crops up repeatedly; she attracts my notice more than the others, because her hair is entirely gray, and with her young, pretty face gives her an extraordinary appearance. Gray hair is said to be quite general among the Mandan—a sort of family misfortune, not due to severe illnesses. In this village men set more value on personal adornment and good appearance than do the girls; they take especially good care of their hair, even wear false hair glued to their own, but that is done only by those men who are accredited with "coups." The hair of the Herantsa Indians is not smeared with grease and has therefore a rough, reddish-brown look. The men wear their hair either hanging loose or coiled into a knot above the brow. La Longue Chevelure, as his name implies, is distinguished by his own unusually long hair. I saw him only once when he allowed it to hang down, and that was the time he delivered the address of welcome to the Sauteurs. He wore black clothes throughout and a black hat—not even a white shirt. He let his hair loose over his dress coat. In fact, the Indians think that, aside from the uniform, black clothes, such as are worn by the President of the United States, are most fitting for ceremonial occasions.

Since Indian women are accustomed to the nudity of Indian men and look upon that condition as in the nature of things, to be taken as a matter of course, no immoral effect is produced on them; while the men, who have opportunities all the time to see naked women, children, and girls in bathing,[27] are just as little affected. They regard clothes more as protection from sun and weather. Girls go naked even to their third year; boys, to their sixth. Often both are also sucklings at that age. When girls are in bathing one can usually see from their manner whether they are still innocent in the real sense of the word (in a moral sense). An innocent girl is not ashamed—knows no reason why she should be. Perfectly nude, she runs about, pursues and splashes her companions, shouts and laughs as joyfully as though she owned the world. Not so with the self-conscious maiden. She knows—what she knows. She stands in a posture à la Venus; she laughs no longer in a carefree way but muses upon that of which she is aware, upon what she desires or fears.

August 4. Between 9 and 10 o'clock the *Robert Campbell* returned from Fort William. Mr. Kipp did not leave on that boat, though he has often spoken of going. The old man does not know what he will do. Mosquitoes are still unendurable; unless a man wears clothes of deerskin they drive him raving mad.

Unless one makes a Hades of one's room every evening, with the smoke of sweet sage, one cannot possibly sleep at all. Do these pests prefer the blood of a white, unsmoked body? Inasmuch as scenes in my neighborhood have little variation, I am now attempting to perfect my first sketches and therefore I am paying especial attention to details.

August 7. The weather is again getting cooler; one is already sensible of the lengthening of the evenings and the nights. I long for the winter, that I may observe the hunting in this region. Just as a variation from my usual life here, such a little adventure would not be undesirable. If I had only taken some courses in chemistry, I might amuse myself in a delightful way with the Indians; they would regard my experiments as "great medicine"—something supernatural. To get on in the wilderness demands, generally, a knowledge of many widely varying subjects not fundamentally acquired. Chemistry, pharmacology, languages, agriculture, cattle breeding, trade, hunting, and every possible handicraft one should have, at least, a sufficient knowledge of to put to practical use. With a musical instrument (for this region, particularly, a loud sounding one) one might afford much entertainment, both for oneself and other people. I am frequently sensible of this lack in my own training; I have given myself too exclusively to painting; but, on the other hand, to perfect my work in art I have quite enough to do.

August 8. Have been thinking much about the past—how much I have endured. My aims are nearer their fulfillment. At last we begin unpacking and verifying commodities consigned to this post.

---

[27] It is certain that half-concealed nakedness excites the senses more than a completely nude condition.

August 10. For some time I have been occupied with the thought of painting an especially beautiful buffalo robe, but not with the intention of depicting my "coups." On the contrary, I will paint thereon Indian scenes in my own manner. Today I have the plan complete: Across the robe at the top, an Indian village; below, a fort; on one side, at the bottom, the outstanding periods in the life of an Indian brave, from youth to old age; on the other side, the life of an Indian woman; in the center, "coups" of my heroes. Heroic exploits and adventures of my heroes will include, necessarily, the most important wild animals of the chase. Not a bad idea! I gave an order to Pierre Gareau for the hide, complete and whole, of a buffalo bull, including the head, tail, and legs. Such hides as that rarely come into trade for the reason that, on account of their size and thickness, they are too difficult for the women to handle. Furthermore, such hides cost as much as three of the usual size, because the hunter, when flaying the animal, has to be so extremely careful that twice the usual amount of time and trouble is required. Bellangé is of the opinion that a buffalo hide may offer good material on which to sketch if it is shaved perfectly smooth. Perhaps that is true of cowhide, but the hide of a buffalo bull?

Such fancies often lead me astray; if they prove to be practical, then they become a definite aim; if not, I put them out of mind. One profits by experience. My ideal of the perfect human form was at first only such a notion. As I progressed, however, in my studies from nature and from the antique and with my investigations in the field of aesthetics my conception of the high purpose of the fine arts gave to that early fancy a more and more definite and lofty direction until it became at last worthy an artist's life purpose—his ideal. To create the human form in its highest perfection, as reflecting its living spirit or, in the language of Holy Writ, the image of God, became my high ideal. While my present aim to reproduce this Indian life in art is merely a preparation for my ultimate life achievement, still the two purposes are inseparably connected. I must find a setting for my Adam and Eve, a paradise that bears the character of early nature in a warm climate. I must become acquainted with the mode of life among primitive people in order that I may truly represent them. The ideal of a modern painter must urge him on to loftier aims than were achieved by the Greeks; loftier than those of the Christian Middle Ages, when an artist's ideal was to personify certain attributes in the character he represented. This might be called the ideal of blind faith. The modern ideal of man must comprise all good attributes.

We find beauty in everything where the form corresponds to the indwelling idea; still our loftiest conception of beauty is man in his first perfection, as perfect soul, embodied with noble feeling in an equally perfect form.

The ideal of the Greek sculptor (and most probably of the painter also) was perfection of the human form, not actuated by the spiritual; a serene being undisturbed by passion or struggle. Their gods served as the loftiest ideal to which they could attain in the representation of human perfection in bodily form. But what gods they were! In what a slight degree they differed from men whom the artist commonly saw! To be sure, gods could make themselves invisible—could at their pleasure transform themselves to other shapes. Not infrequently they made use of that godlike advantage to convert themselves into men. Did they exemplify nobler qualities of mind than men possessed—more lofty thinking? Were they not as a usual thing subject to the base passions of hate, envy, sensuality, insatiable desire for power, of deception, etc.? The Greek deities, as well as those of the Romans, exemplified lower standards in thought, in feeling, and in morals than were practiced by the men of that day, and they were actuated in their dealings by less worthy motives. They did not distinguish themselves for high qualities of soul; the artists of the classical period therefore found it impossible to take a more lofty flight.

That perfection to which the best of them attained has always been a marvel—all the more so as the people of that age, notwithstanding their high degree of cultivation in art, lagged far behind in other respects.

When Phidias, one of the famous Greek artists—one may say the greatest of all antiquity—first attained his ideal in "classic repose" that was not to be surpassed, a number of celebrated sculptors in Greece and Asia Minor attempted to portray states of feeling, as in the Niobe group and the Laocoön. That marked a certain advance, but did not go beyond those few works.

The ideal of Raphael and his famous contemporaries is just as far beyond that of the Greeks as the Christian God is exalted above pagan deities. However, Raphael was also a child of the time in which he lived: His Christus and his Maria are representations of blind faith; with all their moral purity they reveal no vibrating intellect, no creative intelligence, no free will. Good characters and bad are portrayed, to be sure, in a manner distinctively excellent, but the greatest of the artist's creations are but passive instruments in "their Father's hand."

We artists of the modern day desire, first of all, free will; for, without choice, to what virtues can we attain? What is the use of withstanding temptation if one is only the tool of a higher, invisible power? What purpose is served if one assumes that victory or failure is already predestined in his own behalf or for the good of others—therefore inevitable? Furthermore, of what avail are pre-eminent talents if, upon every great discovery in the realm of science, upon every triumph anew over material things, the cry is raised, "That is tempting God." And then, later on, "It was the will of God."

Such blind belief is, according to my view at least, the standpoint of one in subjection. The temptation of our Savior would impress us as a silly farce if He had not of His own free will resisted the splendors of temporal power. Moreover, the miracles would have little significance as direct emanation from divine omnipotence; yet that must be true if the intelligence of Christ dominates matter to such degree! How much higher order of being is man, endowed with intelligence and made an agent of his own will! How much more lofty such an ideal than that of blind faith, than that of "classic repose"! How little we are moved by Minerva, goddess of wisdom, who is all-wise yet impotent! How stupid seems amiable Venus! How lacking in spirit the meek Madonnas of Raphael!

Would the Christian ideal sacrifice beauty in the least degree if the artist conceived his perfect being as endowed with divine intelligence, with independent will? If he represented human beings as more godlike rather than gods in the form of man? Certainly not.

My ideal is the human creature, in whom are harmoniously combined lofty intelligence, noble mind, and ardent feeling, represented in corresponding form; difference in sex being taken into account—that is, without debarring other qualities, man must be portrayed with more spirit and energy, woman with more noble feeling.

But for the necessity of representing the figures fully clothed, I would embody this ideal of mine in Christus and Maria. Clothes are ever an indication of weakness and shame. My ideal is to have no cause for shame—in my ideal, mind and heart are pure. No clothing is to be needed, for in a tropical landscape protection from cold is unnecessary. Aboriginal man! Primeval world! My vision of man in his perfect state shall be embodied in the nude, with such beauty, such nobility of form, that the perfection of the figure, the purity of line, and chaste delineation of feature will permit in the mind of a beholder of cultivated taste not the least vestige of sensuous appeal. I said "a beholder of cultivated taste" because one needs a public made up of individuals who have been accustomed to such figures in antique art and are not inclined to redden at the least suggestion of nudity, to avert their eyes in order to conceal embarrassment, or, perhaps, to cry out, "Fie! For shame!" for the reason that in contemplating the nude figure, most beautiful of all created forms, they are sensitive only to physical attraction.

However, it is not primitive man in his life of untroubled ease that I shall attempt to reproduce in painting; I will represent him under circumstances that test his faculties of heart and mind—his force of character. For that reason I am studying American Indians; for, if I acquaint myself with their way of life, I can later on portray also aborigines of the white race.

The scanty drapery I shall employ will most likely give offense to the general public, but that attitude toward my art shall not deter me from pursuing my aesthetic aims. An artist, conscious of his trained abilities and singleness of purpose, is not to allow his course to be determined by popular approval; on the contrary, he is to assist in the artistic cultivation of the populace. To that end he must necessarily assume an independent position.

How difficult the task! What a long period of time and study, what perseverance is required for the accomplishment of my purpose!

Here I am interrupted by La Queue Rouge, who has watched me a long time, wondering how I dare continue writing such a great while without taking notice of him. At last, as I raise my eyes trying to bring other thoughts to mind, he asked: "Sagiz?" (Enough?). "Tampa!" (Don't understand!)

August 11. This afternoon a cool, brisk wind from the west has considerably lowered the high temperature of the morning. À bas les maringuins! [i. e., down with the mosquitoes]. Yesterday I swapped coffee and sugar with a young girl for a queer sort of embroidered needle case. Today the same girl brought a friend with her who had what seemed to be a bodkin case; swapped with her also. The girls wore these as ornaments pinned on the front of their deerskin shirts.

So I passed the time bartering goods I had brought with me for objects of Indian make. To Pierre Gareau I gave a bolt of calico for a man's buckskin shirt, elaborately ornamented, and a woman's shirt-dress made of two whole bighorn pelts; each of these, at the current price, was valued at $12. Bellangé's Assiniboin wife will supply me with a similar garment, made more simply and untrimmed, for 18 pounds of coffee. From Bellangé himself I bought a pair of ornamented trousers made of buckskin for $10; they are cut according to European mode and trimmed in Indian fashion. Finally, from Mr. Kipp I received six beautiful arrows for my elk-horn bow. I gave him in return a flask of cherry brandy and two pounds of candy "kisses" for his Mandan woman. I shall probably pay the further price of a sleepless night, due not only to my joy in my new possessions but to the possession, on the part of the "boss" and his wife, of the flask of cognac!

Ugh! how the rain pours. How agreeable here in this Indian country, so far withdrawn from the stir of the world, to dream of the ideal toward which I strive and to philosophize. Yes; my ideal human form shall be embodied in the nude; not for the purpose of asserting, however, that the highest ideals can not be attained otherwise. On the contrary, in certain instances, the highest art requires that figures be clothed. My Adam has no world to discover, as had Columbus; his paradise is ready for him.

But his intelligence must show that he is capable of the loftiest endeavor possible to human genius; like Daniel in the lion's den, he must be able to quell wild beasts with a glance. While in primitive man genius is merely existent and offers no difficulty to the artist except in the portrayal of nakedness free from any suggestion of sensuous appeal (otherwise, the artistic purpose would be lost; the work of art pernicious), in civilized man genius in its fullest development reveals itself in the greatness of character and presents that most difficult effort, on the part of the artist, to show the effect of those lofty qualities upon the outer world. If I were not so enthusiastic for the nude human figure in art, I should not have thought it necessary to travel so far in order to find models for the perfecting of my studies, for a handsomer or more intelligent race of men does not exist than our highlanders. Neither can our natural scenery be surpassed in any other land, except perhaps in Mexico, where tropical nature is varied with magnificent mountain scenes and lakes of equal beauty. Primitive conditions exert an irresistible charm upon me. Here I may clothe the figures only so far as to make my pictures acceptable to the greater number of people. The most beautiful of garments can not serve the purpose in art as well as the perfect human form; garments are beautiful, in an artistic sense, only when they reveal to advantage the human form.

Our Celtic forefathers would appeal to me as models for my paintings if their nether garments were not so inartistic. If I should leave them off what an outcry I should cause among the archeologists! O Diviko! How picturesque our highlanders would appear without their pointed skull caps; our women without their stiff sleeves. Such trivialities often bring an artist to a standstill, because he must be true to nature!

Whether I shall attain to this lofty ideal is another question. I do not doubt that in the course of time—after a long time—I shall accomplish my aims, for the same qualities of mind and soul that enable me to conceive such an ideal will empower me to embody my vision in forms. Now I need only to perfect myself in the technique of painting. Up to this time I have only made studies—very few paintings. When I shall have mastered technique I will then venture to undertake the poetic, the aesthetic principles of art that will enable me to achieve my aims in composition and expression. When I have reached my ideal I may assume that my taste is refined. Inasmuch as the pictures I would create have long been distinct in my own imagination and during the six years I have already devoted to the study of composition in rough sketches, my enthusiasm has never grown less, but, on the contrary, has ever urged me on to higher aims as my studies progressed, I am encouraged to believe that, if I live and am granted the blessings of health and independence for only a few years longer, I shall accomplish the ends I have in view.

An artist striving for a certain aim must have an ideal beyond his grasp, else he might think he had attained perfection. That would bring cessation of effort and result in retrogression. That which is difficult to attain inspires to higher and more enduring achievement than that which is easily accomplished.

Earlier in my career I believed that I must, as artist, perfect my conception of the form as well as the godlike mind of Christ. But who knows in what form God is to be conceived? Can not the human creature be distinguished for lofty qualities of mind and heart without being considered, necessarily, the tool of a higher power with no will of his own? Since my ideal has, luckily, survived my change of faith I have no longer anything to fear.

August 13. Toward sunset yesterday I heard an outcry from the direction of the village, followed, as usual, by the howling of all the dogs. Everything was in commotion. I hurried out to the gate, curious to know what was going on. The trouble was that some one from Yankton had carried off four horses belonging to an old Crow Indian. He could not find them anywhere. In a trice young braves, mounted and armed, were galloping across the prairie. By the time they reached the forest, however, night had fallen; to follow any trace was therefore impossible. Until late at night they were heard singing and firing off their muskets as they returned home. Today they say the horses have been found. Only a little excitement for the Indians and me. This entire day there has been rain and nothing but rain.

August 14. La Grande Chevelure paid me a visit today, bringing one of his friends with him. He entreated me, with signs, to open my sketchbook for them that they might see with their own eyes and decide whether my sketches were really the cause of the sickness so prevalent among them. Owing to the absence of Quatre Ours, who is with Mr. Culbertson and the Assiniboin chiefs at Fort Laramie, La Grande Chevelure is now chief of the Herantsa.

He is distinguished for his intelligence as well as for his gift of eloquence; Quatre Ours is accredited with more "coups", having 14 to his account. La Grande Chevelure finds in my drawings nothing in the least to warrant suspicion. He will talk with his people.

He is a middle-aged man of dignified and imposing presence. He has fine eyes, a well-arched chest, and small hands. He wears usually an old buffalo robe and carries in his hand an eagle wing for fan. His breast and arms have tattoo marks. As president of the council he is regarded the most notable personage in the village and as the war chieftain of Quatre Ours he is most influential. While he was looking at my drawings, I studied his interesting features and, as soon as he left, I made a sketch of him immediately from memory. I must, however, get a more exact likeness; here, with Mr. Kipp, I shall have opportunity to do that, for I can see him almost daily. Of the two chiefs he is superior to Quatre Ours, who is not distinguished for personal force and valor. By the way, Quatre Ours has a perfectly beautiful wife, with the most finely chiseled features that I have seen for a long time.

August 15. I hear daily that Schmidt, the bourgeois at the opposition company's trading post, dins into his children's ears continually that the great company brings among them all the devastating diseases so prevalent and that the painter especially is to blame, for all those whom he sketches fall ill. That is perfidy, pure and simple, and may in the end place me in a most undesirable situation.

What will trade envy not contrive! A girl of doubtful character stole from me today my last Regensburg pencil; she committed the theft in revenge because I was indifferent to her. This is the second time articles belonging to me have been purloined by women. The first time the theft occurred while I was at supper; an old Iowa woman carried off some drinking glasses. As Witthae was present I soon found out who the culprit was and went at once to her tent across the river to get them back again. The woman lied. Nevertheless I unpacked her leather pouch in spite of her gabble and found the glasses snugly hidden among old clothes. I am surprised not to have been robbed more frequently, especially as old women are represented by certain writers as a thievish rabble. When one considers their poverty and the fascination of that which glitters and sparkles, indispensable objects in their eyes, one must admit that, for these people, such temptations are more than they can resist; besides, stealing from an enemy is, according to their view, not only permissible but honorable. They do not steal what would serve them for food, but objects that have for them an irresistible attraction. The pencil with which I made sketches was "medicine" for the Indian woman; the bright, glittering cut-glass tumblers exerted, more or less, the same effect.

Pierre Gareau put me on my guard concerning "the blonde," i. e., the gray-haired girl, because he sees her so frequently here and she is said to be married. She is certainly not yet 14 years old, and already a wife.[28] She belongs to an old man who brought her up in order to have about him a young, invigorating person. If he finds out anything about our relations, he may rightly claim all I possess,

---

[28] Indian girls in America mature at a very early age. I knew Creoles in St. Louis who were married at 14; one, in fact, at 11 years old. Her husband (Marey) played the rôle of doctor when the Americans occupied Santa Fé.

and I may indeed be satisfied if that is all he demands; a jealous man, really outraged in his love, might make an attempt upon my life. That would be for me a pleasure dearly bought. Perhaps this is in reality a trap the old sinner lays for me, after having seen, not long ago, the contents of my boxes. Who would have thought that so young a girl could be his wife?

Have not sought its companionship hitherto, but this fragrant blend pleases me well. My pipe will not get me into trouble. And as I am required for politeness sake to smoke with men who visit me, I can also resort to the same means of passing the time when alone.

August 16. The wife of La Longue Chevelure is suddenly dead from cholera, I am told; she suffered violent spasms of colic and vomiting. Is it a coincidence that cholera should first make its appearance here now just after we have opened those bales of goods that we brought with us?

Mr. Kipp says that heretofore the attacks were caused by the eating of too much unripe fruit, by that ill-smelling pond in the midst of the village, and by breathing stagnant air confined within the stockades, through which the wind never blows freely. Hot sun and cold wind may be the cause of some illnesses. Schmidt, on the other hand, tells the superstitious Indians they have cholera, a disease they have caught from the great fur-trading company. And I am inclined to believe that Schmidt is this time right; the conditions I have mentioned above would produce cholera any time.

Bellangé seems moody; one evening he can not have enough of relating his adventures; will talk to me until late at night; another day he will not say a word. It is a matter of indifference to me; besides, it is not for one in my position to be familiar with him and pay no attention to my chief. Day before yesterday he was quite content to conclude some advantageous bargains with me; yesterday he hardly recognized me, for fear, most likely, that I might decide not to trade; today he wishes my double-barreled shotgun at any price. As long as I live in this region, however, I can not let him have my gun. He offered me just such a buffalo head as the most famous warriors appear in when they perform the buffalo dance. He will, however, have great difficulty in getting one, for they are very highly prized; so he must himself order such a head made ready for me by his Assiniboin wife.

Then all at once he has a desire to learn reading and writing, in order that he may, in the course of time, displace P. Gareau and perhaps steal a march on me; for, he says, I can see in one year all that is of interest to me here—every year is merely a repetition of those gone before. Skirmishes and affrays will most likely end once for all when these Indians agree to the treaty with Uncle Sam. Oh, yes; I smell the rat!

August 17. Sunday. This recent epidemic is getting the upper hand—not a day but somebody dies in the village. The Indians have such dread of the disease that they have determined to hurry away to the hills; they would like to take their families with them and live in the huts they build for summer on the Knife River. This would afford me an opportunity to sketch the village as well as the place of sacrifice and Indian catafalque. Take advantage of every thing, even that which is unfortunate.

August 18. Diable! Here I am confined to the house! At 9 o'clock this morning Mr. Kipp came and begged me to put my drawings away—to allow no Indian to see them ever again. They talked in the village of nothing but my sketches. I immediately put them under lock and key. Then I went out to help Reith, one of our engagees, with the tedding of hay.

Soon Le Corbeau Rouge came to me and gave me to understand, with signs, that I was to go to my room and stay there; my looking at everything and writing down what I saw was the cause, he said, of so much sickness and death in the village. His signs were unmistakable. I replied that, though he was, to be sure, a most highly esteemed brave, he was no chief, least of all my chief; i. e., he had no authority over me. Nevertheless I went later to the bourgeois, who said my own safety demanded that I remain in my room, or at least inside the fort. The entire blame for the cholera epidemic was cast upon me. Relatives of some of those who had died were exasperated, almost frantic, and when and where I least expected it an arrow might pierce my ribs. While the trading company would not regard it a matter of principle to revenge an injury done me, still by exposing myself to danger I should, if attacked, be the cause of much disturbance and ill feeling. He might forbid their eating raw pumpkins, turnips, berries, and green maize as much as he liked, but superstition was so deeply rooted in the Indians and the old wives were so constantly telling of earlier cases that they could account for in no other way than in the remarkable coincidence of my having sketched portraits of the persons dead, and in doing that had necessarily taken away their life—otherwise the drawings could not be such exact likenesses. His supplies of medicine had aroused their anger, etc. I hope all of them will go up on the plateau; otherwise I shall, sooner or later, be obliged to leave.

To travel down the river alone in a boat made of buffalo hide would be most romantic, it is true; but since the Arikara and Mandan are even more incensed against me than the tribe here, such a journey would be too dangerous a venture. I have, moreover, some friends to defend me here, but there I have none. Once I was on the river the

Arikara would receive news of it before I could reach there and would watch for me.[29]

After dinner I told Mr. Kipp that I was ready to leave at once if the interest of the company or his own interest, in particular, made my departure advisable. All right, he said; but wait a week longer and see whether the disease spreads or not. It is to be hoped that out on the open prairie the epidemic will lose its force; in that event nothing more will be said.

If the worst comes, then something can be done at once, if I hold myself in readiness. In any case I am not to go outside the fort. If I do, he has no means either to protect me or to revenge an attack on my life. The sick who were left behind will by and by recover or they will die; in either case their people who are taking care of them will go away. Then I shall again enjoy liberty. Let us have a smoke; time brings good counsel. I find it strange that cholera broke out here for the first time upon the unpacking of those bales of goods; yet the same disease was prevalent some time before among the Arikara south of us. None of the boats, at least, had anyone on board suffering from cholera when they landed either at Fort Clarke or at this place.

August 19. The wind has shifted from east to WSW.; it brought us fine cool weather. The sick people are better; those in good health and the convalescent are going away. In violation of orders and against my own conscience I had to yield, notwithstanding, to the desire to draw. The morning was so insufferably long; the thought of having to leave the fort, to say adieu to the Upper Missouri, perhaps, even in the next hour, was hard to endure.

Quickly I drew the water tub [30] against the door and through my grimy windowpane I made some sketches of the interior of the fort. My two sketches finished, I put everything very quickly in place again, and over a pipe of blended tobacco I reflect upon what conscience is. Earlier in life I was taught that conscience is the voice

---

[29] That the disease is really cholera I have no longer the least doubt; that this outbreak of the epidemic is due to the opening of those bales of goods that were packed in St. Louis while cholera was raging there I doubt just as little. That I did not catch the infection in St. Joseph, on the *St. Ange,* nor yet here I ascribe less to regular diet than to lack of fear and, most of all, to a happy frame of mind due to my having realized the aims for which I took the journey—to the joy of being at the work I had long desired to do.

[30] In all of the rooms that are occupied there is kept a large tub or cask filled with water for daily use and also as a means of protection in case of fire. There are neither fountains nor cisterns at the forts; as a consequence, when Mr. Kipp, the bourgeois, went on a visit to the Blackfeet his fort was burned down. Water is brought from the turbid Missouri, which stream is within easy distance of the fort, yet too far to supply water for a burning building without the aid of a fire-engine hose. This lack of water near at hand would be much more serious in time of war, because most of the forts are on heights and can without the least difficulty be cut off from all approaches to the river.

of God, but now I consider this inner monitor to be but the result of moral training, according to which our standards shift and change, inclining always in the direction given by our education and experience. If conscience were the voice of God, of one God, His voice would be always the same—in every human being the same. On the contrary, consciences differ in every human being. What one deems right another holds to be wrong, and vice versa.

Le Loup Court Queue comes with his nephew to ask that they sleep in my room in order that they may not have to see his mother die. He then has no fear of me; he asked, to be sure, with signs whether I were sick? Did I cough? Have violent pain? Convulsions?

August 19. Made a drawing of the inner construction of a skin boat. Catlin tries to prove from the similarity of these boats to the Irish coracle that the Mandan derive their origin from Madoc's colony. That this boat made of buffalo hide belongs peculiarly to the Mandan is just as unlikely as that winter huts are of Mandan origin. All Indians who dwell on the prairies make use of skin boats on account of the scarcity of wood. Such conclusions, based purely on analogies, are questionable.

Hermann Weiss includes in his admirable work on Costumes of all Nations, page 239, figure 136, a description and drawing of Assyrian river boats that look very much like the skin boat used by these Indians. According to him Herodotus makes mention of them, and according to more recent travelers they are still in use in that part of the world.

Catlin is inclined to see in Madoc's Welsh colony also the builders of Indian mounds in Ohio on the Muskingum, from which place the latter's descendants were driven out and appeared later as Mandan on the upper Missouri. If he had been acquainted with the thorough investigation of these highly interesting remains made by Squier and Davis he would not have hit upon that strange idea, for the Mound Builders had left their dwellings in the Ohio Valley long before Madoc could have landed in North America in 1170.

What Catlin calls blonde hair among the Mandan is nothing more than sun-burned hair that is not continually smeared with grease. Black horses become somewhat brown if they are not well cared for and are exposed to all kinds of weather. My horse, Fashion, was a striking example; I bought her for a bay and by painstaking care gave her the lustrous coat of a splendid black horse. I may mention, also, that the lighter color of some Indians' skin (not only Mandan) is easily traced to the "whites."

August 20. Of all the occupants of the fort, only Reith and I are in good health. When he went after stovewood, therefore, I assisted him with the flatboat, with loading the carts, and with the bags, as he brought the loads up the steep river bank. Mr. Kipp consented unwillingly to my serving as clerk. I replied to him, however, according to his own statement that, with nothing to employ my time, I should become peevish and ill. I had expected, I told him, to be of some service here, not to live as a lord. Whereupon he assured me that he understood perfectly well; that I should soon find quite enough to do, when he went away. In winter, moreover, I am accustomed to have a horse at my service, by the hour, so that I can take part in the hunt and extend my opportunities for observation and study. My willingness to remain here disposed him so far toward liberality that he added further, what he had always forgotten heretofore to mention, that if I should get hungry between meals I was only to go into the kitchen and order something to eat. That may be done; for instance, the married engagees receive so much meat for their families and this, they find time, always, to eat during the interval between meals, while I have nothing at all from 6 o'clock in the morning to 2 o'clock in the afternoon, a condition against which my empty stomach often cries out in protest.

Mr. Kipp speaks of undertaking a journey to the States on horseback in the autumn. Not at all probable.

Our courtyard is crowded with old men and women who were unable to go along when the others departed. Concerning their age, they can estimate at least that they are certainly more than a hundred years old—or I would better say a hundred winters, because they can reckon more easily by snows that have fallen; more than 60 or 70 years they do not attempt to count, for they have not the least interest in knowing their exact ages. These old crones are disagreeable creatures. I look upon them as sentinels; each possesses, unfortunately, one or more pet dogs, some young, some old, that make the night hideous with their continual howls. Sleep is impossible. Bill, the cook, rose up in his wrath and sent an arrow through the body of one of these canines and then threw him over the palisades. That rash act made an enemy of the old woman; she is now quarreling unceasingly about us.

Toward evening Jim Hawkins, a negro from Fort Union, arrived here. Mr. Culbertson intended at first to take him as cook to Fort Laramie, but left him behind temporarily at Fort Union, where he was also obliged to serve as cook. He says Dennik,[31] the bourgeois there, is a hard man, liked by nobody, not even here; he keeps two Indian wives, Jim says, and squanders all he has on them; begrudges anything paid the employees, oppresses the engagees with too much work, is never satisfied, etc.

[31] I. e., Denig.

Jim ran away—took a boat that belongs to the great company. He must have related his story to Mr. Kipp with highly pleasing embellishments, for the latter put him in the kitchen forthwith and sent Bill, who has been our cook hitherto, to the hayfield.

Jim was at one time in the employ of Mr. P. A. Sarpy in Belle Vue, where I knew him quite well. All he earned there he squandered on old immoral Indian women; consequently he could not be kept longer. He is really the slave of someone in St. Louis and is required to pay a certain sum to his master every year; the balance of his wages he may spend as he likes. Here he is free, it is true, but the company must be responsible, more or less, for his life.

Jim had bad luck today on the Missouri; having been already nine days on the river, his provisions were exhausted. He was obliged to go hunting, but dared not trust himself far from his boat, so shot nothing. He found instead, however, an abundance of wild cherries, carried a goodly portion to his skiff and this morning, in perfect ease of mind, was gulping down one handful after another, stones and all, when his boat struck a snag ("gigot" in French) and was upset, throwing him, his stolen booty, and his rifle into the water.

Luckily he swam to the shore on this side of the stream. After shaking his wet clothes and looking sorrowfully but in vain for his lost belongings, he was then obliged to work his way through a wood full of bogs, from which he emerged at last on a hill and saw in the far distance the glimmer of something bright. That he took, rightly, to be our palisades and wandered on in this direction.

La Queue Rouge, my language teacher, comes along with Le Loup Court Queue to share my room with me. Just for the fun of the thing he put on a superb military cap adorned with all sorts of horns and plumes in order that I might have a model for a sketch. His friend wrapped a costly mantle of otter skin about his bare legs, which made a sorry appearance in conjunction with his richly ornamented leather shirt and the imposing headgear. At first I was reluctant to make a sketch of La Queue Rouge; I asked him whether he were not afraid of falling ill. What was I talking about? He laughed at the idea of such a thing! Extraordinary, what different views these people take. Did he, I wonder, wish merely to give proof of his bravery—his fearlessness?

August 21. Le Loup Court Queue has gone. The only men from the village now left here are La Queue Rouge and a brother of Quatre Ours; the former is nursing back to health his convalescent wife, who is so weak she can scarcely stand. Her fever rages to such a heat that she wears no clothes at all.

After she had lain perfectly nude for a long while today on her buffalo robe in the shadow of the palisades, she wished to come alone into the courtyard; fortunately I met her just as she grew dizzy from weakness and was about to fall. I assisted her to her relatives in the court. Two more people have died in the village (one of them the mother of my language teacher). Else I might make a sketch of the settlement. I will steal away to the river shore instead and sketch the boat landing, the watering place, and the bathing pool.

Jim was tortured to-day by the cherry stones; he suffered so terribly from griping pains and cramps that he lay down across the corner of a packing case in the courtyard; then he fell to the ground, writhing like a wounded animal. By means of a very strong emetic he was relieved.

August 22. Since our Indians went away there is no fresh meat. We have only cured meat served. I am entirely dependent for what I have to eat upon the mood of the bourgeois. Though P. Gareau is keeper of the meat house, I am less dependent upon his humor, for the reason that he orders his two wives to cook what he likes. If Mr. Kipp has a good appetite he searches for the best of everything in the storehouse and we live in luxurious abundance, such as one would not dare expect in these wilds.

If, on the other hand, he is not well, he assumes at once that the rest of us need no more to eat than he does. A short while ago we were served a heavy soup with rice or beans, excellent rib roast, fresh griddle cakes, buffalo tongue, and in addition cakes with dried peaches or apples. Now, a sudden change of menu: cured meat and hard crackers—so hard that in an attempt to bite one a man can easily break his teeth. Nothing more.

August 23. Dorson and Beauchamp, of Fort Clarke, arrived here. Those women killed at Fort Lookout were in reality Zephir's wife and daughter. For 30 years Zephir had lived happily with his wife. Next autumn, when the Herantsa and Mandan are on the chase, the Yanktonai will revenge that deed. They would find the present their best chance to wreak vengeance, but even Sioux are afraid of contagion.

Today has been the hottest of the entire summer. All the mosquitoes and flies in the village have come over here for what they can find to nourish themselves. Neither by day nor by night do we get any relief from mosquito choruses and mosquito bites; furthermore, the pests bring with them the stench of the village slough.

Aged Indians and the sick are encamped in front of our fort in tiny huts constructed of boughs and twigs. They make use of these shelters at the same time for taking their vapor baths. They produce steam by heating stones red hot in a great fire prepared in front of the huts; then, having tightly closed the one they wish to use, they carry the stones inside and pour water upon them. As soon as they have converted the place into a sweating box at a high temperature, the sick people (sometimes those in good health also take vapor baths) crawl naked into the midst of the heat and steam; whereupon a profuse perspiration ensues. This, Indians think, is highly conducive to health. It appears to be their only treatment for cholera—at least I have heard of no other remedy—and yet all their cholera patients have not died.

At first, for want of other medicine, Mr. Kipp served out small doses of whisky, but his supply was soon exhausted, for the reason that he is so very fond of that remedy himself (greatly to his own hurt, for he has had already the chance of two fortunes and of being regarded a rich man in the States but has ruined himself by immoderate drinking).

Our surroundings have the appearance of a hospital—eight decrepit old women squat beside one another in the sunshine along by the palisades, pick off the lice from their bodies, and eat with relish the flesh of wild animals. The young sister-in-law of Quatre Ours lies naked in a corner of the bastion, while her husband continually goes to and fro, bringing her fresh water from the river; a blind girl, convulsed with cramps, pounds her abdomen with her fists in an effort to get rid of the dreadful pain. I met her today tottering along the palisades toward the gate. Suddenly she sank to the ground and I hurried forward to lift her up, wrap the buffalo robe about her nude form, and carry her inside the fort. To me her body seemed of too bright a color for "pure Indian." If an old woman dies, there is nobody to bury her except ourselves. We have already sent two down the river in perforated skin boats—left there to go to the bottom.

August 24. Another aged woman is dead; she starved herself to death because she saw that she was a burden to her family. Though she did not lack food, she refused obstinately to eat. This hospital of ours, our fare of dried meat, and the mosquitoes prove too distasteful to Dorson and Beauchamp; they intend to leave this morning.

Dorson, the bourgeois at Fort Clarke, is trying to get together here the necessary tools for some building he wishes to do.

August 25. In their "patois" the Canadians use two queer expressions I never heard before: "Jongler", to waver between two propositions; "se tanner", to labor hard for a thing.

August 26. Have made a sketch of the great place of sacrifice dedicated to the sun and moon; a bepainted buffalo skull, set on the summit of a small mound, is encircled by other skulls of buffaloes and of enemies. In front of every skull a bit of white down is placed on a small stave. Beside the circle of skulls stand two posts to which bearskins are hung. Fastened to the posts above are bundles of fagots; above one of the bundles lies a fur cap to indicate the man, while the other is to represent the woman—that is, the sun and the moon. Made a sketch of the Indian catafalque or scaffold for the dead.

Two young Indian women have taken up quarters with me to avoid exposure to the weather; a violent, cold east wind is blowing. As night came on a heavy rain fell and the good women did not know where they might find shelter, for they would not go to the village. One of them is a sister of Loup Court Queue and the wife of Tete Jaune, who left her and his boy here so that she could take care of his mother—now dead. The other is the blind woman whom I have mentioned already, a young wife deserted by her husband, since, during this illness, she lost her eyesight.

I visited also the village, now deserted. Entrance to the huts was barricaded. Saw the cask that is said to represent the Ark. Among the clay huts stood a small blockhouse. The casklike structure (correctly represented by Prince Max von Neu Wied) was not found, however, in the principal settlements but in a smaller one, probably in the land of the Mandan, for the Herantsa tradition includes nothing relating to the flood, consequently the presence of a simulated Ark among them would be an incongruity.

August 28. This morning the sight of seven buffalo bulls on the road leading to Fort Clarke relieved somewhat the monotony of our existence at this hospital. With our telescope we could note their age; they were, according to the current expression, "cayaks." That means they were thrust out by the young bulls and nevermore allowed to approach any herd of cows. Such animals, excluded from the herd, range in small groups by themselves; their flesh is not used for food. Later in the day great droves of buffaloes appeared, coming down to the river from the distant western hills. P. Gareau and Bellangé mounted their horses forthwith to go in pursuit of them. Mounted huntsmen followed with pack horses to bring back the meat.

Meanwhile, on the other side of the river herds came continually into view, emerging from glens and valleys and descending slopes on their way to the river.

Having been left undisturbed for 2 weeks or more in this region, they dared come within a short distance of the fort. At 4 o'clock our hunters returned from the chase laden with meat. P. Gareau shot a cow, Bellangé wounded a calf, which Gareau killed after it had been driven about for a long while by Mr. Kipp's small hunting dog, Schika. Forthwith, on all sides, everybody began to roast meat; after our recent scanty fare we found delicate, tender rib roast an unrivaled dish; nothing could be better, we thought.

August 29. Today old Gagnon, of the opposition fort, came back from a visit to the Arikara. He says eight people dièd there in one night from the same disease that is prevalent here and called cholera; the symptoms are violent cramps and vomiting, and usually death results in a few hours. Gagnon was guilty of a mad act in running his Arikara woman away from here to Fort Clarke; by so doing he spread the contagion in the Arikara village. Dorson thinks as I do, however, that cholera was brought in those bales of goods that we opened. Perhaps he welcomed the occasion that Gagnon's arrival afforded him to throw blame on the opposition. Gagnon had to make his escape by night when he realized the results of his imprudent act. The Arikara have also abandoned their village for the most part and are seeking another distant location.

I saw running about here today for the first time a young wolf that an Indian youth drove out on the prairie last spring with a cord tied tight at the end of his backbone to accustom the brute to pain. The animal's movements—now leaping about, now standing still, now bounding away, now trying to squirm himself free—can give some idea of the pain inflicted. Another was made to drag, in addition, eleven buffalo skulls a mile over the prairie. Behind the fort stands a queer sort of scaffoldlike contrivance from which, upon occasions when sacrifices are offered to invoke good fortune on the hunt or in war, men are suspended, tortured, and starved [31a]; thus, young lads are prepared by enforced endurance of pain and by deprivation for bloody undertakings.

Toward sunset four buffalo bulls came out on the sandbank with evident intention of crossing the river. As the river shore on this side is high and steep they fell down several times while attempting to ascend and sank deeper and deeper into the mire. While I was amusing myself watching their floundering I heard a rifle shot. Turning my head I saw an Indian on a dun-colored horse coming toward me at a gallop; it was La Queue Rouge. His wife is dead, his daughter is still sick, but this does not seem to have put him in a particularly melancholy state of mind. The Herantsa have divided their people into three bands and are said to have gone far north, even as far as the Knife River and regions lying contiguous thereto. The old people at the encampment on the river below us are said to be in good health.

They were left there because they could not travel to the new settlement on foot and the horses were needed for other purposes. La Queue Rouge, while reloading his gun, told me about a "banneret", or young Indian, who, upon finding a group of wild cherry trees, began to sing their funeral dirge, jeered at them as enemies, then—

[31a] This statement refers superficially to the rites of the Sun Dance.

bang! he shot at them, and fell to eating cherries greedily, under the impression that his "medicine" had robbed them of any harmful effect. That same evening he was a corpse. Seventeen more have died among the Herantsa since they went away.

August 30. As our sick people increase in number rather than diminish, on account of the return of old women and little girls from their camp on the river below us, my prospects for a longer stay at this place do not improve. Therefore I went to the upper cornfield to get a good view of the fort for a sketch and I finished the drawings I had begun of the place of sacrifice and burial scaffold. If I could only have studied buffaloes, stags, elk, and bears, I should not trouble myself about the rest. For the present I have enough of the antique.

September 5. Fort Union.

I was obliged to flee 3 miles beyond the mouth of the Yellowstone; perhaps I shall have to travel farther still—as far as I like.

Last Sunday—the Sabbath is not distinguished from week days here by the ringing of church bells and the preaching of sermons but merely as rest day for the engagees. Last Sunday I took Bellangé with me to the upper cornfields to shoot ducks among the inundated willow bushes. Though for 6 hours we waded about in the water, oftentimes up to our chests, in our efforts to steal upon the ducks, he succeeded in killing only a pair. On the way Bellangé came near shooting me. He was pushing through the thick willow growth, just in front of me, when one barrel of his double-barreled gun was accidentally discharged, the entire load just passing my left ear. When we returned at 2 o'clock in the afternoon we heard bad news from the settlements both above and below us. The Herantsa are dying in great numbers; 50 deaths already estimated; a proportion of 1 person in every 14. Seven hundred souls in 84 clay huts. Some of them, they say, are in a rage about my presence here, because so many of their people are dying. Two "bannerets" have come from the Arikara also and report an even worse condition there than here. Arikara and Mandan are said to be dying like flies under the first winter frost; those who survive swear that they will be revenged on all whites. Dorson has closed his fort, so I am told. The opposition is without fear, because they are the instigators. At evening Bellangé came to mé and said that the "old man" had the intention to send him and me to Fort Union.

I was to remain there; he was to conduct me thither and at the same time get a new supply of medicinal drugs and bring them back. What he did not especially like was the necessity of making the return journey alone. By land the distance, as the crow flies, is about 170 miles; by the river route more than twice as far.

On Monday, September 1, therefore, everything was in readiness to start in the evening on horseback with just as little luggage as

possible. As I was obliged to leave my boxes behind, together with
the goods I had brought in them, I began to exchange on the spot
or to barter on a credit whatever articles I was unable to take along
and yet could not leave packed for an indefinite time. At evening
we mounted our horses and bade our acquaintances heartfelt adieu.
I was of the opinion, however, that my departure was due less to considerations for my own safety than to the desire to be rid of a
superfluous man, since the bourgeois could no longer consider taking
his journey. Moreover, Queue Rouge was greatly astonished when I
said good-by and gave him some tobacco as a farewell gift. Besides, we were provided with the worst horses at the fort, which did
not by any means guarantee my safety. Our double-barreled guns,
heavily loaded, we laid across the saddle in front of us; we were well
provided with powder and shot—and each of us carried a scalping
knife which we stuck in our belts; my cloak, together with a sack containing some changes of linen and a zinc drinking cup, all fastened
to the back of the saddle, made up my total equipment.

In place of underwear, Bellangé carried our provisions, our coffee-
pot, and a blanket. So we rode across the prairie into the West,
cutting off the circuitous route of the Missouri. The first day we
saw nothing but prairie chickens, blackbirds,[32] and, in the evening,
several shy antelopes. We camped at night beside a spring; tethered
our horses to tufts of tall grass. Except for the howling of wolves
and the chorus of mosquitoes, a deathlike silence reigned.

Before sunrise on Tuesday morning we saddled our horses and resumed our journey, always riding at a slow trot. About 8 o'clock I
enjoyed my first prairie breakfast, cooked by a fire made of buffalo
chips. Bellangé forgot the meat, so we had only biscuits and hot
coffee. He consoled me by saying he had his gun, which would keep
us supplied with game. I allow myself to be easily comforted when
I am enjoying myself; when on an adventure and in happy mood I
disregard hunger. If our pads had been better travelers, the sense
of my romantic situation would have sustained me beyond any
specified limit.

Constant danger from lurking enemies, the vast prairie, bounded
only by sky and sea; buffaloes and bears in prospect; perhaps a
violent storm by way of variety; fine health and tense anticipation—
what more could I desire? Every dark spot amid the green might
be an Indian, a buffalo, an elk, or a bear;[33] any bright spot might be
a wolf, an antelope, or a deer. My glances wander everywhere; what
my eyes cannot distinguish my telescope brings within my range of
vision. I would not have exchanged this journey for the one I had

---

[32] Here blackbirds (Brewer's Blackbird, *Quiscalus breweri* Aud.) take the place of
sparrows and finches.

[33] Elks and bears are rarely seen in the vicinity of Fort Berthold.

in mind to Salt Lake; there I should not have seen any fur-bearing animals and not nearly so many Indians as at Fort Berthold. Nude Indians, with their beautifully proportioned figures, their slender yet well-formed limbs, their expressive eyes, their natural, easy bearing—that is what I am seeking, and not the bepainted types wellnigh overburdened with excessive decoration. We started our first buffaloes on that day. Bellangé wished to be sure of having the Knife River (Riviere aux Couteaux) behind us before the evening in order to get out of the Gros Ventres' district. So we had to cut across the Big Bend [34] (Grand Detour). Finally Bellangé found the trail which our Indians had marked out with their tent poles. Traces of a wandering band of Indians are essentially different from similar trails left in the wake of white travelers, for the reason that the former have no wagons.

The tracks of a wagon and team make one road; the travois forms three deep paths or furrows parallel with one another, that is, a middle path along which the beasts of burden, whether horse or dog, travel, and two outer paths furrowed by the tip ends of the carrying poles. This trace we followed from the prairie down toward the river, then for a time along the bank of the stream until we came again into a plain. Near a "cut-off", i. e., a lake (frequented at that time by great numbers of pelicans),[35] which was earlier the bed of a river that had now taken another direction, we found skeleton twig huts, over which the Herantsa had merely thrown blankets, and abandoned fires. This was a trace somewhat too fresh for Bellangé's comfort. He began to fear for his skin. We left the trails, therefore, and, turning from the river, we trotted off to a distant prairie surrounded by a chain of hills. After a time my horse refused to trot longer, while Le Vieux Blanc, a well-seasoned traveler, kept steadily his even gait. So, in order that Bellangé and I might remain together while traversing the wide stretch of country that we had yet to cross, I was forced to urge my jade forward with a hazel rod. After we had forded the Coquille at noon we dismounted and lay down for a little while in the tall grass in order to stretch our legs and to allow our horses to recover breath.

Our midday meal consisted of half a biscuit. We were in the Herantsa's own hunting ground. We dared not fire a shot or even show ourselves too openly for fear of attracting unnecessarily an attack from the so-called enemy. Besides, hostile Indians frequently approach such places by stealth in order to number yet another "coup." We might, therefore, be in more peril of the Sioux than of the Herantsa.

---

[34] A bend of the river 50 miles in length ; direct route hardly 10 miles.
[35] American white pelican, *?Peleconus americanus* Aud.

As we were proceeding across the plain in a direction that cut off the Big Bend I called Bellangé's attention to a graceful cabribuck (prong-horned antelope) that came trotting forward from a glade and peered curiously about, without getting scent of us, because we were traveling against the wind. Bellangé, bidding me be still, slipped off his horse, took my double-barreled gun and aimed at the fat animal, which had approached near enough to have been killed with an ordinary pistol. When Bellangé fired the beast paid not the least attention to the rifle shot, but trotted gracefully about us, still without gaining any warning from the wind. Bellangé's second shot was aimed much too high; the buck, now alarmed, fled swiftly away with prodigious leaps and bounds. Bellangé said, by way of excuse, that, as a matter of course, for hitting an object at that distance the gun was too heavily loaded. I did not think it necessary to inform such an excellent huntsman as he represents himself to be that one can hit a mark whether distant or near with the same charge, according as one takes high or low aim. As sportsman he has rather lost my good opinion.

He is wont to console himself, moreover, with this saying, that people applying derision to Canadians because among strangers they speak in such exalted commendation of their country when there is, after all, nothing to warrant such exaggeration:

Je suis du Canada (I am from Canada).
Je me font de ça (I am a part of it).
J'ai des pommes de terre (I have potatoes).
Pour passer l'hiverre! (enough to pass the winter).[35a]

In the evening we had to climb the coteaux or hills near the Knife River; they were so steep and so often intersected by deep-lying brooks that we were forced to lead our horses. From these heights we had a magnificent far-reaching view of a range of hills beyond the Missouri, where the land swarmed with buffaloes. The sun was setting as we waded the Knife River. We saw in the distance the former village that the Herantsa inhabited before they chose their present abode near Fort Berthold, which, to say the least, is much better situated for defense. On a high, steep river shore in a wide-spreading plain they are much more secure from surprise attacks than here in the midst of so many deep, narrow valleys. We reached at length the high woodlands that are usually found along the banks of the Missouri. We unharbored a herd of white-tail deer; they paid no attention to the approaching horses until they saw quite near them that most dangerous of all animals—man.

We selected a spot on the river bank for our camp in order to have water and, in the second place, to get rid of the mosquitoes by means

---

[35a] The rendering of these French lines into English has been supplied by the editor.

of the strong breeze that was almost continually blowing toward the stream. A mug (tin pint cup) of coffee and a cracker (biscuit) was all we had for our supper. In order to avoid attracting enemies, either by firelight or smoke, we extinguished our campfire. But we kept no watch; wrapped in our blankets we slept peacefully with our saddles for pillows, while our nags, tethered with long halters (lassos), were grazing. We had been in the saddle 16 hours that day. As we were in constant danger while crossing this hunting district, we mounted again before sunrise. We were deprived of much enjoyment by the utter weariness of our horses; riding a lamed nag that has to be constantly urged on with the aid of a rod and with digging one's shoe heels into the sides of the beast withdraws one's attention far too much from the beauty of one's surroundings. On the other hand, when one's horse travels willingly without whip or spur, stamps with impatience when told to stand, neighs and snorts when allowed to run, one's spirits become exuberant—one could shout for joy. Such an animal I possessed in Savannah—my Bill. After having traveled 60 miles a day he would still be feeling his oats. My mares, though more rapid travelers for short distances, it is true, and more easy in their gait, for sustained endurance on long journeys could not compare with Bill. To ride a sluggish horse is very much more fatiguing.

We found a piece of sole leather (parflêche) and a bow lying beside it, evidence of Indians having but lately passed this spot, while we imagined they were behind us. We camped for breakfast on the Riviere Blanche. Afterwards we crossed a steep, rocky ridge of hills that would have given an enemy thousands of opportunities to catch us unawares in an attack or to shoot us dead from ambush. We saw cedar trees that had turned to stone—trunk and branch. How very, very old they must have been! As we were descending these hills and came into the skirts of a forest we saw great quantities of fresh dung—in fact, we were evidently following quite close upon a number of bison. Our rifles, always loaded, we put in position under the left arm, so that we might bang at a buffalo the instant he allowed us a glimpse of him within range of our guns. At length we caught sight of several dark humps in motion directly before us, but we were unable to bring our weary nags to a gallop. The beasts escaped; we could only make ourselves merry over the peculiar rolling gait of the galloping buffalo bulls. At every step we were crossing paths that had been traced by those animals from the hills to the Missouri.

We traversed another range of hills that were peculiarly unlike any other in one particular, i. e., red clay soil. From a distance they had the appearance of brick-colored eminences. Entering a deep and narrow ravine that opened upon the plain, we noticed three buffalo steers quietly grazing about 200 feet ahead.

We dismounted at once. I held the horses in the ravine, standing in the dried bed of a stream, while Bellangé crept forward to shoot a buffalo. He took most deliberate aim before he fired, notwithstanding that the beasts were standing perfectly still, grazing. Finally he pulled the trigger, raising dust beneath the paunch of the bull nearest him. The animal looked about him with surprise. Bellangé fired again, this time frightening the buffaloes to the extent that they flaunted their tails angrily and took to flight, but soon stopped again, as they saw no one in pursuit. Not one of them was wounded. Excellent marksman! With his own well-tested rifle he missed a buffalo bull standing perfectly still at a distance of 100 feet; no evasion would serve this time, and Bellangé was not a little abashed. First shot was far below the mark; second shot much too high. After a time, however, he did make a sort of excuse by saying that at this season of the year the flesh of buffalo bulls was not fit for food. "But surely," I answered in scorn, "some parts of the animal are eatable—the heart, the tongue." We came in view of several very large herds of cows encircled by their defenders, the bulls, and followed by the old, worn-out, cast off members of the herd. At this season the bulls fight, stamp, paw the ground, and bellow so loud that they are heard quite a distance away. Oh, what I would have given for a ride on one of the mares I owned in Savannah. Even my little Fashion would have soon brought me near those grumbling males.

All these herds, however great the numbers, fled the moment they got wind of us, but we could not follow in pursuit. Furthermore, we dared not stray too far from our course for fear of losing our way and of fatiguing our weary nags too much. We found, however, a cow recently killed, from which only the tongue and some of the ribs had been cut—evident proof that hunters were living in abundance, when they had cut from their quarry only choice bits and had even neglected to take off the hide. As the animal seemed to have been but lately killed—no vultures, ravens, or wolves in sight—I was inclined to slice off a piece of fresh meat for supper. Considering our scant traveling provisions thus far, I could not be blamed, if I were sensible of my animal appetites and found the meat inviting. But Bellangé pushed on further; Indians were in this vicinity; we should be obliged, therefore, to leave the open plain, he said, and seek out a more sheltered way through thickets and along the dry bed of prairie brooks. As there were multitudes of wild animals here, it was hardly possible that meat would be wanting for our evening meal, etc.

So we rode on into grazing lands that extended farther than the eye could reach and over the wide extent of which were scattered the dusky forms of bison, ranging in herds. This will give an idea of the great numbers of these animals that, at an earlier period, roamed the plains of Indiana and Illinois. All the droves we had met with on that day were coming from the Missouri, whither they had gone to quench their thirst; all prairie streams were dry. To my guide the sight of buffaloes was nothing new; he was on the alert for Indians, because he feared them. To me, on the contrary, those immense herds were altogether novel and my keen pleasure in seeing them made me heedless of any danger whatsoever. Besides, I was in no hurry to reach Fort Union, was uncertain as to what condition of things awaited me there; perhaps I should again be regarded a superfluous guest. I was constantly wishing to stop and observe more closely the motions and capers of the playful calves, how the cows were cared for by their lovers, the bulls, and to study the old stragglers, but Bellangé persisted in hastening forward, perpetually belabored Vieux Blanc, and called out to me peevishly not to lag behind. My only thought was for the buffaloes on the prarie; I was enjoying a sight, indeed, that I had wished a thousand times I might behold!

Then, all of a sudden, we became aware of a herd coming swiftly toward us over the crest of a hill in the direction of the river. We simply could not resist running them.[36] Just as I was pressing on to catch up with Bellangé and call his attention to the unusual speed with which the animals were moving we both saw, at the same moment, a number of Indians on horseback galloping along the flank of the fleeing herd. The leader caught sight of us, wheeled about, and all the wild huntsmen disappeared at once behind the hill. The buffaloes swept by. Another mounted Indian appeared at the hill's edge and turned about immediately when he saw us.

"They have discovered us! We are lost!" Bellangé exclaimed anxiously.

You see, he had been apprehensive the entire day of our meeting with some misfortune, because his left elbow had been constantly itching. I counseled him to put his confidence in those balls of lead that, in defiance of superstitious Indians, he wore around his neck as talisman—his "medicine"; what is more, they were said to have been consecrated by a priest to the purpose of preserving him from peril. For my part, I relied more on my own courage and the double-barreled shotgun. We were on an open, perfectly level prairie.

It was probably about 4 o'clock; the sunshine was glaring and hot. The grass was not sufficiently high to make a surprise attack possible. For my part, I was not at all concerned about danger—least of all

---

[36] Buffaloes move slowly forward, always, when grazing. They lie down only to chew their cud or to sleep ; hence, they never remain long in one place.

from the Herantsa; and even though we were beset, has not danger a part in every romantic adventure? Even love dissociated from risk and hazard would lose the charm of romance. My guide now took my telescope to spy out any suspicious signs of the Indians' approach, either openly or by stealth. The terrain to our left was distinctly to our disadvantage: there was the Missouri, several miles distant, to be sure, bordered with thickets and copses where the enemy might conceal themselves and get the start of us or else keep watch upon us, note what course we took, and take us unawares by night. At last we neared a group of low hills which we had long seen through the distant blue mists ahead and which Bellangé had mentioned as our camping place for the night. In their vicinity, he said, was an old house, where, at an earlier date, Mackenzie, clerk at Fort Union, had traded with the Assiniboin. In fact we were now in the hunting grounds of the latter tribe, which, I assumed, was all the better for us; we had nothing more to fear from the sick and afflicted Herantsa, and as for the Assiniboin they were friendly redskins whose language Bellangé had learned from his wife.

We were just speaking of this and he was telling me how he had first seen his Assiniboin wife at Fort Union, where he was employed as engagee; how he had later bought her, a prisoner, from the Crows, because at sight of him she wept for joy, etc. While talking together in this way we came unexpectedly to a steep bluff and saw with astonishment that two Indians were standing on the other side of a small stream at its foot. We were still more surprised when they waved their red blankets, a sign that we were to come over and join them. And they called to us, "Maregna! Maregna!" (Friend.) Bellangé answered: "Oui, oui, crapauds, pas cette fois ci." [37] He shouted to me that they were Sioux, who were on the watch at this place for Gros Ventres; whereupon he whipped up his white horse and off he went at a gallop. My mare wished to follow, but I was not of the same mind. While I was forcibly holding her back my portfolio was wrested out of place and, as a result, sketchbook, paint box, writing utensils, journal, everything, lay scattered on the ground. Abandon my sketches and drawing materials—never! To dismount and pick up the most important articles required only a moment, but my portfolio was all awry, and I was obliged to keep hold of the horse's rein with the same hand with which I was holding my rifle.

So, finding that I could not get the sketchbook in, I thrust it under my arm, and my riding cloak, which had also fallen off, I threw again across the saddle; whereupon the confounded jade sprang back, jerked the rein out of my hand, and off she went at a gallop. "Ah, I see now you can travel quite well", I said, "Just wait!" The sketch-

---

[37] Yes, yes. You toads! Not this time.

book with my colors, brushes, drawing paper, compass, etc., all restored, and the portfolio put properly in place, I threw my cloak
over my left arm, cocked the rifle, and, holding it with both hands
ready to attack, I awaited the "savages" that were now coming
speedily forward from different directions—all armed and riding
bareback. But instead of holding their hands to their mouths to
make the war cry resound, the leader called to me again, "Maregna!
Maregna!" Meanwhile Bellangé had seen my mare running around
loose and he came galloping back in order that he might share(?) my
danger. He found me surrounded by acquaintances of the Herantsa
Tribe with whom I was shaking hands and making much sport about
his having run away. While he was greeting, in his turn, Le Tete de
Loup and Le Tete de Boeuf, I tried to find the rest of my belongings
that were scattered about on the prairie. Some Indian lads rode after
my horse and brought her back. The Herantsa found our meeting
most edifying; not so Bellangé. He was exasperated with me because I had not followed him at once.

Now we must go with the Indians to their camp, "bon gre, mal
gre!" I should see Tete de Loup was bent on mischief. All of us
rode together down the bluff and through the stream to the camp,
which consisted of a number of shelters built of twigs over which
blankets were thrown. We dismounted and sat down before the fire
in the circle of our red friends—or foes. Bellangé bade me keep my
gun in my hand; otherwise, I was lost. Several children, who knew
me and to whom I had frequently given sugar in my room, came
bounding forward and offered their hands in the friendliest manner.[38] Though I did not believe we were running any risk, I laid
my gun across my lap. Then the Herantsa told how they had been
watching us for a long while, as we approached across the prairie,
and they laughed at us for the way we constantly looked about us;
called attention to my metal water flask that glistened so—it had
dazzled them at a great distance. It was plain that if they had had
evil designs they could very easily have put an end to us with an
arrow while totally unobserved themselves.

There could be no question, moreover, as to their chances of over-
taking our weary nags with their fresh runners on which they were
mounted to hunt buffaloes. We could only have concealed ourselves
in a dense coppice and have halted there, but we could not have
relied on that protection for any length of time. Herantsa knew
something of our weapons from an earlier time: Tete de Boeuf had
often admired the arrangement of my gunlock: a smaller hammer,

---

[38] Indians greet one another neither by shaking hands nor expressing good wishes.
Upon meeting, they talk together or give some sign, either by outcry or by a movement
of the hand. Iowa say "hou" which white people in their neighborhood often imitate
instead of wishing one good day or good night. When an Indian offers the hand in
greeting, therefore, it is in imitation of our custom.

like the cover of the priming pan, covered the fuse, in order to protect it from dampness and at the same time to prevent any untimely discharge. Well, the pipe was passed around, each of us taking several whiffs. In the meantime Bellangé related to his friend Tete de Boeuf, who always called the former's wife "sister" in token of the great friendship existing between the two families, that the purpose of his journey to Fort Union was to take me there to stay; to get medicinal drugs for "Ikipesche" (for Kipp; P. Gareau the Herantsa called "Mi", Stone, from his name Pierre) and to carry them back on his return. He entreated him to do us no harm, for I was much too fond of Indians to have any will to destroy them by pestilence. He heard that some of them intended to put me to death but he hoped to be treated as friend by the brother of his wife. Tete de Boeuf answered, for his part, that they were on their way to the Crows, to pay a visit to their relatives; that I had nothing at all to fear from them, though they believed me to be "bad medicine."

Hereupon, the Indian women brought choice bits of fresh meats, a great quantity of which was hanging out to be dried by the sun. In return we gave them coffee to boil, and sugar with which to sweeten it, so that all might have a share in our luxurious repast of juicy, tender meat and sweetened coffee.

After the meal was over, although the two men invited us to spend the night and ride the rest of the way to Fort Union with them, Bellangé insisted upon pressing forward. He gave as excuse that he was in haste, but he was really urged on by fear only. I cut for my use a jolly good willow switch with which to teach my mare how to behave, for I was much provoked with her for running away from me. Our friendly hosts gave us enough fresh meat to last several days longer, and, just after sunset, we took our leave. Bellangé conducted me to a beautiful spring 2 miles from this camp, where we had near at hand clear, cool water and good pasture. After we had secured the horses with long halters, we lay down to sleep, but not before I made clear to my guide the disadvantageous situation of the place he had chosen and warned him that if he did not really trust the Herantsa he should not have selected that kettle-shaped burrow.

Here we were virtually entombed in the midst of encircling heights behind which the enemy could creep upon us, themselves unseen and unheard, and shoot us dead. There was no longer any cause for fear, he replied.[39]

---

[39] Bellangé was wholly contradictory with regard to our "danger." He would not keep watch at night; he fired his gun as opportunity presented itself, yet he forbade me to do so, though every shot from his rifle was just as easily heard, of course, as from mine. He was wanting in courage, bad humored, and much inclined to give himself airs.

The moon, shining gloriously in a clear sky, was mirrored in the quiet water of the fountain spring. From far and wide came sub- dued sounds of the bellowing and pawing of combative bulls. An old "cayak" passed near the grazing horses, grumbling and shaking his shaggy mane. How was it possible for a person to go to sleep? The moonlight was so brilliant that I could read by it. I looked into my portfolio to find out what articles I had lost; my seal, "fier mais sensible," a valued gift from my brother Louis (in Paris, 1838), a small inkhorn from my friend, F. Studer, some percussion caps, pencils, compositions on loose paper, and other trifles besides. Only one pencil remained for my use during the remainder of my jour- ney—not a comfortable state of things if Fort Union offered me no better supply of paper and pencils than I found at Fort Berthold.

At last I, too, lay down, wrapped in the riding cloak I set so much store by. Hardly had I fallen asleep when my mare sent forth a loud neigh. As I looked up Bellangé said he had long ago heard talking. "Those toads of Indians" (ces crapeaux de sauvages) "are following us; the mare has the scent of their horses and is calling to them. I hear distinctly the cracking of the boughs," he said. The mare neighed again, but the old white horse was silently grazing. Though I heard nothing, I thought Bellangé was probably right, for my hear- ing had been much affected during my service in the artillery at an earlier time in my homeland. "Cayaks" continued to pass quite near us, bellowing and lowing. Finally the moon went down; it was dark! When the sky began to brighten in the east we saddled our nags, mounted, and rode across the brook that flowed from our spring. Then we heard the voice of someone behind us calling "Maregna" again. Without halting we turned and saw on the height the shadowy forms of Tete de Boeuf and his boys. He called for us to wait for them; they wished to make the journey with us. But Bellangé re- plied, "Adieu, barbarians!" We went swiftly forward, for our clothes were damp and we were chilled by the night mists.

Thursday. The sun rose brilliantly upon a vast rolling prairie over which innumerable buffalo herds were grazing. We came several times quite near the fighting bulls, but in their rage they did not see us; only ran away when they heard the report of a gun. Then, cov- ered with dust and foam, they fled swiftly in the wake of the herd, their tails lashing their flanks or else raised vertically aloft, as a threat, most likely, that they were about to begin the struggle anew. I should have thought that, under circumstances such as these, the bulls at least would be inclined to stand at bay upon the approach of men, but all of them fled from us.[40] We found a little pond inhabited

---

[40] On the prairie they escape the moment they get scent of human beings, unless the herd is too large to evade hunters. It is only in narrow woodland paths that they try to run over people or knock them down. However, if, on the hunt, a person comes in close

by a multitude of ducks. Here we dismounted, watered our horses, looked about for buffalo chips—though we might search far and near, we found not the slightest sign of wood or straw—and lighted a fire to boil the last of our coffee. Moreover, we wished to fry the meat that was given us, for it was not yet dry enough to be palatable uncooked. We found the taste of it by no means impaired by our having used buffalo chips for fuel; on the contrary, we ate it with great relish.

After breakfast we hurried on. Saw a great many antelopes and wolves. Passing through a little valley, we noticed, as we rode by, a young grizzly bear in his den and frightened him out. Bellangé called him "Ours Jaune", because his hair was yellow and he had a bright ring about his neck. That is the color of one-year-old bears only. This fellow ran from us, too, but we could easily have overtaken him and peppered him with shot if, unfortunately, our horses had not been such poor beasts. However, even though they had been good travelers, to run our horses for such a purpose would not have been wise, for opportunities to test their fleetness of foot were too frequently tempting. For instance, as we were slowly climbing a hill we noticed the dark hump of a buffalo moving along the edge of the summit. He was a powerful fellow, and hardly 100 feet distant. Bellangé was now to have the final test of his marksmanship. We stopped. I was eager to have a crack at this bison from my horse's back—his heart offered a near and sure aim. But Bellangé sprang down, crept forward in order to get nearer him still—a bout portant (with muzzle clapped to his breast). He fired. I could see plainly where he wounded the animal's shoulder. As the beast was escaping I took aim and fired, just that I might say I had one shot at a buffalo.

His movements showed that I hit at least his hinder parts. No shot that missed the heart would kill. Bellangé had so badly acquitted himself this time that I could not refrain from remark. In retaliation he made some observation concerning my lack of skill in horseback riding, because I was not able to keep up with his white steed. I asked him whether his idea of horsemanship was to bruise his beast with blows? After fording the Bourbeuse we came to a prairie that was utterly barren; it was flat, rocky, and sterile. Not an animal showed itself, not a bird was to be seen throughout the entire extent of this plain, which to me seemed endless. Finally we caught sight of hills again in the distance; behind them rose still another ridge we should have to cross before we arrived at Fort

---

contact with a buffalo, the animal butts against his pursuer. Buffaloes never attack ; a bull defends himself valiantly against bears, but a cow has less courage. It appears odd to me, therefore, that these beasts are not tamed. Our breeding bulls in the meadow are much more fierce, and angrily attack strangers.

Union. So I asked Bellangé whether we should not have done better to spend the night on the Bourbeuse and allow our horses to rest. He replied that he still hoped we might sleep at the fort that night, for the region we were traveling through was very dangerous ground; Blackfeet were said to be often roaming stealthily about, lying in wait for Assiniboin who passed this way constantly, one by one, as they went back and forth between the forts and their various settlements. We had to make haste. I would have been glad to sleep one night more in the open; the weather was so enticingly clear, and, moreover, we still had some meat.

My guide became more timorous and more hurried the nearer we came to Fort Union. He did not halt even at midday; therefore, in order to allay thirst as well as hunger, I thrust a piece of half-cured meat into my mouth to chew on. My arm was tired from administering blows upon the mare, but we had still 25 English miles to cover before reaching our destination.

Finally Bellangé, becoming more and more disquieted, alighted to exchange mounts with me. He bade me ride the white horse with all the luggage, whereupon he whipped up the mare unmercifully and away went the poor beast trotting with a limp. He laughed at me, saying the only trouble was I was no horseman. In reply, I asked whether it was his habit to ride with one stirrup shorter than the other. He had not noticed that one stirrup strap was shorter by two holes than the other; in consequence, I was forced to sit sidewise. In order not to be delayed on that account I rode with my legs hanging free. Now, our way led through plains that became constantly less broad and were more frequently traversed by streams that had worn a deep bed, to be sure, but at that time contained little water. On our right there were always hills; on our left flowed the Missouri. Evening came on apace; to me it seemed no longer possible to reach the fort that day. At length we came to a prairie at the verge of which Bellangé pointed out a bright spot.

With my telescope I discerned a white bastion. That was Fort William, trading post of the opposition. Five miles farther, 3 miles above the mouth of the Yellowstone River, lay Fort Union. Bellangé smacked with his tongue and licked his lips. The reason for this was his anticipation of a drink when he delivered a letter he carried from Schmidt to Joe Picotte, bourgeois at Fort William, nephew of our Mr. Picotte, but employed by the opposition company. The letter and my close acquaintance with Joe gave Bellangé hopes of getting a dram. Soon we came upon the track of a wheel. We were at Fort William. Roulette, clerk and interpreter, received us, took possession of the letter, thanked us in behalf of his bourgeois, who at the moment was on the river fishing. Without dismounting we continued our way along a good smooth road to our fort. The sun went down and a golden shimmering light spread over the landscape. Soon the stockade was visible and the white bastions, over which appeared the top of a tall flagstaff, that stood within the court-yard. At length we rode up to the gate. Bellangé was immediately surrounded by his many acquaintances. I was most heartily glad to stand once more on my own legs.

Bellangé delivered the letter he brought to a small, hard-featured man wearing a straw hat, the brim of which was turned up in the back.

He was my new bourgeois, Mr. Denig. He impressed me as a rather prosy fellow. He stopped Bellangé short, just as the latter was beginning a long story he wished to tell; on the other hand, he ordered supper delayed on our account that we might have a better and more plentiful meal. A bell summoned me to the first table with Mr. Denig and the clerks. My eyes almost ran over with tears! There was chocolate, milk, butter, omelet, fresh meat, hot bread—what a magnificent spread! I changed my opinion at once concerning this new chief; a hard, niggardly person could not have reconciled himself to such a hospitable reception in behalf of a subordinate who was a total stranger to him. After we had eaten he apologized for not having a bed in readiness for me; that night I must content myself with buffalo robes in the interpreter's room; better arrangements would be made next day.

The inside of the room presented an appearance rather like an Indian's habitation. On the floor near me were three beds for three couples of half-Indians and their full-blooded wives—visiting "barbarians." The wife of Spagnole, the horse guard, was a Mandan; Smith's wife was a Cree; and Cadotte's [41] an Assiniboin.

The last two men had been obliged to accompany as guides the transport of goods to Fort Benton in the territory of the Blackfeet and had not yet returned. In spite of this promiscuous company I slept quite well. I dreamed of milk, for the reason, I presume, that I had been so long deprived of it; for, until that evening, I had not even tasted milk since I left Belle Vue. No cows were kept at Fort Berthold on account of the cornfields; the law prevailing there gives Indian women the right to kill any animal that strays into their fields. Once I saw a splendid 2-year-old colt half killed by an Indian woman because it had escaped from its keeper and was bustling about in the midst of the growing corn. There is no Indian village near the fort. The Assiniboin are roving hunters without fixed abode. The tribe is separated into various bands that

---

[41] Both hunters were Cree half-breeds and at that time absent.

live apart from one another, for the reason that a great number of people move slowly from place to place and find greater difficulty, moreover, in providing sufficient food.

That night, after supper, Joe Dolores, the horse guard, played the leading role in a comic action: He galloped up to the gate shouting: "Blackfeet! Blackfeet!" R. Mack and Pattneau swung themselves at once upon the backs of their respective runners in order to corral the grazing horses and assist in defending the fort.

Everybody was keen to help. Blackfeet were reported to be sneaking secretly about the garden coulee (dry gully). With great trouble the men got all the horses together just as a man emerged from the spot where the enemy was suspected to be in hiding. Who should it be but our negro, Auguste! He had been looking for berries, simply as a means of diversion. Joe was so ridiculed that he took refuge in flight.

This morning, after breakfast, the room in which I am now writing was put in order for me and furnished with bedstead, two chairs, and a large table. Here I am alone, the more agreeable arrangement always for me. I do not find company a necessity. I have always something at hand with which to occupy myself, so I am not lonely, though I may be alone. What is more, Mr. Denig has found some work at once for me to do. He has here, for instance, many oil colors (neither very good nor complete) with which I am to paint, first of all, the front of the house, and then I am to decorate the reception room with pictures. At the same time I shall not fail to execute a life-size portrait of himself that is to hang in the office where it will strike the Indians with awe. All this work is to be done before Mr. Culbertson returns from Fort Laramie, because Mr. Denig wishes to prepare a pleasant surprise for his chief and, furthermore, because he expects that Mr. Culbertson will take me to Fort Benton.

All colors, crude or ground, were searched for in the principal building, in the warehouse, in garret and cellar; a marble slab with a grinder was put on a special table, five measures of oil were procured, and all spare shaving brushes were collected, in order that the painting may begin tomorrow. Today I am still free to do as I like. I employ the time writing.

A young grizzly bear and a war eagle, both alive, are confined behind the powder house. A number of Indian trinkets are displayed in the reception room and there are, besides, a stuffed Rocky Mountain sheep (female bighorn), black-tailed deer, large white owl, prairie hens, and pheasants, all of which will afford me, meanwhile, sufficient models for sketches and studies.

September 6. Before breakfast Bellangé began his return journey to Fort Berthold. Denig was provoked with him because he had to leave two good-for-nothing nags here, and wished to have in exchange a thoroughly good traveler. He received, however, a pack horse with the notification that his commission had been executed. Bellangé wished very much to be allowed to take my telescope with him, but I could not spare it; I must give him something later, at all events, as a return for the fear he endured.

This entire day I have been painting, with the assistance of two clerks, Owen Mackenzie and Packinaud,[42] the balcony and reception room; besides, I have ground some colors.

September 15. Morgan has gone again to the "Chantier," a place in the forest up the river where workmen and laborers under his direction are getting beams ready for the palisades.[43]

He was only on a visit here; therefore was lodged in my room. Now I am again in quiet possession. Last week I worked hard: ground colors and painted the pickets in front of the house. Mr. Denig expressed the wish that I paint also a sideboard in the mess hall; it was not sufficiently glary when finished, so he decided to improve its appearance himself. As paint of that sort is an abhorrence to me, I praised his work highly in order to be rid of it once for all. But I was interested in painting the entire outside of the house to his satisfaction, for in his relations with me he is most kind and agreeable. Every evening he sits with me, either in my room or in front of the gate, and relates experiences of his earlier life. As he has held his position in this locality for 19 years already, his life has been full of adventure with Indians, particularly since the advent of the whisky flask. He wishes me to paint also a portrait of himself and his dog, Natoh (bear), a commission I am very glad to execute. In return he promises, in the interest of my work, to enable me to have the best opportunities for studying wild animals. Now that I have found out what I need to know about Indians, I would like to vary my investigations by making just as thorough a study of wild animals. My plan is, not to write a book on the history, religion, and customs of the Indian race, but rather to depict the romantic life of Indians, either in oil paintings (my gallery) or in prints; therefore I find it necessary to study animals of the chase, although, as a matter of course, that is by no means my chief purpose.

---

[42] He was called Packinaud, which is said not to be his real name; as he can neither read nor write he is himself not sure.

[43] The palisades of this fort are not driven into the ground, as in Fort Berthold, but are fitted into heavy beams that rest upon a foundation of limestone. At this place palisades are further secured by supports of crossed beams on the inside, so that they cannot be blown down by the wind. Nevertheless, it happened once during my stay that on the western side, where the supports were badly decayed, a violent wind did force them down before the new beams were ready.

My recent transfer to this post I may regard as the most fortunate event of my life in this country. I am indebted to Herantsa superstition for my removal from a most unpleasant situation; for a highly interesting journey to this place, where I find congenial surroundings, and where I can make myself useful and not be regarded as the fifth wheel of a wagon. As to the personality of my new bourgeois, who was represented at the fort below as being a disagreeable person, I find myself most pleasantly surprised. Kipp is a man approaching old age who is forced by necessity to begin life anew for the reason that he has lost a good fortune on account of his addiction to strong drink. This makes him unhappy, dissatisfied with himself, and morose. Denig, his former clerk, has, on the contrary, come rapidly forward, owing to his commercial knowledge, his shrewdness, and his courage at the posts where he was earlier employed; therefore he has aroused the jealousy of his former chief, whom he now disregards. Fort Berthold, which is really under control of Fort Pierre, is not a trading post of much consequence; trade is carried on with only one tribe; and, moreover, business is done, for the most part, on credit, which frequently results in loss.

Here, on the other hand, Assiniboin, Crows, Cree, and half-breeds do their trading; and, besides, Fort Union is the depot or storage house for the more distant posts, Fort Benton and Fort Alexander.

It goes without saying that a bourgeois who occupies the position of responsible warden, chief tradesman, and person in highest authority at a trading post far removed, where he has fifty men under his direction, may regard himself of more importance than a man who directs five men. To conduct such a post as this requires more ability. In winter there are established from three to four byposts. Moreover, in this region where there is neither the rule of law nor an established police force, it is necessary for one to know these engagees in order to understand the difficulties in managing them. They are workmen employed by the year; they represent all nationalities—Canadians, Americans, Scotchmen, Germans, Swiss, Frenchmen, Italians, Creoles, Spaniards, Mulattoes, Negroes, and half-Indians, and come, for the most part, from St. Louis, where they have found no means of earning a livelihood. Canadians are in the majority; but these men are not to be mistaken for those commendable sailors mentioned earlier, the "Coureurs de bois", who were fitted for their employment under the strict discipline of the Hudson Bay Company.

The men here are called "Mangeurs de lard" because their chief occupation is the eating of pork. According to their talk, there are no workmen more capable, but when it comes to work they are neither industrious nor skilled. To make such people work, when one has no recourse to police control or to any outside assistance, is no small matter; one has to manage them with ability, courage, and tact. The more capable among these engagees advance immediately to better positions; if they are really skilled craftsmen they are employed as such, their wages doubled and better board and lodging provided; on the other hand, if they are qualified in the mercantile line or in languages and prove to be honest and shrewd, they are advanced to clerks, bourgeois, or agents. In this region every man works up from a lower position, for many years' experience among Indians— to become familiar with the Indian character, habits, and tongue— is required at the more important trading posts. One has not much respect for the ordinary engagee; one has to be constantly at hand when he is assigned work, for he takes no interest in the success of the fur trading company, and runs away upon the least suspicion of danger.[44]

As a matter of course, Denig keeps the subordinate workmen strictly under his thumb; what is more, he has to if he is to prevent their overreaching him. He feels, however, that one man alone is not sufficient to enforce good order among these underlings, for every one of them is armed and, though not courageous in general, are, nevertheless, touchy and revengeful. So for purposes of order and protection he has attached to himself the clerks, who stand more nearly on the same level with him in birth and education and afford, besides, the only support, moral as well as physical, upon which he can reckon. In his turn he provides just as willingly some diversion for all of them when they have performed services satisfactory to him; on the other hand, he limits their victuals when they are idle or lazy. For instance, last week under Morgan's direction a supply of hay for next winter was mowed 9 miles from here and piled up in "stacks" (conical heaps); nearly 15,000 pounds of cured meat was purchased at an Assiniboin camp and both clerks have returned with their men and teams. Today they had another laborious and difficult task, i. e., the felling of trees and the preparing of lumber for palisades at the fort.

On Saturday evening, therefore, Denig gave a ball, to which he invited also Joe Picotte, his family, and the people who work with him. We decorated the room as brilliantly as we could with mirrors, candles, precious fur skins, and Indian ornaments. He himself had the hardest work of all, because he was the only fiddler and did not stop until everybody had tired himself out with dancing.

[44] Our Smith (Gagnon) and Zimmermann gave us, more than once, evidences of their spirit; both were thrifty fellows and tried to earn some dollars extra as trappers. One evening in winter they went together into a nearby thicket to set traps for wolves or foxes. One of them saw, in the distance, a person descending a hill; immediately he abandoned both friend and trap and ran breathless to us, crying "Indians! Indians!" The approaching foe proved to be merely an Indian woman accompanied by her dog!

Indian women and men were dressed according to European mode. From my point of view, the ball on that account lost much of its character and the picturesque interest that one might have anticipated in this region and under these conditions. Only the spectators, who were in Indian costumes, gave one to understand in what part of the country the dance was taking place. The cotillion, which the squaws went through with much grace and far more correctness than I should have expected, seemed to be the favorite dance.

Indian women manifest the same preference for dancing, however, that is common among our white women, and most of them have had much practice in the art with their white husbands. Figures of the cotillion represent what is most pleasing to me, in general, in the way of a dance; to me, the waltz seems nonsense; it corresponds in no way to the purposes of dancing, i. e., developing a graceful body, suppleness, and ease of manner. As I do not dance myself, I beat the tattoo on the drum.

It is odd, yet worthy of note, that just such engagees, clerks, and even bourgeois, upon their return to the States or when they go back there on visits, cannot have enough of distinguishing themselves as "Mountaineers", of attracting attention in their highly ornamented buckskin clothes, of performing Indian dances and imitating Indian war cries, in order that they may be regarded as the hardy, fearless, jovial "Mountaineers", a name synonymous with famous huntsmen, distinguished warriors, bold and crafty trappers such as are described in books. While they take pleasure in making themselves conspicuous among their white brothers as savages, they try to make a forcible impression upon their red brothers here as white men. He knows— at least, the usual engagee knows—that he is unable to do this except in the matter of clothes, which the poor Indian cannot get, for the former has none of those qualities one ascribes to the "Mountaineer", while, on the other hand, the Indian possesses them all in a high degree.

I must mention here that, since beaver pelts have fallen in price, that far-famed class of trappers is almost nonexistent. Throughout the entire territory of Blackfeet, Crows, Assiniboin, Cree, Chippewa, Herantsa, Arikara, Dakota, the trappers are no longer found at all.

Beaver skins used to be their principal branch of industry; other pelts, like ermine, fox, muskrat, otter, and Alpine hare, are either too rarely obtained or else not sufficiently profitable to justify risking so many dangers. The risks, deprivations, and adventures of trappers have been enough related by storytellers and most excellent authors. The same fault is committed, however, almost universally: They treat the Indians, the rightful owners of these lands and of all beasts of the chase, the redskins' only source of food found therein, as robbers and murderers if they defend their property against hunters who are not entitled to poach there. On what authority do huntsmen and lovers of the chase base their right to follow that sport in Indian territory, to rob Indians of their only means of providing food and clothing? Do they first ask permission? Not at all! But if the Red Men make reprisals, either by cunning or force, then there is raised an outcry, both excessive and unjustified. So it comes about that writers who relate those stories treat first one nation and then the other as arrant knaves, as the meanest plunderers, just as they have frequently shown themselves to be among the Pawnee and the Crows. Is that just? Moreover, the same can be said concerning the behavior of the emigrants.

In many cases they could make necessity their excuse, it is true, but the greater number of animals they killed not from necessity but merely from love of sport. If, then, the right of the strong hand is to prevail, let the same right be granted the Indians, and with whatever measure one metes, let it be measured to the other. Indians defend their domain as it is distributed among the nations according to fixed boundaries, and they maintain their supply of food, their existence, as well as they can. Are not the fruits of the field, the grazing herds, even the beasts of chase, protected in civilized states by laws? Furthermore, is it not lawful in many Christian countries for the owner of land to fire upon a trespasser?

In return for Mr. Denig's kind invitation, Joe Picotte invited us to his fort the next day (yesterday). As I can neither dance nor play any musical instrument, I looked forward to the visit with little pleasure; especially as I am just now occupied with ideas other than amorous adventures. I would much rather have spent Sunday studying the young bear than to have gone to a party at 10 o'clock in the morning, but Joe Picotte seemed so much pleased to see me again, I thought mere courtesy required me to go.

Besides, though I was well acquainted with him in St. Joseph, I had perceived already on the *Robert Campbell* that he did not like seeing me with an opposition company. At about 11 o'clock at night we returned from the ball as merry as it is possible for people to be who have indulged in such gaiety without the enlivening effects of love and wine. The ride home in brilliant moonlight was splendid, a real delight. Morgan, firing off his pistols, rode in front with his dogs. Mackenzie on Toku, his superb courser, whose plunging and rearing as well as the great speed at which the spirited animal galloped home, made Mac's wife, riding behind, anxiously clasp him round! Denig's younger wife, riding a pony with Smith's wife, followed with me. I was mounted on a pony belonging to Denig's older wife, who expressed a wish to drive back. The two women were constantly trying to tempt me to run a race with them and see which could first reach the vanguard. They would remain behind a moment, then shout "Oppaheh! Oppaheh!" to me, whip up the pony, and away they would go. Behind us came the two-wheeled cart, drawn by two mules, carrying the bourgeois and his family and the musical instruments. Pattneau, astride the gray, brought up the rear.

Today Joe Picotte came over to ask how we had passed the night. At the moment I was engaged in no duties; so Mr. Denig said I might paint a portrait of Joe in water color. I immediately set about it. It seems strange to me now that I used to find it so difficult to get a good likeness when I attempted a portrait: my attention was so much engrossed with outlines and gradation of colors that I lost the expression of the sitter. I could not see the wood for the trees. The same difficulty befell me in the study of composition: I had always had rather too much imagination than too little, but if I tried to embody an idea in a sketch I took such pains to draw the forms correctly, either people or animals, or to give them proper positions or movements, that, in my effort to perfect the execution of my work, I lost the idea. A painter dares not give his attention so exclusively to technique that he fails in the expression of spiritual qualities. He must be so practiced in drawing that he can embody his conceptions on canvas with as much ease as the poet expresses his thoughts in writing by means of words. With outlines the painter reproduces a likeness or conveys his idea in composition, and no matter how often he may erase the lines in the execution of his sketch, he will easily recover them, for the salient features that convey the true character of his subject are, to him, far more important than perfection of line and color.

If he excel in the latter only, without being able to portray life truly, he produces pictures that are lifeless; if he excel in the former alone, even though he produces but caricatures he will give expression to that which is truly alive. To grasp the true meaning of his subject and to portray that conception with ease and charm bespeaks the master. If I shall be able to paint a portrait without sittings, merely from observation, I shall be content. But to succeed in doing that a physiognomy must make such an unusual appeal as to put me in a particularly fine mood.

I received today, as a gift from Mr. Denig, a [buffalo] cow's hide most excellently prepared and decorated. The hair is as fine as silk; the under side like velvet. Across the middle of it runs a broad band, decorated with beads, porcupine quills, and tiny bells that hang from rosettes. He got it from the Crows. Though it is so smooth, I found it impossible to adorn it further with fine drawings, still less with drawings on a large scale; so I shall not be able to paint my robe after my own style, Mr. Denig says.

In return for the portrait Mr. Picotte promises me something rare in Indian design. He possesses elk horns [45] of remarkable size and attached to the skull. If I could get such a pair I should have quite an addition to my collection.

Since I came here I seem to be at perfect peace with myself. In the first place, I am quite unexpectedly so much nearer the accomplishment of my life purpose that I have little more to worry about. My youthful dream of journeyings in strange lands, of horses, Indian women, and collections of Indian rarities I have enjoyed in reality.

If I can spend my later life in the painting of pictures that portray the American Indian, if time and strength remain to me until I have realized my ideal, then my cherished aims will have been fulfilled. In truth, I do not desire to create perfect human forms for the sake of attaining fame, but merely to satisfy an impulse from within, a longing for pure beauty. It is therefore a matter of indifference whether I succeed in the fulfillment of my purposes before the end of my life. Unfortunately an artist rarely receives his true valuation until after he is dead. Then it may be his works are bought at colossal prices, while during his life, perhaps, he has suffered want. Who knows whether he may not have lived in penury! Are we to call those people who pay enormous sums for paintings by deceased artists, but who, ignorant of the true value of master works, allow equally gifted contemporary artists to starve—are we to call such people patrons of art? They are votaries of fashion, neither connoisseurs nor patrons of art.

September 16. There was a downpour of rain the entire day; in consequence, no work out-of-doors. I spent the time sketching the head attire of a Cree chieftain captured by Blackfeet. This Cree partisan and eight of his braves were attacked by a superior force of Blackfeet, and when the former saw that they were going to be overtaken they quickly dug a hole with their hands and knives in the side of a low hill. [46]

---

[45] The difference in the size of elk horns is so considerable that I attributed the smaller pair of horns on our bastion to a smaller species. The hunters maintain, on the contrary, that they were taken from young elks whose antlers up to a certain age have only a given number of tines, and afterwards increase both in weight and size.

[46] In his Account of a Voyage up the Mississippi to Its Source, Lieutenant Pike gives a more detailed description of such a dugout: "Mr. Frazier showed me, on this prairie, holes dug by the Sioux when in expectation of an attack, in which they first put their women and children, and afterwards crawl themselves. These holes are generally round and about 10 feet in diameter; but some are half moons, and quite a breastwork." The moment the Indians "apprehend or discover an enemy, they commence digging with their knives, tomahawks, and a wooden ladle; and in an incredibly short space of time will make a hole sufficiently deep to secure themselves and family from the balls or arrows of the enemy. They have no idea of taking these subterranean redoubts by storm, as many men might be lost in the attack, which, even if successful, would be considered an imprudent act." He saw, later on, when examining huts that had been abandoned by Chippewa, similar entrenchments with boughs lying by, in readiness to cover them (whether as abattis or to protect their bodies is a question).

That was their only means of shielding themselves. All died valiantly, fighting to their last breath. The chief's headgear is estimated to be worth as much as a pack horse; therefore, not being in a position to purchase it, I content myself with making a true copy. My funds are spent; my merchandise has been disposed of; my credit with the company is good only for wearing apparel. At this place the cost of necessaries is very high—out of proportion to the increase one might expect on account of the distance things have to be transported. The price of coffee is 100 cents a pound; brown sugar, the same; meal costs 25 cents a pound; seven ship biscuits cost 100 cents; one pound of soap costs the same; calico is 100 cents a yard; to get one shirt washed costs 25 cents, etc. On an average, prices are nine times as dear as in the States.[47] If I had bartered my wares at such prices at Fort Berthold, I should have done a better business than I could have managed with cash. The value of a dollar is insignificant; what one receives for it is of no consequence. Even in the States 20 cents is not worth reckoning. In the Western States there is no smaller coin than a 5-cent piece.

And if I lose the collection, what benefit do I derive? Since I lost such old and valuable memorials upon the occasion of that great scare on the part of the Herantsa, I trust fortune less, if that is possible, than I did earlier. Have I ever had any good fortune? How have I arrived at my goal?

By overcoming a whole series of misfortunes, by struggling on in spite of disappointments. For lack of money I had to leave Paris and go back to Berne; owing to the death of old Fellenberg I failed to get a pleasant position as instructor in his famous institute; failing to sell my paintings, I became convinced that a man could not earn his livelihood as artist in Berne, not in all Switzerland, where political affairs absorb all man's faculties, all expedients, all lofty thoughts; where one looks upon art as luxury, for the simple reason that one has no taste for it. But for bilious fever I should be still in St. Joseph; but for bad luck with my horses I should be now in Savannah or in Deseret; but for cholera I should be still at Fort Berthold. I shall be obliged to leave this post, because I am superfluous here. That is my good fortune! Notwithstanding, I shall be consoled, in spite of all these adversities, if, in the future, I get a comfortable income from my Indian pictures, either by editing a work on that subject or by the sale of my paintings.

If I were a fatalist I should be forced to the conclusion that I was predestined to produce a collection of picturesque scenes in what was formerly called the Far West—my studies have taken a direction so completely unforeseen.

---

[47] He was in the Territories then.

By means of my exhibitions, I may be able to contribute my small share in the cultivation of people's taste and in the advance of science. My chief purpose was to study the antique from life. For the reason that persons who are accustomed to being nude assume postures different from those who are habitually clothed, I had to come to America in quest of Indians who could serve me as models. For preliminary studies, academic models served well enough.

September 17. Worked at painting the house this morning. Began a pen sketch of the house this afternoon for Mr. Denig. A band of Assiniboin came from their settlement on horseback, bringing dried buffalo meat for sale. They were invited to partake of sweetened coffee, which must now replace the whisky that used to be served. Mr. Denig thinks a portrait worthless unless the eyes follow a person who gazes upon it, no matter on which side the beholder stands; furthermore, a portrait must be drawn life-size and painted in oil, he says—otherwise it is of no value as a true representation. A water-color, it appears, has no worth.

Mr. Denig came up the river in the same year in which the Baron von Barneburg, alias Prince von Neu Wied, came; then it was that he and Mr. Culbertson arrived in this region for the first time.

I have several anecdotes from them concerning the Prince and my friend Bodmer; also in connection with Catlin. This last-named painter is regarded here as a humbug. He is said to have compromised the gentlemen who were then at Fort Pierre with a book of stories that they had written. Catlin took the steamer only as far as this point, went back on the same boat to Fort Pierre, where he remained three months and painted pictures of the Indians. Could never paint at all unless he were perfectly comfortable with easel, camp stool, etc. During the three months at Fort Pierre he requested the bourgeois and clerks to put down in a book, over their own signatures, accounts of interesting moments spent in that region. Many of them related their adventures in the Indian territory as he had asked them to do. Later on, so it seems, he published the book, retaining the names of the writers, but greatly distorting the narratives for the sake of effect, i. e., to make as tense as possible the interest of the reader. I had heard Mr. Kipp complain of Catlin. Though the painter knew hardly a word of the Sioux language, he is reported to have given lectures in New York on that subject. Yankee humbug! Since writing the above I have read the book myself. With the exception of several instances where the author talks big, the book contains a great deal that is true. The drawings, on the other hand, are for the most part in bad taste, and to a high degree inexact, especially the buffaloes. Indians never go on the hunt arrayed as if for war. That scene where wolves surround the dying bull is a silly make-believe; that one of the Indian vaulting upon a single bull is another. (The latter may possibly occur in a thickly crowded herd, when the hunter is hemmed in on both sides.) His buffalo herds, moreover, consist of nothing but bulls—no cows and calves. Bodmer makes the same mistake. What astonishes one in Catlin's sketches, particularly in the English originals, is that the faces are grotesque; what is more, they are faces of the same Indians whom he extols constantly, and justly, in the text for possessing the rare beauty of the antique.

He is said to have sold certain paintings of Indians to the United States Government with the understanding that no copies would be made; but, far from keeping his word, he copied them in secret before they were delivered and exhibited them later in London.

Mr. Murray, former English envoy here in Berne, told me he had procured from Catlin in St. Louis the means to make the voyage up the Missouri. Mr. Murray is the author of the interesting novel Prairiebird, a later edition of which, in another form, is called The Trapper's Bride. He took much interest also in my sketches of Indian life.

September 19. I had a most interesting ride to the little or upper Bourbeuse and back again. Yesterday, after our midday meal (here we eat at least three times each day), the bourgeois sent me with Carafel on a horseback ride to the little stream mentioned above, in order that I might have a chance to see my comrade set his beaver traps. Carafel is a skilled beaver trapper, an occupation that requires much patience and cunning. A ride of 10 miles over prairie, steep slopes, and many rivulets brought us to the upper Bourbeuse, where we saw several beaver dams.

While I made a drawing of the one most solid and complete, my companion, with the least possible noise, laid three traps nearby in the water and baited them with castoreum that he carried in a small horn. We took a farther ride about that neighborhood later with the hope of coming upon some buffaloes. Our horses were not prepared for a run; Carafel was riding my former mount, Vieux Blanc. Though "Old White" is no racer, he is nevertheless a most useful animal; he has no bad faults; he is capable of great endurance, and can be left standing untied at any place where he finds forage. As the few buffaloes that we could find were too far away, we went in search of a comfortable place where we could camp for the night. We found just such a place in high grass between two beautiful ash trees. I went immediately to work on a drawing of that spot, while Carafel lighted a fire and made tea. There were mosquitoes, to be sure, in great numbers, but we enjoyed our meal in merry mood, just as well-proved hunters and trappers are wont to do, because they are content with little and blessed with good appetites. While our horses grazed nearby we chatted together until it was dark, then wrapped ourselves up and went to sleep, dreaming the dreams of lucky mortals. We ate breakfast this morning at our camping place, saddled the horses, took a drink, mounted, and rode again to the stream where the traps were set.

I finished some sketches, but we caught no beavers; they are too sly, having been too frequently disturbed by Indians that pass that way. We saw several of the animals, however, but at the slightest sound they disappeared under water. We came home at a quick pace; saw nothing more of interest except a fat buck that we scared away from his lair and an arrow cut at its upper end in the form of a bird. Around the arrow was a wide circle, where the ground bore the impress of dancing warriors.

Toward midday we arrived here, full of enthusiasm for life in the bush; for horseback rides over stock and stone, through clear streams and across the plains; for dreams of the night, as we lie wrapped in our mantles beside a crackling fire, while our horses are grazing beside us and our loaded rifles lie near at hand. But the keen eyes of a hunter, his principal asset, I lack.

Of all the situations at the fort Morgan's appeals to me most. To be sure, when he is out in the wilds he does not have the benefit of as good meals as we enjoy here, but what advantage have we in comparison with his free roving through meadow and forest, over mountain and vale, hunting deer, buffaloes, bears, ducks, and geese, trapping beaver, foxes, and wolves in the service and under the protection of the company.

He sleeps and dreams in his tent of skin. His life as hunter offers a much more varied existence than even that of the huntsmen regularly employed at the fort; the latter go on the chase only once a week, when fresh meat is needed. Even then they hunt only buffaloes or elks, shoot and kill as many as they have need of, load the pack horses that are taken along for the purpose; quickly flay the beasts, cut off the best portions of meat, which they bind together and lay across the pack saddle, the weight equally balanced on both sides, and hasten home, not taking time even to smoke a pipe.

Morgan was talking about going next year to visit "auld lang syne" and see his mother and sister. Who knows whether his leaving might not give me an opportunity to remain here as overseer of the engagees? For that purpose I do not need an especially keen eye, nor any knowledge of the Indian speech. On the contrary, European languages and tact suffice for association with such people as they. I feel so well here. I am no sufferer from nostalgia. If I can only sketch here and there, I am happy.

What delights can civilized States offer an honest, industrious human being not certain as to how he is to earn his bread? How unhappy I should be to find that even my pictures of Indians would not provide an income—to have my sheet anchor fail me.

I should be perfectly satisfied where I am if I could have my two boxes; one of them is 2,500 miles distant (at St. Joseph), the other 170 miles away, and both in danger of being gnawed to pieces by mice and moths or else of being lost. Such a situation causes me to reflect much upon conditions at my old home. How unjust it seems that any active and industrious person should be uncertain as to his means of earning board and clothes. A wrong arrangement of things in human societies.

In appreciation of Mr. Denig's many kindnesses I copied for him my sketch of the interior of the fort.

September 20. Mr. Denig has again contrived some employment for me, i. e., to paint the picture of an eagle, life size, on cotton cloth; then to sew thereon stripes of red and white cloth in alternating stripes about 15 feet long, thus providing flags for Indians. They are to pay the handsome price of 20 robes apiece for these standards; so only the wealthiest among them can afford to enjoy the distinction of possessing one.

Mr. Denig likes to look on the while, and he talks to me continually about Indian legends and usages. As he writes the best of those stories for Père de Smet, by whom they are published, there is no need of my preserving more than some bits of memoranda.[48]

After a few studies from life and further understanding as to the position the eagle was to have in relation to the peace pipe, I set to work at once.

Not the golden eagle but the white-headed or bald eagle is the national emblem of the United States. The last-named bird is not known, however, on the Missouri. The first is a brave well known to the Indians. Whether the fur traders, like Franklin, thought the noble golden eagle a more desirable emblem for the coat of arms of the United States than the common bald eagle I do not know. It is highly probable that they chose that one because it alone was known to the prairie Indians. Audubon referred to Franklin's opinion concerning the unfortunate choice of the national bird and expressed himself as in full agreement. Unluckily, the character of North Americans, as a Nation, corresponds to that of the bald eagle. It is unnecessary to offer further proof of that than was made evident in the recent commercial crisis of 1857 in the United States. Did not the Americans say then to their leading creditors in Europe, "We have your goods; we will not pay you for them; go to

---

[48] If I had only written them in full! Then the book would have been known to myself, at least, and to others on this side of the Atlantic. Even now I like to recall some of the stories he related to me about jugglery : A wager an Indian made with him as to which of them was the most sharp-witted. It was the true exploit of that illustrious chief of the Assiniboin—Gaucher.

smash, like ancient and honorable folk; we are young, your ruin does us no harm"?

As Franklin's opinion, as well as that of Audubon, reveals nobility of character not possessed by the majority of Yankees, I append his words here.[49]

He said today that he never wears anything at all that belongs distinctly to Indian dress, for the reason that Indians take pride in procuring for themselves clothes according to our mode and have an ambition to appear dressed as white men, because they regard our garments more fashionable and expensive. A white person in Indian costume inspires no especial respect among the tribes; on the contrary, he rather lowers himself in their estimation. Furthermore, if he is a white man in the Indian garb of a different tribe he runs far more risk of being killed, because he may not be recognized in that disguise as a pale face. That is possibly Mr. Denig's real reason for discarding buckskin clothes, which are certainly more serviceable for life in the bush and on the prairie and serve as better protection against sun and mosquitoes when one is on horseback. However, he rarely goes outside the fort any more. The clerks who will stay here for years, indeed, for the rest of their lives, perhaps, in the employ of a trading company, endeavor, of course, to oblige the latter; they wear, therefore, clothes made of materials that the company carries in stock and on which a considerable profit is realized. For that reason such an arrangement is acceptable to them. Most of the engagees bring with them quantities of clothing for which they paid much less at the place whence they came and which affords them a good article for trade among themselves.

The "Mountaineer" costume, in which they array themselves in St. Joseph and St. Louis, they have made before their departure for the purpose of distinguishing themselves. Such suits of clothes are made up and sold at Fort Pierre. Buffalo hides are said to be prepared there and marked for sale.

September 21. Have finished the eagle. This is my first oil painting during the entire 5 years I have been absent from home; the

---

[49] The words are not appended in the Kurz manuscript, but the author refers, presumably, to the following taken from a letter Dr. Franklin sent from Passy, under date of Jan. 26, 1784, to his daughter, Mrs. Sarah Bache [translator]:

"For my own part, I wish the bald eagle had not been chosen as the representative of our country; he is a bird of bad moral character; he does not get his living honestly; you may have seen him perched on some dead tree, where, too lazy to fish for himself, he watches the labor of the fishing hawk; and, when that diligent bird has at length taken a fish, and is bearing it to his nest for the support of his mate and young ones, the bald eagle pursues him and takes it from him. With all this injustice he is never in good care; but, like those among men who live by sharping and robbing, he is generally poor, and often very lousy. Besides, he is a rank coward; the little kingbird, not bigger than a sparrow, attacks him boldly and drives him out of the district. He is therefore by no means a proper emblem for the brave and honest Cincinnati of America, who have driven all the king birds from our country; though exactly fit for that order of knights which the French call Chevaliers d'Industrie."

smell of the paints gave me both pleasure and pain. I brought no oil colors on the journey with me, because they are too circumstantial; occupy too much space and take far too much time to dry. Water colors are much more practical to take along when one is traveling. Otherwise I should greatly prefer colors in oil. In the first place, I might have more practice, and, secondly, I find that objects covered with hair, like animals, are portrayed in a much more lifelike manner when painted in oil. In the matter of technique, painting in water colors is distinctly more difficult than oil painting. When working with the former one has to be sparing with white and come forward gradually with the dark colors; consequently, the artist must be sure of his subject beforehand—idea and effect must be calculated with utmost exactitude before he begins; for with too much washing the freshness of the colors is lost.

On the other hand, in oil painting he may put in the white after he has disposed the rest of the tones; he need not calculate so exactly beforehand points of high light but can decide that definitely thereafter. Furthermore, in oil painting mistakes can be much more easily corrected than in water colors. With the spatula he can remove what is wrong without injury to the canvas, while by frequent applications of water to the paper he may change an individual part of the composition in a picture already dry. When working in oil an artist has the further advantage of producing transparency in color, the utmost degree of radiance, while to achieve that extremely difficult aim with water colors, to produce colors that are soft and transparently clear, he must have had long practice and have gained an exact knowledge of the science of mixing his pigments. English artists are preeminent in water-color painting. But in producing their effects they use also quassia, oil colors, and crayons.

What one is capable of doing with a beard brush, ink brushes, and with no lacquer or Guimet, anybody who has the least knowledge of this subject can readily understand.

I gave general satisfaction with my eagle, however, and am therefore content. If I had refused to paint the bird because of the lack of necessary materials I might have been thought ill-natured, and that would not have been well. It might perhaps have also been whispered about in secret that I could not paint the eagle and had evaded the task by a subterfuge. This much is certain: that while a pretended painter can produce nothing worth while even when equipped with the best materials, a real artist, though he cannot acquit himself as well, of course, as when he is supplied with everything he needs, will reveal something of his capability even with the worst materials.

Mr. Denig has been reading to me again from his manuscript, which is extremely interesting. He is very well educated, and he has made a thorough study of Indian life—a distinct advantage to him in trade. He is so fond of the life in this part of the country that he is averse to any thought of going back to his Pennsylvania home in the United States.[50] On this occasion we talked a long while about the future of the Indian race. To be sure, the Americans are much to blame for the present unhappy state of things among the Indians on the borders, but it is, one may say, their heritage from the English, Spanish, and French.

From the time the Western Continent was known those nations contested claims to land in North America without regard to the aboriginal inhabitants. They laid claim to tracts of land where white man had never set foot; the boundaries of which were wholly undetermined and therefore the constant cause of petty jealousies, disputes, and war. When the Colonies declared their independence a new power came upon the field which, from the standpoint of geographical position, was permitted to make more pretensions to the land than foreign nations for the reason that this was the home, the native land of the Americans. Moreover, the fact that the English and the French made use of the Indians as instruments in their pretexts for war, in order to assert their right to property unlawfully obtained, had so deeply involved the colonists in the Indian wars, had aroused such hostility between themselves and the original inhabitants, that it was difficult, nay, impossible, to conclude peace with them immediately after their Declaration of Independence. For that reason it was impossible for the new government, because it had not yet sufficient power, to prevent emigration to the West (nor was it desired). Already, as colonists, those highly religious but most un-Christian Anglo-Americans looked upon Indian territory as their own possession and the Indians themselves as their enemies.

"It is not right for Indians to own so much uncultivated land while white 'gentlemen' are forced to live in want." As is well known, Indians in the East planted maize and tobacco, turnips and beans in abundance; bands of marauding colonists went out against them with the express purpose of destroying villages and taking possession of their stores as well as of laying waste the young corn and lately sown fields. They did not learn the culture of those fruits of the field from the white race, but the growing of maize, tobacco, and potatoes they

---

[50] Not for the reason, as he says, that he may have 2 wives here, but to avoid political carryings-on that disgust him. J'accord! Owing to an accident, his old wife is of no service; so, according to customs in this part of the world, he might be divorced. For the sake of his kind feeling toward her and of keeping her here as companion for the younger wife, so that the latter may not seek amusement at the homes of the clerks' or engagees' wives, he will not cast her off. Furthermore, he has a son and a daughter by her. His boy is being educated in Chicago, but the girl is at home with her mother.

learned from the redskins. So that reproach about the latter's leaving so much land uncultivated misses the mark utterly, so far as the eastern nations are concerned. The Indian war, just as Negro slavery, is the colonists' heritage from the British, a curse that Englishmen left behind them but which seems not to have satisfied them, for they continued during a period of 30 years (up to the Black Hawk war) by presenting gifts to the Indians and holding out promises of assistance to incite the tribes to uprisings against the Americans. It is not extraordinary, therefore, that the latter still harbor feelings of hatred toward the Indian.

Still, whether with the help of this nation or that, Indians have the right to defend their domain, and, now that Americans have grown so mighty, forcing England to discontinue her former practices, it would be more worthy a great nation to treat the tribes in a better way, to make their future secure, to grant them equal rights, allow them the same privileges that the white race enjoys; in a word, allow the two races to intermingle. Other things being equal, difference in color is no reason for keeping them separate.

Whether the United States Government has any higher purpose in calling together so many tribes at Fort Laramie than merely to negotiate a treaty for free passage through their territory on the way to Oregon and California only time will prove.

If only the eastern nations had been united, had made peace with one another for the purpose of driving back covetous enemies, had trusted no white nation nor made compacts with any of them, they would have been strong enough to repel all intruders. But hatred was too strongly indulged among the different tribes, unfortunately too deeply rooted, to admit of united action.

September 22. Yesterday the thought never once entered my mind that it was Sunday, and yet I keep a journal with great regularity. Rain fell in such streams all day and all night, and penetrated through the roof and ceiling into my room in such quantities, that I was forced to the constant occupation of placing water basin and empty paint pots beneath the leaks in order to prevent an inundation.

Today I painted a good-sized picture of my bourgeois' pet, Natoh, whose image I represented so true to life that his master was perfectly satisfied and the women especially delighted. I took pleasure in the work on my part, because it has been so long since I painted in oil that I feared I might get out of practice. I have always found, however, that by varying the kind of work I do, by allowing my several senses or faculties some relaxation, I invariably gain. Just as perpetual eating fails finally to nourish, but, on the contrary, does damage to the stomach, so continued painting dulls the color sense, incessant sketching makes less exact one's sense of form, too prolonged and unvarying application to the study of composition renders less keen the imaginative faculty. When food has been digested, appetite restored, and desire for further nourishment awakes, then one eats with zest and food contributes properly to strength and sustains health. The same applies in the matter of mental nutriment—mental occupations. My first experience as student in Paris impressed that truth for all time; for 8 months I worked with ardent zeal from 7 o'clock in the morning until 10 o'clock at night, resting only at night and on Sundays.

The result was that, even though I made considerable advance for some time, my faculties were so exhausted from fatigue that I saw neither colors, forms, nor proportions truly; in consequence, I imagined that I should never succeed in art and determined to give it up. In disgust I fastened a stone to my collection of studies and from the Pont de Jena I threw them into the Seine. Every artist eager for success suffers at times such miserable states of mind. Then a long period often intervenes before he recovers himself again. The more keenly he suffers the more gradual his restoration. After a 4-months' trip, including a stay in Compiegne (St. Jean les Deux Jumeaux), Havre, and Brittany (at Fouillee), I was fully restored to my former energy—I might well say, to proper understanding. But those studies I threw away were a great loss—a loss I shall never cease to regret, notwithstanding I have now replaced them with another collection made among the Indians. Precisely for that reason, i. e., the resulting detriment to myself, I learned from that experience this lesson I shall never forget: Never again to bring about by overfatigue such a wretched state of mind as that which I overcame with such difficulty and at so great a loss of time.

September 23. This has been a splendid day in my experience; I have been on the chase for the first time and shot my first buffalo. Sketched my first buffalo from life.

After breakfast old Spagnole, our cattle herd (doesn't look like a shepherd) brought news that huntsmen from the opposition fort [51] were running buffalo on the lower prairie. At once Mr. Denig, with much kindness, offered me the pacer so that I could chase buffaloes with Owen Mackenzie and so have an opportunity to study them. Mackenzie rode Condee. We were therefore admirably mounted, and having no orders to bring meat back we followed the hunt with no other object in view than our own pleasure. Mackenzie was to kill a fine specimen so that I might have the chance to make a sketch. My equipment consisted of my sketchbook, carried in my pouch, which was swung over my shoulder, a rifle laid across my lap, hunting knife stuck in my belt at the back, and a bullet pouch hung beside

---

[51] We called them dobies, from the word "adobe", because their fort is built of sun-dried clay.

the powder horn, also suspended from my belt. Mackenzie had returned only this morning at breakfast from a buffalo hunt of several days in another region; it was therefore most kind of him to ride out again with me before he had taken any rest.

How different are one's sensations when sitting a fiery courser whose desire is always to advance beyond the pace, which one must constantly restrain, lest the animal be carried beyond control from excess of high spirits, from sheer delight in the chase—how different from riding a weary, melancholy nag that one wears oneself out with beating and prodding without getting on any faster. What a difference it makes in one's feelings! When provided with an excellent mount, the blood courses more rapidly through one's veins, one's heart leaps for joy; Nature seems entrancing! We could not have chosen more beautiful weather—warm sunshine, clear air, a cloudless sky, and the wide, wide horizon, in the far distance, merged in blue haze. The ground was dry—no dusty stretches, no bogs or fens. We had to go 5 miles at a brisk pace before we reached the herd we were in pursuit of. We were beginning to think that the "dobies" had spoiled our sport when, near the so-called Butte de Mackenzie (named for the father of my companion on the chase), we came unexpectedly upon a small group of both old and young bulls. Some of them were lying in the grass near a spring at the upper end of a coulee; others were comfortably grazing round about them. We changed our course at once, rode around the hill, along by thickets of wild cherry and plum trees that covered the coulee, in order to fall upon the buffaloes unawares. But the sound of hoofbeats had already warned them; those we had seen lying on the grass had sprung to their feet, and, with tails aloft, speedily took to flight.

At a mad gallop we crossed the brook and followed close upon the fleeing herd. Even the horses shared our eagerness and tried to outdo each other, but I allowed Mackenzie to get ahead so that I could observe him. With his keen eye he had already selected his victim, approached within 2 feet, and fired. So true was his aim that the animal lay dead as I passed on a gallop. It might be truly said that suddenly he fell to earth. In the grip of death he groaned, beat the ground with his hoofs, and rolled over on his side. So accurately had the ball pierced his heart that I thought at first he had fallen from sheer fright. But we went much farther. I had a great desire at least to shoot at a buffalo. Mackenzie bade me follow him; we set out again at a gallop and came up with the herd. He singled out a bison for me and forced the animal apart from its companions. I pursued it over the rolling prairie until I was so close I couldn't miss aim. At my first shot the ball entered just a little too high; he turned in such a way that my second shot struck his right knee. Then Mackenzie rode forward and in passing the old fellow sent a bullet into his heart. The pouch swung across my shoulder was a great hindrance when I was shooting, because I was forced to keep it in position with my left arm and yet found it difficult to do that and at the same time fire a gun.

While in full chase, drawing nearer and nearer the fleeing herd, we reloaded our rifles. Mackenzie was laughing the while at the wounded buffalo, who was trying to run, notwithstanding a bullet in his heart. In truth he was killed! He could go no farther. All at once he stood as still as a block and looked angrily toward us, his nose dripping with blood. I reined in my pacer and took aim, intending to shoot the animal in the head and bring him down. My horse, all in a heat from the swift gallop, could not stand quietly; he snorted, he foamed, he pawed the ground; as a result, my shot went amiss, merely grazing the forehead of the monster. He hardly moved his head. But he began at last to sway, placed his feet wide apart to balance himself, but nothing could help him more. He was obliged to come down, first on a fore knee, then on his side. The beast was too thin to serve me for a model buffalo; therefore, we left him lying there and rode back to the first one we had shot. We dismounted, tethered our horses with long halters, and allowed them to graze while I made as exact drawings as I could, showing different views of the fallen bison. As soon as I had finished my sketching, Mackenzie cut out the tongue and other choice bits of meat to take to his wife. Then we galloped home. What joy!

On our way home Mackenzie pointed out to me on the left bank of the Yellowstone a prairie where several years ago he caught a wild mare—an adventure that came to a tragic end. He was riding the fleet-footed John at the time and found that he was some distance ahead of the pack horses that were to carry the meat as usual to the fort as soon as he should have the luck to kill a buffalo. In the distance he saw a drove of dark-colored animals grazing; he directed his course so as to gain the wind and take them by surprise. He made ready his rifle and gave fiery John the reins as soon as he thought the distance favorable. But when he got sight of the herd again he saw that they were not buffaloes at all, but wild horses. As the horses took to flight immediately, for they were just as shy as the former, Mackenzie laid his gun across his lap and seized his lasso of twisted leather, fixed the noose, and pursued the fleeing herd at a riotous gallop. John soon drew near his wild blood relations and Mackenzie selected from among them a black mare that was accompanied by a young foal. He rode after her and with his right hand swung the lasso, catching her head in the noose, while, with his left hand, he held fast to the other end of the rope. He drew in the thong, choking the imprisoned animal by a violent jerk backward that forced her to stop, while at the same time he reined in his own horse. The foal turned back and kept near its mother, now brought to a stand by means of the choking noose and thereby subdued.

Then, with the assistance of Spagnole, who happened to be hurrying by, Mackenzie bound together the mare's feet, so that he could leave her lying there while he followed the chase, for he dared not return home without meat. Unfortunately he did not find buffaloes as soon as he expected and his return to the place was delayed until the next day, when he found only the colt's head, tail, and feet. The mother also, his captured mare, had already fallen a prey to wolves.

To have had such a ride and to have made the sketches! As my shot did not bring down the second buffalo, I returned without trophies.

In the afternoon we delivered Joe Picotte's portrait. Mr. Denig insisted that I demand a flask of whisky in return, and when I refused to bite, because I would rather have had a pair of elk horns, he himself, as a "wink" to Joe, sketched in a whisky bottle at the bottom of the picture. But it was of no avail; there is no longer any whisky to be had at the adobe fort. Joe Picotte offered to give me any Indian curio that I would mention. I would have liked to have asked for the horns, but what would Mr. Denig have said about that? I was thinking only of myself. So we both came away empty-handed. Bear meat, juicy and tender, was served at supper. Ramsay shot bruin on a headland (projecting point of wooded land) quite nearby. The "dobies'" fort is more favorably situated for hunting than ours because it stands between two densely wooded forests.

September 24. Began a portrait of Mr. Denig—life-size, knee-length. This work is to be finished before Mr. Culbertson's return from Fort Laramie for the reason that he may possibly take me with him to Fort Benton.

Bears, big with young, if frightened, smoked out or in any manner driven from their dens during their winter sleep, are said to bring forth their cubs often prematurely. Ducks, when hotly pursued on the water, are said to fix their feet firmly to the grass below the surface and expose only their bills for air, in the hope of escaping the eye of their pursuers. Indians on a stag hunt disguise themselves by covering the upper part of the body with a wolf's skin, the head with antlers and tufts of wormwood, in order to deceive the animals. Some of them turn somersaults, tumble over themselves, and gesticulate like mad to arouse the curiosity of the antelopes. But in order to be successful they must keep themselves always in lee of the wind. If a buffalo shows an inclination to fight, shakes his head and threatens pursuit, which is very rare, one is to shoot him in the nose. The shock will stop him for an instant; that the hunter must be quick to profit by and get away.

If it so happens that one's gun is not loaded, one is to prop it firmly on the ground, so that, in running, the beast will strike his head against it. This is to be done, however, only at times of extreme danger, because the gun will be broken to pieces by the hurtling of the furious colossus, and, furthermore, one runs the risk of being trampled underfoot. The Assiniboin were called by the Cree Indians Assinibuaduk, i. e., stone eaters [correctly, Stone Dakota],[51a] because, it is said, they followed the custom at an earlier period of cooking meat not in the fire but on hot stones. Absaroka they call Crows, i. e., Crow Indians.

In Indian combat the intensity of the struggle, the most violent fighting, centers about the dead or wounded, as in the Trojan wars. An Indian's greatest glory is to distinguish himself as a warrior; that is why the various tribes have been in armed conflict among themselves for so long a time that, as a rule, they can no longer recall the first cause of strife. Their real motive springs less frequently, therefore, from a desire to wage a war of extermination than to gain an opportunity to win distinction as braves. To kill an enemy from a distance bespeaks no courage, is not regarded as the deed of a hero, is not accredited as a "coup"; on the other hand, to strike down your foe in hand-to-hand combat requires force, skill, bravery, and cunning.

Inasmuch as some proof is demanded of the victor's having touched his vanquished enemy, if no one is present to bear witness to the fact, he takes off the scalp of the one slain; that is, he cuts off the skin of the head, together with the hair, or, in fact, only a part of it. To do that requires time, and to expose himself so long to the rage or vengeance of enemies demands courage. In an encounter where many witnesses are at hand no scalp is required as evidence of valor for which a "coup" may be accredited, but the hero must have touched the fallen enemy either with his hand or with his weapon. This explains the press about the fallen foe. Furthermore, it is regarded the worst ignominy, the utmost disgrace of a band, especially of a chieftain, if the enemy captures the body of one of his men, treats it with insult, cuts off the limbs, delivers them to women for their dance of triumph, and finally throws them to dogs for food. Therefore the furious onset in defense of a fallen savage.

Bands of equal strength seldom attack each other unless the war is waged out of plain hate. To expose themselves to a loss without the certainty of gain is not "smart", as the Americans express it, i. e., not crafty, not shrewd. And shrewdness is the better part of valor.

[51a] That is, Buanŭg, the Dakota, not "eater," in Chippewa.—Ed.

If a band of limited numbers is set upon by a superior force, every one fights as courageously as a lion, even to the last man—not one attempts to escape.

To provoke one another by jeering, to challenge one another, is much the practice among Indians; it affords them an opportunity to signalize themselves in the presence of their own people. Also reminds one of the Greeks and Trojans. Generally speaking, however, the heroes described by Homer are in no sense like Indians. Assiniboin (Dacota, also Nacota, Hoha, or Hohe, called the disloyal by their related tribe, the Sioux) rarely take prisoners.[52] They kill everybody who comes under their tomahawk: the old, and gray-haired, women, children, and young girls. All are enemies—have begotten foes or will beget future foes.

Girls from the best Indian families are strictly guarded, and upon going out at night are required to be closely muffled, because young "bucks", when in the humor to run the risk of a fray or to expose themselves to the danger of being stabbed, are allowed to try their luck when and where they please. Such practices allure lads of mettle, because of the danger involved, and afford them, according to their point of view, a sort of preliminary preparation for military exploits that are to be seriously undertaken later on. When once recognized as braves they no longer stoop to such larks. They are men. They respect themselves as such and act accordingly. As a brave may have wives, ad libitum, as many as he is able to support, he buys (marries) the girl that appeals to him.

I am told that some time ago a daughter of Ours Fou, chief of the Assiniboin (now with Mr. Culbertson at Fort Laramie), hanged herself, because, notwithstanding that she was so closely muffled and so strictly watched, one of these young fellows succeeded in taking advantage of her. He made a boast of this and, from chagrin, she hanged herself. Whether she was driven to the rash act by his ill-mannered boastings or by his bold misconduct the story does not make clear. In consequence of her death the boy was forced to go away and join another band for a year, and his relatives had to give horses and other presents by way of atonement for his wrongdoing.

Accidental injury or death to a member of a tribe demands the same vengeance or propitiation as death or injury inflicted purposely. The only exculpation held to be valid is the wounding or killing of a man in the disguise of an animal skin that Indians adopt to decoy stags or antelopes. Such an accident is pardonable, because one must shoot on the instant one is aware of the slightest indication of an animal being near. For the further reason, also, that there is the possibility

---

[52] Quatre Ours was taken prisoner by the Assiniboin.

of an enemy concealing himself under that disguise in order to play the spy.

Assiniboin, Cree, Crows, Blackfeet, Flatheads—none of them have any idea of the great numbers of people that make up the white population or the least notion of the power of the United States Government.

The few white fur traders and the people employed by them, Indians look upon as poor men who find no means of earning a living at home. Even though one of the chiefs makes a visit to the States to inform himself, none of his tribe believe what he tells on his return. They are unable to comprehend the marvels he reports. A son-in-law of our bourgeois was murdered for no other reason than his refusal to allow himself to be called a liar; consequently, he shot down the offender at once. Then he was also killed by the revengeful tribesmen. These are facts I have picked up during Mr. Denig's sittings for his portrait.

September 25. The portrait is finished. The old man is perfectly delighted that he possesses something new to excite the wonder of the Indians. "Who is that? Do you know him?" he asks Indian women and children. As everybody recognizes the likeness as his own he is very much pleased. Redskins do not understand how a picture of a man can be painted exactly like a given person whom they know. That cannot be done by any natural means, so the spectacles must surely have had something to do with it; for not one of all the other whites is able to paint, much less to wear spectacles.

They comprehend quite clearly that the human figure can be represented with special sort of clothes; they themselves have practice in such hieroglyphics. In their drawings they designate a man by representing the figure with legs; a woman, by a long skirt; in other words, a figure without legs. But to paint a face that every child knows for Minnehasga (Long Knife, Indian name for the bourgeois as Americans), that is most extraordinary. The picture of Natoh was amazing, but now, a very man! What pleases Mr. Denig especially is the remark of his wives, that, stand wherever they may in the room or walk wherever they will, his picture constantly looks at them. "Ehah, wakan!" What witchcraft is this!

Since his portrait has proved such a success Mr. Denig takes much more interest in my ideas concerning a collection of pictures representing Indian life. He is now convinced, also, that I have sufficient ability to execute them in the proper way. He approves of my plan: Six landscapes (forest, prairie, river, coulee, a view in perspective, crags); six animal pieces (buffalo, bear, elk, stag, antelope, horse); six scenes from Indian life (the dance, sport, combat, family, hunt, a group about the council fire). "Only they must be large, very large," he said; "small pictures produce no effect."

The above plan was a fancy of mine when I was preparing for my American studies. No repetition, nothing to amaze or shock, animals to enliven the landscape, and the latter to be depicted in a characteristic manner as background for the figures.

But my greatest difficulty was lack of money; I was in need of an independent income in order to put my plans into effect; furthermore, to enable me to vary my studies, to enrich and enlarge my collection of paintings. In any case, such a plan is of great advantage on an artist's professional tour, because he recognizes at once what his objective is, what he needs to do, then goes systematically to work on his studies without losing time with futile attempts here and there. During the first year, accordingly, I studied nothing but landscape; several years thereafter only Indians; and finally wild animals; the last-named came last, because they are found in regions farthest removed from my starting point.

We had great fun this evening with our grizzly; he broke loose from his chain and, of course, had to be caught again. Mac. and Spagnole threw their lassos but their efforts were long in vain, for bruin was always prompt to ward them off with his paw. They succeeded finally, however, between the two, in holding him fast between the nooses. While we drew in the lassos to confine securely the sly and supple bear the old cowherd stood behind him and seized his ears, in order to keep his head still while his collar was put on. The old man then ran out of the way, and our prisoner amused us with the clever manner in which he slipped off the nooses.

Natoh, the dog, nipped him several times on the back but was wary enough never to attack him in front. Natoh knows the effect of a blow from bruin's paw or a bite with his sharp teeth. Three such dogs would cause a 2-year-old bear little concern.

September 26. During the winter season the Assiniboin and other tribes construct in the neighborhood of their villages so-called parks or enclosures, into which they entice buffaloes and kill them in droves in order to provision the settlement with meat for a long period. Such occasions afford the spectacle of a hunt more vast than one can conceive and accompanied with much tumult and noise. On ground suitably chosen for their purpose, they throw up a widespreading circular enclosure of heavy logs and dry boughs. They leave a small opening through which the park is entered. They then set up two rows of stakes that diverge from either side of this entrance and thus form, when completed, a passageway of sufficient width for a herd to pass through. As soon as the hunters are aware of a nearby herd, one of them, disguised as a buffalo, goes out to meet it, and by imitating the cry of a calf, by bellowing, by shaking his buffalo robe, and resorting to all sorts of motions endeavors to attract the attention of the animal nearest him, and then approaches by slow degrees the entrance to the park.

If the decoy can but excite the curiosity of the buffaloes in front and set them in motion toward him as their ringleader, the others follow of themselves. The members of a herd always follow their leaders en masse, kept together by the timidity of the cows, their solicitude for their calves, and the jealousy of the bulls. The crafty hunter moves slowly, never hurries. If he make but one bungling movement he may betray himself, startle the animals, cause them to take flight, spoil the hunt, expose himself to ridicule, and lose his reputation as skilled and practiced huntsman to whom only this most difficult undertaking might be intrusted. Not every one possesses that exact knowledge of the ways and habits of buffaloes, the exceeding cleverness in imitating them, or the craft and courage to expose himself to their horns and hoofs which insures success in ensnaring a herd. As soon as the foremost bison have come near enough to the narrow opening leading into the enclosure to bring the entire drove between the two barriers, then hunters on horseback as well as swift runners reveal themselves in the rear to cut off retreat and by their presence to keep the animals moving forward. Not until the disguised hunter has reached the "medicine pole" in the center of the park, has presented his buffalo hide as offering, and suspended it there along with other decorations and painted objects, does the commotion and noise begin.

The decoy rushes out of the inclosure by an opening on the other side and the bison, attempting to follow, are driven in with wild outcries and renewed tumult until the inclosed space is entirely filled. Then, for fear that the ensnared beasts might attempt to break out, all noise is hushed and the entrance is barred. Huntsmen, standing around the inclosure, either shoot their captives or kill them by hurling spears. When they have slaughtered the herd to the last beast Indian women enter with knives, wash themselves in the gore of their victims, grub into the moist carcasses, dexterously cut off the twitching limbs, drink warm blood, and if very hungry, eat the raw flesh.

When on a general hunt, "mikawua cerne," the hunters shoot in full gallop. They count only the arrows or balls that miss their mark. Women follow close behind them, fall upon the first victim, and carefully rip off the hide, which is all that the hunters require. The meat belongs to those who cut it up and haul it to the settlement in travois drawn by horses or dogs.

Indians of both sexes are passionately fond of games, particularly of those that still survive from their age-old free and independent life. In social intercourse they have no important subjects for discussion, such as political or financial matters, religious questions, their own history, past and present, as compared with that of other remote nations, or of other peoples varying widely in civilization, etc.

Their isolated, lonely existence in tent or village offers few subjects for conversation. They are daily employed in war or hunting; their interest in those adventures is already dulled by too frequent repetition. Their language, utterly lacking in flexibility and grace, is not favorable to the cultivation of wit. Consequently they turn to games as the only excitement their quiet way of life provides. Their object in view, no matter how trivial or insignificant, they strive eagerly, enthusiastically, to gain, but never contentiously. They have no games that offer opportunity for cheating; they indulge in no strife in their play. I have never seen or heard anything of the sort.

The Iowa are fond of card games (poker: the one who holds the highest cards wins). But on many occasions I have seen two young people sit down on the ground opposite each other, take off their moccasins, and place all four in a row between them. Then one of the players thrusts his hand into each shoe, leaving in one of them his finger ring or some other small object. His opponent has now to guess in which shoe it is to be found. He is allowed only one chance; accordingly as he guesses right or wrong he wins or loses the game.

At the Omaha village I saw Indian youths hurling light-weight spears full tilt through revolving rings—a very difficult feat, but one that affords superb exercise for the body, because throughout the game the players run continually up and down the course and at the same time bring their bodily muscles into further action by practicing the swift hurling of a lance at a mark that is in constant motion.

Herantsa are fond of the so-called billiard game, which, when weather permits, they practice constantly in and about their village. They play the game with a billiard wand that they throw with full strength toward a hoop rolling along the ground. This wand or cue has four markings indicated with leather and at the end a pad made of leather strips, scraps of cloth, or, for want of something better, even bunches of grass. The winner starts the hoop, both players run along beside it and throw their wands, the flight of which is retarded by the pads, called idi by the Herantsa, so that they do not take too wide a range over the smooth course. To be sure the ground is not as smooth as a floor; it is uneven, but cleared of pebbles and filth. According to that mark on the cue or wand on which the hoop in falling rests, they reckon the game. Oftentimes the players throw their wands so uniformly that they fall one upon the other, making it impossible for the contestants themselves to decide which wins.

Whereupon, without wrangling or the least suggestion of contention, they appeal at once to the older spectators, whose decision is accepted. Although they always put up some small or trifling object at the beginning of the game, the stakes are steadily increased in value until not infrequently they mount quite high; for instance, from bows, arrows, knives, moccasins, to buffalo robes, ornamented leggings, mitasses, richly adorned leather shirts, tobacco pipes, guns, horses, tents, and it sometimes happens that the players even venture their elder wives. Some members of the Herantsa Tribe devote themselves exclusively to this game—never take part in the hunt.

The "boss" (Meitzer, Schutz, bourgeois) has told me quite a little about games that are enjoyed among the Crows and the Assiniboin. The former are said to be much given to cheating and swindling, the latter are reputed to be generous by nature and good-tempered (?). They take a shallow wooden plate, put in it some beans or seeds of corn that have been burned black on one side and add thereto a magpie's claw, one talon of which is distinguished from the others by a white line drawn from the root to the tip; they put in also, if they have them, some brass nail heads. Then they turn the plate quickly upside down.

According as the black or bright side of the seeds lie upward, but especially as to the position taken by the white tip of the magpie's claw, they reckon the count. If the loser is obstinate or his means considerable the game is sometimes continued for several days without interruption. So long as he has something still to stake he is ashamed to withdraw. In such a case, for the sake of giving the loser further chance to continue the play, and also to prolong the sport, the following rule is observed: The winning player puts up a stake in opposition to the one that has been advanced by the loser twice the value of all that he has won. When the excitement of play is at its height they stake tents made of skins, women, nay, sometimes their own lives. When one loses everything and no longer possesses a dwelling or a family he may well be ashamed to live longer. His life is never taken, however; he becomes, instead, the servant of him who won, i. e., he must serve as hunter. Values range as follows: two knives equal in value a pair of leggings; two knives and leggings, a blanket; two knives, leggings, and blanket are equivalent in value to a rifle; two knives, leggings, blanket, and gun, to the price of a horse; all of those objects taken together equal in value a tent made of skins; and, finally, all the last-named group in combination are reckoned to be worth as much as a woman.

From a bundle of peeled sticks about 2 feet long a handful is quickly separated, even while the player passes them from one hand to the other. His opponent must guess the number taken out.

Mr. Denig declares that the Indians dress themselves much better now than in earlier days. When he became acquainted with them first (speaking, of course, of Indians here) they were either nude or else clothed in soiled, shabby, ragged skins. Only very seldom, upon special occasions, were they rigged out in their finery. Nowadays they are more cleanly, bedeck themselves with beads and blankets, own horses, and, according to their own fancy or their needs, they make saddles that are beautiful as well as practical. In short, along with much that might be spared, Indians have received from the fur traders a very great deal that is beneficial to them.

Whether I shall include in my gallery the modern Indian or limit my productions to representations of the primitive savage I have not yet decided. If I adopt the latter plan I lose too much that is picturesque—the majestic folds of the woolen blanket, the war horse with his splendid, impetuous rider. To represent Indian life truly I would better mingle, perhaps, the ancient and modern, thus representing in my pictures life among Indians as it reveals itself today. That affords more variation, more action and character.

All redskins who live along rivers or lake shores are always clean, because they are not only admirable swimmers but all of them—men, women, and children—are passionately fond of that exercise. Herantsa and Arikara go in bathing every day, preferably twice a day than not at all. Even during the influenza epidemic, notwithstanding high fevers, depleted strength, and coughs, they took one another into the water. The mother bathes herself and her newborn babe in cold water, so long as the water is not cold enough to freeze. It is owing to the lack of such opportunities and due to conditions only that prairie Indians are ever uncleanly. They have no liking for dirt and filth; such a disposition is not in keeping with their fondness for personal adornment or their excessive desire to please.

There is another question I have discussed at some length with Mr. Denig; that is, whether the American Indians are a happier people since their association with the white race. That depends, he says, upon the conclusions arrived at by modern philosophical thinkers. If human happiness consists in ease of mind, in contentment, then the Indian is no longer as happy as he was in former days.

Now that he is acquainted with articles made of steel, such as knives, axes, rifles, etc., with tinder boxes, the hewing of logs, with horses, blankets, all sorts of materials for clothing and ornamentation, and with the taste of coffee, sugar, etc., he regards these things as indispensable to his needs; he is no longer content with his former implements but regards ours as incomparably more profitable to him. His life of contentment in the old days deteriorated into a humdrum, lazy existence, yet was the direct result of a mind satisfied. Now that kind of happiness he enjoys no more. But is such a state the end and aim of human destiny? If so, then all activities are unnecessary except those that provide bread—or rather food—and protection against heat or cold. Art, science, handicrafts, business enterprises are then extravagant undertakings that may be dispensed with. Only the hunter, the land proprietor, the shepherd, those who contribute adequately to bodily needs, are really necessary to our well being. Now the question is: Does the human being find his best satisfaction in eating, drinking, and sleeping? Is our decision to take into account the whole of human needs or only a part? Is man to be accepted as a mere animal? Is he not endowed with talents that enable him to rise above and dominate animal instincts? To gain the mastery over inanimate matter? To rule over the animal kingdom? Are not joys of mind and spirit more profound, more enduring than pleasures of sense?

Are not mental achievements just as indispensable as those occupations carried on by bodily exertion? We have, then, to provide nutriment for the mind; we have to take care that our mental faculties are properly cultivated. In our modern society, increasing in numbers daily, this becomes a need, an absolute, unqualified necessity. In our overpopulated States we are forced to be dissatisfied. Only the Indian, in the midst of a limited population inhabiting extensive tracts of land, can afford to be contented with his lot; but he also is sensible of his need of mental exertion, of the necessity for mental accomplishment.[53]

So long as he is satisfied he will remain what he is; but for however long a time he does nothing but hunt, he roves about, having no settled habitation; he fails to improve his land by cultivating the soil. The human being, however, like other species of animals, is by nature sociable; he must live in association with his fellows. The more numerous the inhabitants in a place, the more densely populated a community, the more difficult to find resources for getting on. Man is obliged to cultivate his land and he settles near his fields. He gains thereby a fixed dwelling place to which he is more closely attached than to hunting grounds. As we know, Indians who inhabited forest lands in the East were able to provide themselves early with stable habitations, because they had timber at hand in abundance and were not obliged to follow roving herds. As a consequence, the tribes in the East, notwithstanding their having been forced into wars with increasing numbers of encroaching foreign nations, reached a higher degree of civilization.

---

[53] Why does every one of the tribes retain its enemies, even though the first cause of strife is no longer remembered? Only to preserve some means of employing their minds. Among prairie Indians war takes the place that the school occupies in our civilization. War serves to develop their intelligence and to prepare them for their highest purpose in life. As long as the chase suffices a man merely for his support he makes no further exertion.

Mind assists body; invention strengthens mental faculties. Inventive power replaces instinct, raises man far above the lower animals, stamps him a human being, and distinguishes him from all other creatures.

This creative faculty of the human mind must necessarily be put in action by compulsion, by discontent, and as a result of the struggle man himself becomes creator; but in such striving to a higher state that quiet self-content of primitive man and his consequent satisfaction with his lot is forever lost; his earthly paradise is foregone. When the human being has but once tasted fruit from the Tree of Knowledge his earlier carefree existence no longer satisfies him. He has experienced new delights, he is ever longing for those enjoyments, for the fulfillment of his new desires, for the attainment of a further aim. This incentive is the germ from which culture of mind and soul proceeds; together with this inner impulse to better his condition comes dissatisfaction with things as they are. The complex social conditions under which we live make it impossible for us to be happy, at least for long at a time. There are moments when we experience unutterable joy! How rare those moments, and how dearly we have to pay for them!

Civilization has so increased our material necessities that those of us who are not wealthy spend the greater part of our time working for a livelihood—to provide food, clothing, house, and home. And happy is he who finds joy in his employment. Nevertheless, in the cultivation of our minds we have pleasures infinitely above those enjoyed by primitive man; the satisfaction we find in an excellent composition, in our work, in invention, is incomparably greater than that of the hunter in shooting down a wild animal.

The majority of mankind look upon this terrestrial existence as a hard school and take comfort in the thought of a future life, when, after death, they will be able to enjoy unending peace and happiness. They console themselves for the difficulties of the present in anticipation of future bliss; for reality they substitute likelihood. This belief in a better future fate has become an imperative need. In proportion to their faithfulness in service, their fortitude under suffering, they are to be rewarded. That is their consolation.

Indians believe, also, in man's continued existence after death, but in an existence only slightly different from their life on earth. According to their belief, physical needs are to be satisfied as well after death as before. Their happy hunting ground will provide them with wild beasts in superfluous numbers. They will suffer neither cold nor hunger there. They believe also that warriors and huntsmen who have distinguished themselves on earth are to have a life apart and enjoy higher privileges than those conferred on cowards or sluggards. As a matter of course, such ideas are consistent with their manner of life here below, where their highest efforts are put forth for pleasure of sense. Of striving toward spiritual perfection they have not the least notion.[54]

We have different ideas concerning Heaven. According to our view, not personal courage alone but purity of soul entitles us to heavenly joys. A striving for spiritual perfection! This conception does not presuppose that our earthly existence will be made more difficult thereby or less happy. That one finds the means of earning a livelihood so difficult oftentimes, even with the best intentions, well-nigh impossible, on account of the increase in human population, reveals false deductions; shows a condition in human affairs out of accord with Nature's law, an imperfect arrangement of things in our would-be Christian nations. That any person should be able at any time to provide honorably the necessities of life by honest and profitable work seems to me a fundamental principle in the organization of a state; for it can hardly be expected of such a person that he strive for spiritual perfection while he constantly suffers want. That entertaining of idle hopes concerning future splendor has never yet fed the hungry or clothed the naked. Notwithstanding the Christian's exhortation to put your trust in a kind and merciful Father, great numbers die every day from starvation.

Nevertheless it is a true saying that necessity is the mother of invention. To necessity we are indebted for marked advance in science and in art. It is much to be doubted, furthermore, whether without concern for the future people would exert their best energies; whether their idealism, ambition, or competition would effect as much; whether, in fine, liberality and Christian love might not abate in fervor, even languish altogether, if there were no want. I know well that perfection cannot be attained in this world, but I cannot understand how it is that, notwithstanding the promises given in the Sermon on the Mount, results in reality are so totally otherwise. Or, if one is to accept only that food which is spiritual, one may well ask why so many of the "well-intentioned" are spiritually lost.

I do not mean to say that I think the Indians' conception of Heaven more just than ours or that their life on earth is more fortunate. I mean only that more real happiness would enter into our manner of living if less emphasis were given to holding out hopes of future compensation for hardships and sorrows endured during our earthly existence—in a word, if the great amount of trouble and pains one is bidden to take by way of preparation for an unsure future be

[54] Speaking always of nomadic tribes in this part of the world, not of the eastern and Mexican Indians of an earlier period; the latter reached an advanced degree of civilization.

devoted to the improvement of temporal conditions—our material prosperity.

It is all very well, after a night's untroubled sleep, followed by a delicious breakfast, to preach to hungry people that they are not to set their minds on earthly comforts. First feed the hungry, as Jesus did, before you begin to preach.

By nature an ardent idealist, I am not one of those who give material welfare an importance above mental and moral advancement. I regard one equally essential with the other. Since it is true, however, that mental powers are capable of their finest development only when the body is sound and when bodily needs are satisfied, we must admit that material well-being is fundamentally important. When we have given proper care to our physical health we are able to turn our attention all the more effectively to those matters that conduce to our spiritual advantage, thereby becoming a happier, better-contented people, not dependent upon being consoled with hopes of happiness to be realized only in life beyond the grave.[55]

September 27. This afternoon about 50 Cree Indians, men, women, and boys, came from a nearby village to pay us a visit. La Rossade de Cou, La Velle Jamb, Le Couteau conducted them. These are the first Cree I have seen. They came to beg rather than to barter—their real purpose is to try and find out at which fort they can get the best price for their skins and furs. They have to be attracted with gifts and much liberality, else they trade with the Hudson Bay Co. No Indians are admitted to trading posts in charge of English fur traders—only what they have to sell is received there. England's commercial policy is here revealed in its true light—spread of civilization affords a fine pretext under which to advance trade interests.

September 28. Nearly all of the Cree have left. They wear their ancient and original dress almost entire, i. e., garments made of dressed skins, and buffalo robes. These people thought Mr. Denig's parrot a great curiosity; they found it hard to part with him. Old and young, chiefs, braves of rank, and men of low degree were constantly laughing at the bird's remarks; though they could not understand his English "How do you do?" "Pretty Polly," etc., yet the fact that he had spoken was sufficiently amusing.

---

[55] I have come to the realization that a man is much more prone to idealize, in his meditations concerning the betterment of human society, if he is in comfortable circumstances than if he is forced to beg, not knowing even from one day to the next where he is to sleep, where he will find food, wherewith he is to be clothed. Then the poetry of life is lost sight of in bitterness of heart and in sorrow. Then the future is so overclouded that not one bright ray from the clear heavens pierces through the gloom to give promise of relief. Neither faith nor poetry relieves an empty stomach; sympathetic words just as little.

A bird that talks must be a miraculous bird—"great medicine." His crying, laughing, coughing, scolding, carried them out of themselves; they could not help laughing aloud. That Indians are invariably stoical is an erroneous idea pretty generally accepted. Certainly, under given circumstances, they are; for instance, when torture is inflicted. Furthermore, in their deliberations no interruption when one is speaking would be endured. But in their social life they talk and laugh as we do. That an esteemed brave respects himself and guards against doing injury to his own dignity by unbecoming behavior, such as overloud talking and inquisitiveness, boyish laughing and chaffing, I think is perfectly proper. That is neither stoicism nor the assumption of an official mein, but simply shows respect for his own worth, his inherent dignity, his noble pride.

Cree are said to be most valiant warriors, excellent marksmen with the rifle, but very cautious and pertinacious in trade. Assiniboin excel in shooting with bow and arrow (but it must be taken into consideration that they get fewer good rifles from Americans than the former receive from the English). "Indians at this post place little value on us whites," says the bourgeois [Denig].

They maintain that we are capable of doing just anything for the sake of getting buffalo robes—we lie, we cheat, we work in the dirt even, just as their wives do. We are poor people who could not exist without them, because we must have buffalo robes or we should perish from cold. To impress them, therefore, on our part, we think it best to assume a proud, reserved attitude, to act as though we take no notice of them, and refuse to imitate them either in dress or manner. The instant we should seek them, treat them in an intimate free-handed manner, they would only believe that we were courting their friendship for the sake of protection, and accordingly would give them a more exalted idea of their importance and a more significant proof of our own helplessness. In that event we should have to pay dearly for their friendship and their so-called defense, for there would be no limit to their demands. Among themselves, Indians value liberality, "largesse", very highly as a virtue; in consequence every gift is designated, even as a "coup", on the buffalo robe. But generosity on the part of a paleface wins neither their friendship nor their respect. They do not look upon a white person as one of themselves or as a recognized friend; his liberality shows his dependence; he seeks protection. The paleface owns no land; he is obliged to get permission to found his fort, to trade with the native race; and he is required to pay formal tribute for the privilege. Accordingly, if one presented an Indian with a gift every day in the year—this morning, a horse; tomorrow, a gun; the day after tomorrow, a blanket; the next day, a knife; and so on until the last day in the year—and then might forget or simply neglect to give him anything at all on the 365th day, he would be all the more angry on account of the omission. The same is true of an Indian woman; the more one gives her to win her good will, all the more convinced is she that the donor is in her power. She does not respect him, much less love him; only treats him kindly for the sake of the gifts. An Indian woman must fear her husband; she then esteems him for his manliness. She desires a warrior—no good-natured pantaloon. Therefore several sound lashings or other rough treatment is necessary from time to time to keep alive her respect and affection. Besides, an Indian woman loves her white husband only for what he possesses—because she works less hard, eats better food, is allowed to dress and adorn herself in a better way—of real love there is no question. After the third or fourth child, when they are getting too old for their Indian dandies, they begin to devote themselves entirely to the father of their children. If an Indian woman runs away, one is not to pay the least attention to her nor to show the least grief; one is to forget her. To go after her, to beg her to return, is beneath the dignity of a brave—is not considered to be worth while.[56]

A brave regards his wife as a purchased commodity that he may throw aside when he chooses; that he may keep in as large numbers as he can afford to buy and support by his hunting. The better huntsman he is the more wild beasts he kills and the greater number of hides he brings home. Buffalo hides when tanned constitute his wealth, by means of which he provides himself with all that he needs. Moreover, the more excellent the huntsman the more wives he finds necessary; women are most skillful and quick in the preparing of skins for sale and the buffalo meat they can use for food. It is not strictly true, therefore, that he refuses to look at a woman unless she be young or beautiful. He aims, to be sure, to have always apart a dainty one for his own private pleasure, but the others are for the most part working women—old maids or widows—who are glad to belong to a family, for, owing to constant warfare, it all too frequently happens that children lose their fathers and women lose their husbands.[57]

If a man marries the eldest daughter of a family he has also a priority claim on her younger sisters. If he presents one of them with a blanket or some other more valuable gift she regards herself

---

[56] The Sioux, especially, regard it a very great honor to cast off as many wives or sweethearts as possible; in other words, to break off marriages. I think, however, that as this is an old-age custom, the "little wife", for her own part, takes the matter not too much to heart—perhaps is glad of a change.

[57] Polygamy among Indians is no indication of sensuality, but simply shows their system of labor. I have known many Indians who had only one wife and had never had any other.

at once as bound to her brother-in-law; she belongs to him. He may surrender her to someone else, but she is not allowed of her own accord to listen to any other man. On the other hand, if he bestows no gifts upon her, when she reaches a marriageable age she is free.[58]

The more sisters a man has for wives the more successful the marriage is supposed to be, because they are not acquainted with such a thing as jealousy; they will not fight one another.

Men in charge of trading posts like to marry into prominent Indian families when they are able to do so; by such a connection they increase their adherents, their patronage is extended, and they make correspondingly larger profits. Their Indian relatives remain loyal and trade with no other company. They have the further advantage of being constantly informed through their association with the former as to the demands of trade and the villiage or even the tent where they can immediately find buffalo robes stored away. For a clerk a woman of rank is too expensive and brings him no advantage, for the reason that he is employed at a fixed salary and receives no further profit. If he falls into debt he is brought under obligation to the company.

Today I saw a Cree woman with the upper part of her body entirely uncovered, a sign, they say, of mourning for the loss of a child. She was walking and wore a buffalo robe. The Cree woman's garb is like that of the Sauteurs women; i. e., shoulders and arms bare, skirt held up by means of bands or straps.

When the weather is cold they put on sleeves that are knotted together in the back at the nape of the neck and on the breast. Assiniboin women wear frequently only one sleeve, leaving the right arm free; they wear shirtlike skirts that, instead of being held in place by special straps, are made to extend over the shoulders.

September 30. Have been hard at work. Had to paint, from a medal, the portrait of Pierre Chouteau, Jr., in the gable over the house gallery. All day long I had to work in a most uncomfortable position on an unsafe scaffold. Pierre Chouteau, Jr., is one of the oldest and wealthiest shareholders in the great American Fur-trading Company to whom Fort Union belongs.

Indians think cedars and firs the shrewdest of plants because they keep their foliage for the winter. Not bad reasoning. A shrewd and

---

[58] Dauxion La Vysse in his Voyage à Trinidad, vol. 1, p. 344, says in connection with the Caribbean: "Ces Califournans sont polygames, comme la plupart des Indiens, et ils ont ceci de particuliers que lorsqu'un d'eux a spouse l'amie d'une famille, il a le droit d'epouser les soeurs cadettes a mesure quelles viennant a l'age de puberte." The Caribbeans called themselves Californians and claim to have come originally, at a very remote period, from another land. For that reason D. La Vysse thinks they trace their origin to the Aztec. He finds, also, marked similarity between the Cherokee and Gonarovun; on p. 364 he gives instances of certain experiments in language by which S. Baron de la Hontan attempted to trace the origin of the Algonquin speech from the Ibero-Celtic; on p. 380, D. L. refers to the same habit among the Caribbeans of pulling out any hair that appears on their bodies that is common among North American Indians.

intelligent manager of a house, for instance, would have as his emblem a green sprig of the fir tree. Heretofore, in our interpretation of the flower language, only feelings, not intellectual gifts, have been represented.

Mr. Denig asked me, among other things, whether I do not consider that the Indian, in destroying all reminders of a deceased relative, in never again speaking of him by name but as "the one whom you know", shows more delicacy than we do in preserving remembrances everlastingly, in perpetually talking of grief, nourishing sorrow, taking satisfaction in such indulgence, and thereby wasting much precious time in wailing that should be turned to better account.

I think, really, that his instances are not well taken, for Indians not only wail and howl for a long while by the grave of one whom they esteemed, but, as everybody knows, they carry the departed one's bones themselves along with them for memorial. Furthermore, only those among us who have nothing better or more worth while to do waste their time in lamentation.

I found even less delicacy of feeling shown in a newly married couple's custom of keeping in hiding from their parents-in-law. For instance, if a son-in-law would talk with his wife's father and mother, he must always speak through a closed door or else transmit his message through a third person. He is not allowed ever to look them in the face. In passing them he must conceal his countenance with his hands or his blanket. If he comes unawares into their presence, he is immediately reminded of his mistake. The same thing is required, to some degree, of the daughter-in-law, but only in relation to her husband's parents; from her own father and mother she has nothing to conceal. It is required, furthermore, only during the time before she takes up her abode with her parents-in-law or in her husband's tent. It is very seldom that she leaves her own home during her early married life; a son-in-law often lives with his wife's parents, hunts for them, and helps to support them.

Such cloaking and hiding I find ridiculous, and only indicative of false modesty. It would show much more delicacy if the newly wedded pair conducted themselves in a perfectly natural manner and allowed no allusion whatsoever to their change of state. And such observances among Indians!

To the works of Schiller, as well as those of other writers, and particularly to Schiller's idea of physical beauty as sign of spiritual and moral beauty, I am indebted for my viewpoint concerning the ideal. Schiller's words must be understood, however, in a strictly poetic sense; in nature, beauty of soul and physical loveliness are only in rare instances combined. It would be deplorable if only good people were beautiful and all the rest were not. Beauty is Nature's gift, an endowment that all too frequently gives rise to vanity and leads to a person's downfall. Kindness of heart is also a gift of Nature, but moral excellence is the result of one's bringing up. Personal characteristics are diverse; even from the time one is born good qualities and bad are existent in the germ; training and education give direction to those inherent tendencies and very often produce good results in their proper development. It is when life's struggle begins, when fair hopes of youth are not realized, when moral standards are forced into conflict with temptations, when the joy of life itself is threatened with destruction, when want and misery, when obstacles of every sort put patience and endurance to the test, then it is that character is developed; not until then does the sunshine of inner peace follow storm and tempest.

Fortunate are they whose lives may be compared to a voyage in calm waters, inasmuch as they are spared much suffering; but they will never become great or be capable of great deeds. Rarely does a great soul attain to anything significant except through hard and bitter experience. Now all such severe struggles, as well with the soul's self as with the outer world, leave their trace on the physiognomy. Every talent of consequence, one's overruling tendencies and passions, are connected with the convolutions of the brain and are reflected in one's face and form. As a matter of course, preeminent gifts, such as I have mentioned, are seldom united in one person, but exist separately in different individuals; thus it comes about that one may possess beauty of soul or grandeur of spirit which does not harmonize with one's outer form or expression. Neither Socrates nor Alexander the Great, Caesar nor Columbus, Galileo nor Mozart, Luther nor Shakspeare, Newton nor Raphael, Buonarotti nor Frederick the Great, Voltaire nor Goethe, Schiller nor Pestalozzi, Napoleon nor Byron, Washington nor Vernet, was endowed with an ideally beautiful face and form. Titian and Henry IV are exceptions.

We imagine Christ as representing our ideal of physical beauty, because we are so constituted that, when not prevented from doing so by faithful portraits of the person in question, we delight in picturing to ourselves physical perfection in harmony with perfection of soul, an indisputable proof that our imaginations, even the imaginative faculties of uncultivated people, instinctively associate outward beauty with inner goodness. Hence our conceptions of the angels.

The most famous beauties of the ancient as well as of the modern world were, with few exceptions, neither morally good nor endowed with great gifts. Homer, in the early ages, gives us such examples as Venus, Helen, Paris, etc.; and, in the modern time, we may mention Maria Stewart. And what numbers of handsome men there are, have always been, who, without any significant gifts of mind, have made themselves famous for moral grandeur.

October 1. This morning I put the finishing touches on Pierre Chouteau, Jr.'s, portrait. In the afternoon I was free to do what I liked, so I took my double-barreled gun under my arm and went for a walk on the hill to enjoy the far-reaching view beyond the Yellowstone. Then I strolled around a bit with the intention of finding out what I could about this vicinity. As I was just getting to the top of a hill covered with loose stones I noticed a bright spot in motion on another height. I lay down at once to observe the animal more closely with my telescope. I found it to be a fat cabri buck that evidently had wind of me already, though he could not see me. Hoping to get nearer to him, I slipped backward down the hill and approached through a dell; soon came in sight of a herd of antelopes that, having been given the alarm by the buck, were peering intently about them, trotting back and forth with eager glance, stamping their feet, blowing through their nostrils. Then they started off, one behind the other, turned around again, and finally took to flight, the buck in the rear. What an elegant picture! How quickly lost to view! There was no use my attempting to pursue on foot those shy creatures so swift in flight; I turned from the mauvaises terres and followed the well-beaten path Assiniboin take to the fort.

When, with the hope of starting or finding other game, I was forcing my way through the garden coulee (the deep bed of a dried-up stream thickly overgrown with coppices and bushes, over against which lies our potato garden) the thought came into my mind that this would be an extraordinarily favorable place of concealment for a lurking enemy. Prying sharply into the thick shrubbery on all sides, I sprang across the now insignificant brook and was proceeding with rapid strides toward the horse pasture when I heard a rustling of dry leaves behind me and someone laughed. Turning around, I saw two young Assiniboin leaping out from behind some bushes. I stopped and cocked my gun. The elder, still laughing, offered his hand and gave me a hearty handshake. From their natural, friendly manner as well as from their clean and expensive clothing I knew they were not warriors, still less enemies, though they were doubly armed with bows, arrows, and guns, which weapons were carried at their backs in leathern cases swung over the shoulders. The elder drew these off over his head and gave them into my keeping, with the remark that he would like meanwhile to examine my gun. I thought that most courteous, for, in the first place, he dared not expect that I would suffer an exchange of weapons or expose myself to the danger of being disarmed. But that he perceived this at once and acted accordingly predisposed me in his favor.

As I was walking along between the two brothers (their resemblance was striking), the younger gave me to understand, by means of signs, that they had been watching my approach from a distance and had immediately concealed themselves in order to startle me, just to see how I would stare. On the impulse, I had a good mind to give them a peppering, but I reconsidered, because, I reflected, if they had been hostile, I should have had ere then two arrows in my body without anybody's having seen the murder or, perhaps, ever finding it out. So, notwithstanding that I returned safe from this adventure, I decided it would not be amiss to avoid in future such dangerous places. Upon arriving at the fort I learned forthwith that the lads were brothers of Mr. Denig's younger wife.

During our evening meal I was warned against the peril of lonely rambles—all the more dangerous, they said, because I was not a hunter and therefore did not recognize signs that would betray the possibility of an enemy lurking near. Only this spring, I was told, a woman of the Cree Tribe set out on the longer route from this fort to that of the opposition and, hardly a half mile from here, was slain with arrows by Blackfeet and then scalped. The enemies had concealed themselves so effectually in high grass that even the keen-eyed Indian woman herself did not notice them, though she was only a few paces distant.

Later in the evening Carafel related to me an adventure he had with the Sioux, as a result of which he is still lame in one foot. Two years ago he was told to go on horseback with Ramsay (now with the "Dobies") to a settlement of Assiniboin.

Five miles from here, as they were traveling through some rough ground, they met, quite suddenly, about fifteen Sioux who came over a hill just at the moment they themselves arrived at the spot. The Sioux fired forthwith, wounded Carafel, who was riding ahead, from head to foot, and killed his horse. Thereupon Ramsay ran off at full speed. As Carafel's horse fell to the ground his gun came under the brute's body and he was unable to pull it out; consequently he was without any weapon with which to repel his assailants. So, notwithstanding his severe wounds, he fled also. While running at full speed his feet caught in a shrub or a tangle of tall grass and he fell. He sprang at once to his feet again, however, for his pursuers had already overtaken him. One of them was in the act of discharging a gun in his face, but he had still sufficient strength to seize the barrel and turn it aside until some blows with the butt end of the rifle dashed him to the ground. He felt then that all was lost; and just as he was passing into unconsciousness he said in Assiniboin,

"Sioux, it takes a great many of you warriors to kill one white man."
All at once his murderers fled from the spot. He collapsed. However, he recovered consciousness after a time and crawled to the
adobe fort, the nearest place of refuge. He is said to have made a
pitiable appearance; a bullet had grazed his foot, cutting some
ligaments to shreds. That flight of the Sioux warriors seemed to
me most extraordinary.

Mr. Denig, who had told me of the adventure earlier, explained
their behavior by taking for granted that they had supposed the two
riders to be Chippewa half-breeds, their deadly enemies, and first
became aware of their mistake when they were near enough to see
Carafel's blonde curly hair and blue eyes; for every half-breed has,
invariably, black, straight hair and dark brown eyes. They left
Carafel prostrate and without assistance, notwithstanding their
friendship—nay, blood relationship—to the Assiniboin, because they
thought he was dead and feared they might draw vengeance upon
themselves if they were known to have done the deed.[59]

Indians believe in spirits, and though they have never yet had any
visible evidence of such things, they talk with them and take counsel.
They think that spirits follow them, not on the ground but about 2
feet above.

Mr. Denig says to me frequently: "When you go to the Blackfeet
territory", etc. Dare I hope that I shall go so far, that Mr. Culbertson will take me with him?

October 2. After dinner Mr. Denig came to my room and asked me
to accompany him on a cabri hunt. He had just seen from the gate
seven of those antelopes in one herd grazing on a hill. To be sure,
what he saw were only white spots moving about. But Mr. Denig is
keen-sighted and well practiced in interpreting signs on the prairie;
he takes much pride in the fact that even his wives have not as good
eyesight as he. He conducted me to the garden coulee that we might
get out of the wind, which was blowing over the hill from the west.
We hurried along up the brook bed, but with the utmost caution, in
order to get around on the other side of the hill on which the antelopes were feeding. Having arrived there, the bourgeois took off his
coat and hat, examined his priming pan, and crept up the hill, but not
without first giving me instructions to remain perfectly still, not to
spoil his sport by noise due to overhaste.

Still, in my eagerness to see something, and maybe to get a chance
to take a shot also, I crawled to the nearer entrance to the little coulee,
took my hat off, and lay down in the grass. Some of the animals were
quietly grazing; the others lay unconcerned on the ground. Unluckily, Mr. Denig was obliged to content himself with killing a

---

[59] Ramsay is in reality a metif or half-breed.

female antelope [60] that was in a position that left her flank exposed. At the report of the gun, all the rest took flight, unfortunately, to the other side of the valley.

The cabri that had been shot made two desperate leaps and fell dead. Still the buck was lingering to muster in the remaining doe, but Mr. Denig had got to his feet, had allowed himself to be seen, had not reloaded his gun; the shy buck took to flight. We hurried over to our quarry; the bullet had pierced her heart—had gone directly through her breast. I bound her dainty feet together and took her on my shoulders, completely encircling my neck, and carried her to my room. I felt her warm blood soak through my clothes and flow down my back. Upon reaching the fort I laid her out on the floor and immediately set about painting my first antelope. Mr. Denig's wives were waiting around, most impatient to prepare the little animal for food, but I had not brought it a distance of 3 miles for the purpose of satisfying myself with an incomplete study.

October 3. Just before dinner Packinaud was brought home in a cart wounded. He and Mackenzie rode out yesterday on a buffalo hunt, but found nothing until early this morning. As both of these men are ambitious to be thought the best hunter for buffaloes, they galloped full tilt into the herd. Now, Packinaud, who was riding John, had the advantage of the better mount, for John is an excellent and enduring traveler, only too unruly for some riders.

The instant he is given the reins he is in full gallop; never needs to be urged on; never gradually relaxes speed; his first spring measures all of 21 feet. When, as I said, the two hunters were nearing the buffalo herd, John tore off, neighing for joy. Andre, although himself a good runner, is not so spirited, and therefore more easily guided. Because he is not so impetuous and powerful, his rider is much more sure of hitting the object aimed at—of securing his victim. Well, John, in his mad rush, carried Packinaud into the midst of the herd and crowded him so closely between two buffalo bulls that he could not get his gun in a position to fire. At the same time one of the bulls turned aside, but the other tossed his head with a jerk, made a pass with one horn through his pursuer's left shin bone, and stuck the other into the fleshy part of the horse's breast, bringing him to a halt. Meanwhile, Mackenzie had already killed a cow and was fol-

---

[60] I was much astonished to see no horns among the female antelopes that I have had opportunity to observe at Fort Pierre. I was all the more surprised at this for the reason that both Bodmer and Catlin represent their antelopes (cabris) with horns alike, which in itself seems unnatural. I have seen positively no female cabris with horns. Are there two different species, or are the artists in error? They made the mistake of representing buffalo herds consisting only of bulls—no cows. I must admit, however, that one does see small droves of bulls only, but this does not apply to the cabri bucks. Neither did Audubon know of female cabris without horns. Nevertheless, I am absolutely sure that neither the doe that was killed nor her companions showed any sign of growing horns.

lowing closely behind Packinaud when the latter was stopped, passed him, and fired on the bull, which immediately tumbled over. Our wounded man now called Mackenzie to his assistance. Mackenzie sent the Spaniard immediately to the fort to bring a cart. They think P.'s shin bone is broken.

After dinner nothing to do. Weather ideal; temperature mild. Who could restrain himself from taking a walk?

Danger? Well, anyone who stands in fear has no need to come into these wilds; all the more necessary, being here, that one explore carefully the whole region—know the ground. What I lack in keensightedness and acute hearing I shall endeavor to offset with courage. If I only had better eyesight how I should enjoy this life. Would not desire a better lot than to roam around, now on foot, now on horseback, with sketch book and gun. Just now, when I have overcome the most difficult hindrance and my life purpose is so near fulfillment, it is impossible for me to think that my life should be in peril. He that believeth * * * shall be saved. The image of that graceful cabri buck hovered ever before my eyes. I was much inclined to go in search of him again. As I had seen the little band several times already in the neighborhood of that brackish stream, I turned my steps thither, stumbled upon several wolves, but in the end came across fresh tracks in the sandy soil—they had been made by antelopes! Following them, I mounted the hill. As I was not expecting to meet the animals so near at hand, I was too incautious and showed myself to them really before I was aware of their presence. To be sure, I ducked instantly to the ground, but away they went over mountain and vale, and all was over with my cabri hunt. I reproached myself severely for my carelessness, my inconvenient habit of indulging in dreams, inopportune musings.

After deciding to hunt antelopes, and then giving my exclusive attention to their tracks, successfully approaching and meeting with the animals, even my very habits as painter caused me to frighten them by showing myself too soon and to lose my chance to study the habits and postures of those beasts of the chase. In vain I searched for them with my telescope. I could not find them any more. But I did get sight of a herd of grazing buffaloes several miles off, and I enjoyed watching them. Now, I said to myself, if I am unable to steal up on them, that is convincing proof I have no talent for hunting. Then I hurried through the many dells and tiny valleys and around the hill to the buffaloes. Concealed in grass or shrubs of wormwood, I peered this way and that over a hill crest, fearing that the animals had already run away. Finally, with beating heart, I crept up the last steep incline of a ridge, crawled on my belly to the edge of the plateau, and I saw the herd hardly 30 feet distant from me. There were thirteen bulls and one calf. Several birds, about the size of a dove, with white bodies and blue-gray wings (magpies?) were sitting on the animals' humps in the midst of the thick, shaggy hair, picking off vermin. One of the bulls pleased me immensely with his odd appearance; he was almost totally black and much more shaggy than the others. Tufts of hair on his forelegs, above his forehead, and under his chin dangled about with his slightest movement.

When viewed from the rear, the front part of him, all overgrown with bushy hair that rose high above his hump, seemed to have nothing at all in common with his hinder parts—seemed not to belong to the same beast. For a long while I lay stretched at full length in the grass, completely absorbed in a detailed study of those beasts. In my pleasure as painter I forgot entirely the role of hunter, though I might have had an excellent chance to shoot the black imp through the heart. After a time they went on farther, sliding down the steep descent to a narrow path on the other side that led through a defile. Then I was eager to fire upon them; to forego such an opportunity would, indeed, show lack of skill. Knowing that buffaloes go up hill not nearly so rapidly as they go down, I made a detour over ground covered with rocks and bowlders, through deep hollows, brambles, and thorn, in order to reach the pass and take them in the flank. As the sun was already low and I was a considerable distance from home, I had no time to lose, so I concealed myself behind a great rock just at the point where the defile opens upon the prairie, the place where, as I have already related, Mackenzie shot the first buffalo on the day he went hunting with me. The black fellow was one of the last to pass me. I fired. He turned aside and ran off at a gallop, the others with him.

Expecting to see the wounded bull fall, I remained where I was, neglecting to discharge my second barrel upon him. He refused, however, to do me the favor of falling dead; he continued to run— perhaps he is still in flight. I reloaded and hurried around the Butte de Mackenzie (as the old cowherd named this hill and the nearby pass from the word butto and in memory of Mackenzie's father, who used to be manager at Fort Union) to the road leading to our trading post. There I saw a rider who was waving his cap to me; I waved mine in return, and then I recognized Mackenzie. Ah! I thought, they have also caught sight of the herd from the fort, have mounted at once and sent ahead the pack horses. It was evidently true; other horsemen came into view, followed by the riderless pack horses. Mackenzie, whose chase I had spoiled, of course, caught a glimpse of still another queer old fellow taking his ease alone on the prairie. Better fresh meat, though a little tough, than none at all, he said, and gave Andre the reins. There was a tendril of up-curling smoke, and the buffalo fell to the ground. I had now been discovered by Joe

Dolores, our horse guard, who sprang down from his nag, fastened the long halter to one of the pack horse's forefeet in order to force him to stand, and called out to me to mount and follow. Not a bad idea. To be sure, a pack saddle is far from being a comfortable seat, a lariat a sorry bridle, but walking alone over a wide prairie at night is still less agreeable.

I swung myself upon the horse and he galloped forward, of his own accord, to join his comrades. Upon coming up with the others, I found that they had already stripped off the buffalo's hide on one side, had cut off the hind legs, bound together the tendons and thrown them across a packhorse; had distributed the choice bits in accordance with hunters' prerogatives and were ready to start back to the fort. Night fell. Mackenzie and I hurried forward. The Spaniard took advantage of the darkness to filch from a neighboring hill a tanned white calfskin that had been hung there by an Indian as a votive offering to the sun. He came up with us again at full gallop, however, before we rode into our courtyard.

Mr. Denig was much relieved in mind to see me again; he feared that I might have lost my way, might have got bewildered in the rough, trackless wilds, or else had met with an accident. So, with the hope of directing my attention to the location of the fort he had given orders several times that guns be fired. His two young brothers-in-law expressed the intention of going in search of me at daybreak, if in the meantime I should not have returned. I offered him for excuse my irresistible delight in being in the buffalo region, where I could make a thorough study quite comfortably of those wild beasts.

"That is the way with all you people with your hobbies and favorite occupations; in your eager zeal you discard prudence altogether. Then when an accident happens we have to bear the blame. A report is immediately spread abroad in the States that the dead man was rich, that he was killed for his money, or if he was poor, that his death was due to jealousy or some such motive."

October 4. The Blackfeet tribe on this side of the Rocky Mountains is estimated to have 1,500 tents and approximately 4,000 warriors; Crows, 440 tents and 1,200 braves; Assiniboin in this vicinity, 420 tents and as many as 1,050 braves; farther north on Winnipeg Lake, from 200 to 300 tents; Cree or Knistenaux, who trade here, occupy 150 tents, but the entire tribe is said to amount to 800 tents; Arikara are reckoned to have 600 warriors in 300 tents; Chippewa, 3,000 tents; and Sioux, 4,000. Pawnee and Arikara, and Assiniboin and Sioux,[60a] are not from the same parent stock. Mandan, above Fort Clarke, have 16 tents (lodges), only 7 of which are occupied; together with those who live with the Grand Mandan, among the

---

[60a] Pawnee and Arikara belong to Caddoan stock; Assiniboin and Sioux belong to Siouan stock.

Herantsa Tribe, they numbered 45 men before the recent cholera epidemic.

Mr. Denig came upon me while I was working on a sketch of my feminine beau ideal. He was extraordinarily pleased with the form and wished to have it painted at once, so that he might hang the picture on the wall in the reception room. He could not forbear his bad jest, however, concerning my hard task in attempting to portray a naked human figure so divine, so exalted, that it would make no appeal to the sensual. He made me feel sick; I was, therefore, not willing to expose my ideal to further remark. But I know that I must accustom myself to this conclusion: There will always be ordinary people who see in the nude only physical attraction, not spirit. A moi mon ideal!

October 5. After Mr. Denig and I had washed and dressed Packinaud's wound he brought the conversation round to the name of a Herantsa woman who is called "Fifty." On her account fifty men suffered the penalty [61] because she ran away from her husband twice, all on the same evening. For like misdoing, fifteen paid the penalty on account of an Assiniboin woman. Carafel happened to be in the camp at the time and had been invited to join them but declined.[61a] The latter woman, from indulgence in the practice for such a long time, lost the use of her legs. In Belle Vue I saw a Pawnee woman who had been taken prisoner on the prairie by thirty Omaha braves and so abused by all thirty of them that she remained a cripple for life.

It was there also that I heard the story of fifty Comanche having abused a white prisoner in like manner and then left her in such a wretched condition that she was found again by her people maimed and insane. Indian women do not so easily lose their reason, at least from such causes, because, I think, they are less afraid and defy pain.

Now and then Indians give what is properly called a glutton feast. Everyone invited is served with an unusually large portion of meat. To the incessant tattoo of the drum they devour what is placed before them. The one who first swallows his portion is victor; the one who fails to do so is required to get rid of what is left by paying a forfeit, i. e., by presenting a gift.

Whether from excess of joy over their triumph or from hate, Indians bite into the flesh of slain enemies, but this occurs only in their rage immediately following a battle; they do not go as far as the Aztec and eat their victims.

Mr. Denig came again to see the sketch of my ideal human figure, repeated his obscene remarks, and expressed again his desire to pos-

---

[61] An evident euphemism.
[61a] Briefly, a rape en masse.

sess a painting of it. When he received, on the contrary, a curt refusal, he found only faults in my conception of feminine loveliness—she looked ugly, was much too thin, etc. I replied that I would much rather hear him find fault with the sketch than to listen to coarse remarks. To paint a nude figure merely for the sake of appealing to his carnal passions and those of other men was beneath my dignity. For the painting of other objects I was entirely at his service, but I would not paint this * * *.

October 7. For a moment there arose such unusual noise made by Indian women and children at the rear gate that everyone rushed down to the river bank with the expectation of witnessing Mr. Culbertson's arrival. The excitement was occasioned, however, only by the sight of an Indian with his wife getting ready to swim with their two horses across the Missouri. One of our Assiniboin swam to the sand bank and demanded to know who he was. As we supposed, he was Herantsa, not Absaroka. With the aid of my telescope I was enabled to watch his interesting preparations. He accomplished the crossing of the river in a similar manner to that described by me earlier when I swam across the Papillon. By means of a dried buffalo hide they formed a sort of flatboat on which they placed the saddles and their personal belongings and to which they fastened a long cord. While he was carrying the skin boat and leading his horse into the water his woman, screened by her own nag, stripped herself naked and, driving the horse before her to the river brink, gave over her clothes to her husband, who thrust them underneath their goods and chattels. Then, with powerful strokes, he started over, holding between his teeth his horse's leather lariat and the long cord with which he pulled the boat after him. His wife followed, guiding her nag in the same manner. They reached the shore on this side without the least trouble. For the sake of keeping on good terms with my bourgeois I began to paint another female figure, but not entirely in the nude.

October 8. An Assiniboin to-day brought the first news I have received from Fort Berthold since I left. Arikara are still dying, he says, like flies under frost. The survivors are in a fury; have razed the block houses of the opposition and stolen their goods; Dorson found it necessary to bring into action his great guns (4-pound cannons) in order to protect himself from the same fate. If this be true, Dorson has no further prospect of trading with the Arikara. Nothing is left for him to do but ship his goods to Fort Pierre. No further illness is reported among the Herantsa.

Indians do not value time at all; among them the idea does not prevail that time is money. They estimate the price, therefore, for the work they do, irrespective of the time they take in the accomplishment of it. Besides, they must be doing something; otherwise they would find the days entirely too long and tedious; consequently they work rather to kill time than to derive profit therefrom. They live at random, generally speaking, without purpose in life, so they do not have to regard time as capital; on the contrary, they find it more frequently a burden. I get forward leisurely with my pictures. There is no haste. The more easily I appear to paint, the less my work is valued.

What costs little is regarded as of little worth. We had a proof of that not long ago. An Assiniboin came to get medicine for eye trouble. He expected the charge to be nothing less than a buffalo robe, or perhaps a horse, just as he would have been required to pay to their jugglers or doctors. But, as it happened, he received the remedy as a gift. He uttered no thanks nor would he use the eye water; had no longer any confidence in its healing power. This reminds me of the first English people who visited Switzerland after the fall of Napoleon. In their own land everything was dear; at first, only the wealthy families went to the continent. So at that time they found the innkeeper's prices too low. They were not pleased with anything. They were constantly asking "How much?" "Can't be good at that price." The landlords were not slow to adjust matters; they kept on demanding more, until their meals were relished. Now, it's just the other way—the English come to Switzerland in order to save, for on an income that is hardly sufficient to supply necessities in Old England they can lead a merry life in our country.

Fort Union, situated on the steep bank of a river on the open prairie, exposed to every wind that blows from any point of the compass, is said to be the coldest place of all the posts belonging to this company—even as cold as those situated on Hudson Bay.

October 9. Sitting before a jolly open fire, by the side of the wounded Packinaud, while a cold, strong wind howled in the courtyard without, I listened to amusing adventures related by Carafel, who was today in fine humor. One of his stories interested me more than the others because I know most of the people concerned. The hero is that sly dog Vilandre (Carafel, a born Canadian, always says Vilandra, engagir, une fua, etc.). He is equally well-known for a tiptop trapper, trader, and hunter, and for a reckless spendthrift not overscrupulous as to honesty. One day old Gre and his comrade hired Vilandre to go along with them and trap beavers in the vicinity of Blackfeet (Pieds Noirs) territory. On the way his two masters quarreled all the time, never agreed with each other about anything, and finally brought matters to such a pass that our hero could stand it no longer. He said to them:

"Now, here, this won't do. You two never agree; after this fashion we shall accomplish nothing. Two masters for one hired man is a bad arrangement; it is better for me to employ both of you. Sell me your horses and traps, and I will pay you later on in beaver skins."

They traded. From the hunt they realized an unusually large profit; it was, you see, in the good old days. They brought back between 400 and 500 bundles of ten skins each.

Colonel Mitchell, the present U. S. agent of the Indian Department in St. Louis, was then bourgeois at Fort Union. When he saw the three trappers approaching he went forward to meet the two old traders, paying no attention to Vilandre, who was leading the way with two heavily laden horses. He knew nothing of the later agreement and intended, of course, to make himself agreeable to those who went out in charge of affairs, congratulate them upon their successful hunt, and invite them in. Vilandre passed on by the employées of the company who were standing beside the gate, curiously looking on, while waiting to receive the packets. He carried his head as high as did the bourgeois himself. And imagine the astonishment of the latter when he saw Vilandre haughtily pass the gate!

"What! You will not trade with me?" he asked the old "grumblers."

"The beaver skins belong to Vilandre, not to us."

The expressions of certain faces immediately changed—business took a different turn altogether. Mr. Denig, clerk at that time, was dispatched at once to present his compliments to Vilandre and ask him to unload his pelts here. In the end he relented. As he rode up to the gate he caught sight of a splendid girl, daughter of old Garion by an Indian woman. He was much pleased with her, and said to himself, "This night you shall be mine."

He sold his furs, which were bringing high prices at that time, paid his quasi-employers forthwith, clothed himself throughout in new apparel, assumed the arrogance of the devil, and bought a great number of articles for gifts. When the horses were brought in from the pasture in the evening and corraled (put in an open stall), he took his best runner and, leading him to Garion, said brusquely, "Take him. He is yours!" Garion, suspecting at once what Vilandre's purpose was, demurred. "Holy Virgin," shouted Vilandre, "am I such a poor man that I can't afford to give away a horse? Haven't I still my little gray?"

Thereupon he stroked the gray horse caressingly, without bestowing even a glance upon the beautiful girl near him. But he sent a friend a little later to Garion asking his daughter in marriage. Her father consented on condition that a marriage contract be drawn up in writing and signed. Well and good. Vilandre went at once to Moncrevier (now with the Pawnee), requesting the draft of an agreement that, when read aloud, would contain all the usual expressions and requirements, but with this difference: A provision was to be inserted permitting him to leave the bride whenever he chose.

Moncrevier, a sort of wag, found much pleasure in anticipation of the impending wedding feast and made all things ready. Garion was satisfied; his daughter, who received many presents, was content; and Vilandre on the same night, after his return to the fort, was in possession of his beautiful bride.

How long do you think he kept her? One entire winter. When he determined to send her away he set her on a good horse and presented her with abundant apparel as well as provisions.

"Holy Virgin", he cried, "when I bid farewell to my wife, whom I am casting off, I will not take the shirt from her back. I put her on a horse and supply her with goods. I don't mind the loss of a beaker [62] of coffee."

I have finished the picture I was painting. While working on it I was often set laughing by Mr. Denig's remarks. At every stroke of the brush he found fault, just as with the other one. I let him chatter, because his judgment is in no sense authoritative so far as I am concerned. In other matters I strive to please him.

Finally when the meaning of the picture began "to be apparent" he began to understand and became then just as much concerned for fear I might spoil what I had done well. "Don't touch it again. You will certainly ruin it. Stop! Stop!" And so on.

Indian word for "friend": *taro* (Iowa), *digahau* (Omaha), *kondah* (Sioux), *kuna* (Assiniboin), *marequa* (Crow and Herantsa), *nitschuwa* (Cree), *sihuan* (Arikara), *manuka* (Mandan). *Koki* in Pawnee means "stone"; *gaggi* in Arikara means "bad."

October 10. Have cleared up everything; the bourgeois has all now that he desires from me as painter. Mr. Culbertson is to decide upon his arrival whether I go with him or remain here, and what, on the whole, my occupation shall be in future. To give me an idea of the easy-going manner in which Indians frequently count a "coup", Mr. Denig told how, once upon a time when Sioux and Assiniboin were at war with each other, a band of sixty warriors marched up to the gate before he was able to get it closed. Luckily, aside from the married women there was only one Assiniboin here, a boy whom he confined under lock and key in a small room just above the one I now occupy. The secret was soon found out; a woman divulged it to one of the braves, who came forthwith to Mr. Denig and offered both his gun and richly decorated robe if in return he might only shake the boy's hand.

---

[62] Mug, cup, tin drinking cup, but used also for measuring sugar, coffee, and meal. It holds a pint. Coffee struck off level with the top, sugar or meal heaped up, is reckoned a pound.

He would take no weapon at all with him, and even desired Mr. Denig's presence. But the latter refused, saying to the Indian brave, "If you wish to count 'coup' you are to seek the occasion in battle."

Mr. Denig spent his first year in this business at Fort Pierre under Mr. Ludlow. One summer he had to go out on the prairie with several Sioux to hunt in order to get meat. As soon as they came near the buffaloes they pitched their tents, one for him and his wife, a second for their relatives, a third for the remainder of the company. All the men except himself left the tents and went out at once to hunt buffaloes. As they stayed away longer than was expected, he took a walk about the settlement to find out where the hunters were. Soon he discovered several buffalo bulls rushing directly upon the camp. He hurried into his tent to get his rifle. Meanwhile his mother-in-law had gone in there and was standing nearest him when he entered and called in haste for the gun, which the old woman handed to him. He killed two bulls. For several weeks afterwards he was the butt for all jokes, because he had spoken directly to his mother-in-law. He should have called to her from without the tent, but was in such haste that he did not for a moment realize that he was not speaking to his wife. Jokes are rare among Indians and survive so much the longer. Even from constant repetition they lose nothing here.

Once during a war between the Herantsa and Assiniboin Tribes sixteen Herantsa braves on a visit to the Crows passed here that they might be put across the Missouri as good customers of the Big Company. They had hardly seated themselves in the office when a band of Assiniboin arrived. Mr. Denig was greatly disquieted for fear of conflict when the two hostile bands stood face to face. He required both chiefs to promise him at once that they would regard the fort, at least, as neutral ground. He desired, moreover, to bring about peace between the two nations. So when the most distinguished of the Assiniboin entered the office he offered the pipe. The chief of the Herantsa refused to smoke the pipe, notwithstanding that he was surrounded by the enemy in superior numbers. Mr. Denig threatened to show him the door: "He should make the effort." After the hostile parties had grimly surveyed one another as long as they liked the Herantsa walked proudly but quietly out to the gate with a challenge to the others to follow them.

Fur traders to the same company are brought many times into relations strangely complicated. Indians look upon fur traders who have an established post and carry on business with them as one of themselves, but a fur trader to the same company, established in the domain of their enemy, they regard more or less as a foe. Even the most intelligent among them, such as "Four Bears" (Quatre Ours), can not understand why white people who go from here to the Arikara or Blackfeet, enemies of the Assiniboin, should not be treated by them as enemies; for instance, why Charboneau at Fort Berthold was unjustified in firing upon the same Sioux who came from Fort Pierre; why one is not permitted here to fire upon members of the Blackfeet Tribe merely because they carry on trade with palefaces at another fort, yet do not hesitate to rob any white person whom they might find traveling alone from this fort. Fur traders are not liked; merely endured because they barter things necessary to supply the Indians' wants. They are required by every tribe that grants them the right and the ground for a fort to furnish protection and assistance in any conflict with enemies (inside the fort only). Fur traders are to regard the foes of Indians with whom they deal as their own foes. Only those carrying on trade on their own account, not for a company doing an extensive business, would find it possible to agree to such terms; nor would those independent traders be allowed to deal with any other than that especial tribe and their friends.[63]

On a recent journey from Fort Benton to this post Mackenzie met a war-like band of Blackfeet on the lookout for Assiniboin. He was alone, but fortunately he was riding John, famous among the tribes of this section for the swift pace at which he can travel. As Mackenzie thought he had nothing to fear from the approaching Blackfeet he did not evade the warriors. They surrounded him, asked him all sorts of questions, and, declaring him to be an Assiniboin, demanded his horse, his gun, and his knife. He did not acquiesce in those demands, of course, but sought to get rid of the redskins by cunning and then give John his head. He protested to the Blackfeet that the company's steamboat was nearby on the river; he had been sent to meet the steamer and deliver important tidings. They wished now to see the boat. They rode forward a mile to a neighboring hill, from the summit of which they could get a view of the Missouri. Meanwhile, Mackenzie made them a present of some tobacco. At the first favorable moment he put spurs to John, who with a frightful bound galloped off and away. Mackenzie knew that the braves would neither overtake him on their saddle horses nor make any attempt on his life.

When two Indians who are not hostile meet on their wanderings they stop usually several paces apart and question each other as to whence they come, what news they bring, whether anything unusual was noticed along the path, whether they met anybody.

If either reports news of significance, they sit down together and, if possible, smoke a pipe of tobacco. As a rule the younger offers the pipe to the older and concedes to him also the privilege of beginning

---

[63] After all, it is easy to understand that no tribe likes to see the same company with whom they deal sell arms and ammunition to their enemies.

the cross-questioning. If one of them has before him the way along which the other has come, he is warned concerning every trace, every significant indication of danger near at hand. If he has found no sign of anything to fear, the other goes on all the more unconcerned. Indians never greet each other with handshake or nod; neither do they wish one another good day or good morning. If they are well acquainted, but still have nothing further to say, they give their watchword "hou!"

A stranger who approaches an Indian settlement or village where strangers are rarely seen, has not long to wait before he knows in what direction his course lies. As he can never come unexpectedly into a village without having been discovered beforehand by either the busy or the idle inhabitants, a soldier is immediately on hand to receive him and conduct him to the soldiers' or assembly lodge. This is the largest hut in the settlement and serves as meeting place for their deliberative assembly or council as well as for the soldiers' guardroom. There all important news is discussed and decisions arrived at concerning the chase, war, and wanderings.

No woman is allowed to enter the lodge. There the stranger will be received, then questioned concerning his purpose in coming and the information he is able to give.

A soldier is in every case a brave who has already distinguished himself—counts several "coups." He is always more or less tattooed; i. e., figures, lines, or points are made with a needle on his skin and then rubbed over with powder or coal dust, so that the tattoo marks assume a blue-black color. Indians in this region are not tattooed over the entire body, but usually on the throat and breastbone or over the chest and shoulders, sometimes on the shoulders and arms or merely on the forearm or on the shin, the latter, however, being decorated only with large dots, hoofprints, or spear heads. They never tattoo their backs, for a warrior, as you know, does not manifest by his hinder part that he is a brave. Women and girls wear tattoo marks by means of which they make known the nation to which they belong; for example, many Iowa girls have a large dot between their eyebrows. Frequently they decorate themselves with two dots, one above the other, as Witthae did. One point is said to signify that the person in question has given away ten horses; two points, that she has given away twenty.[64]

That may have been the custom originally, but many of these girls so marked would have been glad to own, once in her lifetime, one good

---

[64] But what did they signify at an earlier period, when Indians did not possess horses? It is certain that pricking or tattooing the skin was practiced in primitive times. Tattooing was the naked primitive man's first means of decoration, of distinguishing himself. His artist was well paid for the work, sometimes receiving even an ordinary horse. When people began to wear clothes tattoo marks were not so much the vogue.

sound horse. Hauwepine was the only girl whom I knew among the Iowa Tribe having tattoo marks on the breast—a trapeze extending from the base of the throat to the pit of the stomach. Sauteurs women, on the other hand, branded themselves by means of one, two, or three lines diverging from the corners of the mouth toward the chin. Soldiers are recognized, first of all, by their tattoo marks; also by their bearing, their dignified demeanor and their especial manner of wearing the buffalo robe or blanket. The latter they throw about the body in such a way that the right shoulder, breast, and arm remain free, and that part of the robe which is supposed to cover the right shoulder they draw under the right arm and hold in place with the left hand. Thus they form a drapery that falls in natural but at the same time majestic and graceful folds, the most beautiful drapery for the human body that I know. Indians, in addition to their passion for ornamentation, are adepts with their small hands in giving the blankets a graceful swing.

They have this art at their fingers' ends. In this, as in other things, practice makes perfect. They take not the slightest pains to produce an effect; rarely arrange their blankets from any motive other than their own comfort. They wear only their ornamented buffalo robes to make a show. The Indians' blankets are never clumsy or unwieldy; whether they hang freely over the shoulders, are drawn up over the head so as to wrap the body closely, or are allowed to drag on the ground, they are always soft and pliable.

All well-proved braves are soldiers; they serve as police force and as advisory council for their camp. Their regulations for maintaining order are strictly observed. They have due respect for their own law. They devise the method also of punishing the refractory—may inflict beatings or even the death penalty. Their decisions are proclaimed by a crier; for instance, suppose that buffaloes are discovered in the vicinity; now, if one individual hunter should set out after them, he would drive them away before the other huntsmen arrived, and so lessen their chances for means of livelihood.

Consequently, individual Indians are not permitted to go on the chase from a settlement or camp except in pursuit of animals found singly—never in pursuit of a herd. As soon as the news of approaching wild beasts is received, the soldiers assemble at once for deliberation as to the time and the manner in which the hunt is to be conducted (it frequently happens that most of the soldiers are on the war path, but some of the older ones always remain at home, the number depending upon the size of the camp). After their decision has been publicly made known, every huntsman, the most distinguished as well as the poorest, gets himself ready and they enclose the herd in a circle. Woe be unto the man who, in overhaste, attacks inopportunely and upsets the plan; his horse will be shot dead from under him or his weapons will be broken in splinters.

Every fur trader selects several of the most highly esteemed soldiers, upon whom he bestows rich gifts for the sake of having their protection both for himself and his goods. As a rule, each fur trader lives in the tent of one of his protectors. When we stopped on the *St. Ange* at Fort Pierre, it happened that a band of Teton Sioux were encamped near the fort.

A group of a dozen soldiers in grand array greeted us first with a salvo, then came on board to welcome their acquaintances, and finally kept watch over the cargo that had been put ashore. What a welcome prize they were for me! A dog was shot instantly through the heart because he was in the act of lifting his leg against the piles of goods. Women and children were standing in a group apart, curiously scrutinizing the white strangers.

Every year upon the steamer's arrival those soldiers are there in their military garb to welcome representatives of the company with whom they do business. Yanktonai were awaiting us on a bluff, where they had raised the United States flag. We found it difficult to land there, but were obliged to accomplish it, nevertheless, for politeness' sake. Those Yanktonnais, in full array, made the most original group I ever saw. The chief, carrying a tobacco pipe in his hand, stood on a crest of the bluff that had been washed smooth like a high pedestal, and round about him, at the river's edge, stood his braves, in various postures. After the warriors' welcoming scene was over the women were allowed to descend first and come aboard.

As a matter of course, every soldier has a family, of which he is chief. He loves his children extraordinarily. His word of admonition must suffice; he never inflicts corporal punishment upon them. He sets a good example for his son as to how he is to conduct himself as a future brave. He impresses upon his daughters the virtues of modesty and chastity but leaves their training, in the main, under their mother's care. It frequently happens that, for the sake of household peace and order, a soldier gives his quarreling wives a beating. In his own tent he assigns to each member of the family a place to sleep and a place at the fireside just as he does for visitors and guests. As head of a family he dares play no tricks in his own tent, especially with his small children. For that sort of thing a soldier's hut is chosen, where neither women nor children come; there he seeks his recreation, laughs, sings, plays, smokes, dances, and thoroughly enjoys himself, so long as there is no matter under consideration before the council. Then "decorum" is strictly required.

When the man of the house, father or brother, has slain the wild beasts and brought them home, his duty as such is done. Women take off the skins and dry them, prepare the flesh for food, get ready the fire, take care of their children, make the clothes—all women's duties and pleasures, in fact, are distinctly designated for them.

No woman has any voice in the council, is ever listened to, or her advice followed, not even one who has made herself conspicuous for bravery, as not infrequently happens when a village is taken by surprise. Women spend their hours of recreation in looking after their children, visiting, chatting with one another, singing, dancing, in making clothes, painting and adorning themselves, and with affairs of love. They have a share in the dressed skins,[65] which they exchange for clothes, ornaments, and dainty titbits. Their sweethearts' gifts are usually dainties and handsome pelts from the hunt. Sisters have a claim on everything that a brother or brother-in-law possesses. For instance, an Indian comes riding into camp and meets a sister (sister-in-law and brother-in-law are called sister and brother, just as uncle and aunt are called father and mother); she expresses a wish for the horse he is riding; he springs down forthwith and gives her the beast, even though it might be his best racer. Such a proceeding, however, is held to be contrary to right and justice. Girls prefer, for the most part, a dappled horse to those of any other color, because they strike the eye and are easily distinguishable from all others.

Men's employments are confined to keeping their weapons in order, making ornaments for the hair, taking care of their horses, hunting, and waging war. That they have bettered their lot by contact with fur traders, the following facts prove: For one buffalo robe they received 60 loads of powder and shot; for 6–10 robes, a gun, which may or may not be a good one but is always fit for use. So for one robe he gets in return a sufficient number of shots to kill at least fifty of the larger or smaller fur-bearing animals. To grind and polish one single arrowhead from flint rock he would require three days— a longer time than an Indian woman needs to prepare a buffalo hide. The latter has this advantage: that it can be discharged without noise and can be used any number of times, but at a distance of more than fifty feet the hunter is no longer sure of hitting a small object.[66]

Mr. Denig declares that the drinking of whisky does Indians no harm whatever. To be sure, here as elsewhere, brawls and murders not infrequently occur as a result of drinking, but wild Indians think nothing of such things as that. On the other hand, they were more reliable, more industrious, and cared more for their personal ap-

---

[65] If one may call the hides prepared without bark, etc., dressed or tanned skins.

[66] Among Indians of the upper Missouri I did not see the leather band worn around their left wrist as a protection against the rebound of the bowstring, as they are used by the Iowa, Fox, and Omaha Indians. Indians on the upper Missouri, however, are more well-to-do tribes and are provided generally with rifles.

pearance at the time when Uncle Sam allowed them to barter for whisky than at present, for the simple reason, universally accepted as true, that people work more diligently for their pleasures than for the necessities of life. They find in whisky, Mr. Denig says, a keen incentive to work; in order to enjoy a drink the man went more frequently on the chase, his wife dressed a larger number of hides. Since that time they have brought fewer skins for exchange, not for the reason that buffaloes have decreased in number but that Indians, so long as they have meat, which is the food they prefer, will not exert themselves at all for bread and coffee. But for whisky they are willing to suffer hunger, cold, and most strenuous exertions for days together.

This is all doubtless very true, but let us consider also the other side of the question. The fur trader's principal reason for wishing whisky back again as a commodity for trade with Indians, notwithstanding the attending peril to their own lives, is the enormous profit they derive from the sale of it—a profit out of all proportion to the one now realized.

They made a gain earlier ranging from 200 to 400 percent; their gain today is not more than 80 percent. Fur traders form their judgments and carry on business as such. They regard civilization of the Indian with detestation, because that means the end of their traffic. They know that when Indians begin to cultivate their land they will become independent. They will no longer follow the chase as their chief occupation, consequently there will be no longer a supply of furs and skins, present source of the fur traders' ready money. Anyone who investigates the history of the dispossessed Indians will find fur traders always among them warning the tribes against the whites, their own countrymen, and yet at the same time abetting the plunderers. What has the Hudson Bay Co. ever done to benefit the Indians since they have had the chartered rights of English fur traders in North America? Nothing! What evidences do we find here of the Englishman's love of mankind? English philanthropists give themselves tremendous airs where trade is not affected adversely thereby. So do American fur-trading gentlemen in all matters that do not affect their financial interests.

They are not concerned about the Indians' morality or advance to civilization, because that state of things would interfere with their trade—do away with their means of earning a livelihood. As long as there are buffaloes to kill fur traders are going to take a resolute stand against the civilization of Indians, not openly, to be sure, but in secret. Americans will see to it, meanwhile, that this vast trade is not allowed to be ruined at the expense of the redskins. Even missionaries, unless they begin with cultivating the soil as their principal work, do not prosper with their missions in the neighborhood of fur traders. However, I have nothing to say against that. Baptizing savages and roving hunters does not make them Christians; loyalty to the soil forms the foundation on which Christian communities rest, just as, generally speaking, the peasantry forms the core of organized states. A man who owns no land feels, perhaps, attachment for his kith and kin, and in a wider sense for his native country. Hunters with no fixed abode are not for a moment bound by sentiments of loyalty to any land or by attachment to the soil or to human associations. To set up a society composed of all mankind, a close relationship in ways of thinking, in sympathies and like aspirations, is the purpose of Christianity.

No civilized nation of the present day rose from a state of barbarism without the uplifting force of Christianity; though they may not have been Christian, yet teachers appeared among the people, inculcating moral principles having a close agreement in many respects with the teaching of Jesus. All European nations were still barbarian before they accepted the Christian religion; from that time on they advanced in agriculture, science, and art. Indians must take the same course, but they should require less time, because they are beginning under conditions so much more favorable, inasmuch as their teachers are heirs to the knowledge and experiences of men during many centuries. But what discouraging examples our so-called Christians! How little they practice what they preach! Can one, then, blame the Indians if they have no faith in such leaders?

Missionaries of different faiths are all agreed that it is impossible to convert Indian tribes where the tribesmen have whisky in their possession. Against the might of that inspiriting drink their faith, their prayers, and teachings are powerless. Yet there are some tribes that, wholly apart from any interference on the part of missionaries, will not endure the sight of whisky among them; for example, the Cree,[67] whom experience has made wise.

When old Dorion, an interpreter among the Sioux, was sent with his comrade, Dufond, from the trading post d'Eau Qui Court to a distant camp for the purpose of bartering whisky for skins and furs, both of them became intoxicated on the way and Dorion murdered Dufond. When their two Indian guides returned to the fire from the hunt Dorion told them, quite unmoved, that he had killed the

---

[67] White people commit the serious fault of finding always some means of exculpation when drunken men are brought before the courts. If a man were made to answer for his offenses when intoxicated just as when he is sober there would be much less drunkenness. Why an Indian under the influence of strong drink is said to be more dangerous than a drunken white man who, as everybody knows is almost always armed with pistol or bowie knife, is something I do not understand.

man. One of the Indians seemed anything but pleased to be associated with such a drunkard, in whose company even his own best comrade was not safe. He raised his rifle, aimed at Dorion's temple, and fired.

The warmth of this open fire exerts its expansive influence upon body and soul. I am inspired with an uncommon desire to write. Just any day I may leave this place (may or must?); therefore whatever facts worth remembering are now floating about in my head I would better preserve on paper; new impressions all too easily efface earlier ones. So then:

An Indian orator speaking before an assembly addresses the audience according to the relation he bears to his hearers. For example, my people, my friends, my kinsmen, my comrades.

If the orator finds it necessary to employ an interpreter he divides his speech into several parts, stops at the end of each section and has his interpreter translate what he has said, counts off on his fingers each section interpreted, and continues until all the divisions or points have been brought forward and transmitted.

The Assiniboin, as all the other larger tribes, are grouped into bands, each of which has its own chief or leader. The more numerous a chief's adherents, the higher his rank; he is valued according to the number of warriors he can summon. However excellent, however valiant, however shrewd a warrior may be, he will never become chief unless he has followers—extended relationships. The five bands of Assiniboin that severally owe allegiance to no supreme chief are named: Band of the Left Handed Chief (Gaucher), Band of the Maidens, Band of the Canots, Band of the Bluffs, Band from the North. Gaucher was at an earlier time the most powerful, the most celebrated chief. Like the infamous Omaha chief, Black Bird (Waschinga-Schaba), he seems to have removed his most dangerous rival from power by means of arsenic. The Assiniboin were then at war with the whole world—with the Blackfeet Tribe, the Crows, Arikara, Herantsa, and even the Sioux, but there is no fighting against great odds; they were compelled in the end to conclude a peace with the Sioux, Herantsa, and Absaroka.

Indians, says Mr. Denig, have the only system of education that makes men out of boys and wives out of girls. They educate children for a definite purpose in life; the boy is brought up to be a good huntsman, a brave warrior, a wise father; the girl, an industrious, faithful, and discreet mother. In the training of youth they have no further object in view. And in such training as this a good example accomplishes more than instruction, high-sounding phrases, and the inculcation of principles one never lives up to. The duty of a father is, on the whole, to prepare his children for happiness under any conditions; to train them to know how to submit to misfortune with shrewdness, with long-suffering endurance and fearlessness at times of assault, or to bear up against them; to give his son occupations adapted to his native gifts and inclinations, in order that he may sustain himself thereby. To supply young, inexperienced persons with large sums of money immediately following their release from school merely leads them into temptations, makes of them swaggerers, spendthrifts, and scatterbrains. Only when his (Mr. Denig's) son shows how he manages with money (his son lives in Chicago) will his father lavish funds upon him.

Rich children rarely develop into capable men: those who have rendered the greatest service to mankind in the professions, as inventors, in high qualities of mind and heart, come from parents in humble circumstances and have worked their way up through hardships. Necessity is the mother of invention. Only from experience comes wisdom, and out of conflict and tribulation virtues arise. On the other hand, he would afford girls the means to make an advantageous marriage; that is only just, because a girl's education involves less expense than a boy's. With a dowry she is all the better enabled to make a free choice and is assured of a better living, because as wife she is not expected to contribute to the support of the family but to devote herself to thrift and to the care of her children.

According to Mr. Denig, there are three dangerous shoals on which young people so frequently run aground: Idleness, love of drink, and card playing. Sexual instincts, he says, lead to no peril. "Love— damn the word!—is a madness in the brain; a contagious disease, like smallpox or measles. I would much rather take a dose of Epsom salts than to recall the folly of first love—pure love. If it is not stopped, that lunacy makes one ridiculous, childish, ashamed of himself." There is always something true and worth while in what he says, only he expresses himself in strong language.

So pass the long winter evenings in this wilderness.

October 11. The sky was so clear this afternoon and the sun shone so delightfully warm that I could not resist taking my gun and going once more to the hills in search of antelope. If the buck would only once allow me to approach near enough to see his horns, I would not thirst for his blood. I had my usual luck; saw nothing that engaged my attention particularly; began to indulge in daydreams and walked straight ahead. A man sees such a great number of bright yellow spots scattered over these hills that unless he is keen-sighted and pays constant attention it is difficult to tell whether the objects he is looking at are rocks or antelopes.

For that keen eyesight which enables one to recognize instantly what one catches sight of suddenly or at a great distance we have in

German only the expression "kennerauge" (eye of an adept or of a connoisseur); the English word "quick-sighted" implies something more—that is, the rapidity with which the eye recognizes what it perceives. And this instantaneous perception or discernment of distant objects the moment they strike the eye is a primary characteristic of the huntsman.

But for this he would miss his chance to conceal himself or to creep forward at the right moment, and, furthermore, he would unnecessarily expose himself to danger. It stands to reason, therefore, that a hunter must have his thoughts fixed exclusively on the hunt. The man at the fort who possesses the keenest, quickest eyesight is a 70-year-old Spaniard, our cattle herder—the most illiterate man among us. Precisely for the reason that his head is empty of ideas, his wits so blunted he occupies himself with nothing but the herding of cattle, and for the sake of finding something to interest him while engaged in those duties, his eyes stray continually to the distance. He talks incessantly aloud to himself about what he sees. His undivided attention is given to this region that he has known for so many years; he knows by heart, so to speak, every blade of grass, every stone, every shrub, every tree, every elevation or depression of the ground, every hill and brook. The slightest variation in the landscape attracts his attention. Our other Spaniard, who guards the horses, is less noted for keen sight; women and the laying of traps share his thoughts and frequently distract his attention. Packinaud glories in his skill in stalking deer as only few Indians can.

The other hunters, who are equally successful as bookkeepers and tradespeople, grant him this claim to the "excellence of the Indian" but tell him at the same time that he is also as ignorant as an Indian, for he can neither read, write, nor reckon, although he was brought up in Canada. Keen eyesight I lack altogether. In the first place, I am not quicksighted and, furthermore, I am so intensely absorbed with other ideas, studies, and dreams—matters that are not only unnecessary but in the highest degree prejudicial to the huntsman.

To-day, as heretofore, I allowed myself to be seen by the antelopes long before I knew whether the objects in front of me were rocks or animals. It was only when I became aware of yellow and white spots moving through the dry grass that I took out my telescope and saw how the frolicking antelopes were making fun of me, playing with one another under my nose until they were chased from the hilltop by the buck, vanished into the valley, appeared again in full speed on a distant height, darted with leaps and bounds across, and gave me the last glimpse of their shining bodies. In vain I followed their tracks. But I did see a wolf whose head and neck looked singularly blue. He was running down to the brackish stream but found no water to his taste.

Wolves are no uncommon sight here, but they are not seen in packs except when one finds a wounded animal which howls to bring others to his aid. When they see or get the scent of people they scurry away and lie down in some sheltered place to find out whether they are pursued.

As they are never reduced to such straits for food in this region as in settled countries, they are not so wild or so dangerous. For instance, I was reading in a St. Louis newspaper that an Indian in the region about Dubuque, returning home in winter with a load of meat, was set upon with such fury by wolves that he could barely save his life, though he threw out all the meat to them.[68] In this region there has been no instance of a man having lost his life from an attack of wolves.

Not only Indian tribes are separated into smaller camps for the sake of moving from place to place with more rapidity and of feeling more secure as to provisions, but these bands are also subdivided into special groups, each of which claims a certain rank. Young men, braves, girls, and older women have their own bands, to which they pay rather large sums in time if they have the means. Each of these groups has its own distinctive name, decoration, and dance.

Its purpose is purely social, offering the members a variation from their usual diversions. The band of highest rank is made up of the most celebrated warriors—The Band that Never Saves Itself. Others have the names of favorite animals, but never the so-called medicine birds and beasts, the flesh of which they do not eat, the skins of which they refuse to prepare for sale; such birds and beasts are not identical in any of the tribes. They exclude as such eagles, bears, beavers, and wolves; on the other hand, they accept buffaloes, dogs, foxes, pheasants, turtles, elks, etc. At these dances eunuchs wear no clothing at all except moccasins, not even the breechcloth. They fasten an eagle feather on their limbs.

Because of the limited supply, eagle feathers are very high in price. For designating a "coup" only tail feathers are worn, and of those an eagle has only twelve; they are a dingy white in color, with black ends. The tail of an eagle costs here as much as a horse or six buffalo robes.[69] Indians take much pains to catch war eagles; they shoot them very rarely, if ever.

To ensnare the birds, two Indians go out into a wild region and dig a hole in the ground deep enough to conceal one of them, who gets

---

[68] The region beyond Dubuque, however, is not thickly populated.

[69] At the fort we have an eagle confined in a cage. He is given, once a week, a large piece of meat. Since he has been here he has never once drunk water.

in, is supplied with food, and then covered over by his companion with boughs and twigs. Care is taken to leave spaces between the boughs through which he can see. His companion then lays some carrion on top of the covered pit and withdraws from the scene. When an eagle swoops down upon the carrion the concealed hunter seizes him by the legs and pulls him down through the boughs and plunges a knife into his heart. Woe to the Indian if the eagle attacks him with beak and talons, for the wounds those birds inflict are terrible. In their sharp-pointed claws they possess greater strength than a bear, and with their crooked beaks they tear away flesh, leaving great hollows in a person's face. The hunter has oftentimes to remain several days in his lurking place, but is happy even then if he accomplishes anything—moreover, if a bear does not fall foul of him.[70]

I was inquiring today whether the pipe of peace was ever put to a wrong use, in order to overreach a friend by treachery and bring about his overthrow, or whether it was always regarded as sacred. Among Absaroka and Herantsa the sanctity of the peace pipe is held inviolable; among other nations it depends; if the end in view be only to get rid of an enemy, all means are justified. So it was, they say, at the time when Crows and Assiniboin were still at enmity with each other but yet were beginning to be weary of war and to question whether their feud was due to any well-defined cause or was merely a heritage from their forefathers that no longer justified real feelings of hatred as a motive to continued hostilities. During that time four Absaroka, in spite of warnings from the whites, insisted upon coming with their families to their relations, the Herantsa, at this fort for the purpose of bartering for corn, or, in other words, to beg. The Crows came actually upon a camp of Assiniboin. Knife, Spotted Horn, Celui Qui Suit le Chemin (Pathfinder), and other chiefs proffered them the pipe in a tent. The Crows, unsuspecting, laid their weapons aside and smoked. The Assiniboin rushed upon them and

---

[70] Later on Morgan and I had a rather severe struggle with our eagle. On account of the cold weather he and the bear were put in a small outhouse. One day I found a frozen pig near the palisades and wished to give it to the bear. When I entered I saw the eagle's cage turned upside down and the eagle squatting on top of it. The bear presumably had picked a quarrel with the bird between the wooden slabs of his box. I called Morgan to assist me. He took an old buffalo robe and I took my wide riding cloak with which to cover the eagle and secure him, without exposing ourselves to sharp beak and frightful talons. As Morgan approached him he flew away. I threw my cloak in his direction in such a way as to catch him in it. We bound him at once with leather thongs and carried him into my room. We had no more time at the moment to give to him. We had hardly gone back to our duties in the store when someone shouted that the eagle was walking about in my room. To prevent his escape through the window it was necessary to catch him again forthwith. I found my cloak torn to pieces by his powerful claws. This time he turned upon us in a frightful manner and inflicted several severe cuts on Morgan's arm with his feet. But for Morgan's good fortune in having on leather clothes the talons would have made a deep wound. As it was, that arm pained him a long while.

murdered them. Their motive seems to have been to get possession of the Crows' good horses rather than their scalps, for they sent the women and children back on foot.

When it came to a division of their four-footed prizes, Spotted Horn had a quarrel with the son of Pathfinder, whereupon the former let fly an arrow that struck the latter in the back and killed him. As a penalty, Spotted Horn was deprived of his share of the booty and made to sweat for other gifts besides in expiation of the crime.

On the occasion of another such peace proposal, twenty-eight braves of the Herantsa Tribe were murdered by Yanktonai. Later the Yanktonai concluded a peace, in reality, but their motive in so doing was to overreach the Herantsa and make victory over them all the more certain. As it was the custom with the latter tribe to leave their village at Fort Berthold in winter and, for the sake of the hunting, to move up to the region of Knife River, the Yanktonai thought they would find at the abandoned village large quantities of maize. A group of them sneaked up. Luckily, the Herantsa had got wind of that villainy, however, and were lying in ambush both in front of them and in their rear. Not one escaped; all were slain.

Crows are noted for the good order maintained in their villages; but we may assume this has reference more particularly to good conduct on the part of men than of the women, since in that tribe women take the liberty of going to the deliberative council,[70a] where they enter the discussions and make the braves listen to reason, a proceeding never heard of in any other Indian nation.

Yet women of the Crow Tribe are known rather more for their industry and skilled work than for beauty of face and form. Young Crows are as wild and unrestrained as wolves.

Among the Absaroka old Sapsucker was, in his earlier years, a soldier of first rank and became their most famous chief. Once when they were ready to go as usual after the harvest season, on a visit to the Herantsa to barter, or rather to beg for maize, yet realized the danger of the venture, because, owing to their feud with the Assiniboin, detached parties were always attacked, old Sapsucker assembled his forces and came as usual over the Missouri to Fort Union. His object was to find out whether the Assiniboin would pounce upon him at the head of his army. He first sent forward twenty braves mounted on picked horses as a vanguard "to feel their way." It was known that the combined Assiniboin bands were in camp between the two forts and that their warriors were on the watch. He gave orders to his vanguard to avoid any encounter, but to find out where their foes were and keep clear of them. They brought the news here that

---

[70a] Among the Iroquois this is a right of the women and the women chiefs.

in a few days their entire settlement would desire to cross the river.[71]

As soon as they had taken some rest and had gained the information required they proceeded farther on their way. Two days later sixty braves came riding along to support the vanguard and to dispatch couriers here, there, and everywhere. Finally Sapsucker arrived in command of a hundred soldiers, the gros d'armee. The other members of the tribe, including women and children, followed on foot, convoyed by four squads of braves. In this manner the shrewd leader reached the village of the Herantsa unperceived and, while conducting his affairs with them, kept his spies on the alert around the enemy's settlement. His return, in reverse order, was accomplished with equal success.

When outlying pickets discover the enemy they give the following signal to their forces in the rear: They gallop up and down and then crosswise the line. If they come upon buffaloes, they ride slowly up and down in a straight line, often throwing dust into the air.

October 12. Saw today some other attractions that afford motifs for pictures. In the morning two lovely girls were bringing water from the river. After we had eaten I went with Mr. Denig on a hunt for antelopes. Saw first an Indian sitting on a hill beside his horse, musing on the surrounding scene. He then mounted and, singing, rode away, a somber figure sharply outlined against the horizon.

Next we saw a red fox that Mr. Denig might have shot if he and I had not been absorbed in conversation.[72] We found our herd of ante-

---

[71] Flatboats are also kept on the river at this place for the convenience of the people at the fort and their customers as well. The "Dobies" below us are situated at the mouth of the Yellowstone, and use no ferryboats.

[72] There is a crossbreed between the gray and the red fox which, on account of its splendid pelt, is most highly prized. In St. Louis such a "cross-fox" brings as much as $80. We have here several beautiful animals of that species, nearly always lustrous black except on the abdomen, where their hair is gray, verging into red-brown. Others appear to be wholly gray—silver gray.

According to Audubon and Bachmann, there is a distinction to be made between the kit fox (*Vulpes velox*) and the gray fox (*Vulpes virginianus*); it is so slight, however, that I would say the difference lies in celerity of movement rather than habitat. The same species of fox must be able to rely more on his fleetness than his cunning on the open prairie where he finds skulking places much less frequently than in forests and broken or overgrown terrain. Neither the gray nor the red fox are reputed to be crafty. On the prairie, at least, no distinction is made between the gray fox and the swift fox.

I am sorry I was not acquainted with the mongrel black crossbreed (*Vulpes fulves* var. *argentatus*) when I came to the upper Missouri. I regret especially that I had not had opportunity to study beforehand the admirable book by Audubon and Bachmann, as well as other valuable works, for I should have derived much authoritative information in regard to natural history. At Fort Union I took the so-called "cross fox" for a crossbreed combining the gray and red foxes, nor was I informed otherwise by the hunters there. According to Audubon and Bachmann, the silver fox is lustrous black with the exception of the tip of his tail, which, like that of the red fox, is invariably white. On the other hand, the tail of the kit fox is invariably altogether black. Other animals of this species are blue-gray or, to be exact, most frequently black with an intermixture of blue-gray hair, sometimes combined with additional red-brown hairs, sometimes not.

Now the cross fox is the hybrid produced by a combination of the silver and the red fox, and is distinguished from the former by red-brown hair on his sides and from the latter by his black neck, shoulders, back, and tail. His pelt is held to be of great value.

lopes again at their accustomed grazing place near the brackish stream. They were obviously on their guard; instead of grazing they were constantly peering around, sniffing the air, giving every evidence of unrest. Mr. Denig crept up the hill on which they were tripping about, beckoned me to come out of my excellent hiding place, where I should have had the best chance in the world to shoot the buck, and reproached me for a blunderer who had again let myself be seen unnecessarily or else had made a noise. On the contrary, I had been as still as a mouse. The instant my companion fired, the beasts fled with amazing leaps, arching their flexible backs in the manner of cats. We discharged our rifles at once upon the fleeing herd, but to no purpose. We had hardly lost sight of our escaping quarry when we were startled by the unexpected report of a gun nearby; friend or foe—that was now the question.

We reloaded our rifles with care and set forward in the direction from which the sound had come. Soon we met, on the trail leading to the fort, a group of Indians we did not know. There were four men and two women, accompanied by several dogs laden with packs of dried meat. At sight of us two of the latter ran off with their travois, and their companions followed them to a considerable distance. Mr. Denig took the redskins for Cree. He invited them by means of signs to come with him to the fort; they laughed and remained standing where they were. Well, he thought, they are going to the "Dobies", customers of the opposition. They wanted whisky. We had none to offer them. After all, they decided to follow us along the characteristic Indian trail with its three parallel paths. Mr. Denig remarked at once to me that it would be hard to bring them over to our side, yet it would be to his discredit if his attempt failed. To be sure, they had nothing with them of any value, but they would make a great deal of fun at his expense when they arrived at the "Dobie" fort and gave their own account of all the things he had promised them. So, when we came to the parting of the ways and he saw them turning off he made signs to the effect that he would give them as much meat and coffee as their stomachs could hold. "Hou!" They followed us. They were Chippewa, who in their speech constantly reminded me of Potawatomi.

October 13. While we were weighing the meat and hanging it up so as to prevent mold and also to keep it out of the way of hordes of mice (there are no rats in the fort any more than at Fort Berthold) there arrived a great band of Assiniboin, including many women, laden horses, and dogs. Inasmuch as these caravans afford me my only chance to observe different groups of Indians in this region, they are always welcome as further means of detailed study, especially their method of laying on the loads and, during the sale of their commodities, of unloading their packs. Upon these occasions there is no evidence of festive array.

Art is not to be regarded as a luxury beyond the reach of "the general"; love of painting is not merely indulging a taste for extravagance; that is not to be said of any of the fine arts. Ideals toward which one strives in art are as lofty as in religion; one's aspirations are the same and the resulting loss just as profound if one falls into error.

That not all artists entertain this view but are merely influenced by their feeling; that the wealthy surround themselves with paintings, statues, music, poetry, and romances, is no reason why we should suppose that art is something rare and rich, to be possessed only by the few; that many people who have a genuine taste for art may even regard it from that viewpoint does not disprove what I say.

Or are we to suppose that beauty serves no other end in life than to please? Has it not the much more lofty aim to inspire us to love the good?

Beauty's sway is acknowledged by everybody, disputed by none. Beauty arouses sympathies and emotions that inflame to good or to evil, to noble aspirations, to cringing humility, or even to animal instincts. His sense of the beautiful sets the human being apart from the lower animals. In brutes that sense is totally lacking. Now, as the perfecting of our nature is the aim of earthly existence and our striving for a future perfect state elevates us above the animal, distinguishing the human being from the brute, then love of the beautiful and quick manifestations of beauty which is inherent in man but nonexistent, one may say, in the brute, points unmistakably the direction to be taken in the culture of the human individual.

Man has no higher task than his endeavor to attain to this perfection by some called Godlikeness. He has three means of approach in his progress toward this aim: Along the way of truth, the way of love, and the way that leads to beauty. To aid him in determining his course, he is endowed with intellect, which enables him to reason and to will; with soul, the source of all higher feeling and ennobling emotions; and with faculties of sense, by means of which he receives impressions from without. These qualities or native endowments the human being possesses in unequal proportion, one faculty being more dominant, another less. He is not uniformly provided with these gifts of nature which render him capable of advancing toward the spiritual perfection he strives to attain, if not in this world, then in a future life.

In his efforts to put his faculties to right use he should find his best guidance in science, religion, and in the fine arts, for, inasmuch as men are not uniformly endowed by nature, what one knows to be true another believes and a third is deeply conscious of, according to his native endowments. So, then, notwithstanding that the means employed are different, the fine arts have no less worthy end in view than faith and wisdom.

As the senses—sight, hearing, smell, taste, touch, etc.—differ one from the other, so the arts which serve the senses are to be distinguished and every form of art—painting, sculpture, architecture, music, and poetry—all have the same purpose. A picture of the external, visible world we perceive through our physical sense of sight, but the soul also possesses this sensitive faculty. We see with our "mind's eye", we hear the singing in our own hearts, our own inward song we speak to our own inner selves. Our outer senses are only a sort of mirror, but the inner mind possesses also a power peculiarly its own—the imagination. Through the magic of this faculty we can recall pictures of the past, make them more beautiful, transform as we choose or create them anew.

Beauty enraptures us, ugliness is repugnant; the same is true of harmonious sounds, the redolence of flowers, etc. Yet beauty does not exist for mere pleasurable effect upon the senses, but for the higher purpose of inspiration, of uplift. Beauty is one of the mighty incentives that excites our human minds, that stirs our very souls.

To evoke noble emotions and lofty aspirations through the perceptive faculties is the task of the fine arts, called the fine or elegant arts for the reason that in each the end is attained through the medium of what is beautiful and fine. Also called plastic arts, because the end in view is to ennoble the soul, to give to the emotions a higher and more definite direction.

The human mind is excited and influenced by impressions received. The arts have the power to convey impressions that lead to good or evil results. Who, then, can doubt an artist's responsibilities and duties? Only those who refuse to acknowledge how important the culture of mankind is, that is, the materialists. Any one who accepts the truth that man's destiny is to rise to higher levels through the perfecting of his entire self must agree that we employ our talent, with which we are more or less richly endowed, to that end.

Why console ourselves with hopes of a future life, the existence of which we accept on faith but cannot prove?

Poetry finds here now, in this life, what the religious seek on the other side of the grave. Poetry reveals ideal life on earth and shows how all created things are in accord with the divine harmony pervading all; accordingly, the heaven striven for in religion poetry creates on earth.

We know that we cannot attain in this life to our ideal of human perfection. From the cradle to the grave we are beset with trials too numerous, exigencies too great. Notwithstanding, each is to do his utmost and console himself with hopes held out to him in religion of finding his reward in a future existence. Then he will be rid of his mortal nature and, his divine gifts of mind and soul thus disencumbered, developing under conditions more favorable, necessities less urgent, trials less severe, will attain to the ideal. We are taught, also, in religion that not until this afterlife are injustices and inequalities in the bestowal of native gifts to be set right. We are to become good through a constant struggle upward to what is beautiful and fine—that is the aim. We find this same end in view in the study of plastic art, i. e., rhythm, harmony, or, in other words, poetry, is meant to be evident in every pictorial representation, whether embodied in language, colors, stone, lines, and contours, or in musical tones. Woe be unto the artist who employs his talents to an evil purpose, directs his efforts to the wrong aim.

No true artist regards as his highest purpose mere reproduction of nature; beauties of nature are daily pleasures from which only the blind are debarred. The artist's task is to improve nature's forms, make perfect her imperfections, strive not only to emulate but to excel her in the creation of beauty. Nature achieves nothing in ideal perfection, but the artist's mind can conceive of ideal beauty and clothe his ideas with correspondingly lovely forms, i. e., idealize them.

By that means the human being rises above that which is usual or commonplace. To inspire their fellow beings is the artist's most lofty aim; to that end they should bend their efforts, each according to his ability.

Inasmuch as we are unable to conceive of spirit apart from body, since even a spirit in space is conceivable only as a separate, individual entity or else as having vanished into thin air and hence formless, and inasmuch as we can conceive of no form more noble than that of man, animated by the greatest minds, or spirits known to us in this world, the perfect human stands for our ideal of consummate beauty. Man made in God's image is not only His noblest but also His most surpassingly beautiful creation. Though animal forms and the grandeur and loveliness of natural scenery have power to excite our admiration, to evoke poetic emotions and yearnings for the better world, neither arouses more lofty aspirations or a higher exercise of will than contemplation of the form of man.

Not reproduction of Nature's work—that will soon be completely accomplished by the aid of mechanical means—not as a luxury for the few; not for diversion; not as a pastime, but poetry—divine poetry—that is our shibboleth.

To inspire lofty emotions, thoughts, and deeds through pictorial representation of noble forms; to put one into the right way to ennoble one's emotions; to think nobly; to search for truth; to be capable of great deeds; to cultivate one's taste—nothing less than this is the end and aim of the fine arts. To improve a person's taste one must so charm him with representations of an idealized world that he desires those pleasures. It is said, to be sure, les gouts sont differents,[73] but good taste is the same wherever it may be found.

Art that can serve so lofty a purpose is not to be regarded as only one of the luxuries of life. That art can do what I claim is proved by the effect of such statues as we find from the best period of Greek sculpture and the purpose for which the original statues and monuments were carved; furthermore, by sacred paintings in Catholic churches that serve to dispose one's mind and heart to piety, to make one receptive to thoughts of a purer life; by magnificent temples and cathedrals, whose towering pinnacles and spires warn man of his littleness and inspire feelings of humility; by the power of music to attune the soul to merriment, to melancholy, to serious reflection, to heroic action in war, to good and to evil; finally, "last but not least", by the art of poetry, that through the medium of language incites to grand deeds, noble sentiments, and pure emotions.

October 14. While we were getting together the goods for Carafel's winter quarters and packing them into uniform bales weighing on an average of 70 pounds each, eight half-breeds from the upper Red River (not to be confused with Red River in northern Arkansas and Texas) came to the fort seeking employment for the winter. They gave an account of a recent attack made on their people by the Sioux. These Chippewa half-breeds have severed themselves from English sovereignty and have come under the Star-Spangled Banner of the United States. They have chosen from their share of Chippewa domain the delta between the Pembina and the St. Peters River. These metifs [74] have intermarried with both full-blooded and half-breed Indians. Their land is not particularly productive; they prefer still the products of the chase to agriculture, for which tendencies their Indian and French blood is chiefly responsible. While their crops are growing they have time for the summer's hunt; after the harvest, for hunting in the fall; in the winter season the men try to earn some money as engagees, scouts, and interpreters in the service of various fur traders.

---

[73] I. e., tastes differ.

[74] Descendants from Lord Selkirk's colony. Among those colonists were also some Swiss from English regiments of the time that, after the war with France, served in Canada and were afterwards discharged there.

On these hunting expeditions the metifs take dried meat, hides, tents, and cooking utensils around with them on two-wheeled carts. Each band chooses its own leader to direct the hunt and to take measures for defense in the event they are set upon by enemies. They are accustomed, when such caravans are crossing the prairie, to require that carts be driven in a certain order and, upon halting, to form a ring or square about the men and brutes as a means of defense. They push the poles or shafts under the foremost carts.

The other day, according to their story, sixty metifs were on a buffalo hunt with their families. During the chase three of them were captured by a greater number of Sioux. The latter counted some 800 tents; hence about 2,500 warriors. Farther back was pitched another camp numbering 600 tents. The Sioux, conscious of their superior strength, were most insolent and yet cowardly. In spite of their power they attempted to trick the metifs and take them unawares. They made the three prisoners believe that their intention was to conduct them back to their carts, shake hands with the other half-breeds, and smoke the pipe. Accordingly the captives, accompanied by a strong guard of soldiers, were taken in the direction of their barricade. The metifs, however, neither the three held by the enemy nor those behind the clustered carts, put any confidence at all in good intentions on the part of the Sioux.

Those in camp had meanwhile driven in their cattle and horses, which they confined. They had further strengthened their defense by filling in open spaces between the carts with heaps of dried meat. raw hides, and saddles.

The prisoners, who were riding one behind the other in the foremost file, where they could be seen by their friends, decided among themselves that if it were possible, as soon as they came within shooting distance of their own people, they were going to take flight. The one in the rear was mounted on a horse of slow gait, so he had poor prospects of escape, but he did what he could to enable his comrades to avenge his death. So, the instant the two foremost captives put spurs to their horses, he shot the Sioux nearest him—that same bullet brought down three braves. He himself was felled on the spot. His fellow prisoners escaped. The metifs behind the carts shot a number of the Sioux. Then the enemy surrounded their barricade and for two days galloped hither and yon in their attempts to fire upon the cattle, but no hand-to-hand combat took place; they dared not make an attack. A Chippewa woman, in the metif's camp, the men said, was beside herself in her desire to do battle. She was constantly trying to rush out and fight at close quarters with the Sioux, and became extremely angry because her relatives restrained her. Finally she took off all her clothes and, standing naked, waved her skirt at the enemy with jeering words.

She sang and whooped at such a rate, they said, that three other women were induced to make like demonstrations.

The Sioux lost 80 men and 65 horses, and many more were wounded. The metifs' rifles kept the enemy at such a distance that their balls fell short of the carts. They were too far removed to use arrows at all. The half-breeds' loss amounted to twelve horses and four oxen. They kept swift horses saddled, ready to make an attack the instant opportunity was offered. Fifteen foolhardy fellows even rode out once and fired a volley with the hope of enticing the enemy to come at least within range of their archers, but in vain. Attracted by the repeated shooting of guns, a larger group of metifs drew near, whereupon the valiant Sioux took to flight. This is the metifs' story. Sioux, in their turn, will give a different account.

Then the wounded Packinaud would also tell his story to prove that he had at least seen a combat. As he does not appear to be a hero in the action, cne is inclined to believe his narrative: Ten Dakota were out on the warpath near the Herantsa settlement; they were discovered in a thicket back of the upper cornfields, where mosquitoes swarm in thick multitudes. Frenzied by the pests, six of them dug holes with their knives in which to cover their bodies and the other four ran off.

The Herantsa [75] were not overeager to seek out the hidden enemy and attack. To expose themselves unnecessarily to certain death they held to be foolish rather than valiant. Suddenly a Cree came galloping along and shouted, "Where is the enemy?"

He was shown the small wood where the Dakota were suspected to be lurking. He galloped thither, and the Herantsa, ashamed, followed him. Five bullets pierced through the skull of the brave Cree, blowing out his brains, and the sixth shot hit the Herantsa next to him. The attacking party knew then, from the powder smoke, where the Dakota were concealed, but had to tread down willow plats before they got sight of them. Many a brave met his death there. When one of the Herantsa shot to death the first Sioux he called out at once that he had slain a foe, whereupon his companions rushed upon the others and instantly brought down four. The sixth plunged into a bog and sank; a Herantsa was in the act of pushing him down when he, a young boy, begged to be shot rather than drowned.

The Herantsa, with a thrust of the knife, sent him into the other world. Now, at that moment Packinaud came upon the scene of action, just at the right time to witness the amputation of limbs for trophies. With increasing heat he brought his narrative to its conclusion, accompanying his words with Indian signs. In a greatly

[75] Their real name is Gens des saules rongés, not Minetaree, which means gens qui traversent une petite traverse [i. e., who cross a small tongue of land, or isthmus], or people of the gnawed willows.

excited state he sat down. He looked really as if all was over with him.

A decrepit woman who hobbles about this place with the aid of a walking stick has lived in a tent before the gates for four generations. She is the widow of that renowned chief of the Assiniboin, L'Armure de Fer, better known as Le Gros Français [The Great Frenchman]. He was the leader of the Gens des Roches [People of the Rocks], whom Lewis and Clark met on their expedition. She must be more than a hundred years old. She hobbles about bent double with age.

Old people have anything but a pleasant life among the Indians when they can no longer be of use. They must be fed when there is a lack of food; they must be carried along when the band is moving in haste. As a consequence one finds all too frequently that on their wanderings Indians abandon old members of the band to a wretched fate, without shelter and without means of support. They are given only a stick with which to dig the pomme blanche.[75a]

Such an aged woman lived a long while just outside this fort, supported by Mr. Denig. She put together a heap of twigs for a shelter under which to abide; snow kept her warm. Two young blades from the band to which she belonged took counsel together as to what was to be done, whether to build her a more comfortable hut or to do away with her. Since she was of no service whatever, they argued, she was not worth so much trouble, and they decided, therefore, upon the latter alternative, and cudgeled her until she was dead. When the old Spaniard went next morning to take her what was left from the morning meal he found the aged woman with head split open. The two young Indians, who were sitting near, told him lightly that she was better dead than alive.[76]

Only the other day a feeble Indian woman came to the fort, after she had been left 14 days on the prairie to starve. She carried only a few pommes blanches that she had got for her scanty fare.

Generally speaking, women age more rapidly than men, for the reason, so it is said, that they smoke less. Yet the Indians' habit of inhaling tobacco smoke and exhaling through the nose results in serious injury to chest and head; consequently, though they smoke a blended tobacco, mild and sweet-smelling, they suffer quite fre-

---

[75a] This is the prairie turnip, or pomme de prairie, of the voyageurs, *Psoralea esculenta* Pursh.

[76] I do not deliberately pass over in silence such cruel acts, because, apart from my sympathy and friendship for the Indians, I have a just comprehension of their feelings. I assert boldly that in proportion to mental and moral training these so-called savages are guilty of fewer acts of inhumanity and cruelty than citizens of self-styled Christian nations. Not a day passes that the newspapers, both in Europe and the United States, do not publish the most bloodcurdling, shameful deeds. I think the Indians' barbarity during the wars of extermination was perfectly natural; their fury and wrath were aroused to an extreme degree. Were the people on the borders less savage? Did they not scalp with equal zeal?

quently from lung trouble. They smoke a brand of American manufacture, the only tobacco they can get, mixed with dried leaves or
bark they procure for themselves. This Indian blend I have now
become accustomed to using (but do not exhale through the nose).
I never smoke that sort of tobacco anywhere else. I find the aroma
very agreeable. To offer a well-filled pipe to the visitor is in strict
accord with Indian etiquette; I am in duty bound to acknowledge
the courtesy, particularly since I do not understand their speech.

October 15. Walked with Carafel to his winter quarters, mainly
to assist him in getting things arranged; his principal lading of
goods will come later. Afterwards I helped him hang up the rest
of his cured meat and to put the store in order.

I much enjoy such exertions at times, for it is not well to devote
one's self exclusively to building castles in Spain, but to give the brain
relaxation now and then and bring the body into action while engaged
in practical matters.

The father of our new trader, Battiste Lafontaine, was the best
mounted buffalo hunter ever known in this region. He ran buffaloes
once with others on the Yellowstone to see which of them could kill
the greater number at full gallop. He covered 1 English mile in
6 minutes and shot, in flight, 12 cows—that is, two every minute—
notwithstanding that cows run much faster than bulls. Lafontaine
weighed 230 pounds, but sat his horse so lightly and comfortably that
the beast was not sensible of his weight. Owen Mackenzie can load
and shoot 14 times in 1 mile, but does not invariably hit the object at
which he aims. Still I do not doubt but that Mackenzie has the skill
to shoot 12 cows in 1 mile if his runner should come up with that
number.[77] Last year he ran a race with Clark from Fort Benton on a
wager and broke his collar bone during the adventure. He was just
getting a start to his goal when his runner stepped in a hole and fell.
Mackenzie went hurtling over the horse's head and came down on one
shoulder. He won the race nevertheless, both in respect to his horse's
speed and the rapidity of his shots.

When running buffaloes the hunters do not use rifle-patches [78] but
take along several balls in their mouths; the projectile thus moistened
sticks to the powder when put into the gun. In the first place, on
buffalo hunts, they do not carry rifles, for the reason that they think

[77] Audubon says in vol. II, p. 158, of his Quadrupeds: "Mr. Culbertson fired 11 times in
less than half a mile's run." That would make 22 shots to a mile. Mr. Denig told me
about the above-mentioned exploit without putting Mr. Culbertson higher; nevertheless
he was at Fort Union at that time, in 1848, and so must know about the instance to
which Audubon refers. Besides, the result in such cases depends also upon the swiftness
of the horse; it is possible to take more time for a half mile than for a whole mile.
Another fact to be considered in the reckoning is that time and distance are not arbitrarily
fixed here by clock and sundial.

[78] Since the introduction of modern breech-loading guns the word "rifle-patch" seems to
have fallen into disuse.—Translator's note.

the care required in loading them takes too much time unnecessarily when shooting at close range and, furthermore, they find rifle balls too small. The hunter chases buffaloes at full gallop, discharges his gun, and reloads without slackening speed. To accomplish this he holds the weapon close within the bend of his left arm and, taking the powder horn in his right hand, draws out with his teeth the stopper, which is fastened to the horn to prevent its being lost, shakes the requisite amount of powder into his left palm, and again closes the powder horn. Then he grasps the gun with his right hand, holding it in a vertical position, pours the powder down the barrel, and gives the gun a sidelong thrust with the left hand, in order to shake the powder well through the priming hole into the touchpan (hunters at this place discard percussion caps as not practical).

Now he takes a bullet from his mouth and with his left hand puts it into the barrel, where, having been moistened by spittle, it adheres to the powder. He dares never hold his weapon horizontal, that is, in position taken when firing, for fear that the ball may stick fast in its course, allowing sufficient air to intervene between powder and lead to cause an explosion and splinter the barrel. So long as the ball rolls freely down there is no danger. Hunters approach the buffaloes so closely that they do not take aim but, lifting the gun lightly with both hands, point in the direction of the animal's heart and fire. They are very often wounded on the face and hands by the bursting gun barrels, which, especially when the weather is extremely cold, are shattered as easily as glass.

The hunters aim always at the heart of the larger beasts of the chase, the surest and simplest method, since the heart is an inevitably vulnerable part. When hunting wolves, foxes, and beavers they aim at the head, so that they may not do damage to the small, costly skins by perforating them with bullets. Buffalo chasers must not only have the enduring qualities of swift riders but they must also be accustomed to the habits of the animals. A buffalo runner must be faultless in pressing close upon his quarry and at the same time be alert to spring aside if a buffalo tosses his head. Otherwise, if he be only a passable horseman, he will find himself immediately upon the ground and may count himself happy if he is not trodden underfoot.

The metifs cannot find words with which to praise highly enough the magnificence of a buffalo hunt, when from 500 to 600 horsemen attack, encircle, pursue, and slay an entire herd, even to the last cow and calf. On such occasions only the hunter who fires the shot that kills has any claim on the animal slain. Therefore each of them has some sign by which he designates his booty; either the arrows are marked, or a certain number of buckshot are mixed among the bullets, or else the hunters throw something from their wearing apparel upon the expiring beasts. As in any case not everyone in such a large number gets a shot—oftentimes many of them are not well mounted—the successful hunters have some portions of meat to spare. They always keep the hides for themselves. Among the Indians, on the other hand, the flesh of the animals is equally distributed.

This evening two old acquaintances from Fort Berthold arrived here: Le Nez d'Ours and l'Estomac de Corbeau, the proudest and most powerful soldiers of the village. They are on the way to the Absaroka; left their companions behind at the opposition fort. Three hundred Arikara, they say, died from cholera. That whole story about Dorson's being compelled to bring his cannons into action was an invention, related just for the purpose of having some story to tell and to get something to eat.

In reality the Arikara killed only one white person, an old man coming from the timber yard. The Herantsa lost 20 braves, among which number 6 Mandan are included. Women and children were not counted. There is no longer any sign of epidemic, so the Indians returned to the settlement at the last new moon. Mr. Kipp is reported to have provided 14 braves with clothes, i. e., clothes of European make. Which act denotes the measure of his fear. Bellangé, they said, arrived safe; boasted much of his excellent marksmanship.

Most of the Herantsa are well disposed toward me; merely a few customers of the opposition talk violently against me. Jeff Smith, they say, has egged them on to bad feeling, less from real dislike on his own part than from self-interest. This Jeff is said to have gone out beaver hunting with a German once and after great success with their traps he murdered the latter for the sake of stealing his horse and beaver skins. Smith is now bourgeois at the opposition fort. Le Nez d'Ours told me how he had come upon 30 Assiniboin from the Bande des Filles and every one at sight of him began to howl and scream because, owing to the present peace, many Assiniboin scalps remain unavenged.[79]

Four Herantsa were supplied with guns as an inducement not to show the captured scalps again. Their leader is Le Loup Court Queue, who once shared my room with me.

During this conversation several of the company spoke of rudeness and bungling on the part of Pierre Gareau. He repels all young men. He refuses to associate with any but the most prominent men; yet those same young fellows will later on be the most distinguished among their tribe. Bad speculation.

One of the aged women was calling her dog: "Kadosch! Kadosch!" As they entice the brutes usually with "Suk! suk!", I asked Mr.

---

[79] During the recent fray between the two nations a young Assiniboin, so Mr. Denig said afterwards, refused to enter the fight at all.

Denig whether Indians name their dogs. "Only as illustrated in this instance", he replied. "Kadosch means son-in-law." Yes; it is a fact; they treat dogs as members of the family. Many people, I dare say, have, unfortunately, chosen life partners no more faithful than a four-legged beast.

October 16. About 10 o'clock Mr. Denig sent me to find out from Joe Picotte when he expects to take up his winter quarters on the lower Bourbeuse. He and Joe have agreed not to be rivals in trade, inasmuch as such competition is of no profit to either of them, but only incurs greater expense in the matter of gifts and disturbs pleasant relations. On the way I met the Herantsa who had been left behind at Adobe Fort and were now, horse and foot, in search of their companions at our post.

I was first spied by a woman who was walking ahead. Instantly she cried out, "Ista uwatse! Ista uwatse!" ("Iron eyes"—spectacles). That was the name I was immediately given by those Indians, because spectacles on a person were to them such an amazing characteristic. Iowa called me "Ista mantugra", which has the same meaning as the above, but the Assiniboin designated me as "Ista topa" (Four Eyes).[80] I had to shake hands with them all; Le Loup Court Queue was friendly and wished to know how soon I would return to Fort Union. He would await me with Nez d'Ours. Under the impression that he would be able to see as well through my spectacles as with the telescope, he was eager to get possession of them. To convince him of his wrong idea I put them on his nose. With his keen eyes he was unable to see anything at all through the spectacles, of course, and became all the more wonderstruck. As this is the only pair I have with me, I could not surrender the inartistic but (for me, I am sorry to say) indispensable decoration. What would I not give for a pair of Indian eyes.

And yet it is much better, perhaps, that my eyesight incapacitates me for the chase; with my passion for horses and for wandering, my inclination toward romantic adventure, I might become an Indian myself, especially since the difficulties in the way of providing an adequate income in overpopulated, civilized States has deprived me of the desire to return. At the same time I cannot tarry here always for the purpose of fulfilling my plans. I have to go back whether I will or no. Is it really for the sake of my unalterable resolution to carry through my plans, to put my ideas into execution? Perhaps I shall never know. If I were sure of that I should be happy, no matter how great the storm and stress.

What sly dogs these Indians are. How well they know the way to put the fur-traders' teaching to their own use. Now, why did Le

---

[80] Remarkable that in so many languages "Ista" means "eyes."

Loup Court Queue,[81] a customer of our company, sleep all night at the opposition fort and allow himself to be entertained there? Joe Picotte says the Arikara destroyed Dorson's fort and, on the other hand, left his intact, because they prefer the opposition to the big company, particularly since the latter no longer grants favors or courtesies to any one. But the Arikara in this region plundered both posts alike. Why was that? No; these Indians simply wish to be accommodated with board and lodging at both trading posts.

One cannot rely on stories like that of Joe's, but I do not credit such lies to Nez d'Ours and l'Estomac de Corbeau,[82] braves with such pride as theirs would not stoop; besides, they conducted themselves as befits loyal customers, came directly here without allowing themselves to be seen at the opposition fort. L'Estomac de Corbeau was most affable toward me; he sat with me beside the open fire almost the whole of yesterday and today, smoked, talked now and then, watched me curiously when I was writing or painting. Their object in making this visit to the Crows, I understand, is to procure horses for themselves and to induce the latter to take maize from them, for they have such an abundant crop this year they are at a loss to know what shall be done with it.

Such laughter, such chattering and pranks I have never witnessed among Indians anywhere as these Herantsa carried on at Packinaud's sickbed. Packinaud lived 9 years among the Herantsa. He is, in fact, connected with many of them through his Herantsa wife, speaks their language well, and can outdo them in singing and howling. Perhaps the Indians are companionable with him for the reason that they have lived so much together—or is it that wanderers are more unrestrained, more crude, more unthinking, so to speak? Perhaps they were expressing their joy at seeing him again.

Packinaud came here for the first time on the *St. Ange* to be employed as either hunter or interpreter among the Crows.

Mr. Denig, thinking he would greatly please the Herantsa, told them how highly he respected their chief, Four Bears. His flattery did not commend him to their favor, however, for every soldier among them regards himself worthy of quite as much respect as a chief. Le Loup Court Queue replied that he, and "Raven Stomach" as well, bring far more robes for trade than the chief brings. The chiefs, they said, are old-fashioned personages, severe, taciturn, unable to see a joke, quick to lay low any young man who opposes them; hence they are not so well understood or loved as they might be. Whereupon Mr. Denig assured them that he knew well they were all gallant war-

[81] The Short-tailed Wolf.
[82] I. e., Raven's Stomach.

riors, but their chief was a man of more understanding, was less super-stitious, and had better judgment in conducting the affairs of a nation.

"Now I will see what they think of the portrait—vas?" he remarked aside to me.

They recognized Mr. Denig's picture immediately upon entering the office, strode up to it, and offered to shake hands. As they found no response whatsoever on the part of the image they were extraor-dinarily astonished. They placed their fingers on their lips in token of their amazement. No living person was standing there; the image was not reflected in a mirror; they found the solution of this mystery beyond them.

Natoh's picture they recognized instantly also, but could not com-prehend why one would pay such honor to a dog. As they had seen the parrot before on board the *St. Ange*, they did not find Polly such a curiosity as did the Cree. Polly came on the same boat with me from St. Louis. After they had inspected the white lady on the wall in the reception room, examining her from every side, even from heels to head, Mr. Denig asked them whether they believed that he or his dog must inevitably die on account of this. Without saying a word, they drew their blankets over their heads and went out of the room. Later on they expressed a desire to see my quarters also, but they found so many things there that they wanted and began to beg so, first for one thing and then another—my knife, tobacco, pipe, matches, comb, mirror, even the clothes on my back—I soon had enough of them. As I am no longer living among the Herantsa, I refused to give them anything; I shall bestow nothing else for the sake of their good will. If I were to give them presents they would think, most likely, that I was actuated by fear. L'Estomac de Corbeau was the only one who conducted himself differently; he seemed to scorn his noisy tribesmen and to prefer the quiet in my room.

Mr. Denig is constantly talking to me about the worthlessness and incapacity of engagees—not an interesting subject; though what he says is more or less true, such conversations are not agreeable. He complains about them so much that I used to think he felt it neces-sary to justify his severe treatment of the "hands" according to the saying: "The dog struck gives a yelp." I observe now that he wishes me to understand how I am to demean myself—what attitude he expects me to take as clerk. He knows how engagees find fault with him from one year's end to the other, have complained about him already in St. Louis so much that employees invariably say, "Only not to Fort Union," as though the place were a convict prison. Why is he in such bad repute? Merely for the reason that he makes them work; because he does not allow them to be idle the livelong day except when they are feeding. For their labor they are paid well and also promptly, receiving as a rule goods from the store to the amount of their wages before they have earned them. If they are allowed to fall deeply into debt, if credit is given them for their year's pay, they abscond and enter the employ of the opposition.[83]

They exert themselves only to escape work by subterfuges and to fill their stomachs. They are idle by nature, and this trait is intensified by dislike of their employer; they are lazy because they know there is nobody in this part of the world to take their place; they are boastful and insatiable. Mr. Denig expects the clerks to support him in every emergency, whether brought about by dangers from the outside or within the fort, to shoot down any person who attempts to lay hand on him, to take part in affairs with the workmen, never yield a point with them, treat them like dogs. Mackenzie told me how the engagees in the lumber yard fled at sight of him when he and the horse guard came near them on their return from the recent hunt. Although they were expecting him to bring them meat, they took for granted, upon seeing him and his pack horses in the distance, that they were looking at Indians, and having abandoned guns and axes, they ran to Morgan in extreme fear, crying "Indians! Indians!" Morgan recognized instantly the supposed redskins, called his gallant band together, and gave them a scolding. Mackenzie left them a full lading of meat, as much as one horse could carry, and they devoured it all in 2 days. He left, in other words, a load of meat weighing 250 pounds, which, divided among 6 men, makes 20 pounds per day for each laborer.[84]

Morgan, their foreman, does not dare wander about with his gun, but must give his attention exclusively to the men, for otherwise they will do no work.

October 17. Slept little last night. First, the Herantsa sang their war song. As I was getting to bed they began another chant in the interpreter's room and accompanied their singing with the drum. Of course, I could not fall asleep. After tossing from one side to the other for ever so long, I lost all patience, and, throwing my cloak about me, went to find out just what the hubbub was about. The room, dimly lighted by the open fire and one candle, was crowded with performers and onlookers made up of redskins, white people, and half-breeds. According to Indian custom, eight Herantsa and seven Assiniboin sat opposite one another on the floor, encircled about a pile of bows, quivers, knives, calico, etc., and were playing a game.

---

[83] Not less than 12 newly employed engagees of the big company went over to the opposition in the following May at St. Louis, after each of them had received, besides spending money, blankets and clothes charged to their accounts.

[84] If one deducts therefrom about 5 pounds for bones there remains still a goodly portion of meat. They are most extraordinary eaters.

Two Assiniboin were making motions in every direction with their fists, or rather with their closed hands, swiftly passing, in the meantime, a bullet-ball from one hand to the other, while the other members of their party sang "e, e, e, eh, e, e, e, ah", keeping time by beating a tattoo with sticks on washbasins and boiler tops. In an excited state of eager expectation, both singers and players swayed their bodies continually from the hips. One of the Herantsa who had laid the stake in opposition to the two Assiniboin had to guess where, i. e., in which of the two players' fists, the bullet was to be found.

When he felt sure that he knew he made a quick thrust with his left arm in the direction of the fist in which he supposed the ball to be, struck violently on his breast with his right hand, and, with a cry, designated the fist mentioned. If he failed to guess the right one, the winners whooped for joy and gathered in their stakes. Then they relayed, smoked reciprocally from the same pipe as a mark of continued friendship. Then other contestants began the same game over again. One of the Herantsa wished to make himself particularly conspicuous. He sat nearest the fireplace. He raked out all the ashes in front of him and concealed the bullet there, or rather he tried to make his opponents think that he did. He moved his fists among the ashes in imitation of a buffalo working his way through mud and mire or rolling over in the dust; he grumbled and bellowed the while like an angry bull, threw ashes all over himself and around him, pawed and groaned like one possessed. His mimicry was unequaled. Hunters are, as a rule, particularly clever in imitating the movements and sounds made by beasts of the chase. They certainly have opportunities enough to study them, and they make use of such in their dances and sports. After an Assiniboin had won almost every stake the Herantsa had put up they stopped the game.

After breakfast this morning the Herantsa took their leave. They were to be put across the river near the timber yard because that is the place where the boats are kept. Therefore, to prevent our valiant engagees from taking flight upon the approach of Indians, Mackenzie mounted his favorite runner, John, and rode on ahead to see that the boats were in readiness. While Mr. Denig was tarrying below the gate for Owen McKenzie's return he saw a large herd of antelopes bounding out of a wooded coulee and on to the prairie. He called me at once from my room. There were forty of them, at least, sweeping along one behind the other, and a horseman was close behind them. We took the rider to be an Indian. But when we saw him in a mad gallop constantly gaining on the cabris we doubted whether any Indian's horse would be able to overtake those swiftest of all wild beasts on the prairie. Indians' runners are too insufficiently nourished; therefore they lack brawn, endurance, and wind. With the aid of my telescope I recognized Mackenzie just as he was turning his course from pursuit of the herd, which had escaped in hollows and dells among the hills. As he turned his horse's head in our direction my heart leaped to see John so full of fire and energy. Mackenzie could hardly restrain him. He had to make him gallop sidewise, which he succeeded in doing with the utmost grace and skill.

Owen is the one and only horseman whom I have seen ride sidewise on this continent. My mustang, Fashion, learned that gait quite easily. How proudly, how lightly and gracefully she threw her little feet. All Americans ride, but how? More often than otherwise they hold on by the pommel of their saddles. If Owen had had his gun, several antelopes would have fallen victim to his skill. He is now provided with half of his supply of goods for his winter quarters on the lower Bourbeuse. While assisting in getting his wares together I was led to reflect how much more simple a matter it is for the bourgeois to say, "Bring that keg of bullets from the powder magazine at the rear of the warehouse", a distance of at least a hundred paces, than it is for me to do it. To carry 300 pounds in one's arms is no simple matter.

After sunset three fat hinds came out of a nearby thicket and took a walk on the prairie. I watched them a long while, and with much interest.

October 18. According to La Bombarde, Indian words in most common use here are all from the Chippewa speech or from the related Cree language: Moccasin, shoe; ihqua, wife; musqua, my wife; wigwam, tent; apischimo, saddle blanket; mikawne, bivouac of a hunting party; papuchs, child; mitass, leggings; wuasch, sink hole; sumite, pemmican.

This morning four Cree came galloping to the fort from the hollow below our garden to announce the approach of a band and to get tobacco with which to welcome the newcomers. They said that while they were concealed behind shrubbery in the sunken stream bed they noticed three strange Indians whom they took to be enemies. As soon as they received the tobacco the four Cree hastened to greet their friends and conduct them to the fort. Joe Picotte, who had already sent out to them 45 plugs of tobacco and 6 pounds of vermillion to entice these customers from us, won only two to his side. It is really to the Indians' interest to deal with the opposition, because, but for that post they would have to pay twice as much for the goods they buy. The two disloyal Cree, however, did not fare so well, for the reason that they did not have as much cured meat for barter as Joe's gift was worth. Joe gave them a piece of his mind when, after having received all of his tobacco and vermillion, which, of course, was a high price to pay for the small amount of meat they brought, the two families desired, in addition, to be fed and lodged at his post.

The two leaders of this band of Cree, Rassade au Cou [85] and Bras Casse,[86] now told how they had driven those three suspected Indians from their hiding place and had spoken to them, but did not understand their dialect.

They were on foot and had ropes bound about their bodies; hence were horse thieves. But, since all Indians have the same sign language, they are always able to make themselves understood, no matter who they may be or whence they come; therefore Mr. Denig supposed them to be Cree from some other band whom these chiefs would not betray.

Morgan came down the river this evening with his two rafts and the flatboat.

October 19. This morning Le Tout Piqué [87] brought in another crowd of Cree, including women and children. Some time ago I painted a flat pipestem white and sky blue in alternating fields, and in the four white fields I painted, respectively, a buffalo, a wolf, an owl, and a bear. This pipe I presented to Piqué. The smoking of this pipe for the first time was to be celebrated with great ceremony in the office; i. e., an address on the part of Le Tout Piqué and the smoking of the pipe on the part of all braves in company with the bourgeois. Mr. Denig had the kindness to invite me to be present.[88]

I found Battiste sitting in the middle of the room as interpreter; on the floor beside him lay a beautiful buffalo robe. Against the walls braves of both bands were squatting in close rows. Rassade au Cou, Bras Casse, and one other were seated on a sofa. In front of them and directly opposite Mr. Denig stood Le Tout Piqué. When I entered and modestly took my seat in a corner Piqué asked Mr. Denig, through the interpreter, who I was.

"A trader from below", replied the bourgeois. I had to sit behind Mr. Denig. A common engagee is no part of a soldier and not worthy of notice. With much dignity of port Piqué now came forward, put the handsome buffalo robe about Mr. Denig's shoulders, and, holding the new peace pipe in his right hand, offered us his left in greeting. Then, grasping his robe with his right hand, he took two steps backward and began his speech. He had been brought up, he said, a patron of this fort, was a loyal adherent, never brought even one skin to the opposition. He had left 50 tents of his band at home; they were awaiting news of his reception here; i. e., they wished to know whether he were treated well. The chief delivered his address in

---

[85] Bead for the Neck.

[86] Broken or Crushed Arm.

[87] Fully tattooed.

[88] In return, Mr. Denig was permitted to pass himself off as painter of the pipestem. He entreated me not to laugh when I witnessed a scene which to me would seem no doubt perfectly nonsensical. But it was only his own air of official gravity, when clothed in the buffalo robe, that I could have found ridiculous.

sections and at the end of each Battiste interpreted what had been said. Battiste did not use English, but only French, which he spoke not by any means well, repeating his words continually and making altogether a bungling effort that was out of keeping with so solemn a ceremonial.

In his reply Mr. Denig promised friendship and fair prices; whereupon a distinguished brave lighted the pipe and gravely extended it toward the bourgeois. Each of us took several whiffs with becoming seriousness, and then the soldier proffered it to his chief, who had remained standing erect and dignified in the same place where he had stood while addressing the assemblage. He took the peace pipe in his hands, held it aloft, and then lowered it, pointing with the tip of the stem toward the earth, toward sunrise and sunset, smoked himself, and returned the pipe to the master of ceremonies. Luckily the interpreter was the last of us three to smoke, for, being acquainted already with their manner of conducting this ceremony, he drew so vigorously as to rekindle the tobacco; otherwise, while Piqué was propitiating the heavens (good spirits), earth, and sun, the pipe might have gone out, and that would have been regarded as a bad omen. The pipe bearer next invited the assembled braves to smoke, each according to his rank, a ticklish business. Then the guests were served baked meats and sweetened coffee, which they were invited to distribute themselves, so that no one might think he was slighted or neglected by a white man.

Every time a band of Indians annoys Mr. Denig with their begging he flees to me and unburdens his heart by calling them names. At such times he bestows much praise on other Indians who are not here but who get their share of abuse also at some future time. He is always in the best humor with Indians when none are around. He longs for them in matters of trade; he then prefers them to all other people, his own countrymen not excepted. Today the red men who were at the fort stood high in his esteem, but since they have shown that his many courtesies only encouraged them to beg, to expect presents, he thinks them good for nothing, not worthy to unloose the shoe latches of Indians who inhabit the eastern domain. They would rather see enemies of their own race go to ruin than to combine with them against the whites. They are more given to superstition than Indians in the East, he declares, less intelligent, not so brave, and, so far as he knows, they have nowhere a regularly constituted leader, etc. But one must consider that tribes of the eastern domain had their wits sharpened through many years of warfare; they received their instruction by constant intercourse with white people of various nations; they became more wise by contemplation of unending losses. How often have hostile tribes of redskins in the East combined

against the common foe, and for how long a time? One may consider, also, the small number of distinguished leaders and counsellors
among them within a hundred years; and, in proportion to their
superior knowledge, the white race has produced even fewer.

Mr. Denig assured me I should count myself happy that, owing to
my nearsightedness, I was prevented from entering fully upon the
Indian mode of life. Unless a white man were rich he became the
sport of savages when he went about naked and wore long hair reaching to his shoulders, as was the practice with some men at Fort Alexander on the Yellowstone. Indians esteem a white person only when
he gives evidence of talents that they do not themselves possess. They
would never respect any white man more highly than themselves as
hunter or soldier. So far as he is concerned, he would never desire to
adopt the life of an Indian unless, by large means, he could establish
important connections through many marriages and win their venera-
tion with the aid of chemistry, medicine, or by the art of jugglery.
What he affirms in this regard has been proved in the case of Neldrum,
bourgeois at that trading post among the Crows, Fort Alexander.
Though Neldrum is a soldier of note, his scalps and his trophies from
the hunt have not won him influence among the Absaroka; he is
esteemed for his prodigal liberality, on account of which he has fallen
into debt instead of accumulating money. He is said to be an efficient
gunsmith, but not an especially shrewd business man. If, through
ambition or vanity, he aspires to take the lead in establishing a widely
extended family connection, certain Crows of consequence become
immediately jealous and go to the opposition or come here to barter
their buffalo robes.

October 22. As Morgan has been sent with a complete assortment
of goods to Vice de Carafel's winter quarters I am going to have at
least 2 days' peace. He is rarely at the fort; so he has no regular bed,
but takes up quarters always in my room. I admit he is a most civil,
well-educated Scot, but he is incessantly on the move, constantly opening and shutting the door, his three dogs following behind. Anyone
who supposes he can concentrate his attention on writing or drawing
under such circumstances, I say only, just let him try it. Last Monday I found on the river bank a pair of fat Virginia deer. Upon the
occasion of our first snowfall at this place, yesterday, I had to carry
a letter to Fort William in the face of a biting west wind.

After our midday meal I helped to bury two papooses that were
brought here by some Assiniboin. An old mourner made a speech at
the grave expressing gratitude, which is said to have shown him to be
a man of much intelligence. In the evening the two hunters, Smith
and Cadotte, arrived, bringing some horses taken from the Blackfeet.
Their Indian women have longed for their return. On the way,

expecting no thievery on the part of Assiniboin, our supposed friends, they did not guard the drove, and in consequence were robbed of ten horses, including some of their most excellent runners.

They brought news, also, of seven Assiniboin who, 3 months ago, were out on the war path against the Blackfeet Tribe to win renown for themselves, and were all killed, as was to be expected. At the same time they had already taken eight scalps from the Blackfeet and had wounded some 20 more of the enemy in the neighborhood of a village. Then one of the chiefs called his people together and rebuked them for their disgrace in permitting such a small hostile force to approach near enough to do so much mischief. At the head of 200 horsemen he overcame the concealed Assiniboin and destroyed them all.

Today Nai, with his wife and crew of assistants, set out for his winter quarters on the lower Bourbeuse, traveling in a keel boat loaded with commodities. They made an attractive picture: Nai was standing at the helm, his young wife was sitting on the covered bales of goods in front of him, holding his gun, three men were at the oars, an old woman was leaning against the bales. On shore two beautiful Assiniboin girls were harnessing a black wolfhound to a travois. Other girls were picking berries among the autumn shrubs.

In so far as natural scenes arouse in us poetic ideas and emotions (that is, by analogy the actual landscape before us suggests thoughts of the inner life and inspires us to serious contemplation and to lofty feeling), they are subjects worthy the contemplation of an imaginative artist. Even this passive, dead scene, so to speak, can, under certain circumstances, make a poetic appeal. Sun, moon, rocks, streams, trees, woods, plain, clouds, springs, storm, mists, night, etc., all have their especial characteristics bearing, in many ways, close relations to our own and therefore serve, respectively, the artist's purpose.

Cadotte, who arrived yesterday from the Blackfeet territory, is regarded as the best stag hunter in this region.[90] He is a genuine "Mountaineer", possessing to a marked degree both their good and their less favorable qualities. He is unrivaled in the skill of starting, pursuing, approaching, shooting, and carving a deer. In other respects he is heedless, wasteful, and foolhardy—half Canadian, half Cree.

Dauphen, another of the same sort, lives an isolated life on the prairie with his two wives. He left the opposition in debt, and now hunts on his own account. Assiniboin look with disfavor on such

---

[90] As they express themselves here, "even beats Packinaud shucks."

independent characters who are without friends and have no business connections anywhere. If he by chance once spoils a hunt which they have arranged he can jolly well count on a good drubbing and the loss of all that he owns.

But for the relatives of his wives he would have been driven away long ago. Although he was formerly a trapper and followed the related business of trader, he can no longer find employment with either of the companies, on account of his questionable character; he has defrauded both of them.

Once, when Mr. Denig was journeying across the prairie with the drinker, Dorion, who was serving him as interpreter, they wandered into a company of hot-brained Sioux. Dorion owned a strong-limbed, bad-tempered pack horse that was being urged on with the entire gang. This animal gave an Indian boy such a kick on his forehead that for quite a while he was thought to be dead. Dorion, of Iowa blood himself, knew at once what he had to do to get himself out of the pickle. He was aware of the fact that Indians do not excuse such accidents any more than they pardon the unintentional killing of a relative. He seized the nag's halter, with no more ado, and gave the beast to the boy's father. Dorion was not to blame for the misadventure, but he was certain that in the event of intense suffering or of the death of that boy, the father would, first of all, slay the horse, and it depended upon circumstances whether he would not exercise his vengefulness upon the animal's owner as well. In order to forestall any such unpleasantness, he presented also his own riding horse, which appeased the father and saved himself from consequences of present or future wrath. A white man would have raised a quarrel, in the event the father sought revenge, or else he would have killed the Indian; but Dorion conformed to the custom of the people among whom he lived.

I was making inquiry concerning that story Charles Martin told me when I met him at Council Bluffs with his Mackinaw boats, about his friend Lambert's having pursued an American from Missouri all the way to Fort Hall in Oregon for the purpose of killing him, because the latter ran away with "his old woman." Mr. Denig holds a totally different opinion concerning that so-called heroic deed. Not that he calls into question the daring of the man, but declares that in doing what he did he turned his ability as soldier, hunter, or, in other words, as Indian, to wrong use. No Indian brave dares take his wife's elopement to heart; at least he dares not manifest his feeling by any outward act; he would be made a laughingstock if he took one step toward bringing her back. Accordingly, if a white man adopts the Indian life and customs he is to take for his models braves of prominence, not young bucks. Mr. Denig maintains, furthermore, that even from the standpoint of a white man, Lambert acted unwisely; for, notwithstanding the fact that his having brought back his run-away wife and having got the better of her abductor bespeaks, in a way, courage, perseverance, and shrewdness on his part, his act did not bring back happiness to either of them.

So the bourgeois thinks it much better for a man to treat the matter lightly when an unfaithful wife runs off and buy himself another at once. Lambert's chase all alone to Oregon was a daring exploit, but what did he gain by going in pursuit of an erring wife, only in the end to take her life? For, as the story goes, after having followed his "blonde", whom he very truly loved, across a wide tract of wild country, through the domain of several hostile Indian tribes, Lambert came at last upon the fugitives at Fort Hall. His wife tried to offer excuses and by flattery to appease him. Meanwhile, she enticed him out on the prairie, where his enemy, the American, came to meet him. By the advice of her lover, the woman removed the bullet from Lambert's gun, but he discovered that treachery, fortunately, before it was too late. Having replaced the ball, he shot his enemy down, to the great amazement and grief of his "blonde." But he brought her down, also, in his rage over her deceit. He took his vengeance—a two-fold vengeance.

Mr. Denig confirms the report, also, that Indian mothers now and then forcibly bring about miscarriages, either by taking a strong drink or by means of the stick with which they grub for pommes blanches.[91] This stick which is pointed at one end and provided with a knob at the other, upon which the weight of the body can be thrown in such a way as to drive the point under the roots with little exertion, they use for killing their infants by pressing the pointed end below the heart at time of delivery or else by pressing the lower part of the body violently upon the knob.

Not infrequently they throw their newborn babes into the river and drown them. Why do they commit these crimes? They have, then, no love for their children? On the contrary, their maternal affection is strong except when, on account of a child, they lose the love of their "hubbies." A pregnant wife is repugnant to an Indian; he turns to another. That vexes the loving wife in her turn, for her husband constantly ignores her on account of her being with child. She tries to shorten the period of pregnancy in order to be again loved. What we call children born out of wedlock had often such a fate as I have described; they are proof of the mother's loss of virtue in an earlier love affair. Such mothers, having been deserted, in their bitterness of heart put their little daughters to death, feeling that they are better out of the world than exposed to the harsh experi-

[91] Prairie turnip, the teep-se-nah of the Assiniboin.

ences of this life. Owing to this same repugnance on the part of their husbands, mothers suckle their children until the fourth or fifth year; it always impressed me as so droll to see boys with bows and arrows in their hands nursing like babes at their mother's breasts.

Tomorrow we begin our domestic plan for only two meals a day: late breakfast, early supper. Days are so short that meals come too near together. Makes the cook surly, Mr. Denig told me, as if he felt obliged to offer some excuse. As if his evident purpose were not to have us eat less. "In cold winter weather one's appetite is keener", I replied.

October 23. Mr. Denig gave me a buffalo horn that some time ago had been polished by Owen Mackenzie for a powder horn. It is very large and lustrous black. Cow horns are too small; those of fully matured bulls are broken into splinters by their fighting. Morgan is back again. While he was away I had to do his work both as clerk and foreman. Packinaud is still confined to his bed; he cannot stand on his broken shank. I have to look after him. So, for 2 days, having been the only clerk besides, I have had a great deal of work to do. But I would rather make myself useful than be a "bore."

October 24. We buried another Assiniboin papoose. Afterwards, when Mr. Denig wished to smoke with the mourning relatives, he could find nowhere any of the small leaves that Indians in this region mix with the commonly known American tobacco. He sent me to a nearby copse to cut some twigs of the upland willow, so that he might show me what sort of tobacco (mixture) is used by the Sioux. I hurried out and, with my scalp knife, cut off just above the root an armful of young shrubs about the size of a man's finger. I brought them back and we first removed carefully with a knife the outer red bark and threw it away; then we beat off the bast, dried it at the fire, cut it up fine, and mixed it with American tobacco. This willow bast fiber is said not to dry out so well as that earlier used, nor is the smell of it so aromatic. At midday Morgan and I were treated with a splendid cold breakfast or lunch. Mr. Denig served crackers and butter, pickles, sardines, cheese, and excellent hardtack—real luxuries in this part of the world. Then we cut another load of ozier shrubs, brought them in, stripped off the bast, and dried it. As smoking in Indian ceremonies is a strict requirement according to Indian etiquette this mixture must be just as scrupulously provided for as food. Morgan occupied Carafel's bed; so, whenever he and his dogs met Mr. Denig and his doggie there was war in my room. Hoka is particularly jealous and vicious. Mr. Denig had to admonish Packinaud again this evening to wash his wounded leg himself in order to make our work less disagreeable. For 21 days, mornings and evenings, I have washed and salved his wound, a service that he or his stupid wife might just as easily perform. He seems never to have once thought of keeping the wound clean, though we have often told him the flesh was as black as a negro's.

October 25. With the remains of a lap dog we entrapped our first wolf. In laying the snare they dig a hole 3 inches deep so that the trap lies even with the ground, and then they cover it with earth, grass, buffalo chips, etc.

A wolf or a fox, attracted by carrion, steps unawares upon the springs and his leg is caught. To prevent his running off with the trap the latter is fastened by means of an attached chain to a heavy log or trunk of a tree. For fear of unnecessarily piercing his pelt, an animal caught thus is never shot, but killed by a blow on the head with a bludgeon.

I spent almost the entire evening discussing religion with Mr. Denig. Though both of us are Protestant, we are agreed that the Catholic religion is better suited to the civilizing of barbarous people than our own Protestant faith. We know that uneducated tribes with their limited understanding find it impossible to grasp purely abstract teaching and, therefore, such appeals make no impression upon them whatsoever. Savages must, first of all, be inspired with awe by means of visible, mystic symbols, and influenced through their feelings. Nor can they be expected to have a grasp of the by no means inconsiderable knowledge of history and geography that is necessary for even a slight understanding of our religion. I was here interrupted by Morgan, who wished me to accompany him to his traps. We found, this time, a gray fox that I struck dead and brought home to paint for Morgan. These animals are full of fleas. Earlier, there lived here for a time a Jesuit, Père Point, who tried to inculcate strict morality. They let him preach without any opposition until he began to reproach Mr. Denig with a plurality of wives.

The bourgeois replied that his older wife was sickly, but he still kept her for their daughter's sake and for the reason that she had always conducted herself well; he was not one of those who think that man was given strong passions by Nature merely to be continually tormented, merely to crucify the flesh without ceasing, because, owing to circumstances, he might not have a wife or, if the first wife was incapacitated, he might not get a second helpmate. A man in his situation would have in the States sufficient grounds for divorce, but he refused to cast off a good woman who was not to blame for her condition. "You join together Indian women and dissolute men with your holy rites, not a word of which the women understand

and just as little the men regard. Since they do not know what they promise in the ceremony, they make false vows from which you are again quite ready to release them upon presentation of a gift. Are not such things done in the name of religion? Do you not thereby give licentiousness the semblance of your sanction?"

When we went again to look after our traps we found that the carcass had been dragged quite a distance away by wolves. Our Spanish horse guard told us in his Spanish-French-English jargon: "Jamme wolf dragge de carcasse way from de trappe. No seen una pareilla chose. Ni now putte horse's snoute on de pickette, de wolf no more carry awaye."

Night scenes here are decidedly picturesque. Armed with guns and hunting knives and provided with lanterns, we moved across the dusky prairie that seems to have neither beginning nor end but to melt into the wide heaven from which it can be distinguished only by scattered stars. About us are the captured animals struggling and gnashing their teeth, the dead just removed from the traps. The concentrated glow of lanterns, while the traps are being set once more, the hunters' original attire, the dark background, all combine to form a picture at once suggestive of animated life and awe.

October 26. At daybreak we found two gray foxes in the traps. Painted a picture of one of them. In the study of hairy beasts water colors are of little advantage, pointed brushes of still less. For reproducing the curl of hair, broad oil brushes are best. By adroit manipulation of the latter the effect is achieved, whereas with pointed brushes one has to draw hair for hair.

As evening came on I was reading Alison's Essays when Mr. Denig entered, much surprised that I was not on the river bank. Herantsa were there to be put across. Morgan had already left some time ago to fetch them. Three Assiniboin, together with the berdache (hermaphrodites are frequent), on their way to visit the Crows, were slain by Blackfeet.

"And you sitting so quietly here by the fire, while all the rest of us are in spasms of curiosity. Man, you are not keeping up with the times!"

Out I went, taking my telescope with me, but I was unable to recognize any Herantsa. There were too many women.

There were also white people, who kept their horses separate from the others. An Assiniboin woman came down to the sandy shore crying aloud, and struck the ground three times with her buffalo robe as a sign that she had lost three of her people. The other Indians were no less distinguished visitors than the noted chief of the Absaroka and his most celebrated braves. That is, this chief, Rottentail, is their leader on this side of the mountains; on the other side,

Big Robert is chief. As Packinaud speaks the Herantsa language, a dialect, fluently and has the distinction, therefore, of being our one and only interpreter for Absaroka, these great celebrities had to be conducted to his room. Rottentail's resemblance to Louis Philippe of blessed memory struck me at once: the same capable expression of citoyen, the same shrewd look of merchant, the same official mien. I was sorry that he did not wear the Indian style of dress rather than the American. His suit of clothes was fashioned from a blue blanket. He wore gray leggings but no shirt, no vest, neither neckcloth nor hat.

As soon as the Crow women had brought in their heavy bundles and everything was in order Rottentail produced a superb military head-dress, which he put on the bourgeois' head, and hung a handsome buffalo robe on his shoulders. Denig looked comical enough, but no one dared laugh. The pipe was lighted and offered by Packinaud to the chief; then each smoked in his turn.

Rottentail began to relate how the Herantsa endeavored to deter them from coming here, saying that we were afflicted with dangerous diseases: the lives of himself and his followers would be snuffed out. However, his heart was strong and his friendship for Mr. Denig not to be shaken. The Herantsa, conscious of their double dealing, took another route in their return home (but the scoundrels had been well treated). While Rottentail was speaking the name Ista uwatse did not escape me, neither did his obvious reference to myself. Packinaud does not interpret word for word, but only what seems to him worth while. Mr. Denig asked that his thanks be conveyed for assurances of friendship and good faith on the part of the chief, and said he should soon be convinced that nobody at Fort Union was sick. While the Absaroka were being served meats, crackers, and sweetened tea in the office I dressed the wound on Packinaud's leg. I asked him, meanwhile, what had been said about me. Nothing. But I was too well acquainted with the Indian sign language to believe that nothing had been said concerning me. I saw Rottentail indicate me two different times with his finger, then make the sign for writing or drawing, then, of becoming ill and dying. Moreover, when I went with the horse guard to examine the traps he said to me: "Crows tell me Gros Ventres say you bringue de cholera up, and make all you painte die—heape die!" So that was it—lies and false reports.

October 27. Caught a wolf. Brought him in to serve as model for a study. There are wolves here of great size and also prairie wolves, which are much smaller; the latter appear to be half fox. Of the large species there are many different colors, varying according to age and season of the year: black, brown, yellow, gray mixed, snow white. To set more than two traps with one carcass is useless, for noise made by the captured animals drives others away. And when the dog used for baiting the trap is consumed one has to strew small pieces of meat over the concealed trap and all round about in order to ensnare the animals.

Bearshead, the chief in command of the soldiers, is a warrior of great ability and power. He gave Packinaud a long account of their journeyings and dangers, their experiences on the chase, their battles and the hunger they endured, since last winter. Every time they are obliged to take the far journey over barren plains and wild mountain ranges to purchase horses from the Flatheads they suffer terribly from hunger. As Bearshead spoke just as distinctly by means of signs as by words, I understood everything; he took much pleasure in seeing me so attentive. The portraits pleased him, also, I feel sure, but upon looking at them he shook his head. When these braves heard the parrot coughing one of them said at once that Polly had the same disease from which they themselves suffered last winter, and they might catch influenza again.

Because Rottentail was given a piece of painted cloth by Mr. Denig last winter, very large and diaphanous, the latter was blamed for causing that epidemic just as I am censured now. Yet Rottentail related with evident pleasure how he had made use of the picture to cover his pillow on which he always laid his head when he went to sleep and invariably beheld Mr. Denig in his dream. The goodly number of scalps (32) which he and his braves took from the Blackfeet he ascribes to that painting. Lucky for Mr. Denig, otherwise he would not only have forfeited their esteem but would have lost their patronage and brought injury to himself besides. Bearshead wished very much to possess the banner with the painted eagle.

The six white men from Fort Alexander did not come over the river in our boats, because they are deserters from this fort. They belong now to the opposition; Joe Picotte sent them over in long boats made of buffalo hides.

We received news from Bruyere, a trader in these parts; he brought some commodities in a keel boat to Fort Alexander, where he must wait at Nedrum's for Mr. Culbertson. In the afternoon the famous Absaroka amazon arrived. Mr. Denig called me to his office that I might have an opportunity to see her. She looked neither savage nor warlike. On the contrary, as I entered the room, she sat with her hands in, her lap, folded, as when one prays. She is about 45 years old; appears modest in manner and good natured rather than quick to quarrel.

She gave Mr. Denig a genuine Blackfeet scalp which she had captured herself. How amazed as well as overjoyed was I when

Mr. Denig afterwards presented the long black scalp to me! A scalp is an Indian curio of rare worth, for the reason that a brave so very seldom parts with those trophies. My former father-in-law, Kirutsche, brought me once, after long pleadings and promises, a piece of leather on which was found some short black hair and would have me believe it was a piece of skin from a human head. I took it to be a piece of black bear's hide. Our human scalp is very thick, to be sure, and difficult to distinguish from an animal's skin, but the short, thick hair is not.

Relatives of the three Assinboin who were slain have planted a pole and fastened thereon two leather pouches that belonged to the dead. There for a long time they wailed and made blood-offerings by cutting their arms, cheeks, heads, and legs until blood flowed. One of the dead men is that Assiniboin who won the high stakes from a Herantsa; he was a son of the Assiniboin chief L'Ours Fou (Mad Bear); the other was called L'Homme de Nord, the same who was relieved some time ago from eye trouble by Mr. Denig and re-paid him by most annoying barefaced begging afterwards; the third was Good Tobacco, a woman. She was taken by surprise while asleep in her tent. The boy, son of L'Ours Fou, was attacked first. He received eight wounds at the first onset and his hips were broken, but he did not die until several days later, in the Crow village; he was not scalped.

Some lads who were not in the tent, but had gone most likely with the berdache [91a] to the Crows' settlement, saved their skins, of course. Absaroka in the vicinity heard the firing, mounted their horses at once, and put the Blackfeet to flight. They followed a long distance in pursuit, and when they came in sight of the enemy at last, found them entrenched on a hill, having concealed themselves in a hole they had dug. The Crows did not risk smoking them out of their improvised redoubt. During the night the Blackfeet were able to get away.

October 28. Absaroka are continually here; notwithstanding their assurances of loyalty they go from one fort to the other, and allow themselves to be lodged, fed, and presented with gifts; they seek the place where they can trade to their best advantage, for they are ex-ceedingly shrewd in business matters—a match for our traders. When Rottentail returned from the opposition he said Joe Picotte himself—not Bonaparte, his Crow interpreter, but the person in con-trol of the fort—assured him repeatedly that I with my drawing and painting spread the deadly infections, diseases; that I was to blame for death among the Herantsa, who drove me away from their settlement; that if he, Rottentail, and his braves should tarry long

---

[91a] That is, hermaphrodite.

in our neighborhood they would be blown to the moon. If that is not carrying trade rivalry to the limit I am no judge of such matters. The miserable wretch would put my life at stake for the sake of a few buffalo robes!

What would one naturally expect of such a liar but that he would sacrifice everything to his own selfish interest. I did not know why he should have anything against me—or was it for that reason he cheated me in St. Joseph? Envy of the big company is not his motive; furthermore, he had the commodities for these Crows sent to Fort Alexander. Now that they are coming here, he has not a sufficient stock of goods to furnish a continual supply to Assiniboin, Crows, and Cree. So Joe would like to have the Absaroka go home, and I am to be used as scarecrow to frighten them away. Crows have no such idea that I shall bring death upon them with my painting, but they might probably think I could do so by other means. Their minds have been too diligently worked upon by our competitors and they are too much dominated by superstition not to be affected in the end by such influences. All this is especially annoying to me, because I shall be the occasion, sooner or later, of injury to this company, to whom, up to the present, I am indebted for much kindness. If it comes to that, I may not remain here, unless I give up my art, and that I will not do. Now that I am so near the accomplishment of my aim, as far as my studies are concerned, I will not renounce the realization of my dreams!

Though the Crows do not know from experience, as do Arikara, the Mandan, and Herantsa, about the devastating epidemics, yet they have heard about them.

The coming of the first artist was coincident with the breaking out of smallpox; though the plague of cholera was without any such coincidence, how can one get these Indians to believe that? This is the third time things have so happened. Is not that sufficient proof for superstitious people? And each time it was either a portrait painter or a landscape painter that brought the deadly disease; the painter of animals (Audubon) did not oppress them with pestilence.

What did Crows say last winter when influenza was so dangerously prevalent among them? That Mr. Denig had avenged the theft of 10 horses by inflicting aching chests, bursting heads, and swift death. They were confirmed in that fear by the fact that already 150 were dead, counting among them some of their most prominent tribesmen, while in the nearby Assiniboin camp there was not a sick person to be found. The Assiniboin were laughing about it. The Crows swore revenge; came here and defied Mr. Denig to his face. He was troubled in mind, but fearless in manner, though he regarded himself, really, a lost man. To prevent further spread of the disease, however, the Indians brought back nine of the stolen horses. Then Mr. Denig delivered a forcible speech in which he assured them he was too good a friend to inflict upon them such a revenge for the loss of a few horses. Nay, more, he was here for the purpose of bartering for buffalo robes. If he should cause so many Crows to die, would that help him to get robes?

But there was one Crow too wrathful, too much enraged by the loss of his best beloved relatives to be appeased. Mr. Denig saw at once what the man had in mind, so he walked up to him, looked him sternly but calmly in the face and shouted: "Shoot, if you dare!" The Indian fired his gun in the air.

A redskin thinks twice before he murders his trader; he is aware of his dependence on the fur traders and of reciprocal interests that unite them. But upon the death of their friends the tribes get beside themselves sometimes, and if such bereavements follow swiftly one upon the other they excite themselves further by wailings and complaints. An Assiniboin brought news today that the mother of L'Ours Fou's boy had hanged herself with a rope because while at the burial of her grandchild she heard of the death of her son, the father of the little corpse lying before her. The shock proved too great for the poor woman! Besides, she felt uneasy about her husband, the chief, who was in constant insecurity among the palefaces at Fort Laramie.

October 29. Absaroka withdrew as soon as they saw there was nothing more to be had by begging. Summer and autumn are the dullest seasons in trade hereabouts. Hides are not yet available; therefore Indians have no medium of exchange. They must make preparations then for the winter hunting, yet have no equipment and seldom have credit. They keep, to be sure, a supply of cured meat, but that brings in only less important things, such as knives, beads, calico, powder and lead, not guns, blankets, or horses.

They beg. They promise patronage. The trader must assist them in turn, else business at his trading post will be dull. He must attract customers; if he does not, the opposition will, and, as a result, Indians will not come near him. They do not look upon the trader as indispensable except for articles that they regard as luxuries and that they come to the posts to get more frequently than for provisions and clothing. Oftentimes a trader feels compelled to lend an Indian a gun during the hunting season, though he knows that he is virtually making a present—entailing a loss. If he presses the redskin for payment, the latter transfers his patronage to the opposition. Ah, it is the opposition that keeps the Indian on his feet. But for competition, he is bound to one trader, enchained, so to speak, to one man's prices. Yet there is proof here, also, that too liberal credit makes no friends.

For some time past I have been thinking that my diary will be suf-ficiently interesting to publish some day in connection with my draw-ings. At first I wrote down ideas, accounts of my own experiences, and some historical facts for myself alone, more as an aid to my recol-lection than for any other reason. As my notes at the present time, however, contribute much that will give closer acquaintance with the fur trade, the life of the "Mountaineers" and Indians as it is no longer found anywhere, the publication of my journal can do no harm.

If I include matters that other authors have already mentioned then my observations serve as affirmation; if I take another view or if what I relate does not agree with what has been published already, then my account can serve as rectification, for I report from my own contemplation of things as impartially as I can or with statements from authorized sources concerning the matter under discussion. But this idea of publishing my journal with sketches and drawings is not to be prejudicial to the gallery I have planned, but rather to serve as descriptive matter relating thereto. A gallery has its ad-vantages and disadvantages over an illustrated work. In the first place, as I work with more facility in oil than in water colors I can execute paintings of larger size for my gallery, while I shall be able to represent my ideas, feelings, and intimate knowledge in my pub-lished journal. To be enabled to paint so many pictures in peace and quiet, however, requires more considerable means than I can ac-quire. It will be extremely difficult to find a purchaser, during my lifetime, for the entire collection. Living artists are permitted to live in want, to starve, to die in misery; after they are dead, their paintings bring, often, preposterous prices. Why is this so? Because the wealthy people who buy works of art have no taste themselves nor independent judgment in such matters, but make the purchase from vanity or vainglory rather than for art's sake.

That is the rich man's way of making himself known, but when he pays a price beyond all reason for the works of an artist long since dead he benefits neither the artist nor his heirs, but speculators. He hopes to win thereby a reputation as dilettante or even, perhaps, as connoisseur. If such men were really connoisseurs, true patrons of art (whether in sculpture or painting), they might easily find living artists who would be capable of painting just as fine pictures for a hundredth part of those unreasonable prices.

A gallery of paintings or a book of prints, that is the question. If the latter, then I must have a publisher, pay down money just the same as for the gallery. Still it is an easier task to find a pub-lisher, a speculator, than a wealthy dilettante. The limits to which I confine myself are so narrow that the more material I accumulate for my paintings the more difficult will be the sale of them. But that disadvantage amounts to little. Time brings good counsel: gallery, works of art, journal, are all but means to the attainment of my chief purpose, Adam and Eve.

An Assiniboin shot at Morgan and me as we were going around the cattle stall (old fort) on our way to the wolf traps. Talking together, we passed quite near a small encampment. An Indian heard us, did not understand the language, failed to recognize the speakers and, accordingly, sent a bullet over our heads. Morgan called out to him that we were waschitscho.

I attempted to write the war song according to its rendering by one of these Assiniboin. He sang without words merely for his own encouragement. The melody has little variation and no significance apart from the words. The "e" is like our "la" in the practice of song. The first syllable of every verse is a high note, shouted from a full throat; then the tones become softer, lower, until they are a hardly distinguishable murmur; then suddenly the loud note of a new verse rings out again. When heard in these solitudes at the darkness of night, those abrupt loud cries in contrast to the slow movement of the verse and gradual softening of the tones produce a most singular effect, like savage exaltation combined with lamentation and words of counsel.

> eh! eh! ahe! e e a, ahe a, ahe ee ee ee hee
> ahe! a! a! ahe ah, e eh, eh, ia a ee e aha
> eh! eh ahe! ae a eh ah ia a ee a a ee ee
> ahe! ahe! ah, eh, eh, ahe, a, ia, a, a, ee, aa,
> eh! eh! eha, eh, ia, eh, eh, ehe, eh, eh, eha, a
> ahe! ahe! e a ae e a a ia ae a eha eh ee.

Ju, ju, hi, haha, like the neighing of a horse, yet often given a tremolo sound by the motion of the hand before the mouth: this is the well-known, much dreaded war cry, with modulation varying according to the nation.

October 30. After he had sent ahead three messengers to announce his coming, the "Knife", brother of Ours Fou, arrived this afternoon with the corpse of his sister (sister-in-law), brought on a travois drawn by a horse.

He wishes her to be buried beside her daughter—the daughter who hanged herself because a "buck" boasted that he had taken indecent liberties with her. Mother and grandchild lie beside each other enveloped in their blankets, then wrapped in a buffalo robe.[92] Inasmuch as the mourners brought with them four packs of buffalo hides—that is, 40 robes—the bourgeois had a meal served them, con-

---

[92] The bodies were brought here because no wood can be found on the prairie with which to erect a scaffold, nor have the Indians picks and shovels with which to dig graves sufficiently deep.

sisting of boiled meat and corn, sweetened coffee, and beugnies, all of which the aged women and the children ate with great relish. They could hardly restrain themselves from looking glad in spite of their grief. With great avidity they cleaned the dishes with their fingers and licked them with craving tongues. As usual, the distribution of the food was left to one of their soldiers, because the task is rather a difficult one to so apportion the same quantity to each that nobody has cause for complaint. Men were served first, then women; children were counted with their mothers. During this feast a coffin was got ready. The family took charge of the body, laid it in the rude box, Mr. Denig spread a new blanket, as gift, over it, the top was nailed down, and six of us carried it to our God's acre, lowered it ourselves into the grave already prepared and then covered it over. "Knife" made us a speech expressing gratitude; whereupon we withdrew, leaving the relatives of the dead to their howling and lamentation. On this occasion there was no need to employ aged women to mourn, for sorrow was sincere and heartfelt, as one could readily believe. Four members of one family dead within two weeks is cause enough for grief. When the first outburst was over "Knife" ordered a meal prepared at his expense for his relatives. This was eaten, however, at the grave, after the deceased had been served her portion. Then lamentation began anew, accompanied by the cutting of their flesh and offering up their blood without feigning or dissimulation. It was indeed a moving sight.

Indians look upon suicide not as a crime or cause for shame but as something natural and right. No one who is conscious of joy in life and hopes for better things in future ever kills himself purposely. As soon as hope is gone the allurement of life is at an end; doubt, disgust, and weariness set in. The equal balance between sensibility and reason is disturbed and a disordered mind is the result; momentary insanity, morally or spiritually, renders such a person irresponsible, not accountable; therefore, his deed is no crime or disgrace. In fact, even the suicide of a criminal for the purpose of escaping the disgrace of a court trial and public execution bears witness to shame and remorse.

Though it may be regarded by some, perhaps, as cowardly on such a man's part to be unwilling to play the principal role in the hideous staging of a public execution, I maintain, on the other hand, that considerable courage is required also to take one's own life in cold blood.

As to a person's right to kill himself, when he is not bound voluntarily to others, I have no doubt whatsoever, no matter how directly I run counter to established doctrine in saying so. The argument that parents bring forward, especially in their efforts to inculcate the enormity of this sin in the minds of their children: that they are to thank parents or God for existence, nay, are in duty bound to make sacrifices in their behalf, is unreasoning egotism.[93] Why are children born? Can parents say beforehand, we wish our child to be so and so: Boy, girl, beautiful, well formed, good, or clever? Is our existence a happy lot? What father and mother can know this in advance? The moments in life when one delights in one's existence are so rare, so dearly bought, and hope of a happier future fate so uncertain, that I recall more moments when I wished I had never been born than occasions when, free from sorrow, I rejoiced in being alive—was conscious of exceeding great happiness.

If, in a so-called civilized nation, one finds no recognition of one's endeavors; if, in spite of diligence and industry, one cannot earn one's bread—what then?[94] To earn a bare competency becomes daily more difficult, more prosaic. Deprived of our hopes for a better state of things in future, of future justice, we sink into materialism. Without hope of a happier life beyond the grave we are no better than animals. Where there is no hope there is no yearning; without yearning, no poetry; without poetry in our souls we are not human. But one cannot live on hope, nor can poetry survive hunger and misery.

Standing beside the grave of a pretty 16-year-old girl of good family, blameless reputation, modest manners, and honorable nature, who, unfortunate through one single act of a dissolute boy, is robbed of a fair future; who, reflecting upon such a fate may not cry out, Is there a God? Where is the God who promises to uphold the righteous? Where is the Protector of the innocent? Where is the Omniscient and Almighty One without whose knowledge not a hair of our heads shall be hurt, not a sparrow shall fall? Where is He?

Ah, here a girl lies dead; elsewhere, great numbers are starving! Where is He? Where?

And the aged Indian woman, far from her husband and he in danger, too soon parted from the dearly beloved children, becomes so sensible of her age and loneliness that she longs to be united with those she loves—she yearns for peace.

October 31. The unexpected often happens. Mr. Culbertson has at last arrived this evening from Fort Laramie. We had heard the glad news in the afternoon from Ours Fou, who had hurried on in advance to mourn with his family. "Uncle Sam" has appointed Ours Fou chief of the Assiniboin; fate has robbed him, during his ab-

---

[93] Rather more for the care of them than for the gift of life.

[94] Had I only realized at the time what severe trials were in store for me I would rather have remained a common engagee in the wilderness.

sence, of his wife, his only wife, his son, and two grandchildren. Anyone who saw this grief-stricken chief would never speak of an Indian's lack of feeling. They love, hate, experience sorrow and joy just as we do. Only in the face of the enemy are they too proud to show the pain they feel. Ours Fou was grieved to the soul, most profoundly affected; gazing before him in a kind of stupor, he wept silently. His hair and his body were besmeared in token of his sorrow. Morgan felt that he must conceal the chief's weapons for fear he, too, might be seized with too great a longing for those he loved best.

November 2. The news from Fort Laramie fails utterly to justify expectations. No treaties were negotiated, much less concluded. Uncle Sam made no display of military power to impress the Indians.

The United States agent, Colonel Mitchell, is said to have been befuddled most of the time from too much drink, to have made great promises to the Indians, to have appointed several braves to the rank of supreme chief without the approval of the respective nations, to have made gifts, such as stores of meal, blankets, etc. Quatre Ours, Bonaparte and their associates, they say were expecting a grand military display in which soldiers of many nations would take part in all of their war regalia, rather than an adjournment of the conference, but nevertheless the instant they were told by the Sioux, representatives from Fort Pierre, about the outbreak of cholera among the Herantsa, the Mandan, and the Arikara, they were off bag and baggage to their homes. Mr. Culbertson says I should be glad I did not go, for, though I should have seen more than 2,000 warriors of the different nations decked out in martial array, I should have witnessed no dancing, because no dancing was permitted or anything else that might incite hostile tribes and disturb the harmony of the occasion. Neither should I have seen a single wild animal nor any hunting. So I am to console myself for losses in a horse trade and breach of faith on the part of my expected fellow-traveler with the welcome thought of wearing myself out in this place. How often I have tried in vain "to make money." Invariably, through some untoward event, I am defeated in my artistic aims.

I should be believed when I say that I am determined to attain my purpose. Is such a belief on my own part an assumption? Is it not much more a recompense for suffering, the result of my striving? Mr. Denig says Mr. Culbertson has been named a colonel by his friend Mitchell, the United States agent, and we are to address him from now on by that title. Colonel of what? Here we have neither Regular Army nor militia. Oh, the passion for titles among these republican Americans!

Our new colonel gave a ball last night. His Indian wife in her ball gown, fringed and valanced according to European mode, looked extraordinarily well. She has much presence, grace, and animation for a full-blooded Indian. One or more tragicomic intermezzos were not wanting—results of liquor drinking. Joe Picotte had to be put to bed after he came near having a fight with our Indians.

Spent the entire day stripping off willow bast, drying it, and mixing it with tobacco. As long as this visit continues I could employ myself day after day preparing the mixture.

November 3. Late last night Mr. Denig waked me up to keep Mr. Culbertson company. Now and then we took a little whisky, smoked a great deal, talked in a sort of desultory way about God, man's destiny, etc., until finally the conversation was directed to the principal subject in view, i. e., where I was to be and what I was to do in the future.

Mr. Denig wished to know precisely in what way he was to employ me; whether he might be allowed to order me to paint any picture he desired. I had expressed my opinion once to Mackenzie to the effect that I was not employed as painter to execute just any picture.

"Now, here is our master. Tell me, have I the right to order you to paint a picture?" demanded Mr. Denig.

"No, sir," I replied. "Not after that agreement with our Mr. Picotte. I refused to paint for you only one of my compositions. You know why. The other pictures I painted because, in the first place, I take delight in such work and, besides, I wished to show my goodwill and my willingness to be of service in any way I could, for before the traders went away to their winter quarters I was altogether superfluous here; therefore I was glad to make myself agreeable and useful."

Then Mr. Culbertson remarked that the portraits I had painted pleased him so much that he would like to possess one of himself and another of his wife. I was to execute, in addition, a replica of the dog Natoh's picture, so that he could take the original to his post in Blackfeet territory. He said further that Mr. Denig will have need of me, so I remain here as clerk. In summer, when Mr. Picotte senior comes up on the steamer, I shall certainly be satisfactorily remunerated. Such a statement I found brief and to my liking.

"Now" said Mr. Denig, "I'll have a rod in pickle for you. Look out!"

So, I am to remain here. I am satisfied. I wonder how long my remark to Mackenzie had stuck in Mr. Denig's throat; a small glass of gin emboldened him to be relieved of it.

Bruyere, who brought Mr. Culbertson's horse on while the colonel himself came down the Yellowstone by boat, is now the only clerk besides Morgan. Packinaud is still in bed. When Morgan is busy as foreman and Bruyère at his trading post on the upper Bourbeuse I shall find enough with which to employ my time this winter. Am now an employee, not a visitor.

November 4. Those Assiniboin who came to visit their chief were hardly gone when twenty other tents were pitched below the fort. There is no end to smoking and feasting. Even as I was closing the gate, one of the duties belonging to my new position, I heard a noise out on the prairie like creaking wheels of old carts. There were nine two-wheeled vehicles brought by metifs from the Red River who come to trade, to get work, or else to seek shelter as independent hunters in this region.

Since I have taken charge of the keys of the fort various and sundry duties devolve upon me: Early in the morning I must open the gates, in the evening I have to close them; at night, if anyone without wishes to come in, I must open them again; if strangers are there I report the fact.

I must keep my eye on the two bastions and their contents; have charge of the press room where robes and furs are stored, and of the hides and skins in reserve; have supervision over the meat, both cured and fresh, and the distribution of the same to families entitled to it; over the vehicles, saddles, implements received, their safe keeping and proper distribution; must look after the tools, see that they are kept in good condition and properly distributed; must see to repairs; am expected to assist at the saddling and un-saddling of horses, as well as hitching them up and unhitching. One accomplishes little traveling about the world unless one becomes a practical person. An awkward scholar knows not how to use what he knows for the good of others. If an artist lacks exact knowledge and practice in such small matters as putting the saddle on a horse in the proper manner, mounting and sitting a horse correctly, how can he represent such things truly in his drawings and paintings?

November 5. Began painting Mr. Culbertson to-day, under the same difficulties due to insufficient colors and wrong sort of brushes: ceruse, black, vermilion, Prussian blue, yellow ochre, and chrome yellow are the only colors I have, while my brushes are those used, in general, for the beard and for flat painting. Art is long and time is fleeting are old adages the truth of which is daily put to the test.

This evening there was incessant knocking at the gates. Assiniboin, encamped outside, think they may be constantly coming in and going out the whole night through. Fine idea of order! What excited them so much this evening was the arrival of a runaway

Indian woman from the camp below, closely followed by her husband in pursuit. He had exhausted his horse and was himself stiff and sore from the long ride to fetch her back. First came her knock at the gate toward the river and before I could let her in and conduct her to the Indian women inside the fort the man was already pounding at the opposite gate. If he makes her eat humble pie we shall have had only a little drama; if he fails we may have a tragedy, unless he becomes a laughingstock and the play ends in comedy. As yet he has only been made sport of by a perfectly respectable crowd. The hero, meanwhile, does nothing more than look exasperated; the heroine is in fear of a beating.

It is queer that Indian women never carry their children in their arms but invariably on their backs. They swing their papooses over their shoulders, standing the while with backs bent, until they have drawn the blanket over the child and closely about their bodies.

November 6. If Mr. Culbertson's Indian wife had not received news of her younger brother's having been shot by Assiniboin I should have had a chance to study one of the most beautiful Indian women.

In token of grief she had her long, lustrous black hair cut short. She would be an excellent model for a Venus, ideal woman of a primitive race; a perfect "little wife." Ancient Greeks, like the Indians, required of the female sex only household virtues, no social qualities; the gentle sex, therefore, exercised no refining influence upon the strong.

One thing I miss among Indians in this region is the pleasant or merry singing that is so frequently heard among the girls of the Iowa tribe. Here they sing only while dancing; there, they resort to song to enliven their hearts when sad or to give vent to their feelings when merry. How delightfully Witthae sang "Hagge, hagge, torike hagreniki", etc., in a duet with her sister! Ah, tempi passati.

November 7. Smith brought me a large beaver he caught in a trap. Another study. What an ugly head!

November 11. Last week I was so busy I could find no time for writing; and even if I should have had a leisure moment or two, there was no open fire to make things cheery, for no wood has been procured; all hands were otherwise engaged.

Last Friday I finished the portrait, which was immediately hung on the wall in the reception room, where it was soon damaged by Indian women and children who insisted upon touching it to convince themselves that the figure painted there was really alive. As I had so many other things to do I was forced to hurry with the painting.

On the same day the Crow chiefs came again to greet Mr. Culbertson and per se to enjoy his hospitality and receive gifts.

Saturday Bruyere rode over to his post on the upper Bourbeuse, where Carafel, in the meantime, is attending to his duties. Pretty soon, when the exchange trade becomes brisk, both will stay there. Now I am the only clerk; I shall have to procure all things needed and look after everything; the two men in charge think more about their drinks than of giving me directions. Shift for yourself! Do the best you can; only leave me now in peace! would be the trend of my mind today if I had time to think my own thoughts. Both complain vehemently of the hypocrisy that characterizes both political and religious life in the United States; they find nothing but strife, deceit, and lies therein. They laud the way of life among Indians. Both are Americans and, if sober, neither would utter such plain truths.

Now that I've got so mixed up with the fur trade, I wish I had some acquaintance who knows at least one of the dialects spoken in this part of the country. In this Babylonian confusion of languages among the representatives of various nations it is hard to master one single dialect: Assiniboin, Crow, Herantsa, Cree, Mandan, and even Blackfeet all mingled together, and then again mixed up with English, French, Spanish, and German.

I think Indian women native here are very badly dressed. Instead of giving out the meat to all at the same time, one has to wait on each one separately (certain clerks have introduced that order of things) in order to substitute something else to favorites. One woman demands "tandoj," another "waschua," a third the same thing in another speech; then a laborer will come and ask for an oxyoke, another will call it an "outil," a third an "apischimo"; then Mr. Culbertson appears to make an inquiry; Mr. Denig follows, bidding me do something different; after him come Indians asking me about this and that, and expressing their desire to barter for something or other. Every moment the language in which the questions are asked varies, yet I am supposed to understand and reply, "It might be done, but it won't do."

Sunday Mr. Culbertson and his family departed. It is cold weather for a journey to Fort Benton.

Tuesday, yesterday, and today I have been constantly engaged in putting Assiniboin and Crows across the river—a cold, damp business. Had to assist the women in unloading their goods and chattels, as well as in loading again, so that I could make the trip across with more dispatch and regularity. Had frequently much ado with horses and dogs that either refused to go aboard or, when on the boat, would not remain quiet—even sprang, sometimes, into the river. Mr. Denig now begins to take a hand. It is well he finds clerks necessary to back him; otherwise, unless he were more decent to the latter, he would soon have trouble with both engagees and clerks combined.

Mr. Denig would be supremely happy to be put in command of at least 100,000 men and empowered to make them do some sort of work. To command is his greatest pleasure; desire to command his most characteristic trait. Stood he really so high that he could look down upon us, he need not so perk up his head.

I have observed several picturesque snow scenes: Indians pitching their tents or breaking camp; the Indian village in the forest on the opposite river shore seen through mist, smoke, or falling snow; groups of Indians engaged in loading or unloading their commodities; and the river covered with floating ice. While busy at work one is less sensible of the cold than when at leisure in a room where there is no fire. Besides, cold, wet weather, weariness, nothing of that sort matters when one is satisfied in mind.

November 13. First, I rowed our hunters across to the opposite shore; then I took several Cree families over. Cree women are more businesslike in transferring their goods and chattels to the boats than Assiniboin are. Around the various campfires men and young lads sit and smoke or else stand beside their horses; boys and girls frolic among their many dogs; children play with puppies as though they were dolls, or carry them like babies on their backs beneath their blankets; the women employ themselves with their chattels, their tent poles, and their beasts of burden.

Thirty tents swarming with Indians are there, thrown into relief against a background of forest, the bare trees of which, blackened by fire or lightning stroke, are now laden with snow. There is a confused din of voices calling, beating of drums, strokes of an ax, crash of a falling tree, whinnying of horses, shooting of guns, and howling of dogs. The barren prairie extending behind the fort on this side of the river has its attractions also; a light fall of snow gleaming through the dried prairie grass creates a bright surface that appears now dark, now golden, now rose hued. This gleaming surface is further brightened by a group of gaily painted tents with their attendant poles from which are suspended trophies, such as scalps, buffalo beards, strips of red cloth, etc. The place is enlivened by human figures; men walking about with majestic mien, some actively engaged, some idle; youths at their games, girls carrying water, women trudging in with wood, cleaning and scraping hides; horses grazing or tethered near their owners' tents, saddled for use; a multitude of dogs eager to steal something, chasing one another about, scampering away with some old bone, a piece of leather, or an ill-smelling rag. These dusky forms thrown into relief against the glistening snow seem almost phantomlike; especially when often indistinctly seen through smoke or mist. There is no strife; no oaths are ever heard.

The incessant drumbeat, the howling of dogs, neighing of horses, now and then a loud call, are the only sounds that come across the sandbank from that village. There are neither harsh tones of dispute nor conflict, neither glad notes of song nor yodel. Only the tattoo of the drum resounds, from beside a sickbed the music of the mountebank, not denoting joy. An Indian's ideal of enjoyment in the home is a feast; tobacco smoking is his diversion; dancing, his excess of indulgence in pleasure.

November 14. While we were bringing Mr. Culbertson's boat to land with great difficulty a beautiful wild goose, with straight, white neck and green head, swam down the river.[95] Not an Indian would lend a hand to assist us with the boat. That would have been far too great a condescension on their part.

November 15. Early this morning we thought the dog Natoh would die. Several days ago he had a fight over his Tschakan, during which he must have injured his back. Morgan's dogs, Bull and Badger, have escaped from their master. Badger showed deadly hate toward Natoh, and fought him at every opportunity.

Though he was younger and weighed less, his fury of attack, his remarkable perseverance and agility more than offset those disadvantages. Besides, he has teeth as sharp as those of a wolf, while Natoh's are worn dull from age. Each dog is his master's dearest pet and were once set upon each other so that they might determine which master had the most powerful dog in all the land. Natoh is now afflicted with a great swelling on his left side, has eaten nothing for 3 days, to the serious concern of Mr. Denig's wives. I advised Mr. Denig to open the tumor, so that it could be drained of blood and pus. He did not venture; the dog is much too surly. Today the swelling burst of itself; whereupon Mr. Denig congratulated me, saying that if the brute had died the Indians would have ascribed its death to the picture I painted.

"Everything will turn out all right if nothing happens to me during your stay," he added. "Otherwise you'd better look out."

Well, I assume the risk; for the present I know nothing better to do. It will soon be insupportable for a painter to stay among these savages. My danger at present is the result of Catlin's coming here, and Bodmer's, though they themselves are not in any way to blame. I could do nothing to prevent even greater difficulties that, on my

---

[95] This species of goose is not mentioned in Audubon's "Birds of America."

account, might befall future artists traveling in this region. The illness of this dog may well serve me as warning to leave nothing neglected that I would like to sketch.

Was told by an Assiniboin, who out of curiosity accompanied his chief to the Platte River (Fort Laramie; the situation is on Horseshoe Creek), how they were given domestic animals to supply them with food. They refused outright to accept the cattle, so Mr. Culbertson had to take over the beasts and give the Indians corn and biscuits in exchange. In the first place, our redskins would not eat pork at all, neither fresh nor cured. This Assiniboin, who for want of a better name we call "Platte man", entertained his friends with various anecdotes; for example, how three United States soldiers were forced to drag along after them, as a punishment, three heavy balls attached to their feet. This he turned rather cleverly to ridicule. He told, furthermore, how some white men were attempting to sell whisky when soldiers broke open the casks and to the great regret of the narrator let the liquor flow out on the ground, where it did nobody any good.

I read also the treaty which the United States proposes to make with the Indian tribes. Again nothing but hypocritical phrases to impose the belief upon a distant public that Uncle Sam takes the Indians' fate much to heart. In reality, it is high time that he did so. In the first instance, to appoint over the nations supreme chiefs who are neither chosen nor recognized by the tribes themselves is of no advantage to anybody; only engenders jealousy among rivals.

In the second place, to promise, on condition that Indians no longer make war on one another or do injury to any member of the white population, to distribute $50,000 annually during a period of 50 years according to the poll among the nations west of the Missouri—what does that mean? How many such treaties would be kept with Indians? What an easy matter to provoke an affront and then to refuse the annual payment. During a period of 50 years! What guaranty have Americans that their Confederation of States will continue for so long a time? Is it not in the power of any new administration to annul this treaty made by their predecessors? Jackson made himself particularly conspicuous in that respect; he resorted to bayonets in his effort to set aside a treaty made by his predecessor, President Monroe.

As I was rowing a chief of the Cree, "Le Plumet Caille", across the river he said to me, looking northward and describing with his hand a semicircle from the point of sunrise to that of sunset: "Tout ça a moi." He repeated these words several times in the presence of Assiniboin who might well understand his signs. Now, the actual domain of the Assiniboin lies between the Yellowstone and Missouri; therefore, the latter tribe were most likely driven across the river by

Crows and Blackfeet upon land belonging to the Cree. Now, I under-stand, also, why Cree set the prairie on fire—to drive Assiniboin from Cree hunting grounds and force them back into their own former territory.

November 16. That I might have something to enjoy on Sunday I took different sorts of saddles that are used in this region and made drawings of them.

November 17. Weather is clear and cold. Have finally decided to order from Madam Bombarde a winter suit made of buckskin. Up to the present time I have worn my summer clothes, with a buckskin shirt. Owing to the exercise I take in the performance of my numerous duties and to my inner satisfaction to be able to paint daily so many interesting studies, I am little sensible to cold. New-comers, they say, endure the low temperature during their first winter better than natives. But the weather is now too severe for my com-fort. I feel the cold more today on account of being unable to get wood for a fire; the oxen make use of Sunday for a distant hike, and by the time they are found, brought back, yoked, driven to the forest and back again with a load of wood night will already have fallen; besides, there will be a great many applicants for that one load. Mr. Denig feels quite comfortable in his large armchair, smoking his short-stem pipe beside his iron stove that glows with a rousing fire. The instant I come in to attend to something or to ask a question, and incidentally to hold my hands over the delectable base burner which attracted me today like a magnet, the bourgeois invariably finds a new task that takes me into the open air, on the theory, I presume, that the best warmth is obtained by constant bodily exercise.

I am continually required to walk down to the river to find out whether that arrogant Sioux [96] has yet reached the opposite shore and to row him over at once.

The Sioux imagines himself of tremendous importance, because he was a representative at the great assembly on Horseshoe Creek and has received a number of gifts. He is so imbued with self-assumption that he boasts of the number of Assiniboin he has slain in battle. He even brags about having killed the mother of Ours

[96] As I pronounce the word "Sioux" according to the French and heretofore have heard no other pronunciation of the word from any American, I was greatly astonished when Mr. Denig made sport of me about it and declared that one said "Suh", not "Siuh." Yet he could bring neither any proof of the word's origin from the Dakota language nor any reason for the pronunciation he claimed. According to Charlevoix, it is said to have been the final syllable of the word "Nadowessioux." Mr. Denig tried also to make me appear ridiculous for saying that certain animals could be tamed by means of salt. Jim Hawthorn, according to his habit to curry favor, was at once ready with his invented anecdote about a hunter he knew who never went on the chase without a bag of salt with which he could entice any herd of buffaloes he might come upon—in fact, some thousands followed him for several days. I replied simply that it was his intention to make me appear absurd; I would give my information somewhere else.

Fou. Unpardonably tactless, for he intends to live here, among his former foes.[97] To give himself airs he presented two good horses for his wife. He had her with him hardly 4 days when she was taken away by her kinspeople in order to provoke him. Now he wishes to get his horses back; whether he will succeed Mr. Denig is very curious to find out.

Natoh was also a cause of much running around on my part. To-day he went early to the woods, most probably to breathe his last in solitude and to spare the women the painful sight of his final grapple with death. For he is dead.

"Knife" and his soldiers, who trade at our winter posts, brought back the horses that were stolen by Assiniboin.

For the sake of producing actual evidence of their friendly attitude and of their desire to redeem their honor these braves bought the horses at their full value from the thieves, who are customers of the opposition. For their trouble they received from the company gifts at the value of two buffalo robes per horse, which is considerably more than the purchase price of the animals, but better, after all, than losing them altogether.

Sitting beside the open fire so long and earnestly desired, Mr. Denig told me how his chief had the jury in St. Louis decide two questions of much consequence to the engagees. For instance, whether the company was bound to pay his entire wage to an employee who had fallen ill and make no deduction for time lost. It was decided that the engagee was to be paid only for the time he worked; he was to be furnished board and lodging, to be sure, but no medicine. This seems hard on a laborer who, by reason of the service he renders, falls ill or becomes incapacitated for work. Still, the company pays an employee his entire wage if they find no cause to complain of him in any other respect. According to this ruling, Packinaud will have all the medicine he needs during his illness charged against him on his account. The second question is whether the company is obliged to pay to an employee his full wage when the latter, contrary to an agreement entered upon voluntarily not to trade as private individuals in buffalo robes and furs, bartered from Indians hides and skins in excess of the demand.

The jury rendered this decision: Pay the man in full for his work, but have him indemnify the company for loss incurred or else give up the hides and pelts. Hint to me: I am not permitted to barter for any robes or fine furs with the Indians myself, but through my chief as agent, in order that he may not lose his profit on the trade;

---

[97] Besides, he was born an Assiniboin but was taken prisoner while a boy by the Sioux and brought up as one of them. As peace is now established between these related tribes he wishes to rejoin his kindred with whom he originally belonged.

furthermore, I am not allowed to possess more raw hides or pelts than one sample of each species or any more buffalo robes than I am in need of for my own bed.

November 18. Toward evening Jim Hawthorn arrived direct from St. Louis, accompanied by another man on horseback. I hope we shall have some news.

I was already reposing under my buffalo robe when Mr. Denig came into my room with Jim Hawthorn and invited me to a little "spread." There is news of the insurgents' march upon Cuba, just as much in violation of the people's rights as was the Swiss radicals' advance upon Lucerne in '45, and like our radicals, the American annexation party, are now raising their voices against the victors on account of the lawful seizure of filibusters, despite the fact that the latter were not shot, as, in accordance with martial law, might have been expected.

Endless dissension because of the Negroes. Negro slavery is an inveterate menace to the Union, fateful heritage from the English, who by lawful decree introduced this system of labor in the colonies.[98] Such a bondage is wrong—a great injustice. How is it to be remedied? By emancipation? But the free States are just as intolerant of Negro blood as the slave States. No, the Negroes must be put out of the United States.

Capital equal to the value of from three to four million slaves, that is, a sum amounting to at least a thousand million dollars must be sacrificed to that end! Or shall they be set free by ransom? Who, then, would offer such an enormous sum? Who would undertake the task of transporting an entire nation across the seas? To keep slaves is wrong, but to declare them free men and yet refuse to treat them as such, to find them unendurable in personal contact, even to sit beside in the Church of God is damned hypocrisy![99] The aboli-

[98] In 1645 the first Negro slaves were brought to the English colonies by a Puritan from Boston. There arose such a universal cry of protest, however, that the Negroes were sent back to Africa at the expense of the State of Massachusetts (Bancroft, vol. I, p. 132). The first slaves were brought into Virginia in 1620 by a Dutch ship of war. The slave trade was soon such a thriving business and so advantageous to English shipping that the abominable pursuit was favored by the British Government up to the time of the Revolutionary War. Nay, they threatened more than once to dismiss colonial officials who agreed to any law in the colonies against trade in Negroes. In 1776 the American Congress forbade, finally, the bringing in of any more slaves. That much, at least, is to be said in praise of the colonial assembly. The emancipation of the Negro race, in defiance of the English, would never have been accomplished by philanthropists, if they had not hoped to ruin, by that means, the colonies of other nations.

[99] That is basing peoples' claim to good birth on the color of their skin. If the abolitionists wish to free the Negro because he is capable of being as good a person and Christian as a white man, they must also grant him the same rights. But American philanthropy goes not so far. Neither do they consider that Indians are their equals. What abolitionists most desire is to clear the Negroes out of the United States. That slaveholders themselves do not put such low estimate on the ability of Negroes is shown by the strict laws against Negro education. The one and only prospect of doing away with slavery in the United States is an insurrection of the black race. A compromise

tionists in America are nothing more than hypocrites. What is the benefit of such a book as Uncle Tom's Cabin? What purpose is served by such writings? None other than to arouse hatred between the different sections of the country and make the slaves' condition worse than before! What plan is advised by the abolitionists? They have none! To what place do George and Eliza flee, ultimately, for refuge? To some port of safety in free, democratic America? Oh, no! They go to Canada, under the dominion of royal England. In liberty-loving America no Negro is allowed freedom, no free Negro is permitted to live as a free citizen. Among these "most enlightened" Americans in these United States, the home of the most liberty-loving, the most cultivated people, no Negro or mulatto, though he be only one-fourth Negro, enjoys the rights and privileges of a citizen: He is neither enfranchised nor permitted to testify before the court!

November 20. Yesterday we had another ball. I thought at first that Mr. Denig had received most satisfactory news from the States; on the contrary, his prospects of visiting New York next year are smashed to bits. But when the younger Madam Denig appeared among the dancers wearing a rose-colored ball gown in the latest fashion, direct from St. Louis, a light dawned upon me.

I was indebted to that new and beautiful frock for the unhoped-for pleasure of beating the tattoo on drum or tambourine. As I cannot dance I have to comply with others' wishes by helping with the music. It's a pity that this ball gown had not been on hand when the reception was given in honor of Mr. Culbertson. How jealously the two beautiful dancers would have looked askance at each other—just like two beauties of the white race at court.

However, rose color goes not well with a copper-colored skin. To be sure, the complexion of a pure-blooded Indian woman is no darker than that of an Italian or Spanish brunette, but rose color is not becoming to them either. The color of a dress must enhance the general effect and brilliance of a costume, not be a detraction.

Before breakfast I learned several words in the Dakota language from Ours Fou, who seeks the solitude of my room, where, beside the open fire, he can brood over the loss of his loved ones and meditate

---

between white Americans will never succeed. Negroes are just as good as we; except that they are either too much accustomed to bondage or else do not feel so much the need of being free as we and the Indians do, they could have won their liberation long ago. Especially at this time, when the free States would rather help than hinder them. A Negro revolution is a frightful means to gain freedom, but it is their only means. Much blood would flow, but the sin of slaveholding can only be atoned for in blood. However bloody, only by revolution can they set themselves free. There have been frightful upheavals from causes less serious. Moreover, those who do not themselves long for freedom and gain their liberation by battle will not procure it by foreign aid. If Negroes wish to be free and deserve liberty, let them manifest their desire. They would be justified in rising here where such abominations are perpetrated daily by Christians.

upon his future eminence. The good old chief seems to take a heart-felt pleasure in my writing down "Minnehasga tokia? Tschauda waschteh, Osmie schitsche", and pronouncing the words after him.

Rowed across the river today for the last time. The stream is so thickly blocked with floating ice it will soon be entirely frozen over. I brought back the Sioux; he found neither his four days' bride nor the two horses with which he purchased her.

To console him Ours Fou found him another "little wife." When we started over a dog belonging to an Assiniboin remained behind. For a long time the woman called, "Kadosch! Kadosch!" The lean wolfhound, discouraged by the bitter cold stream, ran like one possessed up and down at the river's edge, then with arched back and dragging tail began to howl distressingly. The old woman never ceased calling "Kadosch." Who could long withstand that familiar summons? The dog sprang into the freezing water, worked his way bravely through the floating blocks of ice, now disappeared among them, now was forced to bound upon such a float to prevent his being crushed, now swept along with the yet ductile but half-frozen ice layer that almost entirely surrounded him, until a larger and more solid mass, impelled by its own momentum, moved with rapid, whirling motion through that yielding stratum and burst it asunder, bringing the poor brute again into fairway. Finally, after the gallant fellow had again been borne far downstream by the ice-blocked current, for some moments entirely lost to view, he scrambled to shore and was received by the woman with open arms. Had he gone down the old woman would no doubt have suffered the loss of her last and only friend.

Another dog did not fare so well. He was very hungry. He saw a child sucking a juicy piece of meat, and fairly itched to get possession of it. He looked slyly about him to find out whether he were being observed, turned his head this way and that, pricked up his ears. Just then the child pulled the meat out of its mouth. The hound could resist no longer; he snapped hastily for it, but in securing it, bit the small papoose.

He started off with his prize. Hearing the child's scream, its father, whom we call the Platte man, seized his bow and, quick as a flash, laid the thief low with an arrow through his heart.

The Arikara are said actually to have lost 400 souls during the cholera epidemic and to have been terribly enraged against the whites in consequence; however, they have as yet resorted to no violence.

November 21. When the old Spaniard came in to breakfast this morning, he announced to Mr. Denig that, while out guarding his cattle, he saw in the near distance a pair of white-tailed deer.

Cadotte was instantly dispatched. In an hour's time the buck was brought in. Cadotte brought the head all intact with horns for me to paint. My collection of studies increases slowly but surely. Never despair! Today I received my winter suit of calfskin, made with hood, "metif fashion", and sewed throughout with sinew.

November 22. Joe Picotte made another attempt through misrepresentation and lies to alienate Assiniboin from the big company by declaring that his competitor would annihilate them with contagious diseases. How stupid! What profit could be derived from the destruction of one's own customers? Joe is kept in a state of continual provocation because the United States Government takes no notice of his company and yet upholds always the greater corporation. Naturally, this is a cause of friction between competitors! The big company, possessing a large amount of capital, have already put many of their competitors out of business altogether and have absorbed others. These "dobies" have held their own for an unusually long time, but still make inconsiderable profit; only Campbell, in charge of their drinking house in St. Louis, is making a success.

Before I knew as much about the fur trade as I now know I was astonished to find prices so unreasonably high, but as I became more and more closely acquainted with the business and attendant expenses I knew that it could not be otherwise. When commodities are obliged to be transported 9,000 miles, nay, some of them halfway round the world, the outlay therefor must necessarily be considerable.

Wares are shipped here from Leipsig (little bells and mirrors), from Cologne (clay pipes), beads from Italy, merinos, calicos from France, woolen blankets, guns from England, sugar and coffee from New Orleans, clothing and knives from New York, powder and shot, meal, corn, etc., from St. Louis. The company owns factories both at home and abroad for the manufacture of their staple goods; their trade in furs extends throughout the entire Indian domain from the upper Mississippi to Mexico. Their trading posts are spread along the St. Peters River, the Missouri, Yellowstone, Platte, Arkansas, Gila, Bear River, throughout Oregon, California, Utah, and New Mexico. Trade is distributed through the districts according to the location of navigable streams or some other means of communication: upper Mississippi outfit, lower Mississippi outfit, Platte outfit, etc. Members of the company, P. Chouteau, Jr., Sarpy, Berthold, O'Fallon, et al., live in St. Louis, where they have their office, an immense storehouse. From there goods are shipped to the various posts, skins and furs are received in exchange, and are sold throughout the world, especially to Russia. In every district there is an agent, employed at a fixed salary ($2,000) and paid in addition certain profits on sales. He has charge of several posts. He orders sup-

plies from the company but is not usually obliged to pay for them
in pelts. He is at liberty to dispose of the hides and skins that he
takes in exchange in the market where he finds the best prices.

For goods delivered at the factory price plus the cost of transportation agents are required to pay a yearly interest on capital advanced,
together with the cost of insurance. He knows, therefore, what the
approximate cost of his commodities will be and has only to reckon
in addition sums necessary to pay salaries and keep of his employees,
and largesse to Indians, in order to maintain his trading post with
success. Mr. Culbertson is agent for the upper Missouri outfit and
has supervision of three posts: Fort Union, Fort Benton, and Fort
Alexander. Mr. W. Picotte is agent for the lower Missouri outfit,
which includes supervision of Fort Pierre, Fort Lookout, Fort Vermilion, Fort Clarke, and Fort Berthold. Mr. Papin is agent on the
Platte, having charge of Fort Hall and Fort Laramie. A bourgeois
or head clerk is stationed at each post. He receives a fixed salary of
$1,000 and a stated percentage on sales. He buys goods, just as agents
do, at the cost price. The bourgeois keeps his own accounts. He
orders what he needs from his agent and delivers to him all that is
received in exchange for goods sold; whether he makes large profits
or suffers losses depends upon how well he knows how to calculate
to advantage and to regulate his own expenses.

Agents and bourgeois form, so to speak, a company of their own
in so far as they all agree to buy goods from the stockholders at a
stipulated price in which is included interest and transportation
charges.

If skins and furs bring high prices the agents make a surplus
which they divide among themselves and the bourgeois according
to the peltry contributed by each. The stockholders assume responsibility for all damages to commodities in transit; agents are required only to answer for goods received at the destination to which
they are consigned. All shipments are secured from loss by insurance, the premium on which is quite high for goods sent up the
Missouri, because there are such a great number of snags.

The less a bourgeois has to pay for the upkeep of his fort, in
salaries for employees, and for skins and furs, the greater will be
his profit and that of his agents, who are also bourgeois of a fort.
Clerks and engagees are paid on an average the wage they receive
in the United States, but they are required to buy everything from
the trading post where they are employed and at the price demanded
there. Fortunately, they have neither the necessities nor the occasions for spending money that one has in the States; otherwise they
would save nothing. The traders, clerks, interpreters, hunters, workmen, and their helpers employed at the forts and who are content to
buy on a credit from the company seldom lay by anything for a

rainy day. They marry. Indeed, for the purpose of chaining to the fort, so to speak, those who are capable, those who are indispensable, the bourgeois endeavor to bind them down for the next year by advancing sums to them on credit.

For supplies intended for their own use the bourgeois pay the same price that they would be required to pay to the stockholders for the same article, but they demand much more from their employees and the Indians. For a medium buffalo robe they charge an employee $4, for one extra good (prime) $8, for a robe enriched with ornamentation $15; even a higher price than charged in the United States. For the usual robe Indians receive in exchange, for instance, 2 gallons of shelled corn, from 3 to 4 pounds of sugar, or 2 pounds of coffee. The total expense of preparing a buffalo robe for sale, reckoned as one sum, would not exceed $1 gross. In St. Louis these robes are sold at wholesale for at least $2; therefore, the agents and bourgeois can easily realize 100 percent profit if they know the trade. It is not true in every case, however, that a bourgeois is an expert trader; those managers are chosen among clerks who have been trained in this part of the country, and many of them who become efficient clerks under good and careful management are not in every respect competent to conduct a business to the best advantage.

A craftsman or workman receives $250 a year; a workman's assistant is never paid more than $120; a hunter receives $400, together with the hides and horns of the animals he kills; an interpreter without other employment, which is seldom, gets $500. Clerks and traders who have mastered the court language, i. e., the speech of those Indians for whose special advantage the trading posts are established, may demand from $800 to $1,000 without interest. All employees are furnished board and lodging free of charge; that means, engagees are provided with nothing but meat, a place to sleep, and one raw buffalo hide. Hunters and workmen eat at the second table, i. e., meat, biscuit, and black coffee with sugar. Clerks are served with the bourgeois at the first table, which is, on an average, a well-furnished table for this part of the country. We have meat, well selected, bread, frequently soup and pie on Sundays. Everyone must furnish his bedclothes; however, one may borrow two buffalo robes from the storehouse.

If an employee has a mind to save he can under certain conditions put aside almost his entire income. In that case he must have on hand a supply of clothing, must be content with the fare at the fort, indulge in no dainties or feasting, and never allow himself to come within 10 feet of the Indian women.

As these employees are not stimulated to greater exertions by increases in pay or percentages, it is hardly to be expected that they will work harder or make sacrifices for a company that is accumulating great wealth and, at the same time, charging them such extortionate prices. Independently of the equal salaries they receive, head clerks have advantages over traders that inspire them to greater zeal and more willing sacrifices. Clerks and traders, both at the forts and at their winter quarters, are continually beset by begging customers of the company they serve. They are in no sense obligated to give away their small earnings merely for the purpose of procuring a greater number of buffalo robes for their agents, but the bourgeois not only like for them to be generous with the customers but, on the other hand, either directly or indirectly require it of them. Mr. Denig came near getting a sound beating a few years ago because of some such unreasonable demand that he made of one of his clerks. He fled to his bedroom! One must consider that in this part of the world there are no courts, that one must first catch the criminal, whether guilty or merely accused; that, in an entire year, there are but one or two opportunities to despatch the prisoner and witnesses the great distance from here to St. Louis; that even then the finding of the court is uncertain—nobody knows what the verdict will be.

One can easily understand why people in these wilds rarely resort to process of law. Among the promiscuous white inhabitants of this region there are many rough and vicious characters, in dealing with whom one recognizes the need of promoting peace and harmony just as in an Indian camp. Every man is armed; every man protects his own house and his property; with knife or shotgun he requites every insult. One who loves his life guards against giving offense. It is not their idea of honor to challenge the offender and give him still another chance to commit an outrage by killing an innocent person. Fighting duels is no means of obtaining divine judgment. One hears among white people hereabouts, therefore, fewer violent disputes, and witnesses fisticuff fights less frequently than in civilized States, for the reason that, knowing the deadly consequences, people guard against giving cause for strife.

"Knife" brought ill news from our winter trading post on the upper Bourbeuse; 10 Assiniboin died at their settlement in that region of a strange disease that they caught from the Cree on Red River. Blood, they say, flows from the nose, ears, and eyes. As chance would have it, the disease appeared simultaneously with the arrival of horse thieves, and impressed them anew with thoughts of "bad medicine."

"Knife", authorized as one of our soldiers, flogged a "buck" in Bruyere's house, because the young boor insisted on trying to pick a quarrel with Pellot.[1] At a loss to know what to do with himself,

---

[1] By the English word "buck" is meant a young rowdy whose chief business is the conquest of the fair sex, inasmuch as he is yet too young for exploits in war.

he kept on opening and shutting the door to Bruyere's house, as they frequently do at the fort with the dining room door. The ill-mannered fellow was diverted by the singular lock, the noise he was making, and still more by the sheer malicious satisfaction of admitting a draught of cold air into a warm room. Pellot bade him leave the door alone. The "buck" laughed in his face. Finally Pellot gave him a piece of his mind, whereupon the "buck" said if Pellot would come outside he would thrash him. As it happened, "Knife" was also there, and as soldier bound to keep the peace. He sprang up, quickly seized a stick of wood from the fire, lay hold of the "buck" and ordered him to come in and strike the Schajeh. Tomorrow, you say. Aha, you will in the morning? And with that "Knife" dealt him such a blow behind the ears that the fellow lay on the floor as dead. "Knife" was just on the point of dealing several blows more and in his anger would have killed the churl, had he not been restrained by his friends. That "buck" may well be on his guard hereafter against "Knife", the brother of Ours Fou.

Though one is beset by perils in the Indians' domain, the dangers here do not compare with those that threaten one's life in the United States. Germans especially (including natives of Switzerland) have much to bear from native white citizens there. In St. Joseph and Savannah I got into several desperate fights, because some of the rough natives, either drunken or insolent, tried to play a joke on the Dutchman, with the intention of affronting or else of making a fool of me. On one occasion my refusal to drink a scoundrel's health was his excuse to set upon me; another one coveted my woman; a third derided me, every time resulting in a bloody quarrel, because I am not a man to keep quiet and pocket an insult. As everybody knows, household rights are properly respected in the United States— that is one of the finest provisions in the organization of the States.

Have restored Mr. Culbertson's portrait as well as I could.

As the metifs get meat here now, I have learned the word for fresh meat in the Chippewa (Sauteurs) speech. The word is "wiass." [2] Difficulties in learning a language increase daily. * * *

November 23. A ring, a ring! A wedding ring! Quien sabe? [2a] Marguerite La Bombarde came to see me this afternoon, put a brass ring on my finger, saying "Tu la porteras pour moi." [2b] Does she want to marry me?

---

[2] The mention of this word gives me occasion to remark upon the faults committed in the English language in the representing of foreign sounds. For instance, John Carver, in his journey through the interior of North America (1766–68), writes this word viass "weas" instead of "weeas"; now the translator in the German (Hamburg) edition gives the word "ues"! Furthermore, the Sioux word "waschta" (good) is given "woshta" but in German, "uoschta"; "tibi" (tent, house) is given "tiebie"; "mine" (water) is given "mene" and in German, "mene", etc. For an English "e" (i), the translator always uses a German "e."

[2a] I. e., "Who knows?"

[2b] I. e., "Thou wilt wear it for me."

November 24. I painted a large eagle for Bearshead; he has to pay twenty robes for the flag. Today I came upon Natoh's picture in a garret, that serves as storage room for drugs, paints, and crackers! Is it due to delicate sensibilities or superstition that they keep his image in hiding? Since Natoh's death, Mr. Denig has indulged a new fancy: Three splendid wolfhounds, in new harness with bells, hitched to a cariole! This one-seated sled I am now to give a coat of paint; the last supply of oil at the fort is to be lavished on it.

Indian dogs differ very slightly from wolves, howl like them, do not bark, and not infrequently mate with them. Dogs of another type are brought here from the Rocky Mountains—small, lop-eared canines, covered from head to toes and tail with long shaggy hair. In spite of the widely varying species of dogs, a differentiation as marked, nay, even more marked than between the fox and the wolf, some naturalists are inclined to trace all the different breeds, just as they derive the human races, from one original pair.

Why should not every separate country have its own breed of dogs? Why should any one maintain that dogs native to New Holland, to Kamchatka, Thibet, England, Turkey, etc.—that all these various types are derived from one and the same original pair? Indians make use of their dogs as beasts of burden and as guards, never for hunting, because their baying and howling would betray the huntsman to lurking foes. Moreover, these wolfhounds are too wild to be good rangers and therefore useful on the chase; they hunt out every living thing that they might be able to catch with their teeth. To say that dogs, by reason of their toes, are suited for drawing vehicles or carrying loads is a queer statement. It is not by decree of Nature that the horse, oxen, or reindeer are destined for draught animals, but by an arrangement of mankind those animals best suited to such purposes are selected; accordingly, Indians find dogs more convenient as beasts of burden than buffaloes. Dogs are by far the best animals to draw sleds over the snow. There are certain philanthropists, however, who in their zeal for dogs' welfare give them a higher place in their esteem than they ascribe to man, of whom they exact any and every sort of work.

November 25. Last night Cadotte's Assiniboin wife came to my door and called "ti^{n}i."

I opened the door; she had disappeared. He has no longer credit; so, no coffee, no wife! Point d'argent, point de Suisse! [2c] And for this wife of his Cadotte was rash enough to put his life at stake! It happened last year, when Cadotte had to go along as usual with the Mackinaw boat that carried goods for the Blackfeet tribe and, in his capacity of huntsman, to provide fresh meat for the crew who

---

[2c] I. e., "No song, no supper" (a French idiom) ; also "No tip, no porter."

towed the boat laboriously up the river by means of a rope. Harvey was then bourgeois at Fort William. He was attracted to the beautiful Assiniboin woman, and during Cadotte's absence enticed her to his fort. As Cadotte was returning he heard his wife carousing in the Tiger's lair. Equipped as for the hunt, he set out at once in trace of her, entered Harvey's room and in the latter's presence, inside the latter's own fort, he took his woman by the arm and bade her come with him. Harvey was for shooting him down, but was prevented by the people about him. How the Tiger must have glared at the Lion going off with his prize! Harvey is not a whit less daring than Cadotte, who defies the devil, but he was restrained by the feeling that he was in the wrong! Unfaithful women are now become a commonplace—nobody thinks much about such occurrences. Only old ugly women or those burdened with children remain with their husbands; they are exposed to no temptation, no seduction.

However, much depends upon a girl's parents, whether they come of good family and enjoin upon their daughters the duty of being loyal to their husbands. Indian women who marry engagees are not valued at the purchase price of a horse; therefore they do not regard themselves bound in duty to remain. Such Indian women are, as a rule, of the riffraff. Children born of such unions inherit, as a matter of course, bad rather than good qualities of their parents; on the other hand, halfbreed children of clerks and traders are a credit to the white race.

Rottentail and Grayhead are once more on a visit here. The first-mentioned chief regrets much that he did not find Mr. Culbertson's courier, so that he might have gone to the Platte. Then he would have been chief of the Absaroka and not Big Robert; the latter will gain considerable influence through the distribution of gifts provided by the United States; many of Rottentail's adherents will move over to Big Robert's settlement. Besides, Rottentail has not more than 80 tents.

November 26. Received another wipe-down from Mr. Denig today because I gave out lard in too large quantites. Perhaps so; nobody has taken the trouble to give me instructions. As Bruyere was leaving he delivered to me a bunch of 10 keys without showing me the lock to which a single one of them belonged or giving me information concerning any of the duties I was to assume.

The two men in charge were always more or less befuddled; were unwilling for my nose to come within smelling distance of their gin, for my eyes to behold their tragicomic play; hence, were satisfied to let me find out everything for myself. I knew neither what the rations were nor the persons entitled to receive them; consequently, some of the Indian women took advantage of me. Now

I have found out about these matters myself. I had first to learn the difference between tallow fat or suet and market fat or lard, between tender meat and hard meat, packed in the bladders in which Indians bring it to us, and whether the dried strips of flesh were cut from a cow or an ox. I had to watch over 12 men all at the same time and keep them at work, to deliver their tools and implements, the names of which I frequently did not even know, much less the place where they were kept. Ten thousand soldiers would not have given me as much trouble as those few laborers and women. Nor does the great number of different languages in which I am addressed make my way of life in this place any the less confusing. Women eat at no stated intervals, but, if possible, throughout the entire day. Each comes for meat when it suits her. And I am to make no change in that respect. But it is quite a while before one knows all the various terms for fresh meat, cured meat, lard, corn, water, "open the door", etc., in seven different languages.

Tools and implements are scattered everywhere—in the saddle room, in the meat house, in the storehouse, in outhouses, bastions, on the floor—axes are even thrust under the beds. Before I had brought order out of this chaos by my own efforts alone, I was forced many times to scratch my bewildered head. Of course I make many mistakes; for instance, I forgot once to feed the pigeons, to count the pigs, to drive away a woman because she came twice in the same day to ask for meat, in order to give some food to visitors, and I committed yet another error when I gave out lard instead of tallow fat to another woman. Only at that moment was Mr. Denig inclined to vent his spleen upon me; indeed, at other times he has been kind. He is in a bad humor now, because he has found out that when the Crows come here to trade, not only Joe Picotte but he himself has not on hand sufficient sugar, meal, etc. We are already forced to eat bread made from maize instead of wheat, and to drink coffee without milk; soon we shall have no sugar, perhaps, have to put up with meat and water. He brags about how he puts up with any fare; unfortunately, I was destined to catch him eating butter and bread with cheese and sausage on the sly. He stood before me an idle braggart. He supplies all the corn needed for chickens and pigeons that are laying no eggs and, besides, will most likely be frozen to death before winter is over, but none to preserve the strength of horses, cows, and draught oxen in daily service.

My prime fault, which caused dissatisfaction to my chief, was committed on the evening of the ball, when I neglected to praise the new ball gown as much as did Jim Hawthorn, whose only duty is to dance attendance on the bourgeois, to flatter him and submissively cut his tobacco for him. Now Jim came here with the expectation of getting a position forthwith. He finds no employment; I am, no doubt, in his way. Look alive!

Ours Fou, chief of the Assiniboin, sits now beside me on the floor before the fire. What a melancholy picture! A chieftain "in sackcloth and ashes"; greatness in humility! He sits here now, in sorrow, with the same imposing dignity that characterized him as prince in power. He is uncovered; on his head, breast, and legs are incisions in his skin to allow blood to flow as atonement for his deceased wife, his murdered sons, and beloved grandchildren. The good old man has still other troubles to afflict him: His newly acquired title is not recognized. Neither Absaroka nor Assiniboin accept him. For the first time in 30 years, since the war with the Crows and subsequent peace with that tribe, Ours Fou has pitched his camp in the Assiniboin hunting grounds.

Absaroka interfere with him when on the chase; his tribesmen find no food. He talks with Rottentail, who is discontented, on his part, because he was not chosen chief of the Absaroka. The latter is wary, a good businessman, and makes light of the white man's chief in the territory of the Platte. "White Americans lie", he says; "where are their gifts? Where are their warriors?" Absaroka sneer at a chief who is poor. Ours Fou is in sorrow; he dispensed all his gifts long ago; he is poor.

He cudgels his brain to find some way out of his dilemma; he juggles with this plan and that to try to regain his prestige. Among his own adherents he finds rivals who are envious of him. One of them, "Le Premiere qui Vole," Mr. Denig's brother-in-law, is an adventurous brave. He was in the Platte territory and, but for his impetuous temper, might have been chief, in accordance with Indian custom, for he counted more "coups", assembled more tents, brought together more followers, more braves, under his command than any other.

Severe snowstorm, biting cold, and howling north wind. How queer that yesterday this north wind was so mild the snow began to melt. Can it be that the current of air had swept over a warm section of country, bearing forward the warmth of the South? I can defy this frightfully cold weather when I am put in such a jolly good mood by this bright fire in my fireplace.

How the moist wood sputters and crackles as it burns! It is a joy to behold. Or has my blonde disposed me to be gay? Ach, Marguerite, you would be beautiful enough to suit me, and sufficiently industrious too, if you were only not quite so silly.

Made further progress today in "fort-unionization", Mr. Denig's expression. In other words, I had to take 81 buffalo tongues out of salt and hang them up in my room to dry. Then I was told to cut more than 170 fresh tongues out of buffalo heads and pack them thick in a cask filled with warm salt water. It's as though I were living in a pork house, which overhead suggests a heaven filled with joys I dare not taste. Mr. Denig refuses to sell these choice morsels even at a dollar apiece.

November 27. The bourgeois' sled (cariole) I have painted red and black. Another eagle I am ordered to paint tomorrow; these flags with painted eagles are much sought after as significant gifts. So, by means of such presents, that cost him practically nothing, Mr. Denig is said to have attracted great numbers of customers.

November 28. Absaroka and Assiniboin are encamped across the river only a few miles from here and, now that the stream is frozen over, they are continually visiting at this fort.

They transact no business but do a deal of eating and tobacco smoking. I have become acquainted with another Crow chief; his name is Four Rivers. He is a very powerful man, both in regards to physique and in relationships. Le Fourbillon, an Assiniboin, is said to count more "coups" than all the known warriors of any nation in this part of the world. He has slain 24 enemies with his own hand. Le Gras, Le Garonille, the knapper (one who has been scalped though not killed) are only parasites, beggars.

November 29. Engagees are giving a dance at their own expense in the dining room, which is near me. Meanwhile, I peel twigs of the upland willow and weave fancies over an occasional pipe of this Indian blend. Glad I am not obliged to join the dance; but the cotillion affords more graceful figures, I admit, than the silly waltzes.

November 30. Farewell November! If December brings me as many interesting prospects I shall be well satisfied. How soft, how harmoniously blended are the colors on the wide prairie, under a light covering of snow. Yellows and browns, black and rose, among the grasses and weeds with their gray seed pods, blended with the snow, give every variety of hue and shade. On that radiant plain a buffalo with his velvety winter coat of hair must stand in splendid relief.

December 1. This evening an Assiniboin from the lower camp came to me because in the crowded rooms he could find no place to sit or anything to eat. He was tired and so hungry, he said, that his stomach was continually crying out "rygrug." As I have no authority to feed and lodge Indians on my own responsibility, nor had received instructions to that effect, I could not show too much compassion for his empty stomach. I indicated to him that Minnehasga must give him food. In the meantime he sat down by the fire and I filled my pipe for him. We smoked together. How it occurred to him, a stranger, to get at my weak side, I do not understand. He began to specify certain words in the Assiniboin tongue and to give their meanings by signs, explaining that I was to write them down.

I was so delighted with this unexpected civility on the part of a "savage" that my strict sense of duty began more and more to relent as my list of words increased. I hurried out to the storehouse to fetch a piece of sun-dried meat, though the cold was terrible and keys and locks stuck so fast to my fingers that I thought I should pull the skin off in getting them loose. "Osmiedo", he said, when, puffing and blowing, I reentered the room. Yes, it was, really freezing cold. I permitted him to sleep there. His hunger appeased, he rolled himself up in his buffalo robe and fell asleep on the hard floor.

When the Indians are at the fort in such numbers an especial need is felt for a room of good size with a large fireplace, where the redskins can be quartered en masse. As things are now, they have to be crowded into at least five rooms already occupied, an arrangement that is uncomfortable for both the occupants and the visitors. At this especial time of year all of them like to squat about the fire, and they interfere with the cooking. In midsummer they would find the heat and steam all the more unbearable. Mr. Denig is speaking of having an Indian lodge built; by so doing he would not only satisfy a need but also win for himself a great many friends. We have already devoted our combined efforts to drawing a plan for the construction.

December 2. The same old story of an Indian woman I am to marry—if it were only not so difficult to keep her after I get her! They remain just long enough to procure all that a white man is able to give them; the first time he says, "It is impossible", then it is adieu, je t'ai ou, with them. They know that women are in great demand.

To return to my story, as I was coming back to my room, after having closed the gates, I found an old woman and a young Indian girl sitting on my doorsill. They have been living for several weeks in the camp without. I thought they were waiting only to ask me to open the gate again, but I was mistaken; they intended to come into the room with me.

The young girl was quite well-grown, had fine, noble features, soft, languishing eyes, and, for an Indian woman, a very high forehead. Her face was washed clean, a delicate crimson came and went in her cheeks; but, oh, Lord! The rest of her was in such contrast! Her swarthy neck, shoulders, and bust, her doeskin dress, sleek and shining with grease and dirt, her shabby buffalo robe. The old woman talked a great deal, but the young one, though friendly in manner, only sighed gently, then more deeply, then aloud. I understood her quite well, but the family did not appeal to me at all. When they saw that I could not talk to them, or would not, the girl went to fetch the mulatto, Auguste, that he might act as interpreter. I refused to let that fellow have anything to do with my affairs, and sent him for Morgan. To be sure, Morgan does not know any great deal himself about the Assiniboin language, but I wished to have him come just for the fun of the thing. For a long while they discussed the matter, but to no purpose: With the women, marriage was the word and gifts in return for the bride; on the other hand, a poverty-stricken Indian family with an endless family connection to be supported by the groom—fireside joys too dearly bought!

Morgan left. So did the women. I had hardly closed the door behind the latter and was starting over to see Morgan when I heard a knock at the door. There stood the two women again with the blind head of their family. They came into the room. The blind man said by means of signs: "I give you my daughter to live here with you." Fortunately, Packinaud had got wind of the matter, and came limping over to take a part in the trade. He must have the girl, he asserted, without paying a horse. When that plan failed utterly he became angry and sent them all off.

From now on I am allowed to sell buffalo robes among other commodities under my charge. The price has been advanced from $4 to $5 apiece, just at this time when they are most in demand. Mr. Denig claims that he makes so little profit on them here he would do better to send them to St. Louis. Yes—probably.

December 3. From my night lodger I learned additional words in the Dakota speech. When he had taught me numerals up to 10 I laid down another chip, hoping he would tell me the word for 11; but in spite of all signs I was able to make, he refused further to understand; seemed to think I would lead him on to 30, 40, etc. His sense of color was not at all pronounced: Blue and green were one and the same to him; so were brown and black. He assumed that, having done me such an immense service, he was privileged to beg unceasingly for everything that came within his view. I gave him a present of some tobacco and let him go.

As a means of passing the time during these long winter evenings I have begun teaching Packinaud English. If he learns enough to be able to write and calculate in that language he can occupy a higher post. In return, he teaches me words in the Herantsa and Dakota dialects.

December 6. I got from Smith a real live red fox to paint. Smith brought the fellow in just as he was caught, by his nose, with the trap—a very rare occurrence. Animals are usually caught by their feet. According to my observation of Master Reynard in this region, he has not half the cunning of a wolf, for five of his sort are entrapped to one of the latter. As I sat wholly absorbed in painting the frightened animal, that in quiet behavior as well as in form and color afforded me an excellent model, in came Mr. Denig, who bought the fox from Smith at once, had a cage prepared in which Reynard is to live, directed me to take care of him and feed him, in return for which service I am to study him and paint pictures of him to my heart's content. In the meantime I had taken advantage of the opportunity to make a sketch of him, together with the trap. Now that he is behind the bars, happy to have his nose released, I shall make another study.

Instruction in English and Herantsa.

December 9. My imagination is likely to be overburdened in preserving all the new pictures I am storing there; it is now a matter of conservation rather than productivity. My demon of composition will not break loose until I shall have left this place for some years and long for these scenes again.

December 10. Belhumeur's arrival here last night from the winter post below us caused a break in our quiet life. (I am already quite used to seeing great numbers of Indians.) Mackenzie sent him up here to notify us that Joe Picotte, regardless of his pledged word, had sent his traders to the more distant settlements of the Assiniboin and Cree to anticipate us in the purchase of robes on hand. At that news everything here took fire. Morgan had to mount John and race to the horse guard with an order to bring in all the horses tonight. A decision was made at once to counteract by all possible means the treachery, deceit, and dishonesty of Joe Picotte, whatever the cost. The fact is, Joe had only sent his traders out into the lower fur-producing districts. However, he is no longer to be trusted; consequently, Mr. Denig is going to contest his right to every inch of ground and to every hide. He sent away three expeditions with goods today: Cadotte to Knife River; Morgan to the lower Bourbeuse to relieve Mackenzie so that Mackenzie may be able to avert imminent peril to himself, and, furthermore, he sent a courier to Bruyere, instructing him to dispatch clerks in every direction and to strain every nerve in his efforts to bring about Joe's defeat.

Only Packinaud the lame and Istaboba remain with Mr. Denig to protect the fort. The bourgeois is at this time, of course, in a state of great irritation.

After all our feasting, largesse, and advances to Ours Fou, he has brought us, from his camp of 60 tents, only 57 robes. It looks as though Indians so near the range of buffalo herds would never be in need of anything; they have any number of raw hides in their possession, but are disinclined to tan them, because their stomachs are full.

December 14. After a few quiet days we have another great stir in fort and camp. The sugar is out. No more sugar for coffee, no more sugar given away, no sugar either for sale or for buffalo hides. Frightful state of things! What is life worth without sugar? It will be almost half a year before a fresh cargo can be had. The sweet-tooth engagees have well supplied themselves; as soon as they learned from Packinaud that sugar and meal might give out they went with him into the storehouse and had him put 50 pounds, in secret, to their account. In that way several barrels have been emptied without Mr. Denig's knowledge until yesterday, when Packinaud, unable to make the entries, because he cannot write, had to specify the persons whom he had allowed credit.

What dismay in the land of Canaan! Famine was about to set in. What damage to trade! Ten barrels more of meal and 20 barrels more of sugar would have been no appreciable increase in the steamer's cargo, while for want of a sufficient quantity of these commodities several hundred buffalo robes are lost to the company, for the reason that Indians put themselves to little trouble for other goods on sale. In winter they prefer their robes to woolen blankets, and their own sort of clothes made of skin to those made of cloth, because leather is a better protection against wind and cold than wool. Only in water it does not serve.

I made use of my opportunity to paint a black-tailed deer (*Cervus macrotis*). They prefer to inhabit ravines and mountain glens, and are altogether more rarely seen than the elk and white-tailed deer. This species is of larger size than the *Cervus virginianus*, but not so large as the elk. Because these blacktails are distinguished by their long ears, they are called "mule deer"; the other name is due to the black, crinkly hair that covers their throats and extends along the under forepart of the body to the paunch, and the longer black hair of their tails. Their haunches and the under side of their legs are white like the *Cervus virginianus*.[3]

I had much trouble with my water-color sketch. Though I held the water over the fire in a tin cup it froze when I applied it to the ice-cold paper, and soon formed ice crystals on my porcelain pallette.

Bad news has reached us from the other side. Yesterday, two of our metifs who are out of employment went to the Yellowstone with dog sled and two pack horses to hunt on their own account, in order to provision their families with meat and, if possible, to obtain some hides. They were attacked, so the report goes, by Blackfeet. David is severely wounded and Antoine is missing. Without delay, I

[3] According to Audubon and Bachmann, the head of a buck in our public room at this fort is of the Columbia blacktail species (Richardsonii), not the same as the mule deer mentioned above. This head has ears, to be sure, that cover the first branching-off of the horns and are larger than those of the *Cervus macrotis*. In Audubon's drawing the female Columbia blacktail has a long tail, sparse of hair; that does not correspond to his description. His drawing of the female *Cervus macrotis* corresponds just a little to his description. The fictitious hunter-naturalist A (Audubon was really in California, and not in Oregon) in Capt. Mayne Reid's "Hunter's Feast" designates one sort of these deer, *Cervus macrotis* and the other, *Cervus leucurus* (blacktails and longtails). According to him, the difference lies merely in the short, stout bodies and short legs of the blacktails. These last-named he gives, rightly I think, a southern habitat, i. e., California to Texas; the longtails, *Cervus leucurus*, on the contrary, he ascribes to Oregon and the upper Missouri.

harnessed three dogs to the cariole, Mr. Denig got in and had Joe conduct him to the Crow settlement where David is said to be.

Mr. Denig brought our wounded man home. His nose was pierced through in the direction of his left eye and both his feet are frozen. What a wretched outlook to be lame and half blind in this wild region. As yet no trace has been found of Antoine la Pierre. As soon as we had put David to bed, made an examination of his wounds and dressed them, he gave an account of his adventure. They were fortunate enough to come upon a drove of 200 elks and shot 4 of the cows; whereupon their rifles, owing to the sudden alternation from cold to hot, became dripping wet and of no further use. They had hardly lighted their evening campfire, put their meat on spits and stretched the hides as a protection against the rough wind, when some Indians plunged out of a nearby thicket and fired upon them.

Antoine fled from the place at once, or at least disappeared in the darkness. David, momentarily staggered by being shot in the face, could not see how to defend himself. He was only conscious of clamorous voices, as of many Indians running toward him to take his scalp, of the first arrival's crying out to Blackfeet: "A white man," and then sounds of a quick flight. In all probability the Indians took the pack horses with them, and perhaps Antoine also. David, severely wounded as he was, attempted to reach the Assiniboin camp. On the journey his feet froze; his moccasins must have been wet. David's wife and children will have a hard time this winter: David is out of employment, and though he owned nothing of much use, has now lost all his belongings together with the rifle and saddle Mr. Denig had lent him. Nor do David and his wife stand well with the Bombarde family; on the whole metifs are not inclined, it is said, to render mutual assistance to one another.

Mr. Denig was invited by Joe Picotte to dinner at Fort William. His family and I were included in the invitation. Family did not go, so I had to accompany the bourgeois. He drove over with his dogs and sled, conducted by Joe, while I galloped along on Cendre as outrider to the equipage. Oh, how splendid, how jolly to ride a fiery racer over the frozen snow! Sparkling sunshine but cold air! Joe expressed a desire to return to virtue and avert punishment.

As I was indulging my whim to ride slowly to the gates on our return home, I was suddenly aroused by seeing the sled with Mr. Denig seated therein almost under Cendre's paunch; the dogs had foolishly ignored their conductor and run between Cendre's legs. If I had not kept the horse well in hand we should have been thrown topsy-turvy into a confused heap.

December 15. Antoine has at last appeared with his skin whole. His story is as follows: After they had kindled a fire and stuck the meat on spits to roast they took off their wet moccasins to dry them and to warm their feet. Antoine put on another pair right away and told David to do likewise; but the latter, suspecting no danger, replied "à tantot." Antoine placed his gun, which was quite wet, not only from having been fired in such cold air but also from having brushed against snow-covered boughs and shrubs as they traveled along, beside the fire to dry and began to cut up the elk cows they had killed and hang up the meat. As he was thus employed he heard a crunching of footsteps on snow and a rustling of boughs; he called his companion's attention to this. David thought the noise was made by their pack horses; the dogs were not stirring at all. Now they had stretched a lodge skin, made of several cowhides sewed together, one above the other in a row, to form a tent. These tent skins being much the worse for wear from age and long use in the packing of goods had become almost transparent. So, as the men sat beside the fire or were busy at work, their shadows could be seen by the enemy, but not clearly enough to indicate the race to which they belonged.

Suddenly there were shots and then a voice, shouting in Blackfeet dialect: "Advance, my men, and take their scalps!" Knowing well that, sitting in the firelight, they were at the mercy of an enemy concealed by darkness, they ran instinctively into the night, each trying to save his own skin. They were thus separated from each other. David does not know himself how long he was running about through the snow in his bare feet, for he was almost insensible from pain and weary wanderings in the dark when he arrived at the Assiniboin camp. Antoine fled to the Crow settlement, which was not so great a distance as the Assiniboin camp. Yesterday morning Antoine went with a band of Crows to their abandoned camping place. Along the banks of the Yellowstone they discovered 15 different footprints. Antoine met some Assiniboin to whom he related his adventure and inquired after his comrade. He let the Crows follow the tracks on farther, while he returned with the Assiniboin to the abandoned campfire. He found other members of the Crow Tribe in possession of his pack horses; the meat had been devoured and the elk skins had disappeared. The sled, the dogs, everything had found great favor with someone. The Crow Indians maintained that it was all legitimate booty because metifs have no right to hunt in that part of the domain. They consented to give back only the pack horse belonging to our company, and did that purely on repeated admonition of the Assiniboin, the real owners of the land.

The Blackfeet took no booty, merely shot one of the dogs that happened to be with the horses. The other two dogs were lying by the fire, and the only thing that can be said for any of them is that they were certainly very poor guards.

December 16. At breakfast Mr. Denig told me I was to hold myself in readiness to go soon with La Bombarde to the camp of his brother-in-law, Le Premier qui Vole, to trade for buffalo robes, although, so far as that is concerned, he is certain of the robes anyway. How delighted I should be to spend several weeks in an Indian's camp just as one of the "savages"! What a chance to study camp scenes! However, La Bombarde has not yet come back from Blackfeet territory, whither he was sent to bring back a pair of horses. Tonight Ours Fou, his widowed daughter-in-law, and her two pretty daughters are sleeping in my room. In the Absaroka language, "Bearshead" is written "Machetetsi Antu"; "Rottentail", "Tsite Yore"; "Sapsucker", "Ubschita Thash." In Herantsa, "Quatre Ours" is written "Machbitse Topa"; "Queue Rouge", "Sita Ische"; "Langue de Boeuf", "Kirayi Lesche."

December 20. This morning I was forced into a fight with Badger. Morgan sent him here yesterday with other dogs harnessed to a sled, which was loaded with tongues and driven by Belhumeur. Today he was to return home. Out of pure sympathy for the beast I gave him a good breakfast; whereupon, he crept under my bed and refused to come out until I poked him with a sharp-pointed rod in such a way that he became furious and sprang at me.

I had to strike him sharply on the nose to make him mind me. Mr. Denig was outside stamping impatiently, while he complained of the delay. When he was told the reason for it he said that dogs used for the purpose of drawing sleds must be fed only in the evening, after the day's work is done. Otherwise, as I had just seen, if they were fed beforehand, they became drowsy and lazy. I shall let this serve as a warning to me. While Badger was asleep in my room the whole night, his comrade, Bull, refused to be brought in but remained, in spite of severe cold, before the door on guard.

December 25. Christmas. We were very busy the entire day; our only variation from the usual routine being an extra course at dinner of cake and stewed dried apples served with cream. Last Monday, when Rottentail came with his band, they brought 130 buffalo robes. The Absaroka are famous for their robes; in no other nation are the dressed skins so soft and pliable. As I have no robes for my bed except the handsome one given me by Mr. Denig, I was biding my time to choose the most beautiful I could find in a pack of excellent ones, as a model of the best manufacture. As bad luck would have it, I did not find among these great piles a single buffalo robe that satisfied me. On most of them I found the hair imperfect; furthermore, they were cut in two and sewed together in a seam down the middle.

Some of the Crow chiefs, and several girls as well, wore robes of extraordinary beauty; the skins were entire, including both the head and tail; they were not cut at all, the hair was long and silky, the skin as soft and pliable as a woolen blanket. Such robes cost as much, at least, as a Mackinaw blanket. Since the Absaroka have found out that fur traders pay no more for a good buffalo robe than for one tanned just ordinarily well, they take little pains with those intended for trade. And they are right. Fur traders pay more attention to quantity than quality. The bourgeois sell thousands of buffalo robes in packs of ten robes each. Salesmen first examine the packs and sort the robes, including in every assortment, both at this trading post and in St. Louis at Choteau Jr. & Co., at least 1 robe of the best quality in every pack of 10. Sometimes, for the sake of the fine, curly hair, small hides of 1-year-old calves are sold for robes made of cowhides. Raw calf's skins and robes made from scabby skins are not offered for sale. An old robe that has been in use is more sought than a new one, when the hair is in good condition, because, after it has been worn, it shows always whether it was properly tanned, whether it is soft, and whether it can be cleaned.

We purchased from a band of Cree some immense elk horns; they are sold as ornaments for wall decoration or for the manufacture of knives, tobacco pipes, etc. I am itching for a pair, but, as the Canadians say, "je jongle enivre." I am still contemplating the purchase.

They are far too difficult to pack and too heavy to carry; besides, they are dispensable, because sketches can be made from several different views.

We have with us today old Sapsucker, Bearshead, and their adherents. That they may not be obliged to lie down with common folk, the two chiefs are quartered in my room. Honor to whom honor is due! Crows are distinguished from other tribes by individual features of face and form, cut of their hair, vanity, penchant for personal adornment, and marked parental affection. The men, who value wealth above valor, sagacity, or honor, make a great show of their apparel and decorations. In their hair they hang hollow tubes of white and violet-colored porcelain (wampum), and about their necks they wear long ropes of the same ornaments. They decorate with beads their leather pouches and also those broad bands by means of which they swing their bows, quivers, and rifles across their shoulders. Among the Crow Indians originated that singular style of trimming, for women doeskin garments, with rows on rows of elk's teeth placed horizontally across front and back. They use for that purpose the six lower incisors of the elk, which, since they are so few, are very expensive; one hundred of them cost as much as a pack horse, i. e., $20. The women among the Crow Tribe cut their hair short above the eyes and on the neck. Only the men are allowed to make themselves conspicuous for long hair, and to that end, just as do their relatives, the Herantsa, they stick on false hair as a means of making their own seem longer than it really is.

Indians of no other nation so frequently call themselves by name as the Crows. With much self-esteem they place their right hand on breast and say Absaroka! Then extending their arms from the side they imitate the motion of wings when a bird is in flight. Women and children are not subjected to the rigid discipline that is customary among other nations; on the contrary, they are allowed to be present at the tribal meetings for counsel and even to interrupt the speakers with remarks of their own. Such a liberty is unheard of among other tribes. Rottentail's 12-year-old is always hanging around where his daddy is and constantly begging for something or taking part in the old man's conversations. These practices cause the Crows to be ridiculed by friend and foe alike.

David is blind in his right eye; his toes, black from having been frozen, are beginning to drop off. Twice a day I have to rid both feet of the putrefied flesh and dress the wounds with copaiba balsam salve. In return, they beg alms of me incessantly: "un petit brin de sucre; seulement une poigné de café."[3a] How can I gratify their wants without stealing? These people seem, really, to believe that if a man has the keys to a storehouse he may without scruple pocket a handful here and there—that the company can afford to lose it!

The metifs here are the most haughty beggars I have ever seen, an instance where the admixture of Indian blood, which is supposed to improve the white race, has, in reality, made matters worse. They have the opinion that their business is to serve as scouts, huntsmen, or interpreters; to drive oxen or to cut wood is beneath their dignity. David thinks, apparently, that I am here solely for his benefit; that I am to provide food, fuel, medicine, and other things besides for him and his family; yet he is not even employed here and his wife and daughters refuse to sew a stitch by way of payment. Even Madame la Bombarde and her two daughters, who are employed regularly at the fort to make clothes for pay (credit on account), refused Mr. Denig the loan of her dogs to send goods to the upper Bourbeuse. Mr. Denig retaliated by giving her no more work to do; now she has to use her own supply of meat for food.

December 26. I had a quarrel with Jim Hawthorn about "Bearshead." While he was eating breakfast in the kitchen he asserted that I had neither assigned the chief a place to sleep nor provided him

---

[3a] I. e., "A little bit of sugar; just a handful of coffee."

with a buffalo robe. That was not true. I had done both. But after
I had gone to bed "Bearshead" went out to talk with acquaintances
in another room, where he remained quite late. When he came back
he may have found that his place and his robe had been appropriated
by someone else. I could not help that. He said not a word to me,
but complained to Jim Hawthorn, who is always glad to pick a
quarrel with the person whose employment here deprives him of a
position at the fort.

The latter reported the matter, much exaggerated, to the boss with
the hope of precipitating a reprimand upon me; and this he succeeded
in doing. However, I was able to exonerate myself. At supper I
inquired of Jim in a joking way whether he did not know some other
complaint he might bring forward against me. That he made the
occasion for seeking me out after the meal to say he was ready to fight
me with any weapon from "rifle down to needle", if I wished a row
with him. I asked him, only, "Who began with the carping?" I am
not in the least afraid of him; for some time I have been aware of his
malicious ill will.

December 28. My prospects for remaining any considerable time in
a locality as clerk seem daily more uncertain. Joe Picotte is now
convinced that he is unable to compete with the big company. He
has insufficient means; besides, on his secret scouting trip he lost
several horses. He has already recalled the traders he sent out. Joe
comprehends now that Mr. Denig was right when he told him to be
satisfied with what jealousy among soldiers and their advantageous
position with the two companies can bring in. Owing to the competition between companies, for instance, Indians get European goods
at more reasonable prices. Furthermore, a larger number of braves
find employment at a fort as "soldiers" or protectors, a position
greatly desired by Indians and much envied, because it brings with
it not only authority but many fights and other advantages besides.

December 29. Last evening, Antoine La Pierre brought the skin of
a 6-year-old moose buck and the head with horns intact. As I had
a few moments to spare, I made a thorough study of the head in
my room and painted two views of it. Now I shall not find it necessary to buy a pair of elk horns. That much saved. Collecting has
ever been my weak point. As a boy, I was interested in bringing
together seals, armorial bearings, butterflies, fossils, etc.; as artist,
books, pictures, and, at the present time, weapons, apparel, and decorations common to the Indian race. With advancing age I should
become wise and begin to lay by money for my last days. But
when one can spare nothing from his daily earnings, to begin saving
is an art.

The elk is not so gracefully formed as our stag. Brow antlers of
an elk extend to his nose, do not stand upright as those of a stag.

Whenever elks enter a mountain pass, which is very seldom, they go at a gallop. Their hair is long at the throat and underneath on their paunches. In color they are a reddish dun which shades to dark brown on their legs, heads, and along the edges of brighter-colored spots on the buttocks. In winter the color of an elk inclines rather more to gray. If the animals are old it becomes quite dark, verging frequently to black on their extremities.

An elk's hair is longer and rougher than that of a stag, consequently elk hides come on the market, for the most part, untanned. Their hair is much sought by saddle makers.

December 31. The last day of a year that has brought me much nearer the accomplishment of my life purpose. Six months more ahead of me for my studies of animals and hardly any paper and pencils left; there is not one whole lead pencil in the fort and only ruled writing paper. Moreover, it is hardly possible for me to get a new supply of drawing materials before the summer.

As soon as Mr. Denig learned that Joe Picotte and Ramsay had withdrawn from their ill-intentioned enterprise and had really recalled the traders whom they sent out earlier to skirmish for buffalo robes, he had me go to Fort William and ask Joe to sign a written agreement for future dealing. Upon my arrival there I heard bad news: The Blackfeet have again stolen a large drove of horses from the Assiniboin—155 head at one throw! Among them were two belonging to the "Dobies" and three of Carafel's, while La Main qui Tremble, one of our soldiers, lost all of his, including several pre-eminent runners. The Assiniboin brought their remaining horses together in great haste, neither did they spare those belonging to the fur traders, and hurried out in pursuit of the daring thieves. They soon found that the main trail along which the robbers were traveling separated into three, each leading in a different direction so as to confuse pursuers.

For subjects in art animals take a much higher place than natural scenery. Their self-consciousness, intelligence, and sensibility make them more appropriate, therefore, for idealism in pictures. Not only in their bodily structure do animals bear a kindred resemblance to man, but also in their mental faculties and feelings; it is unfortunately true that many an animal is even superior to many a human being. Moreover, animals have their own speech, not a perfectly developed speech, it is true, but a means of expressing their thoughts, their impressions, by means of the voice and the expression of the eyes, etc. That a dog possesses the imaginative faculty is clearly shown by his actions when dreaming. Animals lack the capacity for inner struggle toward an ideal in anticipation of the continued life of the soul after death and attending consequences. Animals of every species present a distinct character of their own, and demonstrate an especial gift; this is rendered plainly perceptible in their bodily form and mode of life. Owing to this analogy between animals and human beings, the former can be represented in art in an allegorical or even a poetic sense. The animal's good fortune to be free, not compelled to bear the weight of custom and tradition, restraints which we cultivated people cannot cast aside in our material progress but the burden of which often oppresses us; the animal's freedom from all this presents a state of things that captivates the human imagination.

Furthermore, beasts have virtues and vices, nay, what is more, inventive genius which, inasmuch as it often brings judgment into play, is to be regarded as of much higher order than mere instinct. These qualities, possessed by animals of certain species, are employed, however, solely in supplying their material needs and in self-preservation. Animals manifest no tendency toward striving to better themselves, apart from training given by man, or to develop themselves for higher purposes in life. According to Audubon and Bachmann, *Elaphus canadensis* is met with nowadays, in regions east of the Mississippi, only in small herds that range a narrow strip in the Allegheny Mountains. This remnant of the large droves that once roamed this part of the country would no doubt have also wandered westward if they had not been isolated in their wild, almost inaccessible mountain retreats west and south of the colonies. Solitary herds of elks are still found also in West Virginia. Formerly they existed in great numbers in all those regions where the buffalo was found.

The Assiniboin, following the way that showed the greatest number of hoofprints, found that it separated also, just as the other did. They came at last upon the worst conditioned of their horses, but saw no Blackfeet. They gave up further pursuit.

Now, Old Year, farewell. At your beginning you exposed me to severe trials, but all is well as you draw to a close. Once more my hopes are high, my courage unabated! If the New Year brings me to the completion of my studies, puts me in a position where I may have the required leisure to execute paintings to my own satisfaction, I shall be quite content.

1852

January 1. To begin the New Year aright I brought from the press room where our furs are kept the most perfect pelt I could find of a grizzly bear,[3b] so that I might complete studies I am making of wild

---

[3b] In shape the grizzly is not unlike our brown bear; he differs from the latter in that his claws are so long he cannot climb. When he is fully grown the hair on his back is gray at the ends; hence his name, a grayish or grizzly bear.

animals now extant in this territory. It took me the entire day to reproduce with exactness the great variety of hues and shades as well as the differences apparent in curly, wiry, smooth, and long hairs. But it must be taken into consideration that I had to attend to my usual duties besides; that the water I was using for my water-color sketch, in spite of my precaution to heat it, often froze on the paper; that I was constantly disturbed by the halfbreed girl with her kisses and New Year's greetings, and frequently summoned by Mr. Denig to write something down, because his sore thumb is giving him a great deal of pain.[4] (The thumb he is in the habit of thrusting into his waistcoat, just as I represented him in the portrait I painted.)

According to French custom, every kiss demands a gift; accordingly, when one asks a girl what she would like at the New Year she replies always: A note, i. e., a bank note. Less than a dollar a man could not offer her; she herself thought that too little. Kisses are dear!

Joe Picotte was here to acknowledge with his signature an agreement that I was required to draw up in writing. The first clause had to do with his sending out traders to anticipate us in acquiring the stock of buffalo robes in those districts that supply our winter trading posts; the second obligated him to pay $1,000 damages; the third, not to employ deserters in any part of the territory over which he has control. This last-named clause is of great importance, because, under conditions therein named, an employee's running away is made so difficult that he would need have the utmost courage to attempt it. Heretofore, people who had played a trick on the opposition were all the more gladly taken into service; their new bourgeois knew how to use their hostility toward the opposing company to his own benefit in the way of intensifying zeal to thwart a competitor. So long as a man was able to find another employer he was, in fact, not looked upon as a deserter; he might even take a hostile attitude toward an earlier master and then, later on, dare go back to him.

Not even while we were drawing up and signing this trade agreement would old dame La Pierre leave us in peace: She kissed, in turn, every man in the office. I came near having an attack of nausea!

January 2. Today old Sapsucker, at the head of a stout band of Absaroka, came marching across the frozen Missouri to our fort. To do him honor, I was commissioned to fire a salute of three guns; that is, I fired three times with our 4-pounder that stands on the gallery above the river gate. As there were neither cartridges nor match cord

---

[4] A great protuberance of proud flesh formed below the nail and later, after having caused intense pain, fell off. For a long while Mr. Denig feared he might lose his arm.

at the fort I had to wrap a load of powder in paper and thrust it into the barrel, then ram it in with shreds and rags of leather, clear out the vent with an iron pin, put powder on the pan and touch it off with a burning brand. And all by myself. It was in loading the gun after this clumsy fashion that old Gareau (Pierre's father) lost an arm. He thought it unnecessary, after having fired, to stop the vent while reloading.

But what does Mr. Denig care? Sapsucker and his entire family are again my guests. This name *Sapsucker* is the usual designation in the United States for the "downy woodpecker" (*Picus pubescens* Audubon).

January 3. This old chief's medicine is dried buffalo dung! When I lighted my Indian pipe and offered it to him he rubbed, from a bullet-shaped substance in his hand, some dry powder over the smoking tobacco.

Thinking he did this to obtain some sort of aroma, yet sensible of no resulting fragrance, I asked him what it was. He laid in my hand a piece of dry buffalo dung, indicating that I must never neglect to put some of it on the tobacco when I desired to smoke with him. Two of his children wear bits of this miraculous medicine in their hair, just above the brow, as talisman.

Today Mr. Denig bartered with one of the Absaroka for a charming pipe bowl of red sandstone and, as he had no use for it, he offered it to me at cost price for my collection. "If my credit is so far good," I replied. "Certainly," he said. So I bought the beautiful pipe bowl for $7 and had it charged to my account. For such a treasure I should have to pay, among the Crows, the price of a pack horse. The red standstone comes from a cliff near the St. Peters River in Sioux territory; these pipe bowls are fashioned (drilled out, shaped, and polished) by the Sioux, but are offered as articles of trade among all the rest of the natives as well.

Le Petit Mandan came today from the Herantsa village. He says great numbers of buffaloes are seen in the near neighborhood. Nevertheless, I am indeed glad to have been driven to this place, even through the influence of Indian superstition. Only I regret not having been able to make a finished drawing of the village with all its medicine poles, while the Herantsa were encamped within.

I had no opportunity at all; even after they had left there still remained several old hags whose tongues were as dangerous as arrows and just as likely to strike one unawares.

January 4. With the hope of being able to complete sketches of several antlered stags' heads that we have on hand, I hurried through my day's tasks, such as the distributing of meat, feeding the chickens, pigeons, etc. But, notwithstanding that it was Sunday,

Mr. Denig did not fail to find continually something else for me to do. He is kept in a sort of feverish unrest by pain in his thumb; proud flesh is causing the loss of his thumbnail. On account of this he cannot write, so I have to serve as his secretary. In intervening intervals he never fails to find fault with something. He is vexed if I cannot account for every rope, every nail, tool, implement, stock, ring, saddle, nay, even every mouse in the fort. I am to keep a sharp lookout in all directions, so as to know what is in stock, what is wanting, what is out of place; I am to know from actual observation everything, even to the smallest objects, that is stored in the attic under the roof, in boxes and chests, in barrels and casks, in the cellar, in places to which I am not admitted, in outhouses, even among dungheaps in a stall; for shovels and hose or something else may be left lying there neglected or forgotten. If I cannot give an account of a thing forthwith—who has it or where it lies, stands, or hangs, as the case may be—then he says "It is too infernal bad."

When I was given the keys there was no inventory from which I could inform myself; so there was no way for me to know offhand whether certain things were here or not, the names of many tools and implements I had not even heard, at least in the patois, half-Yankee, half-Canadian, half-Indian, that is spoken here. The fault with me is not that I am lacking in diligence or punctuality, but that I am undiscerning, or rather than I am not sharp-sighted, lack curiosity (propensity to stick my nose into everything), and what is more, my thoughts are always intent on my studies in art. My day's work should engross my attention; unfortunately, that is not true; art always occupies my best thoughts. Wherever I am, wherever I go, my eyes instinctively seek beauty of form and color, my attention is attracted by objects that are interesting. To be sure, I might force myself to live entirely absorbed in the duties of clerk and foreman if it had to be done for any great length of time. I have no intense desire to tarry here several years, but only so long as I need to stay to finish my studies. In spite of the romantic adventure of my situation I should become bored in the course of time. Besides, I cannot execute my paintings here—finish my collection; I should find that impossible. I notice there are people enough in the land to do the work of clerks. Hawthorn has been hereabouts for a good long time and yet has no employment. My departure is his dearest wish.

There now lies before me a most charming deer's head that lures me insistently to the paintbrush.[5] How delicate, how tender, how graceful the lines of this little head of a hind! How perfectly in harmony with her character—gentle, shy, elusive. No line is per-

---

[5] Under the term deer (Hirsch) one is to understand that virginia deer is meant, not elk.

fectly straight, no line is crooked, no line turns abrupt angles; nothing indicates boldness, solidity, or power, but all is buoyant force and energy. This head is truly beautiful, its form in perfect accord with the character and species of the animal to which it belongs. Were I to idealize the little hind I should say such perfect loveliness of form bespeaks a corresponding perfection of soul (high degree of intelligence, purity of heart, depth of feeling); but we can idealize the forms of animals only by ascribing to them qualities of mind and heart which they do not really possess.

January 6. Mr. Denig bartered again with an Absaroka for an Indian ornament, i. e., a long necklace of 30 bear's claws. When an Indian offers such ornaments for sale one gets them always for much less than when one asks the redskin to set his price.

As a matter of course they never offer an article like that for sale unless at the moment they need something else much more; therefore the purchaser has the advantage. If one proposes to buy from an Indian some object that he highly values and is not obliged to part with he demands in return as much as he likes or else something that he would much rather have. Mr. Denig barters for such trinkets and trappings as an accommodation to the Indians only when he sees that he can dispose of the object in question at a profit, or at least without loss. He offered me the necklace at the cost price ($10). I took it at once.

Ours Fou again with me. To his great annoyance he found a young Crow already installed in my room, because, according to the custom of the Crow tribe, this young fellow dare not live in the same room with his mother-in-law. He dare not talk with her directly or allow her to see his face until his young wife bears him a child. The same custom is observed among the Dakotas, but only at the first marriage.

Ours Fou wished me to send the "buck" away: He sought the solitude of my room for the express purpose of being undisturbed; furthermore, he thought it beneath his dignity to sit beside this young fop and smoke with him. The latter was most richly appareled: Coat, leggings, and hood fashioned from a new Mackinaw blanket; another Mackinaw blanket he trailed negligently after him in such a manner as to display its wealth of ornamentation.

He went doubly armed, as when he arrived: He swung his rifle over his shoulder in a sheath, bow and quiver in two broad bandoliers, the straps of both entirely covered with coral beads in various designs. The sheath was decorated with fringe and scarlet cloth. He carried with him three pouches, all richly ornamented, absolutely covered with beads arranged in different patterns. The largest of these pouches opened at the side; the shot bag, with cover, was attached to his belt in front; a third pouch, closed with long, tapering cover, was fastened to his belt in the back. His knife sheath was just as elaborately embroidered. It was also trimmed with fringe and, like his knee bands, with falcon bells (from Leipzig). The tinkling of those rows of bells behind and before gave him an especial pleasure. In face and form he was quite attractive looking and manifestly the darling of many sisters or else of other girls who hoped to be his future wives.

He was constantly trying to be companionable with me. He asked me how many horses I owned, with the evident purpose of considering whether, if he offered me a present of one of his, I would make it up, later on, by giving him another in return. I did not encourage him, however, though Mr. Denig had advised me to say, if the young Absaroka made me a present of a horse, that next year I would give him a good one in return, when there will be none left. My painter's wallet made of oilcloth appealed to him very much as a novelty.

Inasmuch as I had a good practical pouch made here, I gave the one I formerly used to him; I had experienced, alas, how little suited to its purpose it was when one traveled on horseback.

His stirrups and saddle were also elaborately ornamented with beads and tassels. The Crows' saddles are made without wood and without pommel; they consist of two leather cushions bound together by means of a broad, solid leather girth. They are most comfortable for the rider, and, being soft and pliable, they inflict no discomfort or hardship on the horse. Besides, the Crows never fail to use a piece of buffalo hide with hair, or some other skin as saddle blanket (apischimo).

January 7. Cadotte brought in a cabri doe, of which I painted a sketch.

January 9. Yesterday Grayhead and Bearshead arrived, together with the tribesmen belonging to their respective bands, for purposes of trade. The two chiefs and their families were shown to my room, which became so crowded in consequence that one could hardly stir. So I found no chance to celebrate my thirty-fourth birthday with reflections on this transitory life. Among 130 robes, more or less, I fail yet to find one of the first quality. On most of them the hair, here and there, is like black silk velvet, but they are either tanned in a superficial way or cut in two and sewed in a seam down the middle, or of good, soft skin, lacking the best hair.

As Crows care little for other commodities just now, but demand horses almost altogether in exchange, we are longing for the return of La Bombarde from the Blackfeet territory, whither he went with Mr. Culbertson to trade for a drove and bring them to this fort.

As in every instance the chief of a band as such is favored in the presentation of gifts according to the number of robes he brings, these leaders bestir themselves, naturally, to make their people hurry with the preparation of skins. In their eagerness to get together the number of robes required they pay no attention to the quality of work done. Among 400 that were prepared by Assiniboin and sent in from Mackenzie's post, I was unable to find one to my taste, for though I must admit they were tanned in a painstaking manner on the whole, yet all were sewed together in the middle. This is due to the fact that the women, to save themselves trouble, cut out that part of the hide which, even on a cow's back, is very thick, and then sewed the two parts together with thread made from dried sinews or tendons.[6] Now and then it happens that they sew together parts of hides that were taken from different animals, which produces a singular effect.

When Madame David came to get "le dur" from me so that she might improve some robes Mr. Denig thought too imperfectly prepared for market, I could not understand for a long while what "le dur" could mean. I was conducted by her to the meat house, where she pointed out the liver. This organ, also the brain of a deer or, in case of emergency, fat of any sort, tallow, etc., are all used to soften hides. One woman dresses a buffalo hide in 3 or 4 days just as well, makes the skin just as soft and durable, as our leather dressers do in 6 months. First of all, they stretch the raw hide on the ground and fasten it down with pegs or wooden pins, and with some sharp instrument, or a piece of bone perhaps, they scrape off every particle of flesh, which is eagerly devoured by the hungry dogs. If the skin is not to be dressed until later they leave it spread in the air to dry until it becomes quite hard. If, on the other hand, they intend to prepare the robe at once, they rub the hide for one entire day with liver, fat, or the brain of a deer to soften the skin, leave it 2 or 3 days (according to the season or extreme temperature) until the grease soaks in, then they dry it at a slow fire, constantly beating or rubbing it meanwhile with a stone until it becomes uniformly soft and pliable. This rubbing is of the greatest importance in the dressing of skins after Indian fashion.

As soon as the hide has been prepared in the manner described above and is quite dry they begin the fatiguing process of rubbing it around a taut rope of horsehair or braided leather to make it smooth; then it oftentimes receives a final polish with pumice stone. Such work is most burdensome from start to finish; even the scraping of the hides has to be done in a stooped position that is very fatiguing. As the brain of a deer is finer and more rare than liver or tallow, it is used primarily in the preparation of deerskins (except skins of

---

[6] Canadians call this Indian thread "du nerf." There are different qualities of it. Tendons of the long muscle that extends the length of the backbone are used preferably for that purpose; the finest thread is made from the dorsal muscles of the Virginia deer and antelopes.

elks). Hides of deer are placed in the final stage of preparation over a slow fire covered with green sprays of sumac and smoked; owing to this process they suffer less injury from water, they become golden brown in color, and retain for quite a while the smell of smoke, which repels mosquitoes and moths.

Grayhead was given his name on account of his gray hair, which, however, is a perfect yellow in spots. As he is not grayheaded from age the singularity of his appearance has acquired for him this nickname. He wears always a fur cap with a red feather. He insists upon much ceremony when he joins in the tobacco smoking. First of all, he makes the statement that he smokes only after meals. Then La Queue Rouge, who has returned from his visit, lights the pipe and with his right hand extends it to Grayhead according to custom, the mouthpiece forward. Whereupon Grayhead explains to him that he is supposed to hold the pipe out in front of him, not offer it directly to a chief. When that position is assumed, Grayhead seizes the pipe with his right fist in a backhanded manner (thumb down) as one grasps a cudgel, passes it gently into his left hand and pulls a whiff. Instead of exhaling the smoke through the nose in the usual manner, however, he holds the pipe aloft in front of him, the stem in a vertical position, and blows the smoke upward through his mouth; again a whiff, and, holding the pipe so that the stem points straight before him, he puffs out the smoke in the same direction; then, grasping the stem with his left hand, he takes a fresh draw, holds the mouthpiece aslant, toward his right side, and blows the smoke to the right; he then inclines the mouthpiece toward his left side, blows the smoke to the left, pulls another whiff, touches the ground with the pipe bowl, emits a cloud of smoke as before, turns toward the fire and blows a puff in that direction, and then begins to smoke in customary Indian fashion, exhaling the smoke through the nose.

When Grayhead saw that I carried the key to the meat house he begged continually for meat for his daughters, who, in expectation that as daughters of a chief they would be supplied with food, put aside for their children the liberal portions of mush served them at the feast. I had instruction from Mr. Denig never to let an Indian have meat without his especial permission, so I referred Grayhead to my boss.

The latter informed the chief that we did not buy cured meat from him for the sake of providing him afterwards with other that was fresh. Notwithstanding, Grayhead continued to beg from Packinaud and others, who replied by way of excuse that they were not in possession of the key to the meat house. An Indian regards it a discourtesy not to be duly entertained at feasts and spreads when he comes on a visit to white people. But what concerns us in these matters is not merely our duty from the standpoint of hospitality but the vital question of sustaining life at a fort. If, therefore, we were required to entertain everyone who comes with hospitality due a guest we should soon have nothing but visitors—no trade, no compensation; consequently, we should soon go to ruin or, in other words, be literally eaten out of business.

January 11. In Zimmermann's workroom I saw four Assiniboin women playing a new game. They sat in a row before the fire. They had four disks, 6 inches long, attached to the ends of wands sharpened to a point. On two of the wands there were disks having the figure of a man on the upper surface; on the other two the upper surface of the disks bore the figure of a hand. The under surfaces of the disks were not marked at all. One after another the women would seize the four wands at the upper ends and throw them on the floor with points turned adroitly downward so as to make them tumble over with all the decorated surfaces of the disks turned upward.

Whoever succeeded in doing that won double the stakes of all the others. If all unmarked surfaces turned upward that counted simply a score; if both marked with the figure of a man or both marked with a hand were turned that counted half as much. The stakes consisted of grains of corn; a certain number designating, according to agreement, stipulated objects, such as ornaments, clothing, etc. The winning woman continues to throw until she fails to turn the disks uniformly, then another player throws them in turn. Women play this game just as eagerly as men, perhaps more passionately when they have no other pastime. They play day and night, lose articles of apparel, and it has happened here that they even put up their children for stakes.

January 12. Again a significant instance of the Indian's sense of obligation in matters of trade. Ever since his arrival in these parts on the steamboat *Robert Campbell* an Assiniboin has been living in his tent at the "Doby" fort. During this entire time he has been provided with food, his smoking tobacco, and with many gifts at the expense of the fort. Finally, when he had finished five buffalo robes, he demanded a high price that Joe Picotte refused to pay. Whereupon the Assiniboin brought his hides here and exchanged them at the current market price. Notwithstanding his indebtedness to Joe, he left him empty-handed.

L'Ours Fou is back again with the members of his encampment. He did not venture beyond the other settlements of Assiniboin and Absaroka, hence had slain no buffaloes. This great but do-nothing chief sees ever hovering before his eyes quantities of cured meat packed in our storeroom, together with supplies of cornmeal mush. Since he has been appointed supreme chief of the Assiniboin by the white man's doing let the white man attend to the duty of having him properly clothed and fed. He confuses all of us white men in this region with Americans—with Uncle Sam. Ours Fou appears to me a stupid rather than a mad bear. First, he came and asked that all his followers be provided with food; when he saw that plan would not work he said, "Still, give me food, at least, and let the others go." Then La Jambe Blessé and La Poudrière followed; they only were to be supplied in addition. It was no use; we could not risk the consequences, so were obliged to have them depart with long faces and empty stomachs. If we had satisfied their demand we should never be rid of these beggars; they would rely on us for supplies, no longer hunt at all, and, as a consequence, we should suffer a twofold loss: Constant reduction of our stores of provisions without any return and no replenishing of our stock of buffalo hides.

On the contrary, as soon as they see that no foodstuffs will be delivered to them except as payment they are forced to go in search of buffalo herds. These Assiniboin grow daily more lazy; they urge as excuse for their inactivity the unfortunate circumstance of their owning so few horses fit to run buffaloes. In that case owners of swift horses have a distinct advantage which they should put to good use now by hunting in behalf of their less fortunate comrades in the camp. At an earlier time every man stood on his own feet, everybody had equal chance upon the encircling of a herd on a buffalo hunt. Footmen remained in the rear of horsemen and those riding ponies took position behind the huntsmen mounted on American racing horses. One of our customers has related here how on foot, during an earlier season, he slew 140 buffaloes in one winter, and sold their tongues and hides at this fort. An entire settlement (40 to 60 tents) takes not so much booty in a whole winter nowadays.

Le Gras brought bad news from the Yellowstone. The river is out of bounds, has overflowed its banks and inundated Rottentail's camp. His largest tent, made of 25 skins put together, all his commodities but recently purchased, his stock of raw buffalo hides together with those already tanned, his clothing, decorations, everything was carried off by the high waters. He himself, they say, sits on a hill and wails. Sapsucker lost 2 of his 37 horses.

A Crow was taken so suddenly unawares by the swiftly rising water that he no longer had time to slip out through his low tent door but had to clamber up poles on the inside to the smoke hole in the roof and shout for help. He was later rescued by a friend mounted on a large, heavy horse. Wallace, whom Mr. Denig had despatched with letters to a trading post in Crow territory, lost his steed in the flood; but at that time he had no business at all anywhere near the river.

Mr. Palesieux's plan was a topic of conversation today. He desires to return to this part of the world for a while to indulge his passion for hunting. He said last year, in fact, when he set out with his trophies on his return journey to Ireland that he wished to come back again equipped with his own supplies of goods and provisions—not for the sake of profits in trade, but merely to hunt, and that he would employ people of the region hereabout to assist and protect him. We found his plan impossible, even for so wealthy a man as himself, with an income of several hundred dollars a day. For instance, his idea was to travel out to this territory either by steamboat or on horseback, bringing his full equipment; to have a blockhouse built and to hunt to his heart's content with huntsmen hired for the purpose.

He is passionately fond of the sport, shoots well, but has no capacity for starting the game; he is forced to rely on his assistants to find the wild beasts and show them to him. He can find no spot on which to have his hut erected that is not Indian domain; he must gain the good will of those who own his hunting ground by the payment of money or he will be looked upon as a scoundrel and robber. In that event, if he attempts to defend himself he will suffer the loss of his belongings, and perhaps, nay, most likely, of his life also; if he obligingly leaves everything undefended he will be driven away. He can by no means remain long unobserved; sharp-sighted Indians will discover trace of him by the smoke from his fire. They will immediately spread abroad the news of a stranger hunting on their land, turn to their own profit his unauthorized presence there, using that as a means to obtain benefits by soliciting gifts, supplies of food, etc. They will regularly besiege his blockhouse; they will make such demands on his resources with their mendacity that even with his great wealth he cannot stand it for any length of time; for he is not coming as fur trader but for the love of sport. Woe be unto him if he enters the field as merchant and draws down upon himself the jealousy of other combined fur traders, who are organized into a company with enormous capital at their command, with privileges of trade obtained by purchase and already acknowledged, and with power to ruin him as a competitor.

However, Mr. Palesieux is purely a lover of hunting; he collects trophies merely with his own hand and his Indian women make his clothes. Coming on his own account as independent gentleman, he does not profit by the protection of any fur-trading company, unless he purchases his supplies from one of the companies at their market price, precisely what he is endeavoring to avoid. A man must have untold wealth to maintain an independent existence in these far distant wilds. In the first place, he must pay dearly to the Indians for the privilege of enjoying his favorite pursuit; secondly, it will inevitably happen sooner or later that he can not grant some Indian's request, cannot escape offending in some way or other; consequently, no matter how kind and generous he may desire to be, he will make an enemy. Those who bear him a grudge will seek opportunity to do him injury, to endanger his life. The greater his amount of supplies, the more he will be beset by begging Indians; the more hunters he keeps in his employ, the more independently he conducts his affairs, the more numerous his enemies and the more violent their hostility.

Mr. Palesieux's earlier plan was a better one. He brought with him to Fort Berthold a letter of credit from Choteau Jr. & Co. His intention was to buy everything he needed from the company and to make friends of their representatives at the trading posts.

So, upon his arrival he produced the letter of credit, but Mr. Kipp, who is always befogged with liquor, upon the arrival of the steamboat treated the wealthy sportsman discourteously—irritated him. Mr. Palesieux proceeded to Fort Union, accompanied by several hunters whom he took into his employ. He followed the chase for a while in this region, but was quite sparing in outlay for that purpose. Now he has more extensive plans.

A wealthy man indulging such a hobby would do best to set out in spring on horseback to some trading post or other on the Missouri. The farther he goes up the river the better hunting he will find. For a lover of the chase, wandering across the prairies in that way is more interesting than traveling comfortably with never a chance for a shot. He should take horses, guns, ammunition, and a supply of clothing along with him. He should be accompanied by several hunters and guides who are thoroughly acquainted with the country and who are expert in the use of the Sioux language, most widely spoken of the Indian dialects. Last but not least, he should provide himself with a letter of credit on the company for a fixed sum. Then at every post where he may stop on his travels he will find this letter of credit sufficient introduction to procure all that is lacking in his equipment; consequently he need not carry on the journey thither a greater amount of supplies, such as ill-smelling alcoholic liquors and drugs, except in small quantities for strictly medicinal purposes to prevent taking cold or for use in case of slight wounds or bruises.

Having arrived at the trading post which he has chosen for his destination, he makes an arrangement with the bourgeois for room and board by the month, for heat, and for the care of his horses. He is supposed to be content with conditions under which the bourgeois lives; eats at the first table, not at a table set especially for him, where he may enjoy choice dishes while all other occupants of the fort are obliged to be satisfied, perhaps, with plainer fare; for instance, he must not try to enforce compliance with his desire to have fresh meat served when wild animals are not to be found within a range of 40 miles, or to have coffee, sugar, and meal in excess when supplies on hand are barely sufficient for carrying on the fur trade. As one can readily understand, the bourgeois dare not, for the sake of just one man who is to be at the fort but a short while, endanger his trade interests for the future by causing the defection of customers whom he could win back again only at great sacrifice, incurring a loss that would very soon swallow up temporary profits on some items.

If he depends for food and drink on the bourgeois, he dispenses with all appeals for such things on the part of Indians; he delivers himself, so to speak, from all importunate petitions or, at least, from injury to himself, if he fail to gratify the wishes of Indians.

By purchasing everything that he needs, as well as gifts and rewards, from the manager at the fort, he obligates the latter to render him assistance in word and deed; it is to the interest of the bourgeois to become his friend. Owing to high transportation rates, he would pay just as much to bring his supplies with him as he has to pay at the fort. Furthermore, by taking up his abode at the fort under such circumstances he enjoys the same privileges that are granted the company in regard to hunting on Indian domain. If he has something of value stolen from him the bourgeois through his influence can recover the lost article. At the same time he must take into consideration that a man who occupies the position of commanding officer and responsible manager at a fort is displeased when one does not recognize his authority or acts contrary to his regulations; such behavior would precipitate an immediate rupture. When he is thus allowed to travel from one fort to another under the protection of the company he can always be assured of an opportunity to follow the chase, while if he assumes the responsibility of directing his hunting independently he is compelled to search perpetually for the wild beasts. Only in a Robisoniad do all the different species of animals draw near, as if under the spell of a magic charm; in reality, even a region abundantly rich in animal life is soon turned to no account by a troop of hunters.

January 15. Le Gras brought only two leather cabrets to exchange; as soon as he had received as much as they were worth he came to me and asked for a rope with which to tether his saddle horse. Then came the Platteman (Garçon du Fraissée) and wished something to eat. Mr. Denig answered, "Yes; when you bring hides for my trade."

"But you will, at least, let me have some smoking mixture?"

"The upland willow grows quite near your tent."

"Then give me a flint and steel."

"I haven't one; neither have I any coal, that I might have such a thing made."

"Well, can I get a file? I need something of the sort."

"Good! Then bring in some robes."

Mr. Denig fled to my room, hoping to escape such insistent begging, but Le Gras soon hunted him out.

"Now say at once what it is you want," Mr. Denig interposed before the former could speak. "First?"

"A calico case for my pipestem", Le Gras began, "long enough to hang over at both ends."

"Second?" Mr. Denig went on, counting off on his fingers.

"Eyewater."

"Third?"

"Tobacco."

"Fourth?"

Le Gras could not help laughing and thereupon gave up any further petitioning.

Smith, Cadotte, and Antoine returned this evening from a 4 days' hunt with only two elks; this shows how difficult it is to start game in a region inhabited by Indians in large numbers.

January 16. Painted my first study of the elk. These animals are neither so graceful nor so lordly as our stags; their straight backs and strong legs remind one rather more of the cow. I am very anxious to make my studies of animals from life, as well as my sketches of natural scenes, so thorough that they cannot fail to satisfy the naturalists; I have not roamed so far and wide and endured so much merely for the sake of painting pictures according to my own fancy. I must be strictly true to nature in my representation of forms, colors, and movements.

If we should have a heavier snowfall, say, several feet deep, Indians would wander about here less and wild game in our vicinity would be left in peace. In other winters, so I am told, wild animals have approached the fort within shooting distance; one could stand just outside the gate and kill buffaloes and antelopes. Never give up hope, never despair.

January 17. Notwithstanding this frightfully cold weather, Rottentail, with a number of his adherents, came here to arrange for an advance payment so that he can revive his business.

At the same time he gave us an account of the disaster that befell him. The Absaroka were taken unawares by the Yellowstone flood while they slept. They had heard, it is true, the thunderous roar of the waters breaking through the ice, but attributed the sound to a violent gale that was sweeping through the forest. Occupants of the village lost more or less according as their tents were pitched on high ground or low. Some were put to it to save even their children; others brought away some of their bedclothes also. As luck would have it, Rottentail, his horses, and six fine mules were on the high shore. The berdache lost everything except the buffalo robe in which she was sleeping. Two horses, her supply of raw hides, of finished buffalo robes, commodities, provisions, knives, everything was swept away by the swift stream. She had to struggle against the rushing, ice-cold water to save herself—it came up to her chest, and so chilled her limbs that they became swollen—no wonder. Some of the more daring youths, at great risk of their lives, tried to snatch their most valuable belongings from the stream; repeatedly they sprang back into the flood to rescue something. Rottentail's tent they could not fish out because it was too heavy, and the ground on which they stood was too insecure. But, though it was carried off, they found it again 6 days later entangled in some bushes.

What a picturesque scene: Fathers and mothers struggling to save their children, young men to rescue their sweethearts, oldish bachelors and widows to hold on to their goods and chattels, some few, stripped of everything, happy to escape with skin whole, while brave men mounted on strong horses contend against the current to assist those whose strength is failing, to encourage them anew and succor them.

January 18. Rottentail presented Mr. Denig with a military headdress containing 36 eagle feathers, that is, three full eagle tails valued by Indians at the price paid for three good pack horses. For such a present as that Rottentail expected naturally to receive some gift in return. Indians are never generous toward a white person; they expect always a gift in return, sooner or later. Even among his own people an Indian is liberal with gifts (meat excepted) only to win friends or partisans, to secure for himself a large number of adherents.

Inasmuch as I am not able to pay $36 for this interesting head attire I am going to paint a picture of it.

Rottentail brought nine robes to sell; as soon as he received the worth of them the berdache claimed one as her property. Rottentail laid the blame on his wife; she admitted that the robe belonged to the berdache, but claimed to have delivered to Jim Hawthorn nine robes besides that one.

Now, for the first time, Mr. Denig sees that Jim Hawthorn does not understand the Crow dialect at all. Rottentail is a Yankee: he is smart. Mr. Denig has to pay twice the usual amount for the robe—the flatterer's shares in this joint business are declining in value. Rottentail bade us farewell until spring; he will not come back until he has once more become rich. Now that is sensible of you. Do but go; the fewer Indians we have in this vicinity the more animals are to be seen. For my studies, beasts of the chase are now more welcome than Indians.

January 19. All of a sudden there is profound quiet at this fort; truly a calm after the storm. Mr. Denig most kindly invited me to make a copy of the Indian war headgear in his warm and comfortable office. He had Packinaud come in, therefore, and put it on properly, so as to serve me as model. His countenance as seen beneath the feathers caused much pleasant merriment—flattered his vanity not a little. My studies progress slowly, yet they steadily increase. Indeed, they are becoming so abundant that my first plan for a collection begins to seem impracticable, that is, too limited. Which pictures shall I paint? Which omit? Besides, there is the life of the fur traders, the mountaineers, and the half-breeds, their hunting expeditions, their adventures, their pleasures and their sufferings, their amours, their good fortune and bad, their travels, their work, dangers they face on water and land, in heat and in frost, in a region of redskins and wild beasts—are not all those matters of exceeding interest?

When the last buffalo passes the last wild beast of the chase will have disappeared; furthermore, the last trapper will have disappeared and the last fur traders.

January 20. Smith wants my fire steel for his benefit early in the morning; he is going on a hunt. Throughout the entire fort not a fire steel to be had for its weight in gold. Not a fire steel, a utensil of such importance, and no coal, in so extended an enterprise as this fur-trading business. Hunters find their flint and steel indispensable; matches are too easily affected by dampness to be practical and, furthermore, we have no supply in stock. So Smith is at a loss unless he can get mine; all the other hunters need their own themselves or else, in consequence of the high value placed upon fire steels at the moment, are unwilling to expose so necessary an object to the risk of coming within the reach of an Indian's long fingers. Now Smith can be of great service to me, if he brings back with him the heads of the large animals slain, and the bodies entire of the smaller ones, thus providing me models for my studies; without hesitation, therefore, I made him a present of my flint and steel. In doing this I was perfectly aware of the fact that in this place a man never knows where he will sleep the next night or whether he may not be sent unexpectedly into the open where a fire steel is just as necessary as knife and gun.

Smith says that at this season buck elks live apart from the female elks and range in groups of 4 or 5 to 8; the females range in droves of from 10 to 20, together with the brockets.[6a] He gave me an account also of a large cave in the red earth at the source of the Missouri. Only Blackfeet go into this cave in any great numbers. That they

---

[6a] I. e., 2-year-old stags.

may not lose their way in the numerous adjoining caverns, they make fast a long rope at the entrance, as they enter the cave, and take the other end along with them. Indians find therein, quite frequently, skeletons of men and of animals, which discoveries lead them to believe that those unfortunates got bewildered in the labyrinth, could not find the way out, and starved to death.

For the sake of conserving his stock of dried meat Mr. Denig plans to send some of his men and horses "into the country" where both man and beast can find food for themselves. Although he has still nearly 15,000 pounds on hand he is forced to use at least 60 pounds a day, on account of the multitude of people who eat here, and at that rate the supply will be rapidly exhausted. Moreover, he can get a good price for this meat just now at Fort Pierre where buffaloes are rarely seen. As soon as our men from the winter posts come back many of us will find very little to do here; consequently, some of us should support ourselves.

How happy I would be if I might do that. Then I should get all the chance I want to study beasts of the chase, their ways of doing, their mode of living, how they are traced out, pursued, and slain. For me the mere portrayal of an animal, however true the representation may be, is unsatisfactory when my desire is to paint the interesting scenes in the midst of which the animal lives. I must become acquainted also with details of the beasts' life, how they are grouped, what their characteristics are, their appetites, their virtues, their weaknesses, whether they prefer prairie or forest, coppice or hill, marshes or river, at what season of the year bucks live with their mates and when the females cast their young, etc.

January 21. Spent my whole day painting a sketch of a pair of elk horns. One branch of these antlers is so entirely unlike the other that one would think them two prongs taken from different deer rather than a pair growing on the same skull, but even so the lines are in accord; that is, straight lines interchange with the wavelike, undulating curves—are seldom exactly parallel. Wavelike lines or winding curves never run parallel in animal bodies, nor do they ever precisely coincide in the joints, either at their starting point or at their extreme end. Straight lines, particularly if they are vertical, indicate firmness, stability; sinuous lines, on the contrary, denote movement and energy; circular or curved lines signify strength.

Too large a number of straight lines in any living form causes stiffness or rigidity; too many curved lines brings about bulkiness, hence awkwardness; too many wavelike or sinuous lines indicate lack of principle or fickleness. To assume that there is one definite and distinct line of beauty, as Hogarth asserts, is totally useless, for there is only one standard of beauty. Even beauty supreme as embodied in the perfect human form is compounded of many varied lines, straight alternating now with sinuous undulations of line, now with the rounded curve. Furthermore, the human figure embodies two-fold beauty of form: The virile body of man and the delicate loveliness of woman. These two differing forms can be blended in one and the same figure, as in the representations of angels, only by sacrificing those characteristics which distinguish the two sexes. What one gains in tenderness and delicacy one loses in strength. In portraying the masculine form one tends more to the use of straight lines; in representing the feminine, the sinuous or wavelike curve. As a matter of course, one can lay down a universal principle which transcends special forms and colors in determining our standard of beauty, but one can no more prescribe one single line or one special color as absolute norm than one can determine by rule that all human souls are of the same character and to be judged by the same standard; for beauty is not perfection of form and color, but the expression of indwelling spirit, i. e., of the soul.

Any living creature, any plant in the natural world, even a lifeless body may be beautiful in so far as its form is a complete and harmonious expression of the life principle embodied. Hence there is infinite variety in beauty, both in form and in color. Nor are these widely varying revelations of beauty to be valued in the same degree, but each according to the importance of the idea expressed, according as soul or informing life principle is rendered perceptible to the senses. A body actuated by its own being is, as a matter of course, endowed with nobler form, has a more complex structure, than that of a plant. Accordingly, though any object that reveals a given idea in completeness, that corresponds perfectly in form to the purpose of its being is called beautiful—and this may apply to the most heterogeneous representations, as widely diverse as thunderstorms and lilies, mountains, rocks, doves, dwelling houses, and the sea—yet only those subjects that represent the consummate embodiment of creative mind, independent power of will, depth of feeling, and nobility of soul offer the loftiest ideal of beauty that is possible for man to conceive. So, one who merely imitates Nature's forms ranks below the creative artist who produces poetic compositions according to his own ideal; the copyist is far less esteemed than one who creates. One who merely reproduces what he sees need have only feeling for form and color; may, in other respects, be stupid and untaught.

Not so the artist whose productions are his own: he must be endowed with creative imagination; he must have an exact knowledge of his subject; he must be capable of keen discrimination in his judgment of forms, colors, and harmonies; and, instead of allowing himself to be blindly influenced by his feeling, he must control his efforts and give an account to himself for what he determines to do. To master perspective requires more intellect than

Bitzius, in one of his works, gives a painter credit for. (Jer. ? Golthey.) Because he was acquainted with only one artist, the simple but highly talented Mind, he formed the opinion that one need have no intellectual endowments at all to become a celebrated painter. Mind's cats are famous (but, as usual, not known or highly valued until long after his death) because he represents them in a manner so extraordinarily true to life. He never put in a background, never painted a picture in all its completeness, yet among those who attempt only imitation of Nature he takes first rank.

Eberhard's descriptions in "Abwechslung und Einheit" give me no satisfactory idea of beauty: for instance, a clear heaven and quiet sea are beautiful without any note of alternate change, because they suggest the idea of infinite space; and chaos, without form and void, or a storm-boding sky cannot be truly represented by clouds in glaring colors.

Smith has come back with nothing to show for his pains; entire region inundated. He could find no way out of the marshy depths.

January 22. Several most interesting compositions are taking shape in my brain. I begin to realize that my first plan for a gallery of paintings from Indian life is too restricted in scope; I must extend the bounds I had set, and arrange for a larger collection of pictures. But why adhere to my first plan for a collection? Why not paint the pictures singly and offer them for sale as opportunity offers.[7]

---

[7] (Written on October 11, 1856.) After 4 years of strenuous work I finished last month the collection mentioned above, but for the most part only in sketches. In New York, about the time of my departure, I was seized with ague, and, owing to that ailment combined with seasickness, I had an abominable existence during my return voyage. Though weakened from hunger and illness, I dared not, with my very limited means, even think of waiting in Paris until I recovered, but hurried home, where I arrived long before I was expected. Months later, when through the motherly care and assistance of my beloved sisters and brother I was restored to my former vigor, I began work on the collection of paintings from Indian life with the hope of interesting some art dealer in a foreign country.

The time was unfavorable for my undertaking, owing to wars in the East, and I see now that my project included too large a number of pictures. I was retarded, moreover, in my efforts to execute the paintings rapidly by having my head so overcrowded with ideas. Having met with refusals from several art dealers, I decided to paint for sale several works in water color and in oil to defray my living expenses. Things went badly enough. In the first place, Indian life is of no interest to the public in Switzerland; furthermore, audacious critics, ignorant of the subject, went so far as to contend that my pictures were not true to life—as if I would have devoted 6 years to a genre merely for the sake of indulging fancies in the end. To be sure, I could have followed here the example of Neu Wied and Catlin in their works. This year I have been particularly unfortunate with my Indian collection, but as I have now the position of drawing master and shall be henceforth, I trust, independent of a public composed of pedants, I determined to complete my collection of paintings from Indian life, at least, in outline. This accomplishment relieves my mind in a twofold sense: In the first place, I now feel that, come what may, my journey shall not have been made in vain, and, secondly, my brain is no longer burdened with so many crowding pictures. However, I do not regard this collection as the end and aim of my endeavors, but rather as a means to my advancement in art and, finding comfort in the progress I have made thus far, I look forward to the future with hope that, without neglecting the duties of my position, I shall be able to devote myself still further to my ideals, giving no thought to this public with its petty formalism.

January 24. Mr. Denig gave me Dr. Moller's Symbolik to read. Père de Smet left it behind for Mr. Denig, trusting he will become convinced that the Catholic religion is far preferable to the Protestant. This will occasion further "subtle speculations."

January 25. Water from the Yellowstone River is said to produce goiter, due, it is supposed, to the content of yellow tuff or tufa. Neither the Missouri nor the Mississippi contains this goiter-producing element.

Yesterday evening Bruyère arrived from his winter trading post for a visit and La Bombarde returned at last from the Blackfeet domain, bringing 17 horses with him. As I have mentioned already, he accompanied Mr. Culbertson thither for the purpose of bringing back horses. Mr. Culbertson got to Fort Benton in safety, after a journey of 24 days, and dispatched forthwith a messenger (express) direct to St. Louis. At every post under the direction of this company the expressman will be supplied anew with provisions and, if need be, with fresh horses.

After I had taken care of the different saddles and camp fixings and made a memorandum of everything, I found, to my utter astonishment, upon entering my room, that Master Reynard had escaped from his box and was cutting all sorts of capers in the middle of the floor. He had gnawed through one of the narrow slats nailed across the side of the box and wriggled out. I slammed to the door and seized my buffalo robe with which to catch the renegade. I saw at once that was going to be no easy matter, for he made tremendous leaps, over the table, over the chairs, the pile of firewood, always bearing his superb tail with fine effect. Finally, to my utmost perplexity, he took refuge under the bed, where he crouched in a corner and gave forth sharp, guttural sounds—kschk, keh, kch. I had a hard time getting him out. After we had chased each other for a long while up and down the room, I succeeded in throwing my robe over him; whereupon I seized the crafty fox by his neck and put him again in confinement. It was lucky he did not jump through the window into the open; I should have been severely censured if he had.

January 26. Painted a study in still life of a female elk. Observed in detail her shape, color, quality of hair, and proportions, then her movements, in order to get a correct idea, from actual observation, of the beast and its habits.

January 28. Upon reading Moller's Symbolik I am struck with glaring contradictions in the Bible. In this book both predestination and free will are plainly taught; yet the two doctrines are totally inconsistent. It is a question of accepting one or the other—the two cannot be reconciled. First of all, the Bible teaches that in the beginning God created heaven and earth, the sea, and all that in them is; that He knows all things, everything that goes on in this world that He has made, everything that is going to be, even the number of hairs on our heads; therefore, we are not to be troubled in heart or afraid. Our lives are in His hand; some are chosen, others are left (which is most reasonable); we have no choice in the matter, are not creatures of free will. Faith is required of us; through faith, not by works, we are saved.

On the other hand, we are commanded to subdue our earthly passions, to strive for Godlikeness. We are taught that punishment is inflicted not only on unbelievers but also upon those who do not make good use of their gifts, who do not multiply the talents bestowed. We are even led into temptation in order that our virtues may be put to the test, for without temptation there is no transgression; hence no reward. Yet we are born in iniquity, slaves to original sin. We are to be set free through our unreasoning faith; this applies, however, only to the elect whom the Heavenly Father, so we are told, takes especial pleasure in chastening by the infliction of severe tests.

God created us, knows us through and through, brings us into temptations—wherefore? He knows beforehand what we are going to do. Are we to understand that our Maker watches our poor flounderings and downfall as a means of diversion? What a farce! Yet this was the doctrine taught by Luther and by Calvin.

Romanists place the human being on a higher plane, but their viewpoint is also inconsistent with Bible teaching. Assuming that man is endowed with free will to choose that which is good, to avoid that which is evil; in other words, that the human creature is not the mere plaything of his Maker—Catholics entrenched themselves behind the mysteries—the divine mystery of the world. According to their belief, man by a virtuous life may win heaven, where all God's people are judged alike. Moreover, man will suffer punishment if he does not obey instructions given him in the Christian Gospels or, in other words, if he does not endeavor with all his might to fulfill the divine commands.

But are we endowed with good and bad qualities proportionately? That is the question. Is every human being given greater power of understanding, more moral strength in proportion to his strong passions, in order that he may the better curb evil tendencies and keep them in proper restraint? Not so! Our native endowments are in the highest degree disproportionate.

It is said, moreover, that we are born in sin, inheritors of original sin. God tempts us, guides us, inflicts penalties upon us. In opposition to such omnipotence, how can man exert his free will? Can he be called a free agent when God directs his will? Under such conditions, can there be such a thing as sin, as violation of divine law? If our Maker, knowing beforehand whether his creature is strong or weak, leads him deliberately into temptation, is not God himself the tempter? Is that not to make us mere playthings of fate? Is that not diabolical trifling with our feelings, our struggles and conflicts? Can a devil exist independently of this omniscient and omnipotent God?

What is the Devil, anyhow, but a personification of the evil desires, wicked enticements that God himself causes to exist? This formidable figure of Satan must needs have been created by the Catholics to prove that God is all good and to represent to Christians a personal foe whom they have to combat perpetually—a foe always prowling about, seeking to ensnare God's people and drag them down to hell. But for the Devil they would be forced to ascribe evil as well as good to God; and to teach that the good and merciful God should, in His wisdom, so trifle with Christians would have been a fatal contradiction. That He perseveringly led man astray: Such doctrine was not tolerable; the Evil One had to be contrived. But have contradictions been reconciled thereby? Superficially, yes.

But the question in my mind is whether this power that one must concede to the Devil does not necessarily controvert the omnipotence of an Almighty God. How is it possible that He allows the existence of this powerful rival, ever on the alert to thwart His designs, always trying to play some trick? And must we not confess that the Tempter all too often succeeds?

The shocking and formidable Devil, the frightful agony of burning in eternal fire, are inventions to which the early Catholics were forced to resort in order to bring rude and unlettered peoples to a better morality. They found barbarous folk too much creatures of sense to gain anything at all from the teaching of abstract truth, and so had to make their meaning clear by means of images, concrete comparisons, such as a great and good spirit, a wicked spirit, heaven, hell; and at the same time assist their understanding by means of appearances, visions, as well as other forms of the miraculous. They resorted to this because barbarians have not faculties of mind sufficiently keen or feelings sufficiently sensitive to be able to comprehend the idea of hell as suffering inflicted upon a soul tortured by bitter remorse or guilty conscience.

During centuries of advancement Christians attained to a degree of cultivation that enabled them to understand true doctrine without tangible evidence.

Many of them could not only grasp the truth of Christ's life and teaching without the aid of miracles (even among the Jews evidence of miraculous power was not necessary to impress facts of Christian doctrine), without the aid of material images, impersonations, or intermediary Pontiff, etc., but were also capable of proceeding with vigor according to their beliefs. The first Protestants had no desire to take a different viewpoint in Bible teaching from that adhered to by the Catholics, but only to clear away certain abuses in the church and to get rid of the priesthood. Their differences of opinion in matters of faith as revealed in interpretations of the same law, the same doctrine, became first known during a religious war originated by the Catholics with the hope of nipping this new teaching in the bud. Neither in the promulgation of their doctrine, however, nor by means of other weapons, could they withstand successfully the spirit of the age. But the Catholics are at fault in that, by their incessant controversies, they drove the zealous Protestants on the rocks where, owing to the obstinacy of Calvin and his followers, they are even today stuck fast. I say this because I regard the doctrine of pre-destination taught by Calvin as unworthy of human beings who claim to be Christians. Such doctrine makes each of us a mere plaything in the hand of God; in other words, sets aside any question of virtue or responsibility, does away with sin; hence with reward or punishment; for, according to that interpretation of the Scriptures, we are as irresponsible as puppets in a colossal Punch and Judy show.

Calvin's doctrine is only for those who are sufficiently informed to count themselves among the limited number chosen by God for salvation.

Inasmuch as my ideal transcends that of blind belief, I am, as a matter of course, a champion of free will. It is by the possession of his will power that man takes rank above the lower animals, that he has dominion over all the earth, that he devotes his talents to the accomplishment of his own aims, that he is capable of rising to higher things in his efforts to perfect his gifts. By the direction of his will he puts to use his inventive faculties, is no mere mechanical device, penetrates Nature's secret forces and gains knowledge, hitherto unknown to man, with regard to the origin and movements of heavenly bodies.

This is the great mystery behind which Catholics must entrench themselves if they refuse to acknowledge that human beings are endowed with Godlike minds, that God is only the source of nature's secret forces. The further man progresses, through the power of his own mind, with his discoveries and inventions, the less will his ideas dwell on God's attributes and God's power. If he but lose sight of the personality of God and His close association with man the Divine Being becomes to him a spirit.

If, on the other hand, he conceives God as a remote Being, eternal, all-powerful, and omniscient, then he recedes daily more and more from the conception of our Maker as possessing attributes of love, mercy, and goodness; for how can He be the embodiment of all love and all good if He elects for Himself only a few whom He has chosen for salvation, purposely makes some bad and throws them into the clutches of the so-called Devil, and torments others still with constant temptations?

As the giants stormed the heights of Olympus, according to ancient legend, so the inventive mind of man assails the heavens in this modern day. We no longer fear the thunderbolt as threatening direct vengeance or announcing the visitation of the Supreme Ruler of the universe. Mankind has only one thing of which to be afraid: lest through the agency of man's discoveries the equilibrium of the earth be disturbed, resulting in the overthrow and consequent annihilation of our planet.

Those who must needs personify the living cause of all things as a God may do so. For many, there is much that is good in such a belief; therefore, I would not rob anyone of it. But that there is God who concerns Himself with the destiny of only individual persons seems nonsense to me, because any discussion of such a belief involves too much that is contradictory and unjust.

Phrenology is as yet in its infancy, to be sure, but when this subject becomes an exact science it is bound to support my views on these matters, and furnish the proof of what I have said.

January 29. Last Tuesday evening Morgan returned from his winter post on the lower Bourbeuse. We found the first and second tables so overcrowded with bourgeois, clerks, interpreters, hunters, workmen, and horse guards that Mr. Denig saw the time had now come to send out a "starvation band," together with their half-frozen saddle horses, as he had so often spoken of doing. The nearby region where our garnered hay had been flooded upon the inopportune overflow of the Yellowstone was selected as good pasture and within easy reach of hunting ground well stocked with deer. The hay ricks are surrounded by a great shallow sheet of water covered with a thin layer of ice. As Cadotte, Smith, La Bombarde, and La Pierre, our four best deer stalkers, are among the troop, there will be a gay, jolly rivalry. Those hunters would soon devastate any region, so far as deer are concerned. I would have liked to go with them, and yet I am glad to make myself useful, meanwhile, at the fort; otherwise, my services would be dispensed with entirely too soon.

Today the expressman went on his way, with one fellow-traveler and a pack horse, to St. Louis. A difficult undertaking at this time of year: 2,500 miles on foot all the way to St. Joseph, from which point he may travel by steamer. Hawthorn left also with one companion for Blackfeet territory, where his family lives.

Afterwards Packinaud related to me an Herantsa tradition concerning the origin of that tribe. He began by saying that the annual retelling of this tradition is a solemn occasion among the old Herantsa. The story is never begun until they have at hand a sufficient quantity of tobacco mixture to last the entire length of time required for the narration, i. e., 2 days and nights.

Herantsa believe that they came forth from under a great water (a sea), but only the half of their people; the rest of them remained behind. In other words, they climbed out of a cave and had to swing themselves up to the surface of the earth by the limb of a tree. When a woman great with child seized the branch, however, it bent so far down that the woman stopped up the outlet of the cave. When the Herantsa came out upon the earth they saw the sun and moon for the first time. There lived in the moon at that time a frog and a woman of the Herantsa tribe. The Sun took a piece of coal or charred earth and said to those two in the moon: The one who makes the most noise with the teeth when chewing this I will marry. Whereupon the frog took a piece of coal and began to chew, but the woman, for her part, took roasted corn. She made the most noise with her teeth; so the Sun married that woman. She gave birth to à child—a boy.

Every day the father followed the chase, bringing home great quantities of meat; the mother, meanwhile, worked diligently in the cornfield, producing an overabundance of maize. Now, as the boy grew larger and began to play about, his father forbade his digging "pommes blanches"; [8] if he disobeyed, the Sun told him, he would die. One day, while his father was hunting, the boy went with his mother out on the prairie, where she set to work digging "pommes blanches." He reminded her of what his father had said, but she replied that he need fear no harm. Then, through the hole from which she had taken a "pomme blanche" the mother saw the village where her people lived—the Herantsa on earth. She watched them at their games, at their dances, attending their droves of horses (?),[8a] and at their work in the fields of corn. She was seized with homesickness. She yearned for association with her people. She told her son to entreat his father to bring him all sinews of a buffalo cow the next time he went hunting. The boy did as he was bidden. When his father asked what he was going to do with them he answered that he wished to make a long rope with which to play. His father, the Sun, brought him all the sinews of a cow except one, a short, thick tendon in her hind leg. That one he forgot. The mother then made a long rope and, when her husband was out again on a

---

[8] Prairie turnips.
[8a] Horses were unknown to the ancient Herantsa.

hunt, she took it and, carrying her son, went to the hole where she had dug the "pommes blanches."

She laid a thick piece of wood across the opening, fastened the rope around it, and, taking hold of the other end, let herself down toward earth. But because the rope was too short she got only as far as the top of a high tree. Meanwhile, the Sun having returned from the chase found nobody at home. After searching everywhere for his wife and child he spied them at last clinging to a long rope. He seized a large stone, commanded it to hit his wife but leave his son uninjured, and threw it at the woman, killing her outright.

That stone lies today, so the report goes, at the mouth of the little Missouri. The boy got down the tree and so reached the earth. He had no fear, because he was "medicine", a supernatural child. He rambled about, here and there, seeking something he could eat. Finally he came to a tent in which an old enchanter and enchantress lived. The man was hideously ugly, the lower half of his body being that of a serpent. When the boy entered the tent he found nobody there, but saw an earthen vessel full of boiled corn, which he ate. For several successive days he visited that tent, always found boiled corn, but saw nothing of the magicians. Every evening the old enchantress found an empty earthenware pot from which her corn had been eaten and tried to trace the thief.

She noticed the little fellow's footprints, but, owing to their small size, she was still left in doubt as to whether they were made by a boy or a girl. To assure herself of the sex of this pilferer she laid on one side of the vessel of boiled corn a ball such as girls kick about as a plaything and on the other a bow and arrow. If the child is a boy, she then said to her husband, he will take the bow and arrow; if a girl, she will prefer the playing ball. And so that very same evening she discovered that the thief was a boy.

After that she kept a lookout for him, and upon his arrival at the tent she invited him to remain there with them. The old enchanter was very wicked and of a surly temper. He gave the boy nothing to eat, and in one instance of ill humor he forbade him to eat on pain of death. The child did not know the meaning of fear, however, and assured the sorcerer he would not die. He said, moreover, if he were not allowed to eat he would kill the old man.

"You can't kill me", declared the enchanter; "I am 'great medicine.' Nobody has power to kill me."

"You think I can't kill you? I will show you this instant."

Whereupon, the boy took one of his arrows, placed it against his bow, and sent it whizzing through the old man's head with such force that he fell dead on the spot.

When the old sorceress returned the child told her what had happened. She was not much concerned about it; on the contrary, she made him a present of a new bow and quiver that had belonged to her husband, the enchanter, and which unfailingly struck whatever its possessor desired, even though the object might not be within range of his vision.

"Now," said the boy, "I will bring meat to the tent for you."

And he did supply her with meat in greatest abundance. One day, when he was roving about, he met two men, mighty enchanters, who spoke to him. They were very hungry, they said, but were unable to start any buffaloes.

"Is that so?" replied the youth. "Then I will shoot a cow [8b] for your benefit."

"We see no cows."

"What I promise, I will make good," answered the youth.

He laid a magic arrow against the bowstring and spoke the words "schima etanka" (kill a cow), and it did what he commanded. Following the direction of the arrow, they found the animal soon after, and, upon cutting it up, took out an unborn calf. The young hunter knew this to be his "medicine" (a talisman that had appeared to him in a dream). He ran from the spot, leaving behind his magic bow and quiver. The two enchanters recognized at once the cause of his flight: the calf was his "medicine." They took the unborn calf, together with his bow and quiver, and went in pursuit of him. As soon as he was aware of the weakening of his powers he scurried up a tree. Whereupon the two enchanters hung the tiny body of the calf at the foot of the tree and thereby held the boy under a spell.

Then they went away and did not return until a year had passed. They found their captive starved and emaciated. They told him that if he wished to be free he must make a promise to procure his foster mother for them—one night for each of them. He gave his word. Then they removed the calf and allowed him to return home. His foster mother was delighted to see her young huntsman back again and insisted upon having him relate his adventures. He told her everything, not forgetting to mention the promise whereby he had gained his freedom.

"I know those two sorcerers," said the old woman. "Since the death of my husband they have been continually laying snares for me. I refused to have anything to do with them; I detest them. But for your sake," she added, "I will fulfill the promise you made them; I do this because they allowed you to come back."

The two men came and spread their magic tents. The old witch lay with each of them one night and then they departed.

The youth resumed his hunting expeditions. One day he saw a rattlesnake. Now in those days reptiles of this kind were not yet

---

[8b] Cattle were unknown to the ancient Herantsa.

provided with rattles but had long bills by means of which they dug through the earth as swiftly as they now run. This daring boy shot the snake dead and came home and told his foster mother what he had done.

"Now, my child," she said, "if you go hunting tomorrow you will come upon a nest of those serpents. If you go near them they will certainly kill you."

Nevertheless, conscious of his immortality, the boy walked into the den of snakes the moment he found it and killed a great number, but night fell before he had annihilated them. He wished then to go home, but the night was so dark he lay down on the ground and stuck an arrow upright at his head and one on each side of him; for those arrows possessed the magical quality of becoming aware of approaching danger; whereupon they would fall upon the sleeper and wake him up. But on that night the youth was so overcome with sleep that when a serpent came near, though one arrow after another fell upon him, he made no preparations for defense—took no notice whatsoever of his impending peril.

So the snake ran clear through his body up into his head, where it caused him most intense pain but was unable to put him to death. To get rid of the serpent he asked whether he might be released if he would bring to life all the snakes he had slain the day before.

"Yes; on that condition I will leave you," said the serpent.

He shook his bow, spoke some magical words, and the dead snakes were again alive.

When the youth returned home his foster mother said to him:

"Next time you are out hunting you will see a spring, and near this spring a tent will be spread. Do not enter the tent; you may lose your life if you do."

But this bold lad sought danger; he liked nothing better. So he went at once in search of the spring and its nearby perilous tent. He entered without hesitation. Though it was very dark within he could discern the trunk of a man's body. They talked with each other. Finally the Sun's son asked the man in the dark tent whether, by way of pastime, he could not contrive a game. The latter produced two billiard [*sic*] wands [9] and the two played together. Now it came about that they threw the wands so uniformly they could not decide, in the darkness, which won the game.

The man in the dark corner advised the young hunter to fetch from a nearby tent another man who had been put there by the witchcraft of the two sorcerers mentioned above.

"Call him here to decide."

"What is his name?"

---

[9] Billiards were unknown to the ancient Herantsa.

"Utch."

The boy summoned the other man by the name designated. Utch decided in favor of the youth. The man in the dark corner became enraged and the boy slew him.

"Now," said Utch to the heir of the Sun, "you have begun strife that will never end. Those two sorcerers will be here tonight and they will kill you."

"They have not the power. I am 'greater medicine' than they." Then he told Utch what adventures he had encountered.

"Good," said the latter. "If you wish to overcome the two sorcerers I will tell you what to do. Be on the watch when they are about to go to sleep tonight, and the instant they lose consciousness lay aslant over each of them one of these billiard wands. They will no longer have strength to move, they will be powerless."

As he was now released from the spell under which he had been held he hurried away from the place. The two enchanters came, and the youth rendered them powerless by means of the billiard wands; they were unable to raise themselves from the ground. Thereupon they said that they realized they were now in his power and wished him to tell them what they were to do to accomplish their release.

"Well, I have heard you have a sister enchantingly beautiful, whom you have not yet given to any man. Give her to me and you shall be free."

They promised to grant his wish. He took away the two wands.

Here we concluded the narrative, for I had had more than enough of it. I asked Packinaud to tell me instead something of the Herantsa themselves. Twenty years ago they are said to have been a most powerful tribe, more feared than either the Sioux or the Assiniboin. At that time they took up their habitations in five different settlements:

	Tents
1. Village where now the Mandan live	250
2. Village 1 mile farther up the Missouri	80
3. Village on Knife River	130
4. Village 1½ miles above Knife River	60
5. Village 6 miles from the one last named	30

This makes in all 550 tents, and the tribe reckoned 1,650 warriors. This number was reduced by epidemics of smallpox and measles to 80 warriors. Subsequently it was increased to 150, 20 of whom were carried off last year by cholera. The Teton Sioux are said to have been forced up into this region from St. Louis,[10] the Arikara from Council Bluffs.

[10] According to Bancroft, the Sioux, at the time of La Zotas, are reported to have inhabited the region extending westward from Missouri and the Falls of St. Anthony, and southward even beyond the southern boundary of Arkansas.

The Arikara now inhabit the same village that heretofore the Mandan owned; that is, they chose the same location on which to establish their dwelling place; for under the best conditions clay huts last not longer than 7 years. Mandan and Herantsa have always lived most amicably together.

January 31. Morgan came the other day to barter a choice pelt of the gold fox, ermine fur, and a black pipe in addition for my beautiful pipe bowl.

February 1. That, as Mohler says, the word "Adam," according to its Hebraic signification, means "red earth" might be accepted as sufficient proof, to be sure, that the copper-colored Indian is the original progenitor of the various races of men, irrespective of the color of their skin. That climate might easily have had its effect in changing copper color to black or white may be true, but experience of a thousand years tells against such an assumption. For my part, I do not accept the belief that the human race is to be traced back to one human pair only. In the Old Testament itself I find refutation of such an argument; otherwise, how could it have been possible for Cain in exile, after his brother's murder, to have found populated cities hitherto unknown? Furthermore, I think the Biblical description of Paradise and the creation of the first man and the first woman too highly poetical to lose anything of its significance, even though we do not trace our descent so literally to Adam and Eve. I find nowhere in Moses' account any so positive affirmation concerning our first parents in Eden that would make indefensible my assumption that several races of man may have been created at the same time in different parts of the world. Likewise, I refuse to believe that the so-called fall of man can be referred to relations of sex.

If that were true, why was there a difference in sex? Why the urgent inclination to union of the flesh? If the Creator of the world had desired some other means whereby people were to multiply and replenish the earth, he would have had human beings engendered under other conditions. However, let anyone who, in defiance of natural history, insists upon one and only one pair of human beings as the source of our genus, explain as best he can the rise of the different races of men. So far as I am concerned I attach just as little significance to this belief as to the assertion that the Indian was derived from the Jew.

In the first place I maintain that the invariable copper-colored skin, black hair, and brown eyes that distinguish the primitive inhabitants of North America as a whole afford sufficient proof that they are an individual race just as clearly differentiated from the Caucasian as from the Ethiopian and Malayan races. Now the

Hebrews are Caucasian; [10a] blue eyes and light hair are not infrequently seen among Jewish people, but of copper-colored skin there
is absolutely never a trace. Nevertheless, many scholars as well as
men of little learning trace the Indians' origin to the Hebrews.[11]

These writers claim to have discovered resemblance of features
and similarity in mode of life, both public and private. As for me,
I have never yet seen an Indian who had that distinct cast of countenance we term Jewish; resemblance, in this instance, is not determined by black hair, brown eyes, hooked nose, etc., but must be
sought in those characteristics which reveal the inner spirit of a
people, which may be taken as typical of national character, such
as expression of the eyes, mold of the lips, etc. Of the Jewish propensity to bargain and to haggle I find no trace at all in the expression of the Indian; that is to say, acquisition is not the principal
end and aim of his existence. On the contrary, the redskin is by
nature heedless as to money matters and a reckless spendthrift, the
direct opposite of the thrifty, calculating Jew. His trait of liberality is one of the Indian's chief virtues; no matter how valiant or
how rich their leaders may be, it is only by generous giving that they
attain to positions of prominence. Warriors strive for personal possessions not for the sake of hoarding wealth but to gain great
numbers of adherents by the presentation of gifts. Like most
barbarous tribes, Indians place great value on largesse; as an indication of this, the number of gifts conferred is emblazoned on the
chief's robe of state just the same as "coups."

How different are the Jews! Were not the patriarchs of ancient
days thrifty people, rich in lands and herds? To me it seems
extraordinary, furthermore, considering the pertinacity with which
the Jews hold to their Mosaic belief, that Indians, if directly descended from the Hebrews, should have lost so completely all contact with Judaism. Another unlikeness that occurs to me: Jews,
as we all know, are strong on beards; look upon the beard as more
or less sacred—swear by the beard. Now, there is not a beard to be
found throughout the Indian tribes; not the trace of a beard. But
what surprises me most with regard to similarity in the mode of
life among Hebrews and Indians is that none of the native North
American tribes did anything in the way of stock raising. Though
the Indian drinks with zest the milk of a buffalo just killed or of a
hind or a doe, the idea seems never to have occurred to one of them
to breed these animals for the sake of their milk. Nowhere do I
find any inclination toward cattle breeding, not even for their meat,

---

[10a] The author errs here ; the Hebrews belong to the Semitic stock.
[11] For example, Lord Kingsborough, Catlin, Captain Maryatt in the Mormons. The last
two prompted my writing down the ideas stated above.

which Indians particularly like for food. No, the redskins' only domestic animal is the dog. Is it at all likely that Hebrew tribes, shepherds from the beginning of time, wandering into this part of the world where the buffalo and other milk-producing animals were already at hand, would have forgotten entirely that especial branch of industry? Certainly not. This total neglect of cattle breeding among Indian tribes is to me utterly incomprehensible. It seems impossible that any people who progressed as far as they in the cultivation of the soil and in other important branches of knowledge should never have thought of so simple a thing as the taming of animals and getting milk from cows.

Not only would they have had an abundance of food and clothing but they would have found also abundant opportunities for the employment of their energies in defending their herds from wild beasts. That one striking difference in the way of life among American Indians as compared with that among aborigines of the Old World is alone sufficient proof to me that the former constitute a separate and distinct race of men. Throughout the entire continent of the Americas only Peruvians (Quichua) were shepherds. They found in their homeland the llama and alpaca, which they raised in herds, and used the wool of those animals for the weaving of cloth, out of which they made the garments they wore. In this respect the culture of the Incas and their subjects sets them apart from the neighboring tribes. Aboriginal South Americans have no kindred likenesses, either in color, physiognomy, or in speech, with North American Indians. The Guarani, Patagonians, and Quichua were also tribes totally different, their manner of life dependent wholly upon natural conditions in that part of the country where they dwell. In the pampas, they were roving hunters; in the forests and mountains where great numbers of the inhabitants were engaged in tilling the soil, they had settled habitations.

Just as a people's mode of life is determined by the vegetation and animals abounding in the region they inhabit, so climatic conditions and atmosphere exert an influence upon the bodies of men and affect the color of their skin.

Nor do the few customs and arrangements for the conduct of their daily life among Indians, especially Mexicans (Aztec), and Hebrews furnish any basis for argument. Man in his natural state is everywhere the same, be he white, yellow, red, black, or spotted, hairy or smooth skinned. All human beings have exactly the same bodily structure, consequently they have like needs, are dependent on the same conditions that make existence possible, use the same sort of implements and utensils for hunting, cooking, tilling the soil, fishing, making war, and for transportation. Necessity is the mother of invention the world over; hence, various and diverse tribes living under similar natural conditions hit upon the same ideas. Man got his first sustenance from the fruits of the fields and forests, by fishing, killing birds and quadrupeds. When he was unable to get sufficient food by such means he resorted to agriculture and stock raising. When, in the conduct of affairs, related families lived together as one community, they laid the foundation of tribal or national government under the direction of chosen leaders or chiefs and for the establishment of regulations that would insure better order, security, and success in their undertakings.

The more forceful these associated families were and the more densely populated their communities, the more difficult their communal management, the more complex their organization. This has been found true in all parts of the world; accordingly, one finds among primitive peoples everywhere bows and arrows, knives, spears, bludgeons, slings, shields; boats made of the hides of animals or hollowed out of tree trunks, rafts constructed with stems of trees or, sometimes, of reeds; throughout the world one finds huts built of twigs and branches or of clay, tents of skins, earthenware vessels, and beasts of burden; in all places, the first plowing was done by means of crooked branches torn from hardwood trees or with shoulder blades of the larger wild beasts, and clothes were made from the wool of animals, animal pelts, and of hemp; in place of knives, sharp stones were used for cutting, and fishbones were used for needles. Agriculture is the basis upon which is builded every firmly established state. In tilling his land the savage becomes attached to the soil and loyal to his native land. Upon husbandry depend settled habitations, spacious country residences; as the result of husbandry, business thrives, inventions are called into being, arts flourish, sciences are in demand, and laws are enacted for the better morality and better government that is essential to the prosperity of a state.

So much has been written in contradiction of the Indians' fitness for education, by way of excuse for injustices done them, that I cannot forbear breaking a lance in their defense. I am all the more inclined to do this because they cannot defend themselves against assailants unknown to them who attack them in books, and because I, a native of Switzerland, with no colonial policy to protect, am able to take a view all the more unprejudiced. In their primitive condition the state of the Indians was much the same as that of our forefathers in the so-called Stone Age; they were unacquainted with the art of working metals because they had no need of that sort of thing. Arrow heads made of stone, implements contrived out of bones, served their purposes. As long as they could be sure of a steady supply of food by following the chase they remained hunters; with increasing population they began to till the soil: they planted maize, beans, potatoes, and tobacco. Whether men or women worked the land when they first began to farm is a matter of no consequence. That the Indians did actually cultivate their land throughout the region lying between the Mississippi and the Atlantic Ocean is a fact to which travelers and adventurers who have visited this country since its discovery by Columbus collectively testify—all of them, whether Spaniards, Frenchmen, or Britons.

Yet Capt. Mayne Reid (together with a number of others) attempts to prove the contrary. Will he set aside historical fact, a thousand incontrovertible facts, for the sake of vindicating the right of Englishmen to rob Indians of their land? He says, in his Scalp Hunters:

"No handful of men have the right to withhold from the great body of mankind a valuable portion of the earth's surface, without using it."

Granting that this statement is true, it has no application to the Indian tribes inhabiting the eastern part of the United States, nor can it justify the colonization of this part of the world by Englishmen on the ground that there is a lack of uncultivated land in their own country, for the Indians have as much of their domain under cultivation as their needs require, while, in England, there is even today much land idle—yea, wide stretches of heath and forest set aside solely for the purpose of hunting. I will furnish later the proof of what I say from Bancroft. If Capt. Mayne Reid had made the statement quoted above in that part of his narrative described as "poetically colored," I should have taken no notice of it at all. I should have paid just as little attention to it as to Dr. Bird's Nick of the Woods or Pierre St. John's Introduction to the Trapper's Bride and the White Stone Canoe.[11a] I should have regarded it as "fact enameled by fiction," of which he himself says, "My book exhibits no higher purpose than to amuse," and farther, "If you cannot believe the scenes true, may I hope that you will acknowledge their vraisemblance?" But in the Notes he assumes the role of instructor. Does he not desire, in fact does he not mean to be accepted there as "true" rather than "vraisemblable"?

Such practice on the part of the captain as that to which I have referred above is not only wrong but dangerous, for the reason that his most interesting book will certainly be far more widely read than accounts published in duly authorized histories.[12] If he had pronounced his judgment with reference to the prairie Indians only

[11a] The White Stone Canoe or White Flint Canoe idea was developed from a block of ice, the boat of the Winter Gods. See article Tawiskaron, Bull. 30, Bur. Amer. Ethn.

[12] We find sufficient proof in East India and in China that the aim of Englishmen is solely to extend their trade and their power, not to civilize the primitive peoples of those lands or to provide food for their hungry poor. In India alone there are vast tracts of unimproved land which great nobles will not allow the poor to cultivate.

he would have given his statement some semblance of truth, for they find the land much more useful to them as hunters than as landlords. But prairie Indians have their own good reasons for being content to live by hunting; as long as buffaloes are found in such large herds, it will be impossible to cultivate fields; those animals will have to be well-nigh exterminated before husbandry can be established as an industry. Furthermore, when a tribe of people are satisfied with the environment in which they live they are far more happy, under any circumstances, than populations in civilized states where contentment is unknown; for that reason we envy the savage.

I am inclined to believe, moreover, that in making our chief task in life the civilization of mankind, we lessen our chances for happiness. Nevertheless, we are forced by competition to work to that end; we are obliged to develop all our faculties, to improve our talents, in order that we may be capable of meeting the demands of an existence, the conditions of which are constantly becoming more difficult.

There is convincing proof that the Indian is not incapable of improvement, as his enemies would have us believe: Captain Reid admits as much. That Indian women work the land is not due to racial coarseness or brutality but to the fact that the men regard war as their chief aim in life. By reason of their many wars, moreover, the number of women is in excess of the males. According to the contrary argument, European nations, where country women willingly work in the fields, must also be called cruel and brutal. It is far better for women to till the land, which is no disgrace, than to starve or beg alms. In the course of time, when this country becomes as densely populated and the land as much exhausted as in European countries, North American women, I am firmly convinced, will have to adapt themselves to the same order of things. Furthermore, there are Indian nations where men as well as women work in the fields (See Ralph Lane: Bericht uber die Indianer bei Roanoke).[13]

We find, indeed, a distinct difference in the development of Indian nations, according as more densely populated communities increased the necessities of existence.

Among the nations in the eastern part of the country there were settled habitations, comfortable houses, fortifications, temples and, according to recent investigations in Michigan, ancient copper mines (the Mangoack in Roanoke worked in copper), while prairie Indians used lead to fashion their ornaments—they employed only soft metals in making ornaments. On the Mexican plateau Indian tribes lived in communities even more densely populated; accordingly we find there the organized state, and so marked an advance in handicrafts, in art, in science, and in religion, that one can but wonder at the

---

[13] Ralph Lane's Account of the Indians of Roanoke.

number and variety of their accomplishments. One may readily assume that those nations would have attained in time to a still higher degree of civilization. In every instance, advance to the civilized state requires time and is furthered by necessity. So we may conclude when prairie Indians can no longer satisfy the needs of their existence as hunters, they will of their own accord resort to husbandry just as the Arikara and Herantsa have done already.

We should consider, moreover, how long a time has been required to civilize Germans and Celts. How many thousands of years they remained in the so-called Stone Age. How many thousand in the Age of Bronze. Even today, what would be our condition without the uplifting influences of the Christian religion, without our great and extensive educational advantages? Even now, after nearly 2,000 years of progress and enlightenment, can one assert with truth that all superstitious beliefs, all heathen observances have disappeared from Europe?

Do not our wars, our revolutions, give rise daily to more horrible deeds than occur among Indian tribes? Were not ancient Britons far more barbarous than Indians? Did not the ancient Britons take advantage of their own offspring to satisfy their lust?

When it is a question of the civilization of peoples one has to reckon by centuries, not generations. I maintain that in time North American Indians will make due progress. I maintain further that the coming of Europeans hindered the Indians' continued advance in their slow development. The Aztecs are exterminated and shame on the priests, evidences of their civilization for the most part blotted out of existence. So-called Christians, for all their fanatical zeal, have set so poor an example of the Christian code of morals, and do still, that the Christian religion can but make an unfavorable impression on the mind of the natural man. When all Christian sects, almost without exception, war against one another with shocking intolerance, of which are savages to become adherents? When 20 people are condemned to death as witches or unbelievers—hanged on a charge of witchcraft? When 55 other persons are tortured in order to extort a profession of faith, whereupon some worship before the Cross, while others scoff? And how was it with the Moravians and the Delawares? They were mistrusted and put down by their heathen fellowmen as well as by their Christian brethren! Have fur traders, as pioneers of civilization, ever shown the least concern about moral standards?

Do they not know that among civilized Indians, who devote themselves to the cultivation of their lands, fur trading will cease? How much do those daring officials on the borders care for the enlightenment of Indians? In spite of sacred treaties, the Cherokee were forced to abandon their well-tended fields and give up their lands.

With all their improvements, which even Captain Reid must give them credit for, we shall see how long they will be left in peace in their new domain beyond the Mississippi.

As long as mutual ill-will and hate engendered by earlier conflicts is kept alive among Americans and Indians there is little hope of a better state of things among the red skins. Who was first responsible for armed conflict and consequent hate, historical fact makes indisputably clear; it is high time, therefore, that Americans give some evidence of their being "the most enlightened people." It is time that they grant to the Indians the right to live. Once they are allowed to live in tranquility, the Indians, we may be sure, will adopt whatever advantages are offered them in civilization; then moral and spiritual betterment will inevitably follow. But, first of all, they must have that tranquility which comes with security and peace of mind—then, a better example set for them by these sentimental Christians.

Laws are of little use, however, unless individuals are trained to develop their human organism to best advantage; in other words, the education of the individual has different tasks in view. First, it is to provide training for the preservation of health; secondly, training to fit the individual for earning his bread and, at the same time, to make provision for the development of the mind, cultivation of the feelings, and betterment of the soul. Science, art, and religion are the means to this end, for in pursuing these great subjects the human individual is led in the right direction and capacitated through the best development of his powers for the best accomplishment of his life work; that is, to provide for his own needs by the employment of his especial talents and to be of service to his fellowman.

Now this particular instance is cited that astronomy among the Aztec was much the same science as that developed by the Hebrews. How could it be otherwise when the two nationalities inhabited the same planet and contemplated the same sun, moon, and stars? How was it possible for them to formulate two different planetary systems from a study of the same stars? Those crude peoples divided the time into years according to snowfall, rainfall, or seasons of harvest, and the year into months according to the full of the moon.

When they found, however, that such computations would no longer suffice in a more complicated national organization, they began to regulate time by the rising and setting sun; consequently, no matter how widely different peoples may be or how far removed from one another, their computations with regard to the solar year must be much the same, differing only, in fact, as to the manner in which they dispose of the six hours left over.

In like manner the pyramidal form appears in different parts of the world, because the pyramid affords the most stable base for the greatest height. When all is said and done, our own church towers are nothing but pyramidal. Though the Jews could hardly have been unacquainted with the pyramids in Egypt, yet they never made use of that form in their buildings. On the other hand, why are not the Mexicans, whose teocallis are pyramidal in structure, declared to be descendants of the Egyptians? Why are not the Peruvians with their Cyclopaean masonry said to be descendants of the Greeks?

As to the rest, I do not question the probable migration of tribes from Asia or northern Europe to the American continent. I contend only that such a migration was not necessary in order to establish either reasons for the population of the country or the civilization of the American Nation, because, in due time, population and education follow as a matter of course.

The great majority of native Americans are of the same type and bear no resemblance to any race of the Old World. The few immigrants from foreign countries have been amalgamated, somehow or other, with the native stock. Moreover, one must take into consideration that there are also animals and plants that did not originate on American soil but were likewise transplanted. Just as like plants grow out of the ground in different quarters of the globe, according to the character of the soil and the geographical situation, so must animals that feed on the same vegetation and like animal substances develop into the same species. Why should not the same be true of humankind? Why should it not have been possible for the same natural conditions that produced, in America as in the Old World, the beaver, bison, stork, eagle, hog, wolf, fox, serpent, lizard, monkey, butterfly, squirrel, hare, worm, fish, etc., have had their effect on the American type of man? To be sure, the elephant, lion, camel, and horse are not native to America, but that does not by any means prove the type of primitive man peculiar to that land could not have been produced there, especially since the monkey, which marks the transition from animal to man, is there. Some plants native to American soil and hitherto unknown in other countries are found there also: the potato, tobacco, maize, banana, etc. In conclusion, I must mention that, according to recent investigations, there have been discovered, among antediluvian remains, skeletons both of human beings and of horses which, so far as the natives are concerned, give sufficient proof that they had their origin in the New World.

February 4. Weather usually fine and warm. I was enabled to sketch the interior of the fort from the southwest bastion. Should such agreeable atmospheric conditions continue for any length of time we may expect a slow, cold, or wet springtime, for as yet very little snow has fallen. Smith came in to bring venison. The hunters in the hayfield have already shot twenty-four deer and two elks. They are feeling quite at ease, camping in two tents with their women and eating all the choice portions of the game they kill. They are glad to be where they have not the bourgeois continually directing them.

February 5. Morgan had to take ox carts and pack horses to fetch Mackenzie and his remaining stock of goods from his winter quarters on the lower Bourbeuse. This warm weather has melted the snow, and in consequence the river overflowed to such an extent that the occupants of this winter trading post were beginning to think they might have to be rescued from the roof. Today there is hardly anybody at the fort. The days begin to lengthen. Weather continues warm.

February 8. Mackenzie is here with what remains of his stock of goods and what furs and pelts he has accumulated in his barter trade. His progress across the prairie, accompanied by armed foot passengers, ox carts, pack horses, Indian women, ox drivers, and dogs was, to say the least, original.

He brought me a stag's head which I shall sketch. There are already four tents, occupied by Assiniboin hangers-on, pitched near the camping place of our hunters in the hayfield. The smell of meat attracted them. They make themselves quite comfortable and look on while our white men hunt and our outworn horses drag in meat for them. So Smith has received instructions to keep no supplies there with which to provide food for good-for-nothing Indians, but to send what they do not need to the fort at once.

February 9. Four separate expeditions equipped and despatched: Mackenzie had but arrived at the fort when he was sent off with three ox carts laden with commodities for Bruyère; Morgan with his workmen set out for the timber yard to get lumber ready to build the new Indian lodge at the fort; Boneau and Valette were sent with two dog sleds[14] loaded with maize also to Bruyère; and the fourth traveled to the hayfield to bring up fresh supplies of meat. After all these had been despatched, then commodities and robes brought back by Mackenzie had to be itemized, entered on the books, and put in their proper places.

February 10. This afternoon Le Gras brought news that we were to expect the early arrival of Ours Fou and members of his band, the

[14] It is estimated that a dog, traveling at the rate of from 30 to 40 English miles a day, can haul a load weighing 70 pounds, and can carry a load of 50 pounds. That the dog is not physically constituted to serve as beast of burden or for hauling is a mistaken idea on the part of "prevention of cruelty to animals" advocates.

Gens des Filles, an Assiniboin band, for whom we were directed to make ready a feast of fresh meat, mush, and sweet coffee. Only the chief's commands. As the dark-skinned Indians came forward in the glittering sunlight across the smooth surface of the frozen river, some on horseback, others on foot, accompanied by women and numbers of children, pack horses, and laden dogs, they formed a most picturesque cavalcade. But, as they failed to bring robes for exchange, nothing came of their bidding us prepare a feast.

All appurtenances to flat painting have been put in order and all remaining paints that were left on the floor in the store have been put away, indicating that my duties of official painter are at an end.

February 11. "Mad Bear's" band occupy only 11 tents. Bear would like to sit for his portrait but fears to take such risk, inasmuch as Natoh is dead and, though Mr. Denig's thumb has healed, it is a strange coincidence that such affliction should have come upon him just at that time.

Furthermore, the coincidence was promptly misinterpreted by womankind at the fort. To be sure, "Mad Bear" declares he is not so foolish as to think my paintings exert a perilous influence but at the same time he has to confess that his people believe they do. Instead of painting his likeness I drew for him the picture of a turtle on a piece of wood. Then Mackenzie carved it out and filled it with lead. Now the Chief wears this leaden turtle around his neck for a charm—his "medicine." He dreamed of a turtle. His earlier "medicine" had failed to ward off the death of many relatives, so he wore it no longer. If this charm proves more efficacious he can then say whether it brings good luck.

February 12. In the Indian encampment just without the fort there was a fight today between two wives of one husband as to which of them was the owner of a horse. When the man saw his wives seizing each other by the hair he took bow and arrow and shot the unoffending nag through the heart. Then he gave the woman who was in the wrong a good sound thrashing. He would have been much more sensible if he had inflicted the beating without sacrificing the horse—all the more as it was the only one he possessed. L'Ours Fou is much cast down because the Assiniboin band north of us refuses to conclude a peace with the Blackfeet Tribe. Now that he is supreme chief, appointed by the United States, he thinks the Assiniboin should obey him. But those wild bands, having no conception of the power and extent of the United States, are not inclined as yet to change their condition. His appointment to the rank of supreme chief is, moreover, contrary to their wishes, in violation of their right of free choice, an infringement of their liberties, and in contravention of their ancient customs. As Ours Fou can unite under his leadership only the smallest of the Assiniboin bands, his appointment as supreme chief meets with all the more opposition.

Bear's plan is, first of all, to influence his people to establish a village as the Herantsa have done and to plant acres of corn. But Assiniboin are an idle people, and easily distinguished from the proud, gorgeously bedecked Absaroka and Sioux by their indifference to appearances. So far as clothes are concerned, the Assiniboin would just as soon have his old worn robe as a woolen blanket. He cares only for the possession of horses; he is too poverty stricken to purchase the beasts, so he has to find those he can steal; in other words, he must have an enemy. In the event that the Assiniboin should consent to stop their wars against the Blackfeet, the Crows would necessarily conclude a like peace, for the latter are by no means powerful enough alone to hold at bay the great Blackfeet Tribe.

Without war an Indian is no longer an Indian. War is his means of educating himself. Success in war is his supreme aim in life. By nature imperious and full of energy, he finds in martial exploits his only chance to win distinction. In renouncing war he gives up his chief life purpose; he is forced to rearrange the plan of his whole existence.

No one, whether good or bad, stupid or clever, practical or un-businesslike, can go through life without some object in view. That is true of individual people, to say nothing of entire nations. If one gives up an aim, to the accomplishment of which he has directed his best energies, then he has to replace that aim with some other. Now an Indian, observing the manner of life among highly educated white so-called Christians, finds little that invites him to change his lot. White men have, it is true, many amazing contrivances, make use of many tools and implements of service to them, but, on the other hand, they are harassed throughout their entire life with care and laborious toil in their efforts to supply the multitude of things they require. They are never left in peace either day or night, but work hard their whole life for their daily bread without ever feeling even then secure from hunger and want; for their many "improvements" by no means keep pace with the ever-increasing demands of a steadily increasing population. To an Indian, therefore, the lot of white men in civilized nations, notwithstanding their accumulation of knowledge, is no better than the simple existence of his own race, which enables him to be content with little. White men talk a deal of twaddle about Christianity, morality, sobriety, and honest dealing, and in the meantime serve Mammon rather than God. Above all things else, white people prefer money; money, the value of which

Indians know nothing about, look upon as of no value in itself, yet the white man's curse.

Indians are often taxed with being incapable of improvement, obstinate in their adherence to traditional customs and superstitious beliefs, etc. Why? Because they are not quick to imitate the bad example set for them by white people? Because they do not subject themselves slavishly to a manner of dress that changes at least twice every year, only in rare instances gives evidence of good taste but most often of tomfoolery and discomfort instead? Because they refuse to accept a belief which the whites uphold neither in word nor in deed, but, on the contrary, in defiance of their moral teaching, their printed, too often distorted Scriptural passages, play the hypocrite, lie, steal, and murder? Let him who dares assert that Indians are not capable of being instructed first ask himself whether he affords the redskins a good example of true Christian, noble friend, industrious, loyal husband, good father; whether a savage of practical mind may not recognize what is preached as only fine-spun theories, when his newly acquired instructor and counselor falls so far short in actual observance of his creed, when, notwithstanding the white man's never-ending toil, not infrequently want and even famine prevails among his race. That oft-heard vindication, on the part of the preacher, that the Word of God is nevertheless true and worthy of belief, though uttered by a man in a state of sin, is in itself not wrong.

But, unless such a speaker believes the Word of God himself, makes every possible effort to conduct himself accordingly, shows in his own way of life that it is possible to live in conformity with Christian teaching, that he is full of enthusiasm for Christian living; in other words, if he does not manifest by his own example the intrinsic value of Christianity, the necessity, and above all, the possibility of conducting himself as a Christian in daily intercourse, he may rest assured his preaching will make no lasting impression. When his life is out of accord with his preaching, what hypocrisy. What a farce.

Christian ethics is not a variable moral code subject to momentary change but, on the contrary, an absolute standard of conduct, a positive condition upon which the existence of human societies, i. e., nations, depend. Unless founded upon those principles of right living given first to man by Moses on the Tablets of Stone, then broadened and perfected by Jesus, no State can endure. If it were only for that reason, those Commandments would have to be accepted by us as sacred, not because they are said to have been delivered to Moses direct from God, but for the reason that they are the foundation upon which all enduring lawmaking rests and without which we should live in a state of confusion worse confounded. "As ye would that men should do to you, do ye also to them likewise" is the foundation principle of every State in any degree civilized, whether Christian or heathen.

To inspire the Indian with a desire to live as a Christian one must not rely solely on preaching the Gospel but must make the savage realize, by personal example and by instituting a better order of things, the practical advantages of Christianity.

Just as the stability of a house depends upon its firm base, so the existence of nations, whether small or great, depends upon the principles upon which they are founded, that is, their supreme end and aim. If white men preach peace to Indians whose chief passion is for war, whose existence depends in large measure upon the spoils of war, then white men must prove to the savages that by living in harmony with one another they will have a happier life, that they can live in peace and yet never suffer want, never be bored with the dull monotony of their existence; that, on the contrary, they will find better means of winning distinction by employing themselves in other activities. And, furthermore, white races must stop waging wars on their own part. Ecclesiastics preach the doctrine of peace and brotherly love, yet they more than other men have caused much blood to be shed. I cannot too often repeat that the unworthy examples set by so-called Christians are more to be blamed than anything else for the Indians' slow progress in civilization; the vessel in which inspiriting influences of culture are offered them is far too much besmeared to be inviting. It is unfortunate that the missionary is rarely the first Christian to acquaint Indians with the white race. The trader almost always precedes the priest, conducts his business to his own advantage, unconcerned as to immoral tendencies inherent in his traffic, indifferent as to the passion for display, the intemperance and avarice, that he excites, intensifies, and never suffers to grow less.

Long before the missionary comes to sow his good seed, tares already sown have taken root and sprouted; the man of God finds his field full of weeds.

I have nothing to bring forward against the fur traders; they are no worse than other American tradespeople. It just so happens that their business interests run counter to the civilizing of Indians; in other words, their traffic with the redskins must inevitably cease when the latter become civilized people. On the other hand, I find not much to be commended among the missionaries, at least among those who do nothing but preach and upset the present order without inspiring the savages to attempt better things. If one wishes to clear a field of weeds one must sow seeds in good soil that they may bear fruit and crowd out the weeds by leaving them no ground in which to grow.

We Europeans have developed from barbarous tribes. Our wars have not yet ceased. Though for more than a thousand years we have been Christians, or at least claimed to be, yet who can claim that European nations follow Christian doctrine in their dealings with one another? If we, avowed Christians, have not progressed thus far in love for our fellow man in a thousand years how can we expect Indians to attain to so lofty a plane within a generation?

I will mention just one instance of those seemingly trivial circumstances that prove such difficult obstacles for missionaries to overcome in their noble endeavors: Mr. Kinesey (?), a Protestant missionary to the Omaha, Oto, and Pawnee, told me, in Belle Vue, that the Omaha wished to give up cultivating their fields, because crops had failed for 2 years in succession; the Good Spirit, they thought, favored them no longer and refused to keep His promises.

Jesuits do not forbid Christian Indians entering upon defensive warfare; they forbid their being aggressors in war. The Jesuits are also shrewd in winning savages by impressing them with outward form or semblance.

February 13. Weather so warm today that we could dispense with our open fires and revel in the genial sunshine. If this continues my hopes of hunting buffaloes, antelopes, and stags on snowshoes will not be realized. As those animals, with their thin legs and sharp hoofs, bound over the snow, they sink so deep into the drifts upon making a leap that they can be easily overtaken on snowshoes, and with no trouble at all by swift hounds.

It is an easy matter, therefore, for wolves to catch the more delicate hinds and antelopes in the deep snow. The wolf is not more swift in pursuit, but can hold out longer. On the whole, he is more sly than the fox, though the latter is the universally accepted symbol of trickery and cunning. Wolves in this region, though just as wild and strong as those in Europe, are not so dangerous, because they are never so ravenously hungry. Isolated wolves are frequently seen on the prairie or in the dense forests but never in gangs except when they smell blood and come together mob fashion in pursuit of a wounded animal or to devour the carcass of one just slain.

Their speech is a howl, which varies according to the motive that actuates the beast. When the wolf is hungry or gets the scent of something he dares not tackle he sends forth a prolonged, dismal howl; when he is in pursuit of wild beasts a much more quick, angry note that is yet not the same as the yelp of a dog. Perhaps I might more clearly indicate the difference in sound by saying that wolves use head tones only, no chest tones. By brisk, insistent howls they invite fresh wolves continually to aid in the pursuit; constantly call in new forces. When those that first began the chase become tired and out of breath they lie down to rest until their victim comes back that way, for at every turn the quarry pursued finds enemies anew, called thither by the howling of its pursuers, and finally driven back again to its pasture ground, falls exhausted into the jaws of the beasts waiting there.

The prairie wolf is neither so large nor so strong as other wolves, has a flat forehead and is usually yellow, striped with black on his back, mixed with white on his under parts. Inasmuch as this wolf is a separate species, being a cross between the wolf and different varieties of fox, yet never herds with any of those animals or mates with them, I am inclined all the more to believe that various breeds of dogs may have been originally so derived.

February 22. For a week there has been nothing new to record. Weather continues fine. Time passes quickly. My studies increase in number, because I make a sketch of every little thing that I shall use later on in paintings representative of life in this region. For instance, I made a drawing today of that stuffed head of a Big Horn or Rocky Mountain sheep. The female has horns like a chamois; the buck has horns like a ram. Instead of wool, however, his coat is of coarse dun-colored hair; white on his under parts.

Audubon and Bachmann state, with regard to the geographical distribution of the Big Horn, that this species is not found on Hudson Bay or east of the Rocky Mountains. In that statement Audubon contradicts himself, because he relates earlier how he saw 22 Rocky Mountain sheep at the mouth of the Yellowstone and declares that those animals choose for their pastures the mauvaises terres. On my return journey down the Missouri, Cadotte, on the same boat with me, shot one of those sheep in a herd ranging even farther southeastward. Audubon seems not to have known our wild goat, for, in his account of the Big Horn, he refers to only four varieties of that species, i. e., the mouflon, found in the mountains and on the steppes of Northern Asia; another that is native to Egypt; another in America; then he mentions, on page 223, the ibex and chamois of the Alps (or did this originate with Bachmann? Or did he, perhaps, not include the steinbok as our European scientists do?). That the males make use of their horns to protect themselves in falling or that their horns could serve at best as a protection to their skulls upon an unexpected impact with bowlder or rock, I do not believe. A fall on the head, even when calculated, causes dangerous concussion of the brain; as a matter of course, the much more perilous tumble heels over head would result in more serious shock. Hunters are quite ready to credit any story whatsoever as to the uses which those large horns serve.

Packinaud would rather play poker with common laborers than learn English. I have given him up. That American card game called poker enables only the rich to win, i. e., those who can always put up a higher stake irrespective of the hand they hold. Though the poorer man may have the higher cards, even three aces, three kings, etc., and stakes everything that he possesses on the game, his opponent wins, notwithstanding, if he puts up a still higher stake than the man of less means. As no money is in circulation here the gamesters stake their credit at the store; they gamble their wages or salaries. To keep the score they use grains of corn.

Two Cree Indians brought more than 100 robes, for which they received a better price than is usually paid. This was due, in reality, to the fact that they were heretofore customers of the opposition. The Sioux have the intention to keep the Treaty of Horse Shoe Creek; at least, they are willing to try and keep it for 1 year, so as to find out whether they derive any benefits from it or whether it is nothing more than empty promises—white men's lies.

They have about 80 tents pitched on this side of Fort Clarke. They were visited by Assiniboin who presented 12 horses, laid stress on their ancient relationship and insisted upon the combined tribes using the same speech. Assiniboin, occupying 120 tents, are on a visit to the Herantsa; most probably, to beg corn. L'Ours Fou has already selected a site for his future village, in the vicinity of this fort as a matter of course, and not too far but that he can get the smell of sweet coffee and warm bread. He understands perfectly well that sooner or later he can depend no longer on hunting for a livelihood, but he assumes that, as chief, he himself is entitled to an annual supply of coffee, sugar, and meal at the expense of Uncle Sam, especially since to work is beneath his dignity. Why, of course, molasses will be provided him: He dreams every night of molasses. I am of the opinion that the treacle he so much likes and dreams about is going to displace in his esteem the turtle he wears about his neck. L'Ours Fou is friendly with me. Every time he comes to the fort he sleeps in my room; he talks about his plan to voyage down the river with Mr. Culbertson in the spring and return on the company's steamboat, bringing back with him, to distribute among his people, all the wealth of possessions promised by Uncle Sam.

Woe be unto the white population if that promise is not kept. If representatives of the United States Government are again guilty of false statement their double dealing will have become proverbial among nations in this region also.

Not long ago L'Ours Fou was sleeping as usual in my room. He waked up every now and then during the night, mended the fire, teased the fox, smoked his pipe, and would jab me in the ribs with the pipestem to wake me, so that I might chat with him. To entertain me he would teach me words in his native tongue. For example,

"nuspeh", which means "ax"; "kukusch",[15] which means "swine."
He had great fun teaching me the last-named word. To make me
understand what animal was meant he grunted in such perfect imitation of a hog that I laughed until tears rolled down my cheeks.
Now he always says: "Kukusch, ch, ch."

February 26. Mr. Denig is Swedenborgian and at the same time
he is a Freemason. He mentioned to me that it would be of great
advantage on my travels if I were a Freemason. I am too slightly
acquainted with the order to judge them, but what I do know is
nothing laudable. To be sure, they lend a hand where they can; but
they assist their own at the expense of those who are not Free-
masons, as I have learned from experience. I like the Odd Fellows
in the United States much better. They make less parade of their
benevolence, have no secrets except their recognition signs, and no
distinction in rank, such as embroidered marshals, masters, and
commoners.

While I was sketching this afternoon the Sioux visited me. He
brought two interesting drawings. He was not satisfied with my
work; he could do better. Forthwith, I supplied him with drawing
paper. First he made a drawing of his "coup." Then, with ink, he
drew a buffalo, very well indeed for a savage. In their drawings
Indians attempt to make especially prominent some outstanding distinguishing feature. For instance, in drawing the figure of a man
they stress not his form but something distinctive in his dress that
indicates his rank; hence they represent the human form with far less
accuracy than they draw animals. Among the Indians, their manner of representing the form of man has remained so much the same
for thousands of years that they look upon their accepted form as
historically sacrosanct, much as we regard drawings in heraldry.
We must take into consideration, moreover, that the human form is
not represented in the same manner by all nations; on the contrary,
each nation has its own conventional manner. To prove this, one has
only to examine the different drawings of a man on horseback. In
one the man has no legs at all; in another both legs are on that side
of the horse which is in view; in still another both legs are on the
other side of the horse. My manner of representing a rider was,
therefore, not at all satisfactory to the Sioux.

"But, you see," said he "a man has two legs." That the other limb
was concealed by the horse's body was not the question.

I annoyed him not a little in the end by my remark that among
our people only women ride horseback as he represented riders in his
drawings.

---

[15] French "cochon."

February 29. After several chilly, lonely days I have once more a change of conditions in my room. L'Ours Fou, his daughter, and two of his grandchildren are going to share my quarters with me until the chief departs with Mr. Culbertson for St. Louis. For the time being I welcome their company; the hours pass so slowly just now, since there is nothing to sketch, nothing to interest me. During these last few days we have had a recurrence of such extremely cold weather that there is no possibility of my being able to paint, however ardent my zeal. Our only occupation at the moment is the storing of ice in the ice house. Some of the men cut out thick blocks of ice from the river and bring them up the river bank, others load them, a third drives the cart, and I have to count the number of loads delivered at the ice house and supervise the packing of the blocks. In summer ice is indispensable for preserving fresh meat and for cooling the tepid drinking water brought from the river.

Today Bear's half-starved Assiniboin returned at last to the lower Bourbeuse. They would have liked to be supplied with food and, in that case, they would have felt quite at ease. Not a man in the camp had the least idea of going out hunting; they kept hoping that meat would be offered them from our stores of provisions, which we purchased from them last summer.

Bear himself is much more concerned about filling his own stomach than he is about inspiring his tribesmen by his own good example to be up and doing. Their emaciated dogs, with backs sharply arched and tails between their legs, watched every door, every movement made, hoping for a chance to steal something to eat. Nothing was safe; even pieces of leather that they could snatch were acceptable to them. Since I have the duty to distribute meat to the various employees, I was forced into a constant scuffle with those beasts. If I went toward the door of the meat house I was immediately surrounded. I dared not leave the door open for an instant. Old Indian women were no better. They themselves would have suffered a beating for a piece of meat. We felt obliged to pen up all the pigs and calves; otherwise much fine skill might have been put to the test for the sake of a goodly portion of fresh veal or pork. The Assiniboin complained of our hardness of heart, especially mine. But they should consider that the meat does not belong to me, and, furthermore, that their need is a result of their own laziness. They were not employed here. They have to be made to work; sluggards deserve neither sympathy nor assistance. On the other hand, those who wish employment should never be at a loss for something to do, should never be in need of food.

For the sake of providing more space in my room for my guests I packed my collections. Now I am ready to start on a journey at a moment's notice. I hope the three girls will bring in enough wood, so that we may keep ourselves comfortably warm.

I am glad to have some variation from the employment of every day; life at this fort has become more and more a dull routine, as less that is new or novel has presented itself for my study. There remain yet 4 months to live through before the steamer arrives. But am I certain of going to St. Louis? Is it not probable that Mr. Kipp may find employment for me still 1 year more? I am at his service; there are all sorts of things I should like to study at the Herantsa village. Even though I might not dare to make sketches except in secret, I could devote all the more time to collecting facts concerning Indian legend and tradition, religious belief, social organization, etc. To serve under Pierre Gareau, an unreasonable, self-conceited half-breed, would be most unpleasant. The truth is, I am totally unaccustomed to taking directions from anybody. Still, to accomplish my purpose I can accommodate myself to circumstances, as I have already submitted to greater humiliations. At all events, either here or at Fort Berthold I must get a chance to attend the hunt and take part in everything just as the others do. Wherever it may be, whatever it may cost, I must hunt the stag, the elk, perhaps the bear.

March 1. The Blackfeet call themselves Siksigisqu, i. e., Siksika.

March 2. The Queen of Sheba, as Morgan and I designate Bear's daughter, is gradually overcoming her shyness, or rather her high-bred reserve, in my presence.

She received from Mr. Denig a calico dress; accordingly she took off her soiled black mourning costume of dressed doeskin, exchanged her buffalo robe for a blanket, indigo blue in color, and no longer remains always crouched behind her bed curtains. Mad Bear asked Mr. Denig beforehand whether his daughter was in danger of being annoyed by me. Mr. Denig assured him of the contrary, saying that I was absorbed in other matters. Besides, his daughter is old enough to know how to conduct herself properly and, if need be, to defend herself. The old chief would be pleased, really, to have his beautiful daughter married to a white man who is in a position to keep him well stocked with coffee, meal, and molasses—yea, but that would be a joy dearly bought. His daughter would have to be more richly endowed in mind and heart as well as in beauty of form and feature to induce a man to burden himself with a pauper family of high rank. During the first few days the dark-skinned princess sat behind the curtains, as if she were possessed of beauty too rare to be exposed to profane gaze, but since she sees that I pay no especial attention to her, that I have no designs upon her, she is moved to descend from her throne of buffalo hides and take charge of household affairs at our warm fireside. She has been once married to a young brave who was killed in an Indian fray. In truth the young widow is not distinguished for personal loveliness; she has, it is true, a finely developed figure, beautiful, pensive eyes, splendid teeth, small hands. Between her eyebrows are tattoo marks, forming a half moon.

It is well that my thoughts are absorbed, at the moment, in my studies; otherwise this association with an attractive, unguarded young widow might result quite differently. As all our traders are now provided with wives and as Morgan and I intend to leave in the spring this young widow has little prospect of being married to any man here, the less so as both Mr. Denig and Mackenzie made proposals earlier that were rejected by her father, because at that time he expected a far greater number of gifts than those men offered. Times have changed.

Throughout the whole world wives are easy enough to win but difficult and expensive to keep. At any and all places on this earth opportunities to marry are offered one. As for me, just now marriage would not be favorable to the accomplishment of the purpose I have in view. I do not believe that even my ideal of feminine loveliness, amiability, and virtue combined could induce me to sacrifice the chief aim for which I strive in life. Now, Schitschaka is far from being my ideal; she is not to be compared with Witthae.

No doubt Matoh Mito and Schitschaka will soon find this place dull enough; there is nothing to amuse them, and our fare is neither rich nor abundant. We drink coffee without sugar and eat bread made without lard.

March 4. Le Gras brought the news from Fort Berthold that a courier had arrived there from Fort Pierre. As that is so unusual an occurrence at this time of year Mr. Denig has high hopes that the opposition is crushed.

What a victory! What a triumph! But can it be true? This company has already put down many competitors or else bought them out. They are still steadily extending their trade and increasing in wealth even in their own midst. The opposition, whom we designate as "Dobies," were at an earlier period employees of this company. Owing to some disagreement they withdrew and combined to form a new firm. It seems that their earlier friendship, relationship in fact (the two Picottes), serves to make these two companies all the more bitter and jaundiced in their attitude toward each other. Indians know full well that when there is no competition they are obliged to pay much more dearly for what they buy; so they have good and just reasons for doing what they can to keep competition alive. As to this report, it seems to me, if Primeau, Harvey & Co. have suspended payments, they have in mind only a change of firm, for Campbell of St.

Louis, their principal creditor, who advances their goods, would not allow the business to go to ruin.

March 6. I have just had the pleasant but most unexpected news that I may go with Robert Campbell to the horse camp tomorrow. What glad tidings! There I can sketch and hunt to my heart's content; the only duty imposed is that I am to take charge of the camp when Morgan is absent. He supersedes Smith, because the latter fed too many Indians; owing to his forbearance, several tents were occupied with redskins all the time.

When we first get there I can be all the more free to roam about or follow the chase, because my friend is not just now fit for much hunting and will stay in camp. What unexpected good fortune! How my heart thrills! Just what I most ardently desired, just what I am most urgently in need of to accomplish my aims is now awaiting me. Adieu, Fort Union!

March 8. Horse camp, 12 miles from Fort Union. Morgan and I left the fort day before yesterday, with our bedding loaded on an ox sled driven by Tetreaux. The sky was clear. There was little snow. A sharp, cold wind was blowing, but our blood was warm. As we were supposed to be a kind of escort accompanying the sled we had to adapt our gait to that of the oxen. Five dogs were leaping joyously about us. When the hayfield was flooded, upon the overflow of the Yellowstone, Smith had removed his camp to the forest; so we had to go a little out of our way at that point, in order to take along enough hay for the oxen overnight. We were proceeding across the marsh when Morgan caught sight of a wolf in the distance and instantly gave his dogs the signal; away went the hounds in full cry, raising a whirlwind of flying snow in their wake. We followed full tilt to see the fun. The young greyhound was in the lead, eager to win his spurs. Then came Badger, Castor, and Bull. As soon as Kadosch got scent of the wolf's track he lagged behind. The greyhound soon overtook his quarry and was instantly bitten on the nose; whereupon Badger seized the wolf by the leg. Bull and Castor caught him by the throat and killed him.

It was only a prairie wolf. In spite of the terrible cold Morgan tarried long enough to flay the beast. While he was engaged with that the dogs found another wolf and set out at once in pursuit. We called them back, however, because we dared not stray too far from our course; so they lost that trace. When we came to the hayfield, where Tetreaux was already setting to work, we found the flooded bottom land frozen over; the water was about a foot deep and covered with a crust of ice not thick enough to bear our weight; consequently, at every step we broke through. For the distance of a mile we had to go forward, sinking through the ice crust into the water at every stride, a most fatiguing progress. So we changed our course and blazed another trail.

Four miles farther on we found Smith's camp. It was situated on this side the bois peinture ("painted tree"), at the foot of a steep slope—probably river shore in prehistoric times—at the edge of a forest below the high prairie; therefore, though well protected from the wind, our situation afforded no view at all of the plateau where the horses were to graze. Morgan decided at once to transfer the camp to another spot, so we did not pitch the tent we brought with us but laid it on the ground along with our bedding, brought dry wood, put together a good big pile of it and kindled a crackling fire. We found quantities of meat on a scaffold; Smith had concerned himself little about sending it to the fort.

Nearby on the height above we found traces of several tents but recently removed, the occupants of which, too indolent to hunt on their own account, had lived entirely on food brought in by our huntsmen. We ate our supper with the old Spanish horse guard, then sat down beside our dogs before the blazing, crackling fire, the sparks from which swam high up among the trees. How tall the dark tree trunks seemed in the gloom of the forest! How glorious to smoke my pipe in that romantic place! What a sudden change of scene. What flowing fancies filled my brain, of hunts I was to follow, of studies I was to make, of pictures I was to paint! How could I ever have been able to sleep! The others disturbed us very little with talk; the fact that we had come to relieve Smith of his post, to put a restraint on Cadotte's and Pierre's women, to buy sugar from the opposition in exchange for deerskins, to prevent Indians from consuming meat brought in by our hunters, to spur the Platte-man on to a better use of the powder and lead he borrowed, gave occasion to each for reflections more or less displeasing. Morgan was to put things in order and, inasmuch as he knew no French and the hunters and metifs knew no English, I was to serve as his interpreter as well as assistant.

Yesterday (Sunday) we transferred our camp to the bank of the ice-bound Missouri. We pitched our tents in a beautiful spot that affords an outlook over the hills, the prairie where our drove of 36 horses and mules is to graze, and a far-reaching view of the river.

We found there quantities of dry wood and brought pure river water from a hole in the ice. When we reached our chosen location each selected the place where he wished to pitch his tent and cleared therefrom the snow and underbrush. While the women busied themselves dragging in their household effects some of the men cut down dead trees and others got ready the tent poles.

As soon as ground was cleared for a tent, pieces of bark were laid all around the place where the fire was to be built, so that the apischimos (raw buffalo hides) or whatever was used for bedding would not lie directly upon the wet earth. The size of the tent was determined by the number of occupants; accordingly each required a larger or smaller amount of bark. To construct a tent three or four poles were bound together at the ends, then set up to form the first framework; their lower ends were extended as far apart as the diameter of the tent was intended to be. In the spaces between them other poles were added until a circular framework was formed. Then the tent cloth, made of several dressed skins sewed together, cowhides from which the hair had been removed, was bound fast by its upper edges to another tent pole which was erected inside the framework and fitted in at the top where the other poles join. This awning was then pulled over the poles and fastened together with wooden pins or cords, an opening having been left at the top for the egress of smoke and at the bottom for entrance to the tent.

Along its lower edge incisions were made through which wooden pins were driven into the ground to hold the tent cloth down. The two flaps at the top were sewed together like a pocket and weighted down by means of long, slender rods to prevent their being blown about by the wind in such a way as to drive the smoke back into the tent. This pocket and ends of tent poles left uncovered were frequently used by Indians to display their decorations and ornaments. An animal skin stretched between two staves was hung before the lower opening that served for door, a most uncomfortable arrangement; one had to bend almost double to crawl through under the pelt. As the wind was blowing violently and the ground too solidly frozen to permit our putting much faith in the wooden pins we had driven down, we secured the awning further by weighting it with heavy boughs, even sections of tree stems, in order to hold it fast to the ground. As a further precaution we heaped up snow all around, so as to ward off the wind as much as we could. Our tents were then ready, so far as the exterior was concerned. On the inside we spread our beds over against the fireplace; we put up two posts nearby that were to serve for cupboard; higher up, about 5 or 6 feet from the ground, we extended a thick beam straight across the fireplace, made each end secure to a tent pole, and suspended from this another smaller one with a hole in the middle over which we set our kettle. Opposite the entrance we deposited our stores of meat.

From now on the hunters are required to deliver to us all the game they kill; we in turn distribute the rations due. Every hunter, as a matter of course, is entitled to certain amounts that belong to him by right, according to their accepted laws of the chase; for instance, the head of the animal killed, the heart, stomach, stone, unborn calves, etc.

Morgan and I together with five dogs occupy our tent. The Spaniard, Joe Dolores, his Mandan woman, and Belhumeur live in the one next to ours. In the third Cadotte and his Assiniboin woman live with two Assiniboin families; in the fourth the half-breed, Antoine La Pierre, with his family. Our company is made up of people differing widely as to race and lineage.

Joe had a mind to impress me at once, today, with his courage. Though he is only horse guard, he wished me to believe that he is just as experienced in hunting and setting traps as any other man. He succeeded no better in convincing me this time, however, than when he rushed into the fort just after my arrival there with Bellangé, and shouted "Blackfeet."

Today's bear hunt was all false alarm, I am sorry to say. We found, it is true, in the depths of the forest on the other side of the frozen Missouri, a great hole made by the uprooting of a tree. The mouth of this den was half covered with snow. I fired one load from my double-barreled gun into it but unearthed no bear, either vigilant or sleeping, black or grizzly; at least we saw no evidences of anything astir.

But suppose an old son of a gun had rushed out to attack us, is it likely that we should have given him a mortal wound forthwith? We stood there ready to brave the worst.

To compensate ourselves for not having fallen victim to bruin's paws, as our foolhardy act deserved, we followed quite fresh deer tracks that we discovered on our way home. After having followed the deer for a long time as noiselessly as we could along a course full of twists and turns we were startled by two white-tailed hinds springing out of their retreat just in front of us and taking themselves off with mad leaps over shrubs and fallen trees. We fired instantly, but of course without result. Joe ran on after them, but I crossed the river and came back to our tent, opening a way for myself with great difficulty through brambles and grapevine stems.

Naturally, Smith is not particularly pleased about his removal from command at this camp. He is not permitted now to go hunting whenever he likes. He must take off only the hides of the beasts he kills and keep only those portions of meat to which the hunter is entitled, leaving the rest for Indians or wolves. Besides, he must now go hunting on foot, so as to spare the horses; he has to hunt every day, moreover, unless weather conditions are altogether unfavorable. But I cannot help being grateful for his negligence, since for that reason I am here.

March 9 (?). I went this morning to the slope, where is the bois peinture ("painted tree"), to examine a trap that Joe set. I found therein only a magpie (common magpie, *Pica melanolenca* Audubon). Made a sketch of the tree.

It is a large cottonwood, on the trunk near the foot of which an Indian cut away the bark and, on the bare wood, sketched different figures in vermilion and chrome yellow. As the tree stands near the trail, people passing that way have added various other figures in charcoal, verifying the proverb "A wall is a fool's writing paper." The original drawing of a sun, a hand, an enclosure, and the forms of different animals were meant to record, so it seems to me, adventures on a hunt that the redskin who made the sketch experienced during one sun (day) in this forest.

March 14, Sunday. Clear weather. Sunshine quite warm wherever the abominably cold northwest wind does not penetrate. At our camp things go on as usual. Because he is unfit for active duty Morgan has to take charge of the tent, so I have better opportunity to wander about with the hunters than to sketch or write. Besides, I have covered nearly all the pages of my sketchbook on both sides, so I have to guard against making superfluous drawings, especially when so much of great importance may occur. We have killed 16 elks and 10 deer and dispatched the meat to the fort. Though hunters have turned this region to good account already, they enable us to deliver more meat to the fort now than was sent there earlier. They are no longer allowed to slay the beasts for the sake of their hides only (hides belong to the hunter), but are required to bring the meat here on pack horses.

Hunters are not paid salaries and provided with guns and ammunition merely to go hunting for love of the sport, but they are employed to hunt, in order that business at the fort may derive a profit therefrom. So Morgan has appointed certain days on which the hunters always go out to shoot the game and others on which they bring in the spoils. I am invariably on hand on such occasions and on the lookout for picturesque landscapes, views, etc. To secure the slaughtered animals from wolves, hunters hang the carcasses as high as they can on limbs of a tree or else cover the meat with the hide of the animal in such a way as to prevent the smell of it from reaching wolves within 24 hours. To verify their right of possession, in the event other Indians find the game, hunters hang on a pole or stake set up nearby some article of their clothing or equipment. To drive away wolves or ravens that may approach his booty a hunter will sometimes inflate bladders taken from the slain animals and attach them to the stake or pole where their movements in the wind will frighten the vultures or prowling beasts. To the same end, he is said to strew gunpowder about the place where the meat is left.

If we fail to find sufficient game here to supply the fort with meat we shall remove our camp to a region on the other side of the Yellowstone, where, on account of frequent forays into that neighborhood by hostile Blackfeet, little hunting has been done.

We should have the disadvantage there of being obliged to take the pack horses across two rivers, not expedient except at this time of the year, when the ice is firm. Inasmuch as we can be all the more easily dispensed with when Bruyère and his men return to the fort this horse camp is likely to be maintained for some time yet. But Morgan wishes to go with Mr. Culbertson to St. Louis next month, so that he may make a visit to his Scottish homeland during the summer, when he is free from duties here.

Last Thursday Schitschaka came to see the Platteman (le Garçon du Faissée). She stayed twice as long in our tent. With the desire to do something in acknowledgment of the honor we served coffee with sugar. Later came the Platteman to inquire whether one of us would not like to marry her. Oh, is that it? That is why she came to see us?

March 18. For several days a cold, penetrating north wind has prevailed. It makes me all the more uncomfortable for the reason that, in spite of every precaution, it blows directly on my bed. Besides, we are out of coffee. Our only drink is ice water. The river ice is now so thick we can no longer get drinking water from the hole we scooped out. We have to melt ice either in a kettle over the fire or let it waste away in our mouths. To make matters worse we suffer unending thirst as the result of an enforced diet of lean, sun-dried elk meat; and as a consequence are continually wanting to drink.

If this chill to which our bodies are subjected both internally and externally does not penetrate even the marrow in our bones I know nothing of our human constitution. To get bread at this camp is out of the question; we have nothing but meat, which at this time of year is stale and tasteless enough. Never have I been so tormented with thirst; even in seasons of excessive heat I have not suffered such intense desire for drinking water as now, in this climate of severe dry cold. Even the corn that is now and then graciously sent us from the fort serves only to inflame the stomach. But we shall soon have coffee; we set as much store by the coffee pot as do old wives. If the meat had more nutriment a broth would satisfy our appetites. The worst effect on me of this severe weather is that I see so much, so very much, I wish to record with my brush, while to attempt painting in weather at this temperature is out of the question.

Yesterday Boneau and Valette arrived here to take up their abode for a while; Bruyère has no longer anything for them to do. Smith has to go to that winter post and hunt; all of the Indians are temporarily absent from that vicinity. L'Ours Fou, finding things dull at the fort, sent for the Platteman, whom he wishes to take with him to fetch the Gens des Filles.[16] In this wise, changes have come about in the personnel of our camp.

All my ideas revolve about one central thought: How much sketching I might be able to do if the weather were warmer. Since this excessively cold spell set in my chief occupation has been cutting wood. We attend to everything ourselves in our tent, so that we can be alone and undisturbed.

March 21. Have been here 2 weeks already. Today, all of a sudden, the weather turned warm. Real thawing weather. If the ice in the river should break up we would be obliged to get away from this place and seek a new hunting ground. Even now the hunters are forced to go a distance of 20 miles to find deer; that is too far when the meat must be delivered at the fort. I have decided that, in the event my studies are pretty nearly completed by the end of next month, I shall make an effort to go with Mr. Culbertson on his trip down the river. To feel that I am a superfluous guest makes me uncomfortable in the highest degree; furthermore, there is no prospect of my being able to earn my livelihood in this country; and, finally, the noiseless motion of a keelboat will afford me better opportunity to see wild beasts than if I were to travel on a puffing steamer.

Joe Dolores and his wife have left for the fort; the former will go to the Yellowstone to trap beavers on his own account, the latter will remain at the fort. L'Ours Fou dropped in to see us yesterday, in passing. Smoked with me for the last time. Heartfelt leave taking.

March 24. Owing to the sudden rise in temperature we were obliged to change the location of our camp.

We had to be constantly on the watch for fear that the Yellowstone flowing up from more southerly latitudes might break bounds at any moment, where it empties into the Missouri, and overflow all the surrounding lowlands. Though our camp stood 8 feet above the ice-bound Missouri we did not regard our situation as being any longer safe. Morgan decided upon the old camping ground near the hayricks; we folded our tents, loaded our goods and chattels on pack mules, mounted horses, and rode along with the rest of the drove to that spot. We had to make a detour of 4 miles around a wide bend of the Missouri. Snow was melting everywhere and, as

---

[16] A band of the Assiniboin, the Girl Band.

the water had no outlet and could not be absorbed by earth still frozen, we were compelled to trudge all the way through slush.

We had the luck to find tent poles [17] that Smith had made use of when he pitched his camp here earlier in the season, and quantities of good firewood, but we are surrounded by water. I do not approve this site at all. We spent a horrible night. I lay down early under my buffalo robe and fell asleep listening to an Indian air sung by three metifs in the tent next to ours. I had been fast asleep for some time when Morgan waked me with the shout, "Water! Water!" He had been trying to make up the fire, because he wanted to fry another piece of meat, but though the wood was dry he could not get the fire to burn.

He thought at first this was due to the dampness of the ground where the fire was built and removed the wood to a more elevated place in the tent, but with no better result. Finally the light went out. Morgan started out of the tent and found he was standing in water. It was high time to save ourselves; the river had overflowed its banks and the flood had crept gradually and stealthily upon us without the least warning. We shouted at once to the singing metifs and told them to bestir themselves. We hurried to higher ground, taking with us our bedclothes, books, supplies of gunpowder, and rifles. In one place we waded through water above our hips. We left the heavy tent behind and also our stores of meat. The rising flood came slowly forward until it reached undergrowth and thickets by which it was restrained. We were at least an English mile from the river. In the midst of this dismal scene, lighted but faintly by a crescent moon, our dark forms, enveloped in buffalo robes, were hurrying to and fro, plunging through the water like robbers escaping with their booty. The metifs, meanwhile, kept on singing their long-winded Chippewa song, taking no heed of our warning, and yet they were perfectly sober. Did they continue their song in defiance of the elements?

Having reached dry ground, I bound together all my possessions of value, i. e., my sketchbook, journal, drawing material, etc., and put them in my much-prized calfskin pouch, which serves me regularly for pillow.

We spread our apischimos on the ground out on the open prairie and covered ourselves with riding cloaks and buffalo robes, having first removed our wet clothes. We lay as close together as we could to keep each other warm.[18] We called our dogs to lie on top of us, as

---

[17] This advantage, together with that of having hay near at hand, influenced Morgan to select this place.

[18] For the first time since I left St. Joseph I slept without my trousers, and now, of all times, when the weather is cold.

usual, for the purpose of keeping guard and also of imparting warmth. But those canines were every instant scenting nearby wolves, bounding off with great outcry to fight the beasts or drive them away, then lying down on top of us again, scratching themselves and contesting one another's places. Under such restless, disquieting conditions, especially in our overexcited state, we were unable to sleep at all. Notwithstanding, Morgan and I consoled ourselves with the thought that journeys affording no adventure are worth nothing to a fellow. One must have something or other to relate afterwards, else one would not have a really comfortable feeling.

It was already late in the day before we went to see about our abandoned tent. Several times we had peeped out faint-heartedly from under our bed coverings but dared not expose ourselves to a cold, piercing wind on the open prairie while we put on clothes stiff with frost. Once dressed, I strode swiftly through the water to our tent, where I found nothing to eat or drink, no meat, not anything. Then I went to the metifs' tent to dry my clothes by their fire and to get warm. It was evident that they had removed their tent to higher ground.

During the hours our place was unguarded dogs had devoured all our meat. Morgan came on behind me. Never in all my life did black coffee, without sugar, have so delicious a taste. Never did a fire seem so glorious. Even the intense cold without, in this instance, stood us in good stead; ice is always preferable to mud and slush. Anything but mud and mire, mud and marsh.

Hardly were we through eating when we heard swans passing overhead, the first we had heard. Morgan ran out to see whether they were likely to come down anywhere near. He returned quickly for his gun and hastened away. Meanwhile I sent Boneau and Valette to bring together our roving horses and see whether all of them were to be found. Then I assisted Belhumeur to pitch our new tent, inside of which I am now writing. We have placed this one on somewhat higher ground than the other, but we are still much too near the water. Morgan distrusts wind on the open prairie; not infrequently tents are blown down. After great pains and trouble we have a good fire burning between our two beds. I am at last drying my shoes and hose while I get myself warm. Just now the evening sunshine feels unusually warm. So we are encouraged to expect the early arrival of ducks, geese, and swans.

In summer the neighboring moor must be alive with those migratory birds; with mosquitoes and frogs as well, no doubt. The water now flooding that low ground is purely the result of melting snows.

March 26. Night before last the Yellowstone overflowed its banks and poured into the Missouri with such volume that the ice layer was crushed in. We were forced to remove our own tent and two others to the spot where Morgan and I had such a miserable lodging last Monday night. This bottom land throughout its entire extent is now under water; the flood, carrying blocks of ice, boughs, tree stems, scum and foam, sweeps over it like a wild mountain stream. I hope we may be able to stay for a while, at least, in one place, for this constant breaking camp and pitching tents anew has become a bore. Our present location, in my opinion, is not well chosen. We are exposed to the full fury of prairie winds and while we have, it is true, plenty of firewood conveniently near, we find it hardly feasible to snatch our fuel from this roaring flood; to force our way through a stream blocked with ice and tree trunks for the purpose of bringing only wet, sodden wood from the forest is much too dangerous—at the same time of little use. So we have to go, after all, to the nearest coulee (2 miles) to get wood that will really keep our fires burning. And where are we to find our game? On the wide open prairie, where we can be easily discovered for miles around? Water we have in superabundance, of a certain sort.

Morgan thinks only of shooting ducks; he stands, loaded gun in hand, gazing always southward. Only a few ducks were seen; today they sneak under the willow bushes to escape this cold southeast wind. In truth our prospects for hunting seem rather discouraging at the moment; we have no shot either here or at the fort. I don't see how Morgan is likely to hit fowls on the wing with bullets, especially when the birds are flying singly.

The metifs are employed for a limited term, which ends on the 15th of next month, and they draw their pay in horses. They own now 26 animals in this drove under our care, while only three horses and six mules remain to the company. When the metifs depart with their drove I wonder what is going to be done with regard to our horse camp? During the recent fearfully cold spell of weather an old gray horse belonging to us was nearly frozen to death and in consequence unable to defend himself against wolves that gnawed away the shank of one of his hind legs. And yet the pitiable old creature still lives.

March 27. After a long hunt yesterday Morgan came back late in the evening with only one duck. He said his failure was due to our lack of shot, and, as I am on good terms with Joe Picotte, he wished I would go and try to buy some shot from him.

Morgan has expressed that wish several times before, but I am unresponsive for the reason that I despise Joe Picotte on account of his double-dealing; for the further reason that he would know, since I am no hunter, I have no need of shot myself, but wanted the supply for his competitors; and, finally, because Mr. Denig would say at once I went after bread and sugar or else that, during my absence from the fort, I was currying favor with the opposition. Still, Morgan has shown me so much friendliness I ordered a horse saddled today and rode over to the adobe fort. There I found the Missouri 30 feet above its usual level and rushing by with thunderous roar. The upper Missouri, I was told, rose 20 feet yesterday in 2 hours and, bearing with it huge blocks of ice, overflowed all the lowlands. In thickets and coppices, on the outskirts of the forest, blocks of ice are piled as high as a wall. "The oldest inhabitants have never known the river to be so high or to rise so rapidly." The adobe fort stands 100 feet from the steep river bank; today the stream was sweeping by within 20 feet of the southward gate.

I was received in a most friendly manner. Joe presented me with 3 pounds of sugar. But I could not get any shot. Notwithstanding the fall of night I rode immediately back, because I had concealed something interesting on the prairie and dared take it to our camp only after dark. In short, on my way over I found a medicine doll lying on the trail.

Such images are said to have the power to invoke spirits and also to exert curative effects on sick children. It is a stuffed doll made of the dressed skin of an animal. It is about 2 feet high and adorned with the usual ornaments children wear, i. e., bracelets and necklace of "dove's eggs", made of blue and white porcelain. An Indian woman doctor who attends sick children lost this conjuring doll, therefore I dare not let the women at our camp know that it is in my possession. It was as dark as Erebus on the prairie; but for my horse I should have found my way with difficulty. He neighed to his comrades and, as they came thundering along to meet him, they seemed really ghostlike, for in the blackness of night their bodies could not be distinguished; only their resounding hoofbeats and eager neighing gave evidence of what was approaching. They might just as easily have been taken for stags, which often graze with our horses. After a time I detected in the distance a gleam of light; it was a fire burning inside a tent. I could at last guide my unwilling courser in a definite direction, he being much more inclined to go roaming with his own kind. And he was soon at liberty to do so, for we were again at our camp. The dogs had already scented us and came bounding forward with loud outcry, but they changed their wrathful baying for joyous yelps when I called them by name.

This ride of mine over the wide prairie, with only hunting knife for weapon, brought vividly to my mind a similar uncanny experience I had once when returning on horseback from St. Joseph to

Savannah. It was a hot day in August (1850), I rode my much-prized mare Fashion to St. Joseph. As the heat was extraordinarily oppressive in the late afternoon I delayed going back until night, when I should find the temperature more agreeable. On the way I took much pleasure in observing the odd shapes given mighty trees by luxuriant climbing plants that hung like veils upon them, sometimes airy and unsubstantial, sometimes heavy and thick; here, decayed trees seemed to stretch forth naked arms to heaven; there, uprooted trunks supported their broken limbs on the ground or lifted their huge roots menacingly. As the moon rose I was nearing Savannah on my swift traveler, Fashion. How she was stretching her four legs. How jolly I was feeling. I had thrown my jacket across my saddlebow, for the temperature was still so high as to make me too warm even in my shirt sleeves. Suddenly there appeared before me on the dimly lighted roadway the indistinct shape of a man on horseback. The rider asked where I was bound for. He advised that I turn back with him; in the vicinity of Jamestown, he said, was an apparition that froze the blood in his veins. The stranger then told me how, as he was riding along the road, a knight in armor suddenly appeared, standing on a high rail fence.

He tossed the plume on his helmet and, lifting his bare sword, struck three blows on his shield with such force that my informant's horse became frightened and ran away, thus rescuing him from peril. He urged me to avoid passing that spot, for horse thieves were in ambush there. I knew that entire section was in ill repute; far and wide there was not a dwelling house to be seen; the forest afforded secure hiding places; at night, the road was little traveled; murders were not at all infrequent. But the unknown rider impressed me as even more worthy of suspicion. I was unable to distinguish his features, though our horses stood so close together they could rub noses. His intention, I thought, was to entice me along with himself and, at a favorable moment, to deal me a blow behind the ears. In reply, therefore, I assured the ghost seer that I had no fear of danger, I was well armed, and well mounted; thereupon, I bade him good night, gripped Fashion with my legs, rode down the hill and crossed the stream at its foot. I peered sharply into the dark places sheltered by shrubbery, drew tighter rein, gripped Fashion more closely, so as not to be taken unawares, for, to tell the truth, my only weapon of defense was my little pocketknife. On the high rail fence so exactly described I saw no sign of ghost. However, I did hear the next day that the son of a farmer living in the near neighborhood of "Jimtown" was attacked that night, as he was returning from Savannah.

Some one shot at him with pistols. As luck would have it, he was carrying an umbrella under his left arm (umbrellas are often used by Americans to protect them from the sun). This man's sunshade was perforated by seven bullet shots and he received several slight wounds.

March 28. As Morgan and I were out together on a hunt we met the semisavage Kipland who was bringing us a note from Mr. Denig, in which he gave us directions to remain at the camp, in spite of the outbreak of the rivers, until the metifs left, or better still, until Mr. Culbertson arrived from Blackfeet territory and took us two along with him. If Mr. Denig only knew how little we yearn for his society he would not have been in such a hurry to send that message. He assumes, I suppose, that we are just as sensible of the want of bread as he would be in our place.

As the result of a raw, cold wind, the river is again covered with ice sufficiently thick to restrain the upper current and cake together ice blocks and masses of wood, but yet not firm enough to bear our weight. We had quite a picturesque adventure crossing the wild coulee by holding on to overhanging boughs as we clambered over huge blocks of ice. In a corner of this frozen lake that covers the upper pasture we heard La Pierre frequently firing off his gun.

We therefore hurried across the thin ice crust that overspread the prairie, breaking through at every step and causing a great deal of noise by the constant cracking of ice. This attracted our dogs, unfortunately; they broke loose from the tent where we had confined them and came running along, too. As they were not in the right direction their presence would necessarily only destroy our prospects for a hunt. We drove them back, but they retreated only to a certain distance and there they remained, howling most dolefully. Pretty soon we discovered two hinds, standing bewildered at the brink of the frozen river and looking anxiously toward us; on one side of them La Pierre was unceasingly firing upon a herd that had sunken through the ice crust into the water; in the rear was the treacherous ice; in front of them were Morgan and I; on the other side were the howling dogs. Morgan took my gun, concealed himself behind a clump of bushes, and told me to go around to the other side and drive the two hinds toward him. I ran quickly forward, facing the sharp wind; the dazed animals did not scent me but remained perfectly still until I was within 20 feet of them. I put them to flight by shouting and hurling chunks of ice. How easily I could have shot them if only I had had my gun at hand. Morgan missed aim; the little creatures escaped. For my part I did not grudge them their life.

Then Morgan went in pursuit of his everlasting ducks, a sport that is not worth so much freezing oneself and getting one's clothes soaking wet.

I made my way through the thin ice layer to Marguerite La Pierre, who shouted across to ask that I come and lead the pack horse she had brought, through the water to her father, so that he might load the meat and hides. Up to his knees in water, La Pierre stood far out in the river, where he had slain a herd that was unable to get out of the depths, because, with every plunge to extricate themselves from the surrounding ice crust, the animals sank again into the bed of the stream. I had great difficulty crossing the thin layer myself; I sank through repeatedly into the icy water. Still, I could not expect that girl to do such work. When I reached La Pierre he was already taking off the hides. Standing leg deep in ice water, I assisted him. As soon as the horse was laden (with hides, legs, shoulders, and portions of ribs) I made my way as fast as I could to the tent, for I was miserably cold and even more uncomfortable from the irritation to my skin caused by frozen trousers. The tent I found cheerless and cold; the fire had gone out. I had to return to the frozen river, snatch from it some tree limbs embedded there, split the wood, and build a fire again. In a short time I had a blaze that would have done credit to Hades. For such terrible cold as I was enduring was no joke; I was trembling in every limb, my teeth were chattering, and yet I was obliged to dry my clothes on my body. I was so benumbed that I felt as though I would like to put my arms around that fire and hug the blaze.

April 1. Since last Saturday winter has returned with rigor: heavy snowfall, frightful cold, violent north wind. Everything seems working together to make our life here quite romantically miserable. In such atrocious weather as this one would refuse to turn a dog out, to say nothing of human hunters; accordingly, Morgan feeds the dogs better than usual and diminishes our rations from day to day. He means, most probably, to give the former less inclination to steal. To procure wood for our fire we have to run the risk of slipping down, perhaps falling through the treacherous ice crust at any minute, with our burden on the shoulder, or else wade through deep snow to the distant coulee, cut down an ash or a linden and lug the wood to camp. A hero in peril is, I admit, romantic. But a hero unloved—Does he excite any interest?

Yesterday morning, I can tell you, I was in no jocose humor. Upon awaking we saw what inspired great alarm: the interior of our tent was entirely covered with snow. The vessel containing our meat broth, the fire, bedclothes, man, and beast, everything under snow. What a dreary outlook: to get out of our beds, shake off the snow, clean up the tent before we could light the fire again, thaw our meat broth and make it palatable.

Our prospects become constantly more dreary, more comfortless. Later on, while lying beside the fire beneath my buffalo robe, what visions hovered before my inward eye of the good food, warm living apartments, smokeless fireplaces, dry, well-secured dwelling I had given up for the sake of attaining my life's aim. Never had I been so entranced with material comforts; my imagination as by a conjurer's art brought before me, in mockingly tempting review, all the delicious viands I most relish, all the most alluring situations in life.

"Tante mieux" (so much the better), as they say here, I consoled myself by considering our wretched condition from the standpoint of painter and dwelt upon our picturesque situation. For the time being, life is hard to be sure; but did I not come in search of these experiences? Have I not longed for them as an aid to my study of Indian life, in good fortune and bad, in abundance and in want, in joy and in sorrow, in summer's heat and winter's rigorous cold?

Shall the enjoyment of a pleasant lot in after life compensate me for the pains I now endure? Will my paintings insure me comforts in my old age? Aside from the satisfaction a painter feels in the accomplishment of work well achieved, this is what I most desire. I have no ambition to strive for fame, but only to express in my art the ideal that urges me on.

Patience! Sunshine follows rain!

April 2. Bad news has reached us from Joe Dolores. When he arrived with his laden dogs at his destination on the Yellowstone he found the region under water and had to turn back. He has now been lingering for several days in the tent of an Assiniboin on the other side of the Missouri, opposite Fort Union, until he feels he may risk crossing on the ice. The tent of that Assiniboin with whom he is staying is the only one left of five that were pitched there. The report goes that Blackfeet have killed 25 people.

During last night the waters of the Missouri receded to their normal bounds; the ice crust, after much splitting and cracking, finally gave way. The thick fogs have been dispersed by the sun, which now shines with more splendor and more warmth than we have recently experienced. Under the sun's genial rays the snow is melting fast. Blades of grass are already protruding from the soil. Throughout these recently flooded lowlands quantities of driftwood lie in piles and, what presents a more singular appearance, great blocks of ice rest among the boughs of trees, where they were lodged when carried thither by the high waters. There they remain, along with other heaps of such ice blocks and snow mounds found everywhere among the undergrowth and coppices. Is the winter really at an end? Hardly: the month of April is the most unsettled of the entire year.

Dried venison and suet is our only fare; but we should do pretty well, even so, if we did not suffer so dreadfully from thirst and the drinking of ice-cold water did not so chill us to the bone. Black coffee is a rare delicacy that we drink with all the pleasure of old maids. As a rule we have to make out with hot broth made from dried meat.

April 3. Joe Dolores is once more with us. He told us about his misadventures on the beaver hunt. In the first place, he set out on his trapping expedition one day too late; reached the Yellowstone, therefore, just as the waters burst through the ice and overflowed the surrounding land. He attempted to cross in a skin canoe, but found the stream so full of floating ice he had to turn back. Even then he was forced to abandon his boat in order to save his dogs and the travois, together with three traps, from the raging flood. Then he had to wade a long distance through water breast deep, until he reached higher ground on the prairie. Under a great elm, where he was sheltered by a gigantic ice block lying near, he kindled a fire to dry his clothes and get himself warm. Next morning he walked around to get a view of his situation and decide what he was to do. He came upon an abandoned campfire. Upon such discoveries this question arises at once in a person's mind: Friend or foe? Dolores was unaware of Assiniboin lodges in that neighborhood, so he assumed at once that Blackfeet had recently passed that way.

He loaded his gun, adding, along with his bullet ball, a handful of buckshot, and went cautiously forward. Soon he caught sight of an Indian. At the instant he raised his gun and took aim he heard the whimpering of a dog.

"Blackfeet have no dogs," he said to himself. "That man must be one of the Dacota."

With that, he stood upright and greeted the Indian with the well-known words, "Dagodeh kuna?" (Whither, friend?) The Assiniboin was severely wounded in his left arm, which was so swollen it was all astrut. Joe had from him an account of Blackfeet attack. Seven Assiniboin tents under command of La Main Poque were hunting in the vicinity of a small lake this side of the Butte des Mammelles, where they were detected by a troop of Blackfeet who were lying in wait for Crow Indians. At sunrise the next morning the Blackfeet made a surprise attack on the seven tents, cut three of them asunder at once, sent a bullet into the brain of one Assiniboin, but were unable to get his scalp. On the whole, though they had all the advantage of a surprise attack from higher ground and of superior numbers, the Blackfeet seem not to have fought valiantly. They were reported to have numbered 50 men; but that I do not for one moment believe, because the casualties were so few. They killed one warrior only, one woman, and inflicted severe wounds upon 15 others. They themselves lost three men and one scalp. It is reported that after the first onslaught they made no further combined attacks but merely kept themselves concealed within rifle range behind trees and underbrush. The Assiniboin were protected only by heaps of snow. Perhaps, when the Blackfeet found out that they were attacking Assiniboin instead of Crows, they lost courage.

I must say La Main Poque chose a most unfavorable situation when he encamped in the bottom of that deep circular valley, shut in by hills covered with groves and thickets, while the ground surrounding his encampment was perfectly level. The women lay down flat on their stomachs and covered themselves and their papooses with buffalo robes. That is why so many of these were grazed with bullets on their heels, hinderparts, and shoulders. Bluefoot was the one and only man who did not fight but covered himself on the ground just as the women did. Joe says that he saw the Blackfeet's fortified camp, which was entrenched with the trunks of trees. From the quantities of bones there he formed the conclusion that the enemy had tarried a long time in ambush. If we had crossed the Yellowstone according to our plan some time ago that band would have cost us our pack horses, at least, if not our lives.

To witness such an encounter would not have been an unwelcome experience, so far as I am concerned; at the same time the thought of being crippled or made blind is far more disagreeable in prospect than the possibility of being suddenly killed. To be a burden to others throughout the term of a long life would be a hundred times more bitter than death. Besides, I have no desire to appear as an enemy to the Indians; up to the present time I have had no cause to take such an attitude.

April 7. Mild weather and substantial food has again awakened my dormant imagination. Last Sunday was indeed a dismal, lonely day. We had only tough venison to eat and precious little of that, so Morgan decided to ride to the fort and, under pretext of wanting shot, to purvey the ducks that Mr. Denig so highly prizes for his table, to provide also for our wants. Dejected and lonely, I remained the entire day, lying wrapped in my buffalo robe beside our fire. In the first place the weather was too cold to make the out-of-doors agreeable, and furthermore the long fingers of La Pierre's wife and daughter made it necessary for me to guard our belongings inside the tent. Those two had already committed several bold thefts; once, in the night, they stole a duck that Morgan had been saving quite a while for Mr. Denig; another time they took the last of our parched coffee which we had powdered with a stone and hidden away under my pillow. Upon this last occasion I was aroused from sleep when the skin pouch containing the coffee was pulled out from under my head and I recognized Marguerite from the dress she wore.

Immediately I fell asleep again, and was under the impression later that I dreamed I saw Marguerite. When the pouch was nowhere to be found, however, light began to dawn on me. Both women denied, at first, that they stole the coffee; but soon afterwards my attention was attracted by something moving outside our tent opposite the place where my bed is laid, and then I saw a "beautiful hand" thrust the purloined pouch under the awning. The older woman confessed at once that she took the duck, because, she said, we did not know how to prepare the fowl. That I found much time for reflection, on the dreary day of which I speak, any one can easily understand. To enliven my spirits I drank warm water sweetened with sugar.

On Monday Morgan brought some select portions of dried meat taken from the deponille or fat layers over the ribs, some coffee in return for my money, and corn that had been soaked in lye to remove the outer covering. I could hardly get enough of the dried deponille, such a luxury it seemed in comparison with our daily fare of dried venison, which is all the more unpalatable at this time of year.

Today I had to fabricate for Morgan a novel kind of shot; at least to me it is something new, though this is most probably the sort that was first used.

I had to flatten 1-pound bars of lead into thin plates, cut the latter into narrow bars, from which I then struck off little cubes, threw them into our frying pan together with ashes and sand, rubbed and rubbed them over and over with a flat stone until those small angular pieces had become round. Cadotte is put to the necessity of fabricating his own sort of shot, or rather buckshot. He takes such cubes of lead as I have mentioned, of whatever size his need requires, and rounds them off in his mouth with his teeth. Saw, today, a large herd of elks grazing on the hills. With the aid of my telescope I studied for a long while their different postures and movements.

Only a few moments ago La Pierre brought the news that he saw two Indians running elks on the other side of the river (southern bank). They concealed themselves, however, the instant they caught sight of him. Now our entire settlement is in a state of alarm. Blackfeet!

Once, near Fort Union, Blackfeet Indians drove off a number of horses right under the owners' noses; remembering that occurrence, the men here feel that our drove is no longer in safety. We have loaded our guns afresh, secured the best horses and mules to stakes near the tents, and we make the dogs sleep outside. Now that it is a question of defense, the unfavorable situation of our camp is perfectly apparent.

Out on the prairie we have pitched our tents on the slope of what was in early times a high river shore, while the plain below us is covered with forests and undergrowth, so dense that an enemy could actually conceal himself almost within arm's length of us. By night our illuminated tents expose us just as certainly to their attacks. But white men, when fully armed, have no fear of Indians who have the habit of coming near only for the purpose of stealing.

April 9. Snow again, already. But, after all, snow is preferable to rain. Continual rainy weather would be the most abominable state of things that could be revisited upon us: no hunting, nothing to eat, no firewood, no fire in the tent, and, if the downfall continued long enough, water would flow down even under the beds where we sleep. At the moment things are not going well with our hunters. Cadotte ran a splinter into his foot; he is therefore lame. La Pierre is dejected because he must give up all hope of being employed at the fort. Morgan, enthusiastic and untiring on the hunt for ducks, is ruining his health standing in ice-cold water at some hiding place, and always without success. One day he shot a beautiful otter, and as the animal was being carried down the swollen stream near the bois peinture [20] he plunged into water up to his shoulders in order to recover it; but, as he could not swim, he lost his valuable prize after all. Another time, wearing his horned fur cap, he enticed two dainty hinds within range of his rifle, but his gun missed fire and the animals ran off.

When he shoots a duck, goose, or swan, on the other hand, they fall at some place where he cannot lay hands on them and he has no trained dog to help him. It is due to such mischance, of course, that he is not in a better humor when he comes back to camp, for he is in reality a good shot, only not a cool, well-trained huntsman. When he returns disappointed he finds fault always with me, his fellow tent' dweller. Either the fire is smoking or the blaze is too strong; the meat is underdone or else cooked too long. I pass over such outbursts with patience, since he has often much to endure from my lack of skill in selecting wood for the fire and in the way I cut it up. Besides, in the success of Morgan's plan to put his chief in fine mood by sending him ducks and so win him over to grant our early release, I have everything to gain. I have now observed the manner of hunting game of all species in this part of the world. My supply of art paper is exhausted. Why should I remain longer?

---

[20] I. e., painted tree.

I cannot help feeling sorry for Morgan when, in defiance of frigid weather, hail, ice and snow, high waters, morass and wind, he hunts zealously the livelong day without bringing back any game at all to enliven our fireside with prospect of a roast, and Cadotte shoots enough wild fowl from his own tent to feed himself, his wife, and visitors besides. Cadotte never ruins his clothes, never tires himself out, never gets soaking wet, or benumbed from cold for the sake of roast duck.

So he laughs all the more about Morgan's ill-luck. Cadotte's swift gait, when stalking deer, and his endurance under such strain, is truly remarkable. He can pursue the ambling elks untiringly for 20 miles and turn to his own advantage the curiosity of the animals, their habit of standing still and looking about, etc. However, Cadotte is now lame and must remain in camp.

Elks are not so timid as smaller deer, or so swift in flight. They do not bound and leap as stags and antelopes do, but amble along, stopping quite frequently to look out for pursuers; whereupon the hunter in that case has to hide or else lie down flat on the ground. Even from a distance a skilled huntsman can distinguish the different species of deer by the way they stand. For instance, antelopes and elks, accustomed to range on the open prairie, keep their feet farther apart than the white-tailed or the black-tailed deer that prefer the forests and narrow passes.

April 10. Morgan and Cadotte rode over together to the Lower Bourbeuse to shoot wild fowl; according to report, the birds nest there in great numbers at this season of the year. In the meantime La Bombarde arrived from the fort for the purpose of making an arrangement with Belhumeur whereby he could induce the latter to go along with his family to the Red River.

In other words, La Bombarde is employed by Mr. Denig for another year but his family is not included in the contract. They must go. The metifs leave tomorrow with their horses. Morgan, Cadotte, the Spaniard, and I are to tarry here until Mr. Culbertson arrives. We have to provide for ourselves both food and protection. What La Pierre is going to "land" he himself does not yet know.

April 11. Fifth Sunday in camp, without bread. Belhumeur, Valette, and Boneau have gone, taking all the horses that belong to the metifs. Only three tents remain. Morgan and Cadotte have returned from the Bourbeuse, where they both passed a dismal night. That region is also flooded. Waterfowl in multitudes, but after the first discharge of the guns they were all on the other side of the stream; consequently, if one were not provided with water spaniels the killing of the birds was of no use. This time Morgan came home happy because he outstripped Cadotte.

April 13. Yesterday I spent another utterly miserable day. My discomfort was not due in this instance to scanty fare, for we had roast goose.[21]

But we were thrown into disquiet and confusion by a frightful windstorm that unceasingly howled and, carrying the snow before it, swept across the prairie with a roar, sometimes like distant thunder. Now the sun was allowed to shine, now the sky became once more dark and the air thick with rain or snow or hail. When we found it necessary to secure our tent further by weighting the tent cover down with tree stems not one of us found it possible to stand upright in the storm. There was such a fiendish uproar we could not understand what each other said. Incessant howling of the wind, flapping of the awning, fluttering of the cover flaps, cracking of the tent poles, made it impossible for us to be comfortable inside the tent. We were frightfully cold. We had every reason to expect that the awning would be snatched at any moment from over our heads. That actually happened to the family of La Pierre in the afternoon. To erect their lodge again in such a gale was an impossibility, so they came to us seeking shelter. We detest having them around because of their pilferings; we were not inclined to share goose or coffee, which came so dear, with those common womenfolk; we sent them to Cadotte.

Antoine himself was absent. The old woman, out of pure spite, pushed away a tree stem that we had laid on the awning to weight it down, but we noticed at once what had been done and were able to prevent disaster for the time being. In the evening they had better success with their bad joke. Just as Morgan and I were sitting comfortably together, eating roast goose and drinking strong meat broth, a violent gust of wind lifted our tent and, without so much as by your leave, snatched it from over our heads. At the same instant it drove the fire into our laps and caught up everything together—fire, gunpowder, cloaks, clothes, buffalo robes—in one chaotic whirl. Now what were we to do? It was goodby roast goose and hot meat broth! We had to look out for our goods and chattels flying about our heads and exert our utmost efforts to collect them. We had to regain our fallen awning and pile tent poles upon it, put out the fire, beat sparks out of the buffalo robes, and put the gunpowder in some safe place. There was now no alternative for us; we had to seek protection in Cadotte's tent, the only one left

---

[21] Body gray-brown, head metallic green, throat and breast white, neck indigo blue. The swan in this part of the country is distinguished from the swan in Switzerland by a black cartilaginous protuberance at the root of its bill. The skin of the swan is not used here, but the feathers are made into beautifully decorated fans. Goose (*Anser canadensis*); swan (*Trumpetes novus, Cygnus buccinator*). The ducks were: Pintail duck (*Anasacuta*), scaup duck (*Fuligula valisneriana*), and green-winged teal.

standing. We were so crowded together in that small space that
we were obliged to sit up the whole night through, and to feel
heartily glad, meanwhile, that the gale had not torn away our last
refuge.

This morning the wind fell; the sky is gloriously blue, and the
sunshine delightful. With the help of Garouille's wife and daughter
we pitched our tent again in a very short time; we have had quite a
little practice.

However, we made only a provisional arrangement of things, hoping to be delivered soon from this place. Life in a wigwam begins
to bore me, now that I have no further incentive to make new studies,
no further chance to employ myself except to keep the fire burning
and to gaze into its glowing depths, solitarily, since I possess no
family to enliven my fireside. My enthusiasm wanes all the more certainly under such conditions of inaction and insufferable weather,
since I have nothing more to gain by remaining here.[22]

Morgan and I spent the entire morning drying our clothes, putting
things in order, and helping each other find our belongings. I discovered my gray felt hat hanging on a far distant bush. In the
evening we had Smith and Joe Dolores in our tent. The former
brought with him a fat beaver that he had shot on the way. As he
had furnished me earlier with one of these animals for a model I
could afford to pass over this opportunity to make a sketch. I enjoyed the tender beaver meat, which made a fine dish. Smith gave
me the tail for preservation.

After such dreadful weather, how genial seems the sunshine today.
Its effect is not only to send one's blood coursing more rapidly
through one's veins, but to present the future as brighter, more
smilingly inviting. Never despair! "When sufficient rain has fallen,
then the rain will stop." Days that seem hardest, nights that seem
longest, must come to an end.

They say everything comes to those who wait. Perhaps that is
not universally true. How often I have thought I would have to
give up any hope of attaining my aims because I lacked necessary
funds. How often I have been forced to suspend my studies in order
to earn my bread. For how long a time my thoughts, my fears, my
joys were directed solely to the ideal in my heart of which I dreamed,
on which my life was centered, yet to which, for lack of means, I was
unable to give expression. Now that I am in possession of the studies
I need I look forward to the fulfillment of this dream I have
treasured for 20 years.

The scientific part of my work I have now completed; aesthetic
execution remains yet to be done. Up to this time I devoted myself

---

[22] It would be much more gratifying to me now if I had taken more interest in things;
for instance, in studying the different species of ducks, etc.

more to study; I have as yet executed but few paintings. My plan included the study of all three chief subjects in painting: Mankind, animals, and landscape. It goes without saying that longer time is required for all three than for one of these divisions alone. My studies in America include such a great number as well as such a various assortment that to choose what I shall paint will be no easy matter. Where shall I begin? My head is crammed full of it all. Furthermore, I have still to master by long practice the art of producing harmony and effect in my compositions.

If I may but devote the rest of my life to the execution of paintings; if only the worry of earning my livelihood in future does not dim my enthusiasm; if conflict with need and want does not destroy my idealism. How wretched I should be, what an unfortunate I should regard myself, if I were unresponsive to the inspiration of art. Only not that. I would rather die.

April 14. Very warm weather this morning, golden sunshine, clear bright blue sky. Took my sketchbook under my arm, called Schungtogetsche, our tamed wolf, and wandered over to the coulee to make a sketch of a somewhat grotesque view in a dell. On the way, I heard two cannon shots: Salvo at the fort, but in honor of whom? Culbertson or Harvey? I saw several of our hunters hurrying back to camp, hoping to see the long-wished-for messenger of deliverance approaching at full gallop. I hurried, therefore, all the more with my drawing. As the messenger would have to pass not far from where I was, I remained there. I found, to be sure, that the group of trees, selected earlier in the gloom of a dell washed by wild waters and shrouded in mist and snow, was not nearly so original a subject when viewed under today's bright sunshine. Still the sketch will enable me to recall that first, almost terrifying, scene.

As I now await Mr. Culbertson, I was waiting just as impatiently last year for the blades of grass to spring on the prairie near Savannah, so that I might drive my four-in-hand across country to Salt Lake. The grass grew, but not in my behalf or for the benefit of my four-span.

Will my present expectation end also in disappointment? Will Mr. Culbertson come and go without taking me along with him? If what is offered in exchange prove as agreeable, as much more to my advantage as was my journey up the Missouri in comparison with the anticipated trip to Salt Lake, I shall have nothing on which to base complaint.

The time must be near at hand; I shall soon know what fate has in store.

April 15. Oh! Here I sit in a chair at the table beside the fire in my old room at the fort. Yesterday, no sooner had I replaced my journal in my skin pouch than an aging Assiniboin, his entire face blackened, with the exception of the tip of his nose, arrived at our tent and, in the absence of Morgan, delivered to me a communication from Mr. Denig containing the welcome order to break camp and return, bag and baggage, man, horse, and dog, to Fort Union today. Of what provisions we had, we gave the odd-looking courier something to eat, and fired off our guns to summon Morgan who was over beyond the hayricks lying in wait for ducks.

This morning we had to pack up, break camp, and depart in most unpleasant weather; but for that very reason I left our hunting ground all the more willingly and with no regret.

Had the sun shone warm, had the ground been dry, affording the prospect of one more hunt, of yet other interesting sketches, I might have withdrawn from the scene of our struggles with some reluctance. We were facing a sharp west wind that drove forward, now rain, now snow, constantly recurring storms that made our advance slow and difficult. At the coulee Smith was bitten by one of his dogs. The riders hurried forward with the pack mules. Presently I found myself in the rear, combating the elements in company with old dame Garouille and her daughter. Under the heavy downpour of rain, prairie and sky became blurred and indistinct; sometimes we were unable to see 20 feet ahead. Heavy raindrops, propelled by violent wind, struck sharply against our faces. As ill-luck would have it, my riding cloak was packed with the buffalo robes carried by a pack mule in the vanguard far ahead of us. Under such conditions, facing wind and rain, as I have described, I had to walk 5 long miles through water that on the level and still half-frozen ground could neither flow off nor sink in, but steadily increased in depth and extent until it overspread the prairie like a vast inland lake. The nearer we came to the fort, all the more violent the wind, all the more heavy the downpour, and consequently all the more rapid the rise of water on the prairie. It seemed as though the heavens, provoked to anger by losing so good a chance to inflict continued torment on defenseless men, were moved to vent their utmost fury.

Fortunately, though we found it impossible to look far ahead through the impenetrable rain and mist, we were able to follow a path that had been made by marauders; otherwise I could not have kept my bearings at all. Except for such weather I was in no haste to reach the fort. I did not care to be received by Mr. Denig with the cheerful greeting: "Bread makes you stir your stumps."

On the east side of the fort, where they are protected from the raging west wind, I found a group of Assiniboin lodges occupied by La Main Poque and his wounded braves. Several Indians were walking proudly about the place, parading their blackened faces, with the exception of their nose tips, as evidence of having survived a hand-to-hand combat with the enemy (Blackfeet).

When I entered the messroom I found that my fellow travelers had pretty well emptied the dishes of rice and beans. I saw from my reflection in the mirror how thin I had grown. When I undressed I noticed that my legs were quite stiff from prolonged exposure to cold and dampness and that my feet were badly swollen.

April 16. Old north wind still rumbles and roars as of old, but not to my dismay; in any event it is not likely to snatch this shelter from over my head as he blew away my tent. He cannot penetrate these thick walls and disturb my slumbers. Mr. Denig agreed to my proposal that I be released without further remuneration if Mr. Culbertson is willing to take me along with him.

He presented me with a pair of snowshoes. In such weather as this I am in no hurry to travel down the river.

April 17. I made a visit to the pressroom that I might jot down the names of different wild animals in this section, for the pelts stored there afford a rather complete list of those four-footed beasts which are native here. Those found in greatest numbers are buffalo, elk, Virginia deer, antelope, gray wolf, prairie wolf, gray fox, red fox, mice; then grizzly bear, beaver, bighorn (Rocky Mountain sheep), black-tailed deer, ermine, hedgehog, muskrat, white hare, otter, marten, skunk, and cross fox. Also I came upon the skin of a wolverine: its hair is long and entirely black, except where it merges to dark brown on the underparts along the sides of the paunch; tail is long and bushy, head like that of a pug dog. A living animal of this species has never come under my observation. Among those whose pelts I failed to find are rabbits, squirrels, badgers, rats, black bears, and black and red wolves. Other wild creatures native here in great numbers are tortoises, raccoons, cougars, lynxes, prairie dogs, buzzards, parrakeets, turkeys, doves, fireflies, and bees.

April 18. Fare thee well, Fort Union! Mr. Culbertson arrived by boat yesterday. He will take Morgan and me with him, provided we are willing to pull an oar. Tomorrow morning we shall be off. Adieu, Fort Union! Farewell, ye red men! Farewell, ye wild beasts of primeval woods!

April 19. Left Fort Union at 11 this morning to begin my return journey home. My studies in this country are now completed. From this time forward my thoughts are to be concentrated on the painting of pictures. One half of my work accomplished at middle life and at the expense of my health.

Our keelboat provides a cabin built of wood which will protect us from wind and frost. The door is in the wall toward the prow; two apertures on one side serve for portholes; near the wall at the back stands a cooking stove. Forward, at the left, a bed is placed for Mr. Culbertson and supplies of meat and corn meal. The cabin has a flat roof, on top of which the pilot manipulates the lengthened rudder. In the bow there are three benches for oarsmen, and under those seats is stored our firewood.

Upon setting out we found more people aboard than the boat could accommodate comfortably. Several Indian women took passage as far as Fort Berthold. During that part of our journey we men, with the exception of Mr. Culbertson, had to content ourselves with the roof for our lodging place at night.

April 20. Steadily keeping stroke with the oars I found hard work: My hands were soon blistered, badly swollen, and stiff. Rowing is no joke, even for practiced Canadians, if they are required invariably to keep stroke, never to be put out. First I was too slow, then I was too fast; now I plunged the oar too deeply, now I dipped the oar too lightly; again, my oar either struck the back of the rower in front of me or else became entangled with the oar of another man. Baptiste Champagne was at the helm. Morgan and I, together with Hawthorn, Cadotte, Joe Dolores, and three Canadians, assisted now and then by a young Blackfeet (brother-in-law of Mr. Culbertson), took turns at the oars. Our cook was a Negro. Mr. Culbertson was in command. He was sometimes at the wheel, sometimes pulling an oar, trying to keep himself warm by exercise. Every 20 minutes, at the command "Leve!" [23] the oarsmen were relieved. At night we lay to, collected on shore quantities of wood for our fire, and then lay down to sleep. Very good meals under the circumstances.

April 21. Strong contrary winds; boat moored to shore. Rested. Took a walk. My swollen feet were much in need of exercise.

April 22. We were often interrupted in our navigation today, according as the wind was stormy or calm.

April 23. Rather pleasant sailing. Cadotte killed a bighorn that had left the herd and was clambering down a steep bluff.

April 24. Cadotte and Battiste had a jolly hunt; they killed a buffalo. We had to bring the meat aboard from quite a distance. We are still making our way around the Big Bend. Owing to counterwinds we are often forced to stop. I saw numbers of elks.

April 25. Beautiful weather. Rowed vigorously. Reached Fort Berthold at sunset. Found my large trunk in good order. Indian apparel I had engaged from Bellangé together with three handsome buffalo robes and other things besides were all in readiness for me. I confess I was not a little surprised at this. One of the robes, a

---

[23] I. e., raise.

complete buffalo skin without cut or seam and ornamented with drawings in color, delighted me especially. I was glad to get it, nothwithstanding that I had received from Mr. Culbertson that very day a beautiful robe made from the hide of a forest bison.[24] I have now seven robes and two calfskins.

In exchange for his services Bellangé received my gun with all that belongs therewith, and also other things that I no longer need. For keepsake I gave him my much valued telescope. At Fort Berthold Joe and the three women went ashore; their departure enabled us to be much more comfortable, though the Canadians maintained that the more heavily laden the boat the faster would be her speed. In the neighborhood of the fort I saw a great many tents occupied by Assiniboin and Absaroka.

April 26. Left Fort Berthold at sunrise. This has been the first bright, warm day we have had on our voyage. We came rapidly down the river. Stopped at Fort Clarke; while the bourgeois went to talk with Dorson I watched a ball game played by Arikara girls. We rowed about 25 miles farther downstream, passing by great numbers of prairie fires. At this season of the year Indians set the prairie on fire in order to remove the old, dried grass and provide room for the young, tender growth. Therein consists the Indians' total cultivation of the land their bands are accustomed to wander over. We spent the night at the Cannon Ball River.

April 27. Again strong counterwinds; we had to moor the boat fast to shore. Morgan shot a lynx, which at first we took to be a young cougar, but the short tail and pointed ears were sufficient to identify the species. Multitudes of gulls, either disquieted or bewildered by the high wind, swarmed over the surface of the river. When one sees them flying together over the water and hears the confused din of their cries one may safely reckon on a violent gale. It was on the river that the wind was strong; on shore one notices it hardly at all.

None of the gulls included in Audubon's Ornithologia correspond to these I have observed on the Missouri. These more nearly resemble the ivory gull, but have not the corresponding habitat: Sometimes, by chance, the coast of the United States; frequently, during the winter season, Labrador and New Foundland. Breeds in high latitudes. If the herring or silver gull were not so strong a silver gray in color I might think these were of that family.

April 29. Wind; consequent rest for us. Cadotte, Battiste, and company went into a little glen, sheltered from the wind, lighted a

---

[24] The forest bison and the prairie bison are differentiated according to their choice of habitat. The former are never found in such extensive herds as range on the prairies, but only in small groups. Their hair is more curly, not smooth on their bodies, which is perhaps due to the more northerly latitude of the regions that they inhabit.

big blazing fire, lay down beside it, and went to sleep. In the meantime the dried grass about them caught fire but burned slowly, surrounding them with a circle of flame. Then, fanned by a gust of wind, it spread, driving onward in winding curves. I followed a long way, at an even gait, walking over the charred ground, springing several times across the flames, simply to find out whether prairie fires are really as dangerous as writers declare them to be. Such conflagrations, I think, can endanger the lives of people only when the grass is very high and, as sometimes happens, there is additional brushwood or dried undergrowth. As everybody knows, green, lush grass is just as little likely to catch fire as water is. But all animals, both domestic and wild, flee in terror from the smoke and flame of a prairie fire.

Although the wind was rather high the fire in the dead grass did not spread any more rapidly forward than I could easily follow without walking very fast. In facing the fire one finds the smoke more disagreeable than the flame. The fire was at no point more than 3 feet in depth. It spread in every direction, more swiftly where the wind blew hard; for instance, up the hills and slopes, then descended more gradually on the opposite sides of those heights.

It lingers longer in vales and dells, for it finds more substances there with which to be replenished, but less that is dry and dead, as there is less agitation of the atmosphere.

May 1. Little Cheyenne River. We find here also great blocks of ice caught in the boughs of trees along the shore; they were deposited there upon the outbreak of the high waters. They melt slowly, on account of their great size. On the other hand, the grass is coming out in well-sheltered nooks.

May 2. Great Cheyenne River.

May 3. After much exertion and strain we reached Fort Pierre this evening. Throughout the day I have seen groups of antelopes along the shores of the river.

May 4. Have been held fast here at the Fort the livelong day by a violent storm. Our wooden cabin was broken to pieces, so we had to put up a tent in its place. We expect warmer weather as we sail southward. Here we see hardly a sprig of green grass; no foliage at all; only catkins on the willows. The gale blew with unabated fury even until the evening. After sunset a sudden calm, quite warm weather, and, what is more, mosquitoes. Just at this time Mr. Picotte is sick.

May 5. Left early. About 10 o'clock we passed Campbell & Primeau's new winter trading post. Many Sioux in that section are suffering from hunger; they are now resorting to horse meat.

We found the abandoned Forts Lookout and Nedeune already in ruins.

May 6. We set out again by moonlight before the break of day. Having lost so much time, owing to contrary winds, everybody is now eager to reach the United States. Mr. Culbertson would like to overtake Harvey, who is ahead of us, hastening along the same route in his skiff. If I did not have to be in such a strain rowing and my feet were not swelling so much worse for want of exercise I would be in no hurry at all. During the day we are to make no more stops but will keep steadily on our course until we are forced by darkness to the shore. Foliage! No more blocks of ice among the boughs along the steep river shore. The first whippoorwill [25] and turkeys.

May 7. We overtook Decoteaux, P. Sarpy's clerk from L'Eau qui Court, in his long skin boat, and got some fish from him. While eating supper we passed L'Eau qui Court. I beheld once more that lovely scene at the mouth of the Basil River. I was sorry the trees were not in full leaf, as I saw them last summer; but even though destitute of foliage this is the most beautiful part of the Missouri.

Landry's departure upset all my calculations. Last year I left with him two good horses and my entire outfit for the intended journey to Salt Lake, i. e., wagon, provisions, saddle, harness, etc., to be sold, in order that I might have on my return some funds at my disposal. I reckoned on at least $180. He paid me $40, saying he had sent the remainder in my name to Mr. Mitchell, to whom I was still in debt for goods I bought. This latter statement I found afterwards to be a lie. There was nothing I could urge to the contrary; could only thank my lucky stars that I saw Landry at all. If I had been but 1 or 2 days later I should have lost all my money. My plan was, first of all, to recover my health; then, if possible, to paint some pictures which, in addition to my sketches, I might present to the public as proof of my ability. I could have lived with Landry at very moderate expense.

On the whole, the shores of the Missouri River reveal little that is picturesque. Even so, just the realization that this is Indian domain gives me a pleasurable interest in all scenes along the mighty stream.

May 8. Stopped a while opposite the Isle de Bonhomme, Schlegel's new post. Picturesque landing place. Oaks thrown over a wild brook behind which rise precipitous bluffs.

May 9. In the forenoon we passed Vermilion; later the quarters of Bruyère, the elder; at 12 o'clock, Sergeants Bluff; about 4 in the afternoon, wood bluffs with their burning coal fields; at 7 o'clock, Blackbird's grave. Foilage is advancing in the forests.

May 10. Big Sioux. We came upon one place in the Missouri so blocked with snags, both vertical and horizontal, that we could hardly

---

[25] I wondered whether the whippoorwill had a cry that resembled the sound of its name. I am glad to find, therefore, in Audubon's Ornithologia (VI, p. 350), the real name of this bird: "Nuttall's whippoorwill. Cry: Oh—will."

steer our way through. On the bluffs I saw millions of little swallows (bank swallow or sand martin, *Hirundo riparis* Lin.). First blockhouse. Old Council Bluffs. Toward evening we arrived at the first settlement (Mormons). The Mormons' ferry above was crowded on both sides of the river with tents, covered wagons, throngs of people, and herds of cattle, all bound for New Zion. From one of our oarsmen I purchased for $5 a very beautiful pelt of a grizzly she-bear; from another I bought the scalp of a Snake Indian. Slept in this keelboat for the last time.

May 11. This morning we saw in the distance the funnel of a steamboat at the landing where passengers go ashore for the inland settlement of Kanesville. Owing to the position of the boat we saw only one smokestack; consequently we took it to be the *Utha*, Corby's steam ferry we were expecting from St. Joseph. There was instantly a unanimous hurrah by way of greeting; none of us had dared hope for release from rowing as early as this. We found, however, that it was the *Eloira*, a vessel with two smokestacks, that had brought a great number of Mormons and their vehicles, cattle, household luggage, etc. We thought the captain's charge for the journey to St. Louis was too high, so we waited for the *St. Paul*, which we had already sighted on its way up the river. We could get a more reasonable rate on the *St. Paul*. The captain promised to take us aboard at Belle Vue that evening. Our half-breeds made merry over the "windspiele", i. e., the coquetting of pale, tight-laced Mormon women. At Council Bluffs we found a considerable part of the shore torn away; my former boarding house which, when I lived there, stood a hundred feet at least from the river, was now hanging over the river bank. Had dinner in Belle Vue with my friends, Decatur, Wacoma, Joseph and Mary La Fleche,[26] and Witthae. Witthae expected that I would speak to her, exchange greetings, etc., but I am not the man to offer my hand once more to one who had deserted me as she had done.

When I went into the office she followed, hoping to resume our former relationship. But, showing not the least concern, I read the Frontier Guardian; Witthae wrapped her blanket about her and went away, unwilling to give any evidence of her realization that I regarded her with contempt. At 4 o'clock we went aboard the *St. Paul*, leaving our Mackinaw boat behind. Exchanged souvenirs with Decatur, "the first man to settle in the future Nebraska territory." I gave him one of my necklaces made of bear's claws and he gave me a pair of moccasins (?). To Morgan I gave the first scalp I purchased, which he accepted with great merriment as an acknowledgment of his good comradeship.

---

[26] The father and mother of Dr. Francis La Flesche.

Not long since, I am told, some Oto found, on the Platte, a Prussian named Mullhausen in a hopeless situation, having with him a wagon but no team. He is said to be an attendant of Duke Paul of Wurttemberg who was banished from court, and, so they say, he was protecting his Grace's silverware (?). Meantime, where was the Duke?

May 12. After supper we arrived at St. Joseph. Just 1 year ago I left this town. High water has done much mischief here also. What was once the upper landing had to be placed lower down.

May 13. Accompanied Landry 14 miles on horseback to the first bivouac of his fellow travelers to California.

Saw many picturesque groups of gold diggers with their horses and herds, lodging for the night in the primeval forest, tents on the prairie, wagon trains along the trail, vehicles that had come to grief, horses that had run away, riders out in search of them, herds of cattle, droves of laden pack horses and pack mules. There were also groups of Indians here and there with their begging women, which gave local color to the scene. My bloated legs became inflamed and feverish from rubbing against the saddle. Am I to be afflicted again with dropsy?

Called to see old friends. Gazed once more with all my former enthusiasm upon my favorite scene, a far-reaching view over the Black Snake Hills. Compared past impressions with those of the present, recalling circumstances under which I viewed this scene upon my first arrival here in 1848 as compared with today. My future prospects are anything but favorable if water continues to rise in my trusty legs. In any event I have to reconcile myself to the fact that my most excellent constitution is now impaired. I shall therefore be all the more persevering, perhaps.

My entire collection of Indian weapons, apparel, and ornaments put in order, left a while in the open air, then packed.

May 21. Left St. Joseph.

May 25. St. Louis. Great heat. When I went in search of the Virginia Hotel I found it entirely rebuilt and enlarged by the addition of a new building in course of construction, so that it now occupies the entire block. But I was received, to my great delight, by the same obliging proprietor, J. Sparr von Basel. For the first time this year I am in a perspiration; this is a very great relief to my mind, because it is an indication of better health in future. Even during the time I was engaged in the strenuous exercise of rowing, while still wearing winter clothes, I never once perspired; I was never put to the trouble, as the other oarsmen were, of changing my clothes immediately afterwards. Now, for the purpose of producing perspiration and of exercising my legs (already swollen to my thighs), I visit often my beloved Cahokia Creek and enjoy once more numerous enchanting groups of trees found there. Though the stream itself has been converted by the recent high waters into a quiet lake, in many places entirely choked up with sand, yet I find there the well-remembered trees.

My excursions at present I make with a more scientific purpose in view, i. e., to become acquainted with the names and the character of various sorts of trees and climbing plants rather than merely to enjoy their beauty of form.

I am sorry not to be able to find a book in print that would inform me on this subject. I seek, therefore, to discover through my own investigation the various trees of the lowlands and of the bluffs; to distinguish one from another and to find distinctions between climbing plants, creepers, and parasitic vines. I have found already thirteen separate kinds of creeping and climbing plants, for the most part varieties of ivy that are different as to tendrils and manner of climbing. Of all the high-aspiring sort there is only one, a pinnated variety, that bears a blossom, a red, bell-shaped flower. This vine is said to be poisonous. The most luxuriant and manifold forest growth I saw near Falling Spring, beyond the village of Cahokia, 6 miles from St. Louis. On the cliff out of which this spring gushes there are found every variety of oak and of wild fruit-bearing trees, while at its base ash trees and lindens, horse-chestnuts, oak, hickory, walnut, willow, papaw, cottonwood, poplar, sassafras, sycamore, locust, persimmon, maple, all meet and touch, embraced and overhung by luxuriant vines. Even at first glance one perceives that a distinctive feature of this woodland is its utter lack of any variety of conifers. One finds not a trace of the pines that are common to the Southern States; neither of the cedars that grow in the North, nor of the firs that are found in the East.

I have been told today of some occurrences but recently come to pass that truly characterize conditions in this part of the world. A man involved in debt was mercilessly whipped by two of his creditors. They enticed him by some ruse into the forest, tied a bandage over his mouth, made him fast to a tree and then, taking turns with their cowhides, they lashed him until they were tired out from the exertion of wielding their whips. To rest themselves and renew their strength they went to the nearest pothouse and drank whisky. After that invigoration they returned to their labors and applied the horsewhips anew. As they were proceeding a second time to the grocery, however, their client was discovered by some one and released. The two brutes who scourged the poor man were arrested while still in the grocery.

I heard that Sam Riddle, a rich young business man in Savannah with whom I am acquainted, had shot down a clerk in a store. Sam, although he is a married man, is a fast fellow who piques himself on his wealth and his father's prominence as Senator. As the story goes, he gave utterance, not long since, in the presence of some friends to compromising remarks concerning a lady, a teacher in Savannah. A young clerk, who was a friend of the lady, heard about those remarks and, when Riddle entered the store soon afterwards to see the proprietor, he was stopped by this clerk and called to account. Riddle denied having made any such remarks.

The clerk spat upon him and branded him a liar in the presence of people there. Whereupon Riddle drew a small pistol from his pocket and shot the clerk down. When brought before the justice of the peace, the rich young merchant was required to give $25,000 bail and must appear for trial at the next session of the court. Until the court sits he may go free. Now he is making use of this intervening time to transfer his business interests to his brother-in-law and, when that is done, he will "shake the dust of Savannah off his feet." That is how a wealthy man is enabled to escape the penalty for a homicidal act; for, if Sam Riddle were not allowed to offer bail, if he were not able to make good the security demanded, he would necessarily have been put in the calaboose. He would in all probability be executed, or else imprisoned for life at Jefferson City. The purpose of this law, providing that a person accused of a crime may be released on bail, is to enable the accused to carry on his business, to work for the support of his family until he is declared guilty by the court. In like manner if the accused be innocent of the charge, such procedure averts the injustice of compelling him to spend his valuable time in prison. But crafty Americans know how to circumvent their humane laws in such a way that far more well-to-do criminals are enabled to escape just penalties by producing bail than poor men, unjustly accused, are enabled to secure protection, for a poor man, innocent though he be, derives no benefits from these so-called "humane" statutes.

Another law is, in similar manner, put to wrong use: If a married man fails in business the property of his wife or of his children is never touched by his creditors. Though in principle such a provision is altogether humane, dissembling, crafty Americans know how to twist the law to their own advantage. For instance, a merchant enjoys a period of thriving business; to secure himself from eventualities he buys, whether with good or bad intention, real estate, houses, bonds, etc., for his wife or his children and has titles made in their names. Should the man fail in business, quite a usual occurrence in this part of the world, his creditors are allowed no claims on the property of his wife or children. In that way a "smart" man can so manage as to find himself better off after the liquidation of his affairs than before. One of the best hotel proprietors here lives in the hotel that he bought and gave to his wife, then stopped payment on remaining debts. A shopkeeper can follow the same practice in the retail trade. With cash that he takes in he purchases an excellent farm in his wife's name and pays for it, while he refuses to pay for his stock of goods that he had bought on credit. Likewise, a great deal of mischief is done in the matter of fire insurance. For example, a merchant, conducting what is called a "fancy-dress" store, divides his stock into summer goods and winter goods.

When he has disposed of most of one season's stock (which he can always accomplish by reducing prices), and the time is approaching when, in order to get a new supply, he has to pay for the summer or winter goods, as the case may be, that he purchased on credit in New York, on a Sunday, when all stores, including his own place of business, are closed, by some means absolutely inexplicable his shop burns down. But the sly tradesman had not neglected to insure his stock at its full value. He "burns out." Now he has in his possession cash received in return for the goods sold and, in addition, insurance to the full value of his entire stock purchased but the greater part of which has been sold. Furthermore, he buys at auction, for little or nothing, his former goods now damaged by fire or water; he insures these again and reaps still another profit in the sale of them. Following such a course, shopkeepers of that sort are enabled to grow very rapidly rich; after he "burns out" three or four times he has a handsome sum, for he will satisfy his creditors with the amount of insurance received. I knew just such a man, a German in St. Louis, who was burned out twice during my first stay in that city; the fire always occurred toward springtime or autumn, always on Sunday. Upon the occasion of the great fire in 1848, when 26 steamboats, together with the buildings comprising several streets were destroyed, he burned out again, although his stock of summer goods had but recently been received at his shop.

The same trick is played in the shipping business: when a boat has been in service for 6 or 7 years the insurance costs amount to more than the vessel is worth; therefore it is thought to belong in the rubbish heap as scrap iron.

So the captain lets it run aground, sink, or burn up; then, laughing in the face of the victims, his passengers, he turns his back and collects insurance. Further instances would be superfluous to prove that Americans observe their own laws only insofar as the case in hand concerns them or that the written statutes are supremely excellent from the standpoint of humanity, high moral standards, and freedom of the individual; but in the actual observance of these laws, well, that is a different matter altogether. Proofs are by no means lacking. There is a law in Missouri forbidding the game of nine-pins, or to use the American expression, ninepin alleys. How do the "smart" Missourians manage? They construct their ninepin alley for tenpins. The city corporation not only allows this but are glad to find that means to raise taxes. Likewise, gambling houses are strictly forbidden; nevertheless, are quite frequently found; they yield large profits and afford another source from which, through pecuniary penalties imposed, the city authorities get money for taxes—so much for the first offense, double that amount for the second, etc. But they do not adopt measures to get rid of gaming houses. In the United States every witness, every interpreter is required to swear upon the Bible in the presence of the court that he will speak the truth, the whole truth, and nothing but the truth.

The judge does not ask the man who takes the oath whether he believes the Bible; in the United States that is taken for granted. A set form of oath is read, or pronounced, and the man to whom the oath is administered raises the Bible, not infrequently a much soiled volume, to his lips and kisses the Book (since no one ever takes the trouble to turn the leaves, it might be some other book). Now any person who has no belief in the Bible does not burden his conscience to any appreciable degree by taking the oath. However, the most significant instance of the Americans' hypocrisy is their declaration that all men are free and equal; the statement is not to the effect that only white men in America are equal in the eye of the law, but, on the contrary, all people without exception. Yet Americans grant no civil rights to slaves they own, nor do they allow an Indian to enjoy the privileges of a citizen.

In conclusion I will say that the undeserved fate of the "Art Union" reveals much as to the culture of Americans. Owing to an unexpected increase in the membership of that American art society and the greater amount of money available in New York, I was in high hopes, as I journeyed thither from St. Louis, of offering one of my works for sale and thereby making myself known. Members of the society pay an annual fee of $5, and receive in return each year at least one beautiful engraving, a copy of one of the pictures purchased by the "Art Union." The paintings bought they put on exhibition in New York and raffle them under the supervision of the committee.

From the net proceeds realized yearly upon raffling off these drawings and paintings they have the expectation, or rather they had, of obtaining from the lot at least one production of art. That most pious of States, however, brought action against that raffling of pictures as an unlawful lottery. A bill was introduced and put through the New York legislature. Raffling pictures was declared immoral and illegal; hence, was prohibited. The "Union" was therefore forced to abandon their fine and praiseworthy aim.

Finally, what is the antiliquor law? With the resulting financial ruin of many Germans who carry on retail business in wine and strong drinks, this small trade is forbidden, or at least restricted to certain quantities, i. e., from 30 to 50 gallons. On the other hand, any one who is able to provide himself with that quantity may drink as much as he likes in his own house, under the pretense of using the liquor for medicinal purposes.

On the cliff above this hidden fountain called Falling Spring one may enjoy a splendid far-reaching view in the direction of St. Louis. Along the entire way from Falling Spring to Illinois Town, where the steam ferryboats land, one views continually most charming landscapes enlivened by white and gray herons (great white heron, *Ardea occidentalis* Aud.; great blue heron, *Ardea herodias* Linn.). The season for passenger pigeons (*Ectopistes migratoria* Aud.) was already over. Not less interesting are the old blockhouses of the Creoles; Cahokia or the former Notre Dame de Caho[kia] (known especially in connection with R. Clark's raid in 1778) dates back to the first French settlements and therefore is much older than St. Louis. There tiny barracks are constructed of tree trunks fixed firmly in the ground in a vertical position, not laid horizontally and fitted together at the corners like American blockhouses. Adjoining these small lodges always lie pleasant gardens. That is something one never sees at the homes of American farmers in the West: anything that does not bring in money is regarded by the farmers as a luxury; only in the matter of Sunday clothes do they permit the least display.

When I learned that the position of drawing master at the Jesuit College was to be filled I went to see Père de Smet.

I was kindly received, but my application for the vacant position was deferred, on account of my belief or, what is much more likely, my unbelief. When Heaven grants such proof of Divine mercy and power as was manifested in this pious father I have no longer any doubts. It happened on an earlier journey to the Nez Percé, when Père de Smet wished to enter the harbor at San Francisco on board a ship that was overtaken by such a violent and perilous tempest that everyone thought all was over. Then this missionary, having faith in God, fell upon his knees, there on the deck, prayed fervently for Divine aid and, lo! the wind fell, the roaring waves no longer lashed the terror-stricken crew.

Before a month had passed, without my having been notified, according to the father's promise, when the examination would be held, the position at the college was filled and, I may add, by the appointment of a German architect, an acquaintance of mine. That post would have paid me about $900 a year.

Upon another jaunt up Cahokia Creek on the small lakes near the Indian mounds (burial mounds?) I was delighted to find the well-known water lily and some sedge (no reeds); I have never seen either on the Missouri or the Mississippi. In place of the latter I found tall sea grass and wild oats.[27] Our stinging nettle I have not found at all. Nowhere have I seen any green moss, either on trees or on the ground.

As far as I have traveled on the Missouri and the Mississippi I have never seen beeches anywhere; but beech trees grow in the State of Indiana and farther east.

May 28. A small menagerie made up of one pair of old grizzly bears brought from California, three younger members of the bear family, varying in age, and a cougar, gave me welcome models for study. The old bears are of a bright chocolate color, not of different hues and shades like bears on the Missouri.

August 2. By taking long walks every day this hot weather I have succeeded in reducing gradually the water in my legs without further treatment. I feel greatly relieved in mind to be delivered from this threat of dropsy. It would be really very hard to depart this life just when I have come to the end of my period of study and have reached the point where I shall be able to begin creative work in my art; when life has in store so much that is gratifying and pleasurable, much that will compensate me for difficulties undergone.

As I now dare assume that my studies are sufficiently thorough and comprehensive to justify my executing paintings true to life, yet in aesthetic manner, representing scenes in the Far West (characteristic of life there in former days rather than at present), and as I am offered no better outlook for earning my bread as artist in St. Louis than in any of the other new States, owing to the prevailing lack of interest in painting, I must, though with heavy heart, dispose of a large part of my Indian collection in order to get money enough to travel to New York or to Paris, where I hope to find more encouraging prospects.

To force myself to abandon art merely for the sake of making a longer stay in this region possible by earning my living painting houses, ships, and mural decorations, or by undertaking once more the duties of merchant's clerk, is an outlook I cannot contemplate; my harsh experience in business transactions, heretofore, make such a plan all the more distasteful. Furthermore, my chances for success are better in Europe than in this country and, finally, I regard my collection of studies sufficiently comprehensive to render a longer

---

[27] Wild rice.

stay, in straitened circumstances, unnecessary. After severe mental conflict I decided to part with a large portion of my valuable collection in order to get funds to travel east. Before I let it go out of my possession I made copies of the objects included, so that I might rescue at least that much for myself. It was extremely painful to give up my Indian relics; my heart was so set upon them; I had submitted to so many deprivations for the sake of possessing a collection, as complete as possible, of Indian apparel, weapons, and ornaments. But this is my fatal destiny: I have only to set my heart upon something and, straightway, I am destined to loss. So it was with my collection of engravings, with my love affairs, with my horses. That is the fate allotted to one to whom true, enduring affection is a need; to whom inconstancy and unfaithfulness is shocking.

Truly the few joys of my life have been dearly bought. I am exasperated by such strokes of fate; I might curse my life. Woe unto me if I am to abandon my last hope, chief support of my existence, the ideal toward which I strive in art. Then I should either throw away my life in disgust or else my unruly nature, no longer softened by contemplation of lofty thoughts, would exhaust itself in bitterness, mockery, and rage. What is life to me without art? What is art without an ideal? Is death to be my one and only consolation?

If I had thought for one moment that I should not have been in a position to earn an independent livelihood as artist within a year's time I would have remained in St. Louis, even as house painter or clerk, and then could have kept my much-prized collection of Indian relics. But I cherished too great hopes. As friend of the redskins I was not able to make heroes of Indians among the Americans, therefore had little hope of success in the United States. I should not have appeared in Europe, after such a journey, with only studies and sketches, but with finished paintings also, and executed in a manner to produce the best effect. But up to that time I had devoted myself more to study than to compositions with a view to harmony and effect. I felt, therefore, that I must attain definite results in that.

To accomplish my purpose was all the more difficult because of an attack of ague from which I was long recovering, and for the further reason that I was retarded by the necessity of earning a livelihood here in Berne, where, as in all Switzerland, there was too little appreciation of my genre to keep up my spirits. But for the frustration of my plans by Landry in St. Joseph I should have been successful. With my excellent collection of Indian relics and a number of beautiful paintings representing the principal wild animals that roam the western plains, as well as Indians of the different tribes, treated from an ethnological viewpoint, I should certainly have made money as "showman" in those cities, particularly where many Europeans reside. In St. Louis, however, my first concern was to get rid of the water in my legs. When I was relieved of those symptoms of dropsy I had not enough money to insure several months' leisure and peace of mind during which I might devote myself to the execution of those paintings. For a while, to be sure, I had hopes of being able to fight my way by means of my artistic labors; in other words, I knew a man in the Schultze firm, dealing in books and articles of virtu, who gave me an order for several views of St. Louis and environs. But this man proved to be so little trustworthy that I had to abandon the idea of doing the work for him.

August 9. Returned today from a visit to Highland. Before I leave this land, perhaps forever, I wished to pay a visit to my acquaintances there, but above all to set foot on that farm where, in 1834, I was to begin a totally different career with Doctor Becksel. But for the religious scruples of my dear mother I should in all probability be a farmer now, for at that period many favorite pursuits were struggling for predominance in my mind. In my sixteenth year, it is true, love of painting was already gaining the mastery over me, but had not yet become a passion. At the time of which I speak, agricultural pursuits, particularly the breeding of horses and cattle, would have satisfied me. If I had been accustomed while young to the climate here and to the manner of cultivating land in this part of the world I should have become practical. I might have been a happy farmer, owning numerous herds, fine horses, to say nothing of a family more or less numerous. Now I am an artist, oftentimes indescribably happy, but only too often poverty-stricken, lonely, and peevish. I might yet change my career; I might yet become a farmer. To abandon art now, at the moment when my hopes of success seem more promising than ever before; now, when I have found my ideal, when my enthusiasm was never so keen—impossible!

I wish to determine the question whether every man is to choose his life work according to the measure of his gifts; whether the spiritual and mental development of man is of no more lofty aim than his physical well-being; whether we are meant to be only sons of nature like the Indians or destined to strive for a higher state of civilization. On the solution of those questions I stake my life. Whether I was right to try and make the most of my talents, only the future, perhaps death, will first make clear to me.

There were two routes by which I might travel to New York, both new to me, both equally interesting; the one up the Illinois River by way of Peoria to Chicago, thence across Lake Michigan through the

State of Michigan, Lake Erie to Buffalo, Niagara Falls, Albany, and down the Hudson; the other down the Mississippi to Cairo, up the Ohio to Cincinnati, by the new railway through the State of Ohio to Cleveland, situated on Lake Erie, and so on. As complaints came in from all sides about the low water level in the rivers I decided to go by stage (a private enterprise) to Louisville. I paid a fare of only $12; my luggage, still considerable, was carried free. At 4 o'clock in the morning on August 11 the stagecoach stopped at the hotel for me; we crossed the river and proceeded rapidly across the plains of Illinois. With heavy heart I took leave of the Mississippi, of Cahokia. Even on the first night we had an accident, but with no resulting damage.

At a place where the road ran through a deep cut a bolt sprang out, detaching the swingletree bar, in consequence of which the horses tried to hurry on with that alone and leave the coach with us inside sticking in the mud. If the coachman had not been so securely strapped to the seat he would have been jerked to the ground. But, as good luck would have it, he had a sufficient hold to stop the horses short with the driving reins. He shouted to us to get out of the coach. Fortunately a few more passengers had just got in, so there was a sufficient number of us to be of immediate assistance. We held the horses until the driver could descend from the box and tether them to a near-by fence. Then we had to bring rails from the same fence and raise the vehicle out of the mud. To attach the swingletree bar again, replace the bolt, and hitch the horses was then an easy matter. From Salem, where we arrived the second night, I was the sole passenger all the way to Vincennes. On that night, while we were trying to cross the little Wabash over a very unsafe bridge, I had to mount to the coachman's box and again lend my aid to keep the mettlesome grays in hand while the coachman went back and took away some planks from the floor of that part of the bridge we had passed over and laid them over holes and fissures in the remaining part we had yet to cross. My experience in the management of a four-in-hand stood me then in good stead, for the spirited animals, seeing the river below through crevices in the floor of the bridge, became all the more restive.

August 13. Approaching Vincennes, we came to a kind of ferry hitherto unknown to me. For instance, our boat was not propelled through the stream by a rope suspended across the river and fastened by means of a ring to a tug, but instead of the tug there were fastened together several small rowboats, placed at certain distances apart in the slow-moving current. The boat at the extreme upper end was made secure at a bend of the river where the current was sufficiently strong to produce the desired propelling force but, as a matter of course, the assistance of oars was necessary. In Vincennes I had to wait an entire half day for another stagecoach. I found, however, that the surroundings, from a historical point of view, were interesting. Along the river one sees there still several buildings constructed on piles, which date from the earliest American settlements. They are situated near the former residence of General Harrison.

August 14. On the way to Bleansville we traveled through the first beech wood I have seen. At the place mentioned we made our midday halt and took the railway train from there to Louisville. On the way a rascally fellow who tried to force his passage was run over. At evening we crossed the Ohio River and were soon after in Louisville, where I spent the night.

August 15. The next morning I went by steamboat up the Ohio to Cincinnati.

As the next day was Sunday it was impossible to proceed farther by railway, so I made use of the time to see something of the city. There are large brick church buildings in Gothic style; from a belvedere one may enjoy a beautiful view of the city, the river with its many steamboats at the wharf, the surrounding hills, and over into Kentucky. At the hotel I was amused by the way in which the jovial black waiters formed their lines, simultaneously stacked the dishes, made a complete "about face" and stiffly keeping step, marched off, to return again at once with other dishes and, without a word, repeat the maneuver with exactly the same movement.

August 16. I went to the new railway station in a heavy downpour of rain, and continued my journey across the entire State of Ohio to Cleveland, traveling on a comfortable fast train that made few stops. Among the passengers I found Bruyère from Fort Union. He was journeying to Canada, where he wished to spend some time on a visit. Arrived in Cleveland at 5:30 o'clock in the evening, was immediately transferred to a lake boat under full steam and traveled the whole night through, down Lake Erie to Buffalo.

August 17. It was my intention to make an excursion from Buffalo to Niagara Falls, but upon our arrival there was such godless confusion: every fellow, whether he had a fiacre [28] or whether he hadn't, whether his services were asked for or not, grabbed at once for bags, satchels, or trunks, one of them running this way, another running that way, forcing the traveler along too, but in so doing forcing him to risk losing the greater part of his luggage, as was probably designed.

Although a watchman was there to keep order, he was by no means a match for that throng of loafers; they could easily push him aside. I had to resort to a downright tussle with one rascal before I could make him leave my trunk where it was, so that it

[28] A hackney coach.

would not go to the devil, while another fellow was already lugging my bundle of buffalo robes into a dray. Besides, owing to my recent departure from the Mississippi and the West with all my pleasant associations there, I was already in dejected mood, and became so exasperated by that unheard-of disorder that I was not in the least disposed to gaze in wonder on Niagara Falls. I hurried back at once to the railway train leaving for Albany. Not until I was eating my midday meal at Utica, where I was gladdened by the glimpse of a lovely girl, did my outraged feelings become calm. Everything was conducted with perfect order on that train. Late in the evening I arrived in Albany, where my luggage was surrendered upon my giving back copper checks. I took a cab at once to the Hudson River to get aboard the night boat to the city of New York.

Arrived at 5 o'clock this morning. With a letter of introduction from Herr Mehlgarten, to whom I sold a part of my Indian collection for $150, I went to call on Herr Meyer von Hilburghausen, who publishes the American edition of Meyer's Universum, in order to find whether he could use some of my drawings in that publication. He was sorry, he said, that he could not enter into an agreement to that end; the drawings he would need were already provided for 2 years in advance, some of them on terms for immediate acceptance, the remainder on order. He communicated to me, furthermore, the most unwelcome news of legal proceedings against the Art Union. However, he bought two water colors that I had not been able to dispose of in St. Louis. Then I came at once to the conclusion that I would better take passage at the earliest possible date for Havre. I was further influenced in my decision by the fact that, notwithstanding the intense summer heat, I was always cold—a condition indicating an approaching illness, I feared.

On August 20 I secured a place, on the payment of $20, as steerage passenger on the *Sam Fox*. On the 24th I purchased my provisions for the journey, so as to be ready to sail the same evening. At the moment the boat was clearing the dock I was seized with an attack of vomiting, while perspiration oozed from my body; so, while departing from the shores of America, I lay among my buffalo robes, only half-conscious. Nor did sea air prove the benefit hoped for; on the contrary, my fever mounted and seasickness did not fail to make matters worse. Such violent fever so affected my salivary glands that I was unable to swallow any solid food; my fine crackers remained just so much dry meal. I could not eat them.

So, during the entire voyage of 30 days, I was restricted to food I could take in liquid form. Nobody, not even the captain, had any quinine. It was lucky for me that the steerage passengers numbered only 30 persons; for I was therefore enabled to have sufficient space and fresh air to endure steerage conditions. Upon closer acquaintance with my fellow voyagers I found two young Germans from Boden See. I was much pleased with their manner of conducting themselves, and, perceiving that they were not very well provided with food for the voyage, I thought I might be helpful to them as well as to myself by giving them supplies of dried beef, ham, and crackers from my supplies, since I could use only the tea and coffee. In return, they prepared a broth for me twice a day with some of their meal. That was my only nutriment during the entire voyage. I arrived at Havre half-starved, emaciated, and weak.

My companions in the steerage were, for the most part, persons who "had enough of America" and several Frenchmen who had acquired some means in California. The two young Germans had traveled in company with other people they knew to Cleveland; one of them, having lost his young wife during the plague of cholera, wished to return home at his earliest opportunity; his friend was unwilling to remain in America without him.

A young landscape painter from Basle had an idea that he would be able to lead a jolly life in America without any great amount of work, wherein he found himself soon enough mistaken.

"If I choose to work so hard", he said, "I can live much better at home."

A Jew from Zurzach had but just arrived in New York, where a brother of his was already established; but things appealed to him so little he decided to return home at once. That fellow amused us greatly. Well supplied by his brother with fresh butter and eggs, he did nothing else during the whole first week but cook, and most kindly invited to share his meals a Jewess from Mulhausen who had come on board bringing nothing at all to eat. The girl accepted promptly her fellow-believer's invitation; she must have counted on forming a good partnership, besides. From that time on, those two were very much teased and tormented by the others; all the more so when, on account of throat disease, his otherwise attractive young lady friend became more and more disgusting to him as his store of provisions decreased. During our last week at sea he had no food at all left to sustain him. He remained lying on his bed and daily drew in his belt. Some rollicking fellows would toss potatoes to him in derision, but he was rarely given anything to eat except in some such spirit of merrymaking over his fierce hunger.

There was also an old retired soldier from the canton of Lucerne who caused me much mortification. He had made arrangements with the captain to assist the ship's crew in return for his passage and board. One of his duties was to assist the sailors every morning in scouring the decks. As soon as he was once out to sea he refused obstinately to do that work. The captain could not put him off the ship unless he threw him overboard, but he issued orders that the old man was to be given nothing to eat. Now, this person had made his first passage over with money provided by his parish in order to get rid of him. That he was unwilling to work showed a trait by no means unusual among our old soldiers discharged from foreign service. In truth, the chief benefit Switzerland derives from her citizens' military service in foreign lands is that only those averse to labor are attracted to that life (aside from the anomaly of republicans entering the service of foreign despots who oppress their subjects). As this old soldier showed a like aversion to work, our consul at Havre could not concern himself about the matter but had to send him back home at the expense of the canton of Lucerne or of his parish. That is what we get by assisting the proletariat to emigrate. Who can compel them to remain or, indeed, as one often hears mentioned, to found a Swiss colony anywhere in America? Citizens of Switzerland they wish ever to remain, supported by their native country.

They do not care to transfer their loyalty to a new fatherland. A man cannot serve two masters. Tradespeople, doctors, artists may go to foreign parts to seek their fortune and then return, but the peasant, when he owns land, can seldom follow that course without great losses. The Swiss are fond of travel, it is true; but the gift North Americans have of making themselves at home anywhere in the world as soon as they begin to acquire wealth, irrespective of their attachment to the soil or of loyalty to the region, is rarely found among natives of Switzerland. That explains why the Swiss are given to nostalgia, which becomes particularly severe when things go ill with them and lead them to reflect upon the good old days. In this modern time a new colonist has to burn his bridges behind him, has to cut off every means of retreat; in order to go forward he must not look back, for even the poorest people in Switzerland have their advantages, their good times, and abandon unwillingly their strolling life, while the laboring classes in our country enjoy a freedom they would find no opportunity to enjoy anywhere in the United States, still less in a colony newly founded. But the principal difficulty with Swiss colonists is that they may not be forced to work and fulfill agreements they have entered upon, for there is no army in command; any man may go away, nay, what is more, he may again return.

September 22. Havre. To recover from fever and regain my vigor, taking in consideration, besides, that I had little money left, I had no other recourse but to proceed at once to my home, where I arrived on the 24th, unexpected by my family. To earn my livelihood as artist in Berne. Alas! What a prospect.

APPENDIX

To be able to estimate properly in just how far the Indians are capable of mental development we must consider them, first of all, in their primitive state, and then after their contact with Europeans. In that way we shall understand the cause of development in general and the degree of cultivation to which Indians themselves can attain without the aid of foreign assistance as well as the reason why they have retrograded rather than advanced since their contact with European civilization.

The lowest form of human being among the North American Indians inhabited that extensive tract of arid land between the Rocky Mountains and the Sierra Nevada, in the neighborhood of Salt Lake. Only in the matter of speech did they rank above the lower animals. They were forced to live on roots and locusts, with an occasional hare or other larger animal; for in the sterile region where they dwelt there was hardly any vegetation except wormwood, which, when dried, furnished their only fuel. The barren tracts were equally destitute of the larger wild beasts. There the root diggers lived, like an exiled race, despised by their better-conditioned neighbors.

A slightly higher type of human species were the coast dwellers of California. Their bodies, well nourished on fish, reached full development. However, they could no more provide clothing for themselves from the fish of the sea than could the root diggers from the locusts on their sun-scorched plains; consequently they became so inured to the elements that they scorned any covering whatsoever.

But, notwithstanding their readiness to brave the weather, they were so full of mettle that more than once they stood their ground in single combat against the better-armed Spaniards.

The prairie Indian stands much higher in the scale of human development than those mentioned above. On the vast grass plains he steals upon wild beasts and ensnares those that provide him with sufficient food, clothing, and fuel. To accomplish that on the open prairie requires cunning: To entrap a shy creature like the antelope or bison under a disguise made up of wolf's skin or bison's hide and the head of a stag marks a distinct advance in the intelligence of the hunter. Moreover, in mountain ravines as well as in the thick undergrowth of the forests that are found only near rivers and brooks, he is obliged to bring all his ingenuity into play to take by surprise

349

the different species of deer and stag found in such numbers in those places without falling a prey himself to the formidable grizzly bear or other enemies even more merciless.

As the immense number of buffalo or bison makes any attempt to domesticate the animals a useless undertaking, the hunter is obliged to follow the wandering herds, taking with him his tent of skins and his household belongings, including always his strong wolfhound. In late summer, when the "cattle" are in best condition, he tries to confine an entire herd in so-called parks, slaughters as many as he finds necessary, and cures large narrow strips of meat in the sun. He then packs the fat in bladders for use during the winter.

The only service that the Indians render for the benefit of the herds is to burn the dried grass every spring in order that the young crop will be more abundant.

Inasmuch as roaming about alone is both dangerous and dull, as many members of a tribe as can be comfortable together unite and form a settlement. As the provisioning of a small community is a less difficult task, and their frequent removals upon the prairies are more easily effected, the villages or camps are rarely of considerable size. If the huntsman has procured sufficient provisions for a time he gives himself up to social pleasures in camp, such as smoking tobacco, talking over past experiences, relating stories and traditions, performing gymnastic exercises, dancing, getting ready new weapons; or else he goes on the warpath to win distinction for himself as brave. The womenfolk are left to their common household employment. They make all the clothes, including the ornamentation of them; they supply also their earthen cooking utensils and prepare skins and hides. The last-named duty is the most difficult of all; consequently, to facilitate that work, since there are neither slaves, servants, nor craftsmen among the Indians, the huntsman keeps several wives. To prevent petty jealousies and quarrels among his squaws he prefers to marry sisters. To obtain them he presents gifts to his future parents-in-law; in other words, he purchases his helpmates.

The highest aim of an Indian brave is glory in war; accordingly there is perpetual hostility among the different tribes. His method of warfare is nothing more than a well-planned hunt; any sort of stratagem is permissible.

But as the Indian brave places more importance upon single combat than upon a deadly distant attack, the mere fact of his having touched his enemy ranks as a greater deed of valor than killing a person from a distance; hence the practice of scalping. The scalp is indisputable proof that he has come in personal contact with the enemy and serves him as trophy. Since he scalps a living person only in the rarest

instances he is not guilty of such an act of cruelty as is usually believed. For every scalp taken the warrior is allowed an eagle feather
to adorn his head; in recognition of every such "coup" he is entitled
to have an eagle feather blazoned, Indian fashion, on his robe. The
number of eagle feathers worn designates the rank of the brave. The
one who takes the greatest number of scalps becomes leader or chief
of his band. On the other hand, the chief who is able to assemble
the largest number of tents about him is regarded the greatest chief
of that nation. Therefore this dignity is not only not hereditary but
depends also upon the brave's fortunes in war. Nor does valor alone
win such high respect. The brave who wishes to be exalted among
his people must be liberal. Without largesse he will have no followers.
The number of gifts bestowed he is also allowed to have represented
on his robe.

Here we find the beginning of the representative arts among the
Indians. Apart from his great liking for pompous show, for ornamentation, in connection with which one must mention tattoo marks,
the Indian's principal aim in decoration is colored outlines or contours; the human figure is only a secondary matter.

Therefore, though no one can deny that the Indian has artistic
sense, from time out of mind he has made no advance in his art.
His manner is stereotyped—hallowed, so to speak, through the ages—
like heraldry. Wampum belts serve all the better to call to mind the
most important events of the present and of past times.

The bringing up of boys consists entirely in training capable
huntsmen for the support of future families and distinguished warriors for the glory of the nation. Young Indians, hardly past the age
of boys, subject themselves willingly to severe fasting and cruel torture. They must learn to endure any pain heroically, so that even
as captives at the stake they can jeer at their enemies and prove by
singing under torture their persecutors' impotence to cause them
pain. Only by valor and undaunted courage can they gain their
Elysium. Torture inflicted on an enemy, therefore, is not merely
for the sake of being cruel, but has the further purpose of testing in
a "trial by fire" his steadfastness under pain. The Indian faces
death calmly, yea, with joy, for with the close of earthly life all his
troubles end, while the future abode of his soul offers him the fulfillment of all desires. In addition to the qualities of courage, cunning, and liberality, the gift of oratory is very highly prized and
fostered among Indians. Next to this talent for speaking, the trait
of keeping silent is most valued, for the reason that an ill-advised
remark may possibly at some time or other put one's life in peril.

Girls are brought up to be good mothers and industrious house-
wives. Children are dearly loved by their parents. The future In-

dian brave is never flogged. His sense of honor is developed early in life. On the other hand, parents are loved and respected by their children, yet it not infrequently happens when they are journeying to a distant destination with little means of transportation that decrepit old people are left behind, forsaken.

The goal set for both sexes, differing according to the nature of each, is one that can be attained. Though believing in a life to come, they love and work for their human welfare and enjoy this life to the full. To make their earthly existence a hell, in order to gain after death a still uncertain future bliss, is not acceptable to their distinctly practical sense. To lay down vital principles and yet fail to observe them is just as much opposed to the Indian's way of thinking; he lives in strict accord with the views handed down to him from his ancestors; he gives no promise of wishing to be better than he can be according to his nature. Because he thinks that waging a constant conflict with his nature is repugnant to common sense, he is designated the natural man in contradistinction to civilized people. Still, the Indian knows full well how to master his human desires, when in yielding to them he would run counter to the interest of those dearest to him or to the recognized usages of his tribe. Civilized man is supposed to develop only his spiritual powers and suppress his animal nature, except when he has not sufficient money to get married.

In social intercourse the so-called savage may serve as a model for civilized society in this respect, that he neither indulges in disputes and arguments, using vulgar terms of abuse, nor in brutal fights. On the contrary, he guards against any offense of that sort, because among the Indians every insult is followed by bloodshed; therefore he provokes his adversary only when he is of a mind to enter upon a struggle for life or death. To pocket an affront is to be guilty of cowardice. In such emergencies it is permissible that the weaker antagonist resort to stratagem.

Although the prairie huntsman is familiar with the cultivation of native Indian corn and other cereals, a tribe turns to that employment only when, owing to the greatly reduced number of braves, it is no longer safe to wander about and make head against opposing foes in the open field and, therefore, is forced to establish a village and settle down.

As contrasted with the prairie Indian, the red man of the forests, owing to conditions in that part of the country which he inhabits, may be considered of a somewhat higher order of human being. Westward from the Mississippi, extending beyond the Rocky Mountains even to the Pacific coast, the region is predominantly prairie, abounding in grass, weeds, flowers, and sand, but usually, for want of sufficient water, not capable of cultivation. East of the Father of Waters, on the other hand, the land, with but few exceptions, is covered with dense primeval woods.

Owing to this difference in the vegetation of his domain, therefore, the Indian of the East follows necessarily a different mode of life from that of his western neighbor. It is true that wild game is plentiful in the boundless woods, yet the animals do not exist in such numbers nor are large herds so frequent as to furnish continually a sufficient supply of food. Though the hunter on the chase in a forest finds less difficulty in approaching wild beasts than on the open prairie, he has also this disadvantage, that his game more easily conceal themselves and more quickly escape his eye. So in North America, where there are fewer trees of the fruit-bearing sort than in South America, the Indian of the forests finds it necessary to till the soil. In his part of the country the land is adapted to the cultivation of nutritive products, such as Indian corn, potatoes, beans, peas, turnips, etc.

The brave, always true to his inborn character, prefers war and the chase to the hoe and gives over the labors of the field almost altogether to the female sex. With the cultivation of the land there comes of itself a more settled habitation, more comfortable dwellings, and in consequence a stronger attachment to country (expressed symbolically in "graves of his forefathers") than one finds among the prairie huntsmen. The latter do not bury their dead, but leave them temporarily in the air on a scaffold and, at best, gather the bones and carry them along on their wanderings. The Indians of the forest bury their dead in the ground; usually the body is placed in a squatting position with face turned toward the east and interred with similar ceremonies of lamentation, discourse, food portion, and weapons.

In affairs of state the eastern tribes follow a different custom with regard to the office of chief, which is hereditary and inseparable from their system of revenue. The succession may revert to the female line; that is, to the son of the deceased chief's eldest sister; but in every case it must be ratified by the nation. Apparel and implements are pretty much the same as among the prairie tribes, except that canoes made of the bark of trees or hollowed out of a tree trunk replace the troughlike, portable skin boats used by the western huntsmen.

By way of transition I will mention also the former inhabitants of Cibola in New Mexico, and the nameless Mound Builders in the Ohio Valley. The former, when they occupied the "Casas Grandes", distinguished themselves by their peculiar manner of building cities and in their cultivation of cotton and manufacture of cotton materials. Their dwellings were constructed, and are still, when occupied by Apache and Navaho, inside a great encircling wall 40 feet high. They were built of sun-dried brick and consisted of several stories, the upper stories projecting so far over those below that a broad passageway was left as a means of communication. Access was had to the different stories by means of movable ladders. Gates admitted the city dwellers to the surrounding fields where their crops were planted. The stag and the hart they had in large numbers, but the bison, owing to the warm climate, was not native there. The latter, however, existed in multitudes to the north of them in a region not too remote.

Defensive warfare with stones and arrows was easily conducted from the flat roofs of their adobe houses. Their provisions were stored in oven-shaped cellars. The women were skilled in weaving and kept a great supply of handkerchiefs and mantles. The Apache and Navaho claim to be related tribes to the Aztec, and have preserved, even to most recent times, the same style of dress and the same kind of weapons that were in use among the latter. As the most of the "Casas Grandes" now lie in ruins it has been erroneously assumed that the Aztec might have occupied them before the arrival of the former tribes and have destroyed them when they wandered farther south. Near the close of the sixteenth century, however, the first Spanish explorers found them densely populated, and it was those avaricious Spaniards themselves who, after many years of conflict, destroyed the towns, just as at a later time the Indians avenged themselves by wiping out the Spanish settlements in turn.

I must now mention briefly the early inhabitants of the Ohio Valley, who, for want of a historical name, are called Mound Builders, because of the tumuli they left behind them. Judging from the remnants they have left of their buildings and utensils, they attained to a far higher degree of civilization than any other North American tribe. They worked in copper. The pipe bowls that they wrought in the form of human heads were excellent; so were their figures of animals carved in stone. Their fortifications (in the form of quadrant and circle) show a rather advanced knowledge of military science and of geometry.

These Indians had already proceeded into the Bronze Age when all other North American tribes were still lingering in the Age of Stone. One knows this from the fact that, except for the use of lead in certain ornamentation, they worked neither in copper nor in iron, notwithstanding that both metals lay in greatest abundance beneath their feet.

The Mound Builders have vanished from their early habitations so long ago that even the Indians that came later to that region knew nothing of their having lived there or of their name. From the thorough investigations that have been made by distinguished archeologists in America it seems more than probable that these Mound Builders were one and the same nation with the Toltec, and that the opinion concerning their having been a remnant of the colony settled by the Welsh prince Madoc is altogether untenable, for the reason that these immemorial woods, that have since grown up on their earthworks, were already there before 1170, the year in which Madoc departed from the Principality of Wales. That they were identical with the Toltec, as investigators permit one to believe, is assumed from the similarity of overlapping gateways, of carved pipe bowls, from statements on the part of merchants and tradesmen from Mexico that obsidian is a species of Mexican stone, from the advanced civilization of the Mound Builders, the presence of similar earthworks (even though they are neither so well constructed nor so numerous) in all that region extending southward from Ohio to the Gulf of Mexico during a period of time that coincides with the appearance of the Toltec in Anahuac in the year 648, together with their own tradition concerning their arrival on the earth.

These proofs I have brought forward here merely for the sake of showing, what many hold as questionable, i. e., that the Mound Builders, in the matter of the high degree of cultivation, are much like Indians of the Toltecan family.

That the Toltec reached a high degree of culture is acknowledged by historians both of former generations and of recent times. From them the famous ruins in Anahuac derive their origin (not to be confused with those of Yucatan, Palenque); from them the Aztec, who penetrated into that country from the Northwest 400 years later, learned their science of astronomy in accordance with which at the time of the Spanish Conquest they reckoned their solar year with more exactness than their avaricious Christian conquerors; from them resulted those hieroglyphic paintings for the pictorial representations of their history, of their era, of their calculations, an art that in no way brings their Indian origin in dispute. From them the Aztec acquired a moral code strikingly like that of Christian teaching and derived from them the idea of independent priesthood and of judge, etc.

The Toltec lived for something like 400 years in Anahuac, until, for causes unknown, whether pestilence, wars, or famine, their numbers became so reduced that they were unable longer to defend their homeland from the fresh, warlike hordes that were breaking in upon them.

Among these different invading tribes were the Aztec, who, in spite of their savage nature, adapted themselves readily to the civilization they met with there, but along with lofty morality adhered to their ghastly human sacrifices and the eating of their victims. A most extraordinary anomaly. Only the Acolhuan, known by the name of their capital city Tezcuco, were more peaceably inclined. They came into the country at the same time with the Aztec, in fact were a related tribe, but struggled against this bloody practice of human offerings which, after all, was not carried originally to such a shocking degree among the latter, but became gradually more and more horrible under the exactions of the priests, a class of ever-increasing power. This sacerdotal influence was exerted for the purpose of maintaining constant military exercises; the victims sacrificed were always prisoners of war dedicated to the deities of the underworld. The creator of the world was worshipped without either pictorial representations or human offerings.

In the course of time the inhabitants of Tezcuco, profiting by the Toltecan civilization and encouraged by excellent princes, like the Nezahuacoyotl, made considerable advance, on their own part, in intellectual and artistic matters, especially in poetry and in plastic art, while their neighbors, the Aztec, directed their aims rather more to material development. What especially amazed the Spaniards, partly because of the originality and novelty displayed and also for the reason that the existence of such things among Indians was totally unexpected, were the suspended or hanging gardens; complete collections of all indigenous plants in their well-kept gardens and of all native domestic animals in well-arranged menageries; their careful tillage of the soil and production, by means of irrigation, of Indian corn, bananas, agaves, cacao, cotton, etc.; their special fondness for the cultivation of flowers; their mighty aqueducts and original designs in the architecture of magnificent palaces; the houses built on piles; the dikes, and lake shores connected by drawbridges that they might serve for highways; their schools for boys and girls; the immeasurable treasures in precious metals; their coins stamped with the form of a Latin T; their market places, hospitals, storage houses for tools and provisions; their skill as goldsmiths, feather workers, weavers, etc; and their extensive, highly respectable trade.

Amazed to find such cultivation among Indians, many people are inclined to assert that their civilization was not their own but was based upon certain analogies of European and primarily of Asiatic origin; for instance, the teocallis from the Egyptians; astronomy from the same race or from the Mongols, Persians, etc.; cyclopaean walls, gateway, and window facings from the Greeks; the tradition of Noah and the deluge from the Hebrews; baptism, absolution, the cross and the punishment of burning in everlasting fire, together with moral teaching, from the Catholics; helmet-like coverings for their heads from the Celts; weapons, standards, court singers and court fools, dwarfs, and jugglers, in addition to certain feudal adaptations, from the Romans or else from the medieval knights; consequently, in the end, little remains that is peculiarly Mexican.

This view concerning the part that foreign influence has had in the civilization of tribes in Mexico still gains credence, to be sure, from the native tradition (of Toltecan origin), so harmful in its effect, that relates how, at a period most remote, Quetzalcoatl, god of the air, appeared in the form of a white man with long black hair and flowing beard and taught the inhabitants of Anahuac the use of metals, the science of husbandry, and statecraft. Then, having promised to come back again, he set out upon the sea in a skiff of serpent's skin, sailing eastward to the fairyland of Tlapallan.

Even though the Toltec themselves may have been indebted in part to earlier inhabitants of Anahuac or to foreign influences for their civilization, still in their advance to a higher cultivation they have been always true to the fundamental characteristics of the Indian race and have only improved their own abilities (just as the Aztec, according to their own admission, are indebted to the Toltec for their culture). Their hieroglyphical paintings prove that fact incontestably, while moccasins, breechcloth, kneebands, eagle feathers, shields, bows, arrows, lances, knives made of obsidian, tomahawks, fans, painting the face, antipathy for beards or for any hair on the bodies denote pure Indian; merely a modification in their style of dress appears when, owing to a lack of pelts, leather was scarce and the wealth of metals and precious stones was made use of as a mark of distinction by the splendor-loving Indians. Maquehinte (?) and the dart were peculiar to the Mexican.

Although it is not so much a question here of vindicating the claim of the former inhabitants of Anahuac to a culture of their own as it is to prove their capacity for civilization, yet we may be permitted to mention several highly important grounds for vindication.

In the first place, except among the Quichua (of the race of Incas), who trained the llama and alpaca for domestic animals, there was an absolute absence of cattle throughout the whole of America, even in this part of the continent, where agriculture was carried forward to a high degree and the bison could not have been unknown. Furthermore, there was a universal ignorance as to the use of iron, though an abundance of it existed in that region. If Quetzalcoatl had been a civilized European or Asiatic, which is much to be doubted, it must appear remarkable in the highest degree that he did not teach those two very important branches of human knowledge, and something even as important, i. e., the use of the sail. It may be regarded surprising, also, that, though European and Asiatic influences played so large a part in the development of this people, the horse never appears in the tradition. It cannot but seem utterly incomprehensible that the Hebrews, for example, who are well known as cattle breeders par excellence and were acquainted, in any case, with the profitable uses of iron, should have left no trace of their skill in those useful employments, while they preserved the tradition of Noah and the deluge. The same may be said of the Europeans; only the ancient Egyptians might be regarded an exception, inasmuch as in the construction of the pyramids they had not yet made use of iron and their influence on the civilization of Ana-huac can be said to date only from their earliest period, at least 2,000 years B. C.

Even the great number of analogies found among widely dissimilar peoples of the Old World, in remote ages as well as in modern times, together with the fact that the discovery of the New World came so much later and that the aboriginal Indian is a distinct racial type, affords sufficient proof, according to my view, that the American Indian is a separate race; furthermore, that the civilization of this people is one peculiarly their own. But I make this assertion without any desire to question the possibility of their having had occasional contact with the Old World.

Wherever one turns in his study of primitive man one finds everywhere, even on the most remote, inaccessible island, that such peoples are provided with the same kind of weapons, nourish and clothe themselves in much the same way and, as soon as hunting, fishing, and fruit-bearing trees are no longer sufficiently productive without artificial aid, they succeed in the cultivation of the soil and in the breeding of cattle. With the expansion of their resources, population increases, thereby increasing their needs; so the state is evolved, bringing to the citizens' attention fundamental truths like personal security, protection of property, and more or less freedom in the development of the individual, etc. It is useless to expect from any isolated race of men something entirely original in manner of living; the natural man is, in all instances, provided with the same sort of physical organism; only in mentality is one race more highly endowed than another, etc.

From the foregoing we now draw the following conclusions:

1. That, owing to their ignorance of better conditions as well as to the sterility of the region in which they lived, no civilization could be justly expected among the Root Diggers.

2. That among the prairie Indians, and also among the eastern forest tribes, terrestrial happiness was so completely possible in this world that civilization according to our ideas would make them worse rather than better. They would only lose contentment, that satis-

faction with their earthly lot which, notwithstanding our noteworthy progress in the arts and sciences, and in spite of our belief in a merciful God, we strive after in vain.

3. That the Aztec and, to a degree at least, the Toltec also took their higher civilization from earlier inhabitants of Anahuac and thereby gave adequate proof of the pure Indians' capability for culture as soon as they find it necessary to renounce earlier conditions.

These conclusions apply equally to the South American Indians, whom I have not mentioned for want of space; besides, the stages of development are the same among them as among the North American tribes that are better known to me.

Now we come to two other important questions:

How did it come about that the civilized Indians of an earlier period lost their civilization?

Why was it that they adopted so little of the culture brought to them by civilized Europeans?

The infamous treatment that these natives of America suffered after the coming of avaricious Europeans is known to everyone. It suffices to mention, for instance, that when the Spaniards came they destroyed with fanatical zeal all the native civilization as heretical, as heathenish; in order to get possession of land and treasure, they brought the nations, glorious in earlier times, so completely under subjection that the energy and inventive genius of the tribes were completely lost; then, instead of giving the subjugated people a broader culture the Spaniards made of them only Christian simpletons. One may with justice put the question: Which in this instance proves himself the greater barbarian? For, though it was a good deed to put an end to human sacrifices among the Aztec, the Spaniards are guilty of a still greater number of murders and their inquisition is, in comparison, even more horrible.

Englishmen conducted themselves in a manner little less reprehensible. Jealous of the Spaniards' increasing power, they sought to acquire, in their turn, lands rich in gold. English kings granted patents as gifts or else sold the unknown lands, property of the Indians, in vast tracts, extending from the Atlantic Ocean even to the Pacific coast, in order to prick on their adventurers to the occupation of them. To find mythical Cathay was the first stimulus to cross the ocean; avarice and expansion of power, the second; to find rest from religious and political persecutions was the third. Never a trace of a colony having been founded for the betterment of the native Indians; on the contrary, Europeans hardly set foot on American soil before they were striving against each other for possession of the land, without concerning themselves about the true property owners.

Notwithstanding all this there are Englishmen who assert even now, and Americans after them, that their chief motive in taking possession of the Indians' land was to civilize the primitive inhabitants. Thus they give the lie to historical fact. Moreover, let them name a single instance that proves the truth of their assertions. Other authors ease their sore consciences with communistic utterances to the effect that no one should hold in his possession land that is not in use. To what would that lead? What is one to think of such doctrine from English historians, in whose homeland so much land lies fallow for their noble lords' pleasures of the chase. And from Americans who speculate in land on such a vast scale. Such assertions are made in the face of historical proof that the Indians, whose domain lay east and southwest of the Mississippi, south of the Great Lakes and the St. Lawrence River, as well as along the entire seacoast between the estuaries of that stream, depended quite as much for their livelihood upon the yield from their fields as from the chase. Now that was the manner in which Indians were rewarded for having assisted the colonists almost everywhere with their own provisions, nay, what is more, for having rescued them often enough from starvation.

To anyone who examines impartially the situation that existed between the Indians and the colonists it must be perfectly evident that during the wars carried on for 200 years by the latter in defense of their homeland against the constant pressure of insatiable colonists, and during the struggles among the various nations represented by the colonists themselves, Spaniards, Englishmen, Frenchmen, and Hollanders, into which the natives were always involved to their own loss, it must be unmistakably clear that under such circumstances the Indians would inevitably become rather demoralized. Even to the first 30 years of our own century the English have continued to incite the native tribes against the Americans, to spur them on to war with gifts and pledges of assistance, only, in the end, to leave them in the lurch.

There was also another potent influence I must not neglect to mention: The interests of the prevailing fur-trading companies were greatly furthered by the Indians remaining in their primitive state. In fact that vast trade ceased just as soon as the native tribes found the cultivation of the soil preferable to the chase, and, on the other hand, this tillage of the ground can only thrive in those regions when the bison is extinct as a wild animal.

In contrast to the fur traders who as "pioneers" are often admired for their courage and simple life, the white people on the borders are recognized to be a lawless set, fugitives from justice who hate the Indians because the latter are a hindrance to unbridled license, but surpass the savages themselves in brutality and turbulence. Altogether an ignoble example of civilized man.

Still another and, perhaps, the most important factor that has influenced adversely the civilization of the Indians is the great diversity of opinion among so-called Christians concerning religious beliefs.

Up the the present time this fact has been too little regarded. North American Indians have a universal belief in a great benevolent Spirit whom they worship without pictorial representations. They make votive offerings to the sun and the moon in recognition of comforts and benefits bestowed. They try to appease the thunder by dancing, etc. They accept these beliefs universally; there is never the least hint of disputation among them concerning such matters. It is only in the matter of their origin that the tribes have different traditions.

Now, how was it with the colonists? Every colony brought another belief, and yet all wished to be thought good Christians, each claiming to be even better than the others. Many of them were seeking a refuge from religious persecutions in their native country, yet showed themselves capable of the most frightful intolerance toward adherents of other beliefs in their new homeland. The most rigorous persecutors of all were the Puritan fathers, who drove out of their congregations everybody who did not agree with their view of things. Instead of Christians, manifesting their union at least as such, and taking the lead as sincere and loyal followers of Christ in their good example, the Indians saw Catholics and Lutherans, Protestants and Quakers, Jesuits and Puritans, all good Christians, striving against each other, oftentimes with rage.

Could such behavior have an uplifting or formative influence? Which one was the Indian to join? How different it would have been if the Europeans, instead of coming as conquerors with fire and sword, had settled down as peaceful colonists and imparted the best of their civilization to the primitive inhabitants. Only people of a fickle nature are ready at any time to accept innovations and give up the old order, whether good or bad. The Indian is certainly not that sort. It must be considered not in the least astonishing, moreover, that he did not immediately imitate the accomplishments of his enemies, but adopted only what seemed especially useful to him in his own mode of life.

What could those admirable individual missionaries like Roger Williams, Eliot, Marquette, the Moravians, and other good men have achieved if their assembled flocks had not been more secure than other Indians from the attacks and persecutions of the colonists? If the culture of the Indian did not give him a guarantee against the cruel blows inflicted by colonial whites, which continued even into our modern era? What profit does the Indian derive from cultivating his fields if, in the end, he is forced to give up the results of his labor, his seeds, and his harvest to the Americans? Is it not inevitable that hatred for such a nation, the inhabitants of which call themselves the most enlightened people, but live and deal with others in a manner so contrary to their pronounced and much boasted teaching that well-founded doubts of the benefits to be had from such teaching should become fixed in the mind of the Indian?

Is it reasonable to require of the Indians, in spite of all these disadvantageous conditions, an equal standard of cultivation in so short a time as his enemies possess? How long a time, for example, were the Germans in strife against Roman civilization? How many centuries did it require to bring them to their present high standard? Furthermore, even at the present time, are all superstitions, all heathen customs nonexistent? Have the Germans not lost in energy since they are civilized?

If one wishes really to civilize the Indian, or at least to allow him to accomplish his own improvement, first of all let him have peace; let him not be continually driven from place to place out of his productive domain to the barren prairie; let him be treated as a human being, entitled to equal rights with the white race. He will then prove that he is capable of appropriating in time the highest degree of civilization, as soon as he judges it to be indispensable to his corporal and spiritual advantage. The Cherokee and Creek give proof of this even now. But, in defiance of treaties, in spite of their well-ordered government, their attention to agriculture and cattle breeding, notwithstanding their advance in schools and book language, they are continually forced back into the interior of the country. The American republican is an aristocrat only skin deep and desires that the redskins enjoy the rights of man just as little as the negroes. After having supplanted the Indians and forced them, therefore, to depend for a livelihood upon hunting, the Americans revile them as savages, difficult to approach, and incapable.

Does one not constantly tempt them from their ancient, oftentimes established domains with the bait of new hunting grounds?

However, the Indian has not rejected everything that European civilization has offered him. On the contrary, he has quickly appropriated what he found to be profitable or agreeable, such as firearms, horses, knives, needles, steel, firestone, axes, cooking utensils of iron, woolen materials for clothing, glass beads, and fatal whisky.

The teocallis have little resemblance to the pyramids, for they consist of several terraces with a temple at the summit. One finds them also in the region of the Mound Builders. One might just as well say that pagodas or our own church towers derive their origin from the pyramids. Of all monuments known to me in the Old World, the one that most nearly resembles the teocalli is the tomb of Cyrus at Pasargadac.

According to Prescott, Montezuma told Cortez that the Aztec had occupied that country only a few centuries. They conducted great affairs there and, after they had given laws to the country and governed for a time, they disappeared into the region beyond the sunset. Had Quetzalcoatl two names or is he here confused with Mexi, who led the Aztec to Anahuac? Quetzalcoatl was a mythical Toltecan deity, to whom the great teocalli in Cholulu was dedicated.

Inasmuch as the Aztec founded their system of astronomy upon movements of the same heavenly bodies it is not surprising to find many analogies with the same science among the Asiatic peoples. On the other hand, that like denominations be always found in their system of classification is hardly possible.[1]

In addition to their widely varying interpretations of the Scriptures, another fault to be found with the missionaries, and one that makes a comprehension of the Christian faith more difficult for Indians, is their manner of presenting the subject with all the perplexing details of the Old and New Testaments which, to be properly understood requires a knowledge of history and geography. Instead of teaching Christian ethics in its appealing simplicity they overwhelm the primitive mind with all the bewildering legends, prophesies, miracles, historical narratives both good and bad, with the result that the poor Indian cannot "see the woods for the trees." But the inculcation of "Whatever you would that others do unto you, do ye also unto them" would be too simple, too quickly taught— an unprofitable business. Moreover, that teaching would be in open conflict with transactions of so-called Christians and would not admit of diversities of opinion concerning dogma, the central truth to which so much more appertains.

From our standpoint we may look down upon primitive peoples with disregard as much as we like, yet primitive man, nevertheless, made most important discoveries in comparison with which ours, though justly regarded of great worth, according to my view signify less. I will cite only fire and speech: The Heavenly Father did no more to assist primitive man to make fire or to learn how to express himself in speech than He helped us to invent the telegraph or the steamboat. Early man discovered fire for his physical comfort; also words, and later on writing, either by means of characters or pictorial representations. Certainly that denotes inherent gifts of

---

[1] See Prescott, Conquest of Mexico, vol. III, p. 242.

no low order. Furthermore, this applies to aborigines even in most remote lands. The discovery of fire and the uses to which it was put, the origin of words and formation of sentences is, from my point of view, an achievement so remarkable that all later inventions signify little in comparison, for without those elements our science and inventions would never have been possible. We are so accustomed to fire and speech, however, that we no longer concern ourselves about their origin and therefore regard the matter as of little significance.

REMARKS CONCERNING MY LANGUAGE EXERCISES

The writing of the Indian language presents serious difficulties. In the first place the Indians have no records in accordance with which they can fix the pronunciation of the words and, as usage in language just as any other usage is capable of change, one is often perplexed to find the correct letters for indeterminate sounds. Furthermore, one finds it difficult to make an Indian, from whom one gets the words, understand just what is wanted, for the reason, primarily, that one is limited to the sign language only and this is not always adequate for specific distinctions or detailed explanation. That one can be led astray also by educated traders who know perfectly the speech of certain tribes, is proved by my linguistic experiments in the Mandan language, the results of which are often quite different from those obtained by Prince von Neu Wied, notwithstanding that the words proceed from the same mouth—that is to say, from Mr. Kipp's. It seems that he must not have had the same ear for the sounds as I, for, though I dare not place myself in the same rank with a traveler so celebrated, so thorough, I may be allowed to assume that I have written down correctly these words of the Mandan language—words I am required to repeat over and over again, all the time, to Mr. Kipp and his Mandan wife. He was most anxious not only to oblige his friend Mitchell, Indian agent at St. Louis, but also to be answerable, under his own name, to scholars. The differences that appear, therefore, in the results of our language texts must be adjudged by some competent third person.

As I have not lived among the Mandan I have received my knowledge of their language from one and the same source; consequently, I should immediately concede that I am wrong if I had not found in other languages better known to me just as many differences of opinion between Prince von Neu Wied and myself—discrepancies about which I am perfectly certain that I am right, because I have heard the words hundreds of times and have used them daily myself.

Previously, when I began regularly to practice speaking the Sioux dialect with Witthae, the men remonstrated with me for talking like a woman—that is to say, the pronunciation and manner of speaking among Indian women is not always the same as among the men. Like the former, I gave a softer sound to the consonants r, p, k, t, etc.

Oftentimes I had difficulty also in learning the names of colors in the Indian language for the reason that those words are rarely used as adjectives but are appended usually to a substantive like earth, color, or even blanket, glass bead, etc. Moreover, when naming parts of the body Indians use the word "my"; when naming other objects, the expression "it is." In such instances one can only get the precise expression by a nearer acquaintance with Indian usage and a more thorough study of their speech.

In German one comes nearest to the sounds of the letters in Indian dialects, for our u, k, r, a, ch, sch, h, and c constantly appear. From the French one finds the nasal sounds "an", "on", and especially "que."

For purposes of indicating sounds in the Indian language, English is of no service at all; one merely admits a great number of new letters to the alphabet. Only "th" can I make use of at all, and that for the purpose of being able to produce the sound "ts" with the tip of the tongue between the teeth. The sign ∼ indicates a nasal sound; with the exception of "th" all letters of the alphabet and all syllables written in Latin script must be pronounced as in French.

BIBLIOGRAPHY

BUSHNELL, DAVID I., JR. Friedrich Kurz, Artist-Explorer. Smithson. Rept. for 1927, pp. 507–527, Washington, 1928.

DENIG, EDWIN THOMPSON. Indian Tribes of the Upper Missouri. Edited with Notes and Biographical Sketch by J. N. B. Hewitt. Forty-sixth Ann. Rept. Bur. Amer. Ethn., pp. 375–628, Washington, 1930.

DORSEY, J. OWEN. Omaha Sociology. Third Ann. Rept. Bur. Ethn., pp. 205–370, Washington, 1884.

FLETCHER, ALICE C., and LA FLESCHE, FRANCIS. Twenty-seventh Ann. Rept. Bur. Amer. Ethn., pp. 15–654, Washington, 1911.

HANDBOOK OF AMERICAN INDIANS NORTH OF MEXICO. Bull. 30, Bur. Amer. Ethn., pts. 1–2, Washington, 1907–10.

LOWIE, ROBERT H. Social Life of the Crow Indians. Anthrop. Papers Amer. Mus. Nat. Hist., vol. IX, pt. 2, New York, 1912.

—— Notes on the Social Organization and Customs of the Mandan, Hidatsa, and Crow Indians. Ibid., vol. XXI, pt. 1, 1917.

MAXIMILIAN, PRINCE ALEXANDER PHILIP, DE WIED-NEUWIED, Reise in das innere Nord-America in den Jahren 1832 bis 1834. B. I–II. Coblenz, 1839–1841.

POWELL, JOHN WESLEY. Indian Linguistic Families of America North of Mexico. Seventh Ann. Rept. Bur. Ethn., pp. 1–142, Washington, 1891.

TRAVELS IN THE INTERIOR OF NORTH AMERICA. Translated from the German by H. Evans Lloyd, London, 1843.

366

PLATE 1

Upper left: July 23, 1851.
Upper right: July 17, 1851. Her[antsa].
Lower left: July 4(?), 1851. Sioux.
Lower right: July 13, 1851. Herantsa.

Lower middle: August 17, 1851.
Lower right: August 19, 1851.

PLATE 2

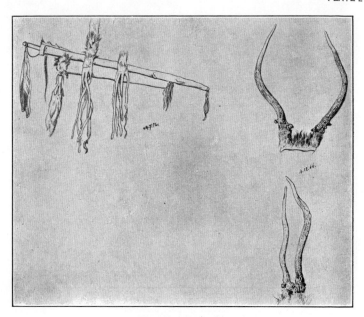

Upper left: July 29, 1852.
Upper right: December 4(?), 1856.

Upper left: August 24, 1851.
Lower middle: Powder magazine, Fort Berthold.   August 19, 1851.

PLATE 3

Lower left: August 17, 1851.

Upper left: February 26, 1852.
Upper right: February 16, 1851.
Lower left: January 27, 1852.
Lower right: February 9, 1852.

PLATE 4

Swimming Across Papillon Creek at the Omaha Village.   May 22, 1851.

Lower left: August 2, 1851.

PLATE 5

Lower right: July 15, 1851. [James] Kipp.

Upper: June 2, 1851. Omaha.
Bottom: Overflow of the Musquaiter. May 31, 1851. Council Bluffs.

PLATE 6

Top: Returning from the Dobies' Ball.
Bottom: Morgan.   October 14, 1851.

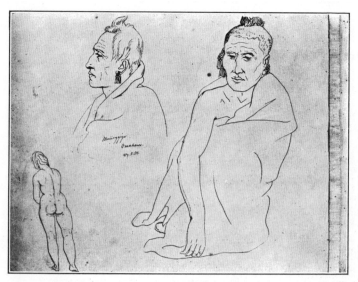

Mannagiga.   Omaha.   Front and profile views.   May 23, 1851.

PLATE 7

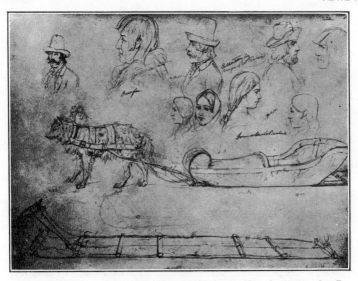

Upper: October 6, 1851.   Culbertson, Bourgeois of Fort Mackenzie.   November 11, 1851.   Ours Fou.
Right of center: November 9, 1851.   Domicila La Bombarde.
Under carriole: November 27, 1851.
Bottom: November 23(?), 1851.

Center: Durham.   October 30, 1851.

PLATE 8

Upper: Mouth of the Big Platte. Nebraska. Niobrara.
Middle: May 23, 1851.
Bottom: ? Mus-lu-la; Wik-wi-la. Omaha.

At horse's heel: August 1, 1851.
At bottom: Herantsa (i. e., Gros Ventres).

PLATE 9

Top: Cree.   December 27, 1851.

Bottom: Crow saddle.   October 5, 1850.

PLATE 10

Middle: Crows. November 29, 1851. Crow women. January 7, 1852.
Bottom: January 23, 1852. (Saddled pony.)

Bottom: August 8, 1851. (Probably ring-and-spear game.)

PLATE 11

Bottom: Californians. Council Bluffs (in the distance). May 18, 1851.

Bottom: August 26, 1851. (Rudolph Friederich Kurz?)

PLATE 12

Top: August 9, 1851. Herantsa. Badger (a dog).
Bottom: Cedar Island, N. I. June 27, 1851. July 23, 1851.

Bottom: August 31, 1850. Fashion (a horse).

PLATE 13

Bottom: February 4, 1852. (Fort Union?).

Bottom: Queue Rouge. August 20, 1851. August 21, 1851(?).

PLATE 14

Upper: October 13, 1851.
Bottom: August 17(?), 1851. Herantsa.

Middle: August 23, 1851.

PLATE 15

Back of horseman: Glaice hair(?).   Habits de Cheffre with Indian ornamentation.
Bottom: Herantsa.   August 1851.   December 15, 1851.

Left (margin): August 12, 1851.
Bottom: Iowa(?).   Probably Chief White Cloud.   December 19, 1850.

PLATE 16

Lower left: July 23, 1851.
Lower right: August 2 or 4, 1851. (Woman with bullboat and paddle.)

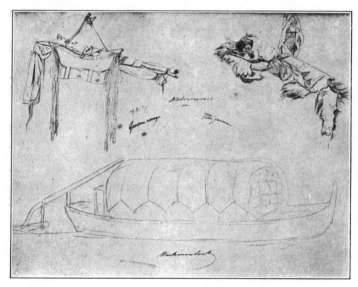

Upper center: August 29, 1851. Medicine Sacs. Queue Rouge. Tête Jaune.
Under boat: Mackinaw boat.

PLATE 17

At bottom: Fort Union. September 7, 1851.

Top: Fort Clarke. Arikara.
Bottom: Young girls' dance. July 13, 1851.

PLATE 18

Top: Gŭthŭmer, i. e., Belhumeur.
Bottom: Omaha.

Top: December 6, 1851. Cree.

PLATE 19

Top right: July 8, 1851. Below Fort Clarke.
Bottom: Horse guard of Fort Berthold.

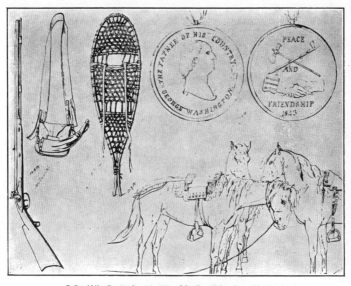

Left middle: September 14, 1851. Mr. Dennick's (i. e., Mr. Denig's).
Foot of snowshoe: September 15, 1851.
Between medals: September 24, 1851.
Bottom: September 26, 1851. Saddled horses.

PLATE 20

Bottom: P. T. Sarpy. Belle Vue. May 16, 1851. "Trading house for the Omahaws."

Upper left: July 12, 1851. Mandan.

PLATE 21

Bottom: Potawatomi. May 21, 1851. Equipment for horseback riding.

Bottom: Sauteurs visiting. August 4, 1851 (left). August 14, 1851 (right).

PLATE 22

Below: August 5, 1851. Herantsa (i. e., Gros Ventres). Ring and spears

Top right: March 12, 1852.
Bottom: February 15, 1852. Saddled Blackfeet pony.
Lower right: October 12, 1852(?). Three breeds of dogs are shown.

PLATE 23

Upper left: February 18, 1852. La Bombarde.
Upper right: Herantsa cutting up a drowned bison.
Lower center: Sauteurs (Chippewa) girl. At her right, July 27, 1851.
Lower right: Herantsa woman.

Bottom: Omaha. Halfbreed.

PLATE 24

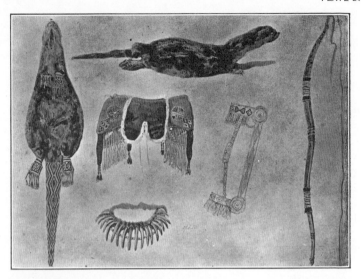

Two medicine pouches, two necklaces, a ceremonial bow, and a saddle cloth.

Left center: Illegible phrase.
On shoulder of upper figure: July 7, 1851.
Under two figures: July 16, 1851.
Lower center: July 16, 1851.

PLATE 25

Under horsemen: August 6, 1851.
Right, under figures: August 7, 1851.

Bottom: Oto Indians with a boat.   May 15 ,1851.

PLATE 26

Upper row: August 10, 1851.   Under second figure, Pierre Gareau.   *Between last two figures:* August 13, 1851.
Bottom: July 23, 1851.   From Fort Berthold.

Upper left: December 27, 1851.   Crow bags (Indian).
Bottom: Iowa.

PLATE 27

Packet boat "St. Ange." August 7, 1851.

Bottom: Mandan. July 14, 1851. (James) Kipp.

PLATE 28

Upper row: July 16, 1851.   (Le Serpent Noir.)

Left: Female bighorn.   January 27, 1852.
Right: February 22, 1852.

PLATE 29

Bottom: July 12, 1851. Herantsa (i. e., Gros Ventres).

Upper left: Corbeau.   August 7, 1851.
Upper center: Herantsa (i. e., Gros Ventres).
Bottom: July 14, 1851.

PLATE 30

Bottom center: Cree.   July 23, 1851.

Bottom center: July 22, 1851.

PLATE 31

Left: Long Hair. Squirrel skin.
Center: July 1851. Herantsa (i. e., Gros Ventres).
Right: July 12, 1851.

Upper left: July 24, 1851.
Bottom: Herantsa (i. e., Gros Ventres). July 23, 1851.
Top, near woman's head: Cree.
Right: August 23, 1851.

PLATE 32

Bottom, left: Engagees.
Bottom, center: August 28, 1851.
Bottom: Trader.

Top center: December 8, 1851.   Ours Fou (i. e., Mad Bear).
Right: Waaschamani, second Chief of the Omaha.   June 9, 1851.
Left bottom: Omaha.   June 8, 1851.   Wäkusche.

PLATE 33

Lower left: Herantsa mourning (shown by wearing stripes of white clay).
Right center: July 17, 1851.

Top left: Under design, Assiniboin song. September 9, 1851.
Bottom: Under figure of Mr. Kurz and horse, October 1850.

PLATE 34

Upper left, below heads: Assiniboin.   December 3, 1851.
Upper center: Ours Fou.
Bottom: Cree.   December 8, 1851.   The drawing includes a modernized calumet.

Upper right: Assiniboin.   November 16, 1851.
Under horseman: Charles Martin.

PLATE 35

Under top house: Council Bluff.   May 19, 1851.
Bottom: In center, May 26, 1851.
Extreme right: Mud lodge.

Under standing figure: May 9, 1851.
At bottom: May 10, 1851.

PLATE 36

Under horse: Sioux. May 25, 1851.
Under barefoot man: Engagee.
Under man with pipe: Trader. June 1851.
Under moccasined man: Guyotte.
Under last figure standing: Engagee Canadian. May 26, 1851.
At right of man's bust: Lambert.
At back of woman's bust: Herantsa.
Under row of houses: Council Bluff.

Right below house: Council Bluff. May 19, 1851.
Bottom: Cree, or the Cree. July 28, 1851.

PLATE 37

Upper left: November 13, 1851.
Lower left: (Illegible).
Bottom center: Fort Berthold. July 13, 1851.

Bottom left: Young Elk, chief of Omaha.
Bottom right: Omaha. May 5, 1851.

PLATE 38

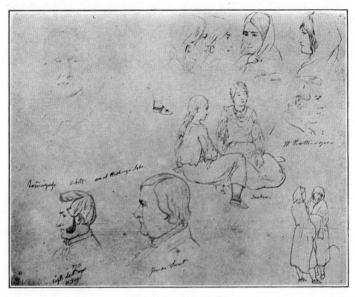

Upper left, below faint outline: Tamegache, son of Washinga Saba, who is called the Young Elk(?)   June 11,
1851.
Upper right: Dakota squaws.   June 24, 1851.
Middle right: W. Picotte and squaw.
Under two seated figures: Omaha.
Left bottom: Captain La Barge of the "St. Ange."   July 7, 1851.
Bottom center: Père de Smet.

Bottom: August 20, 1851.   (Showing warrior with hafted stone tomahawk.)

PLATE 39

Bellangé. (R. F. Kurz?) From Fort Berthold to Fort Union, September 7, 1851.

Bottom: Omaha Village. May 20, 1851.

PLATE 40

Upper busts: Left, [Charles] Morgan. September 13, 1851. *Right,* Four Rivers, Absaroka. November 25, 1851.

PLATE 41

Bottom: August 16, 1851.
Bottom right: Long Hair (i. e., La Longue Chevelure).   August 15, 1851.

Bottom: Crossing at Council Bluff.   May 19, 1851.

PLATE 42

Bottom: July 4, 1851. Fort Pierre.

Bottom: (Rudolph Friederich Kurz). Iowa (Indians). March 20, 1851.

PLATE 43

Upper right: Bull and Badger (dogs).   October 10, 1851.

Bottom: Omaha lodge (interior structure).   May 16, 1851.

PLATE 44

Bottom: Oto camp below mouth of Big Platte.   May 13, 1851.

Bottom: July 16, 1851.   Two young braves returning with their first scalps; their faces, with the exception of their noses, which are painted white, are blackened, to indicate the making of a "coup."

PLATE 45

Center: July 22, 1851.
Upper right: August 1, 1851.
Lower left: G. V.   July 12, 1851.   (Gros Ventres?)
Bottom: July 1, 1851.   Below Fort Pierre.   Garden Island.

Bottom: Omaha Village.   May 24, 1851.

PLATE 46

Left center: Figure in attitude of mourning.
Bottom of burial scaffold: July 28, 1851.   August 30, 1851.

Under horse: February 16, 1852.
Under yoke: February 19, 1852.
Right center: Sauteur (Chippewa).   Methods of making network of cords.

PLATE·47

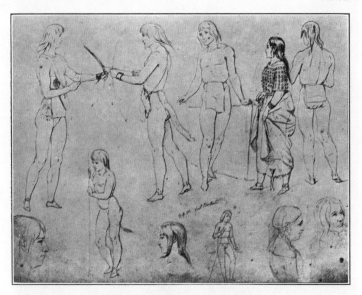

Lower center: Fort Berthold.   August 3, 1851.

PLATE 48

Absaroka (Crow). Probably Chief Rottentail. October 26, 1851.

INDEX

374

378

380